Predicting Technology

Identifying Future
Market Opportunities
and
Disruptive Technologies

Thomas E. Vass

The Great American Business & Economics Press, Inc.
www.Gabby-Press.com

Printed in the United States of America

Published by The Great American Business & Economics Press, Inc.
Printed by WingSpan Press, Livermore, CA

Second Edition

ISBN: 978-0-9794388-0-6 0-9794388-0-2

Library of Congress Control Number: 2007930437

Table of Contents

Index of Exhibits, Diagrams and Tables

Introduction

Identifying New Market Opportunities and Creating the Jobs and Wealth Creation Pipeline In Your Community

In early 2001, Converse Shoe, once the largest private employer in Robeson County, with more than 2,000 jobs, announced it was shutting the plant. Converse had been recruited to the State of North Carolina by the NC Department of Commerce in the early 1980s.

On the day of its arrival in Robeson County, the Governor of the State held a press conference to describe how wonderful the jobs in the new plant would be for the working people of Robeson County. The Governor did not expect to hear these words from one of the Converse workers just 20 years later.

"And I've begged, I've totally begged, you know, for help to get me straightened out so I could go back to work. Find a job and go back to work, but everywhere I went I've just been turned away. We can't help you. And I said, you know, it's a shame, I've worked all my life. Now I need some help and I can't get it."[1]

North Carolina job loss between 1994 and 2000 reached more than 100,000. Robeson County has lost approximately 8,708 manufacturing jobs between 1993 and 2003. The peak years of plant closures in Robeson County were 1998 to 2003, with nine plant closings reported in 2003.

By 2004, regional household income had been reduced by $674 million per year due to the manufacturing job loss in Robeson County. When the plants close, the delayed negative economic effects continue for years. Another worker in Robeson described what happened to her when her plant closed.

"Well, I was drawing unemployment up until the first of December, and all unemployment was cut out, no more extensions or whatever, and I've had not one dime coming in since then. Not one thing, I've been staying at mama's, taking care of her, trying to come to school, taking my grandchildren to school, going back to get them. It's just been constant schedule every day. But it's took a toll on my health...and now I can't even afford my medicine. I can't afford to go to the doctor."[2]

What happened in North Carolina is occurring throughout communities in America. This book is about an economic theory of technological evolution. The primary reason this book was written was to help ordinary citizens in each

1

community understand what is happening to their jobs and incomes as a result of rapid technological change that is occurring on a global scale.

One of the biggest sources of current economic and financial anxiety is the churn and disruption caused by rapid changes in technology and global markets. The uncertainty makes planning for the future difficult for families, and for children today who are trying to make career choices.

The U. S. Bureau of Labor Statistics published a study that showed that workers with less than a high school diploma held 10.6 jobs during the 22 years following their high school graduation. Workers with a bachelor's degree or more held 10.7 jobs after their college graduation. That is a lot of job churn and uncertainty, no matter what the level of education.

When ordinary workers lose their jobs as a result of layoffs and restructuring, the jobs they next find usually pay less and have fewer benefits. Overall rates of employment may have gone up on an aggregate scale, but the individual statistics are not so rosy.

Economic studies describe the lower range of income loss related to job churn as a 10% decline over the course of a five-year period. The upper range of income loss is a 50% decline for the rest of the worker's life. Even that statistic is not as grim as the worst-case scenario where middle age workers lose a job and never work again.

Readers do not need any education or training in current economics to understand the theory about technology described in this book. Understanding economic theory would not help very much because much of contemporary economic theory is based upon a myth that makes economic theory not very useful.

Part of the myth about existing economic theory concerns the benefits of free markets and especially free global trade. Current economic theory always begins with the initial assumption that the perfectly competitive free market forces will adjust supply and demand to end up at optimal rates of social welfare.

This is a myth. The myth is based on a false premise that the real world operates just like the imaginary perfectly competitive market of economic theory. Ordinary citizens who rely on existing economic theory as a guide to creating a better economic environment would be short-changed. The practical advice from current theory is to do nothing because everything will work out for the best, *in the long run, because the real world functions just like the perfect world of economic theory.*

The real world does not operate like the perfect world. Real markets have a tendency to stagnate at low levels of economic activity, especially in metro geographical regions. When the regional economy stagnates, many citizens are vulnerable to job loss and financial ruin. Current economic theory tends to overlook this problem, and most economists tend to shrug their shoulders when asked about economic disruption when thousands of residents in a metro region lose their jobs.

"Its just the workings of the free market," they say. "Folks will find new jobs and things will get better soon." As the cases in Robeson County point out, this naïve optimism about folks finding another job is unfounded. A better approach for economists would be to use their knowledge and influence to create competitive economic environments so that ordinary citizens did not bear the brunt of economic disruptions that could have been avoided.

The advice contained in this book for ordinary citizens may be surprising in the sense that it is based on the idea that more free competitive markets at the regional level is the best way to proceed. This book is not based upon the fashionable liberal political idea that more federal government intervention in the economy or redistributing wealth from the rich to the poor is a good idea.

The current economic system, combined with the current political system of favoritism and benefits based on connections, will not lead to better jobs or fair outcomes for ordinary citizens who play by the rules. More federal government regulation of the special interest political system is not a viable solution for creating the jobs and wealth pipeline in your community.

Competitive markets do create opportunity. But, the competitive markets must be matched by fair political systems. Only a certain type of political and economic configuration of values will work to create better jobs and incomes for ordinary citizens.

Better jobs and income opportunities are created when new markets are created, where ordinary citizens have the greatest chance to benefit from the new flows of incomes and profits. This book describes a theory on how technological change causes new markets to be formed. The theory is primarily related to another theory about biological evolution. Biological evolution is used as a metaphor to explain economic theory.

The theory in this book does not start from the assumption that free markets always lead to social welfare maximums. It starts from the initial assumption that what exists today could have been something entirely different, if prior decisions about economics and finance had been different.

Part of the theory in this book builds upon work done by Clayton Christensen, a professor of business at Harvard University. Christensen has written many books about a topic called "disruptive technology." Part of his work also includes the topic of "sustaining innovations." All of his work, however, is directed to the area of how large multinational corporations handle the issue of technological innovation.

This book modifies Christensen's emphasis on large corporations and redirects the topic to how technological innovation occurs in distinct metropolitan economic regions. In a way, this book asks how metro regional economies function like large corporations.

In *The Innovator's Dilemma*, Christensen shows how technological innovations in products affects large corporations. He suggests that new products cut into the low end of the current marketplace and eventually evolve to the point where the new products displace high-end competitors and their reigning technologies.

Christensen's main policy advice is directed to the senior managers at large corporations. He is primarily concerned with how large corporations with established products should respond to potentially disruptive technological innovation. Christensen writes that even the best-managed companies, in spite of their attention to customers and continual investment in new technology, are susceptible to failure no matter what the industry,

Christensen suggests that senior managers in large companies usually follow the conventional market wisdom that the "customer is always right." The conventional wisdom leads managers to place too much attention on satisfying customers' current needs. By focusing too much attention on current customers, the large companies fail to adapt or adopt new technology that will meet customers' unstated or future needs.

When companies are blind-sided by the new competition, Christensen calls this phenomenon "disruptive technology." Christensen's thesis is that great companies blow it precisely because they do everything right. He explains why top companies that had listened hard to customers and invested like crazy in new technologies still lost their market leadership when confronted with disruptive changes in technology and market structure.

Most ordinary workers and many local elected leaders are also "blind-sided" by economic disruption, even when they are doing everything right. Part of the theory explained in this book is about disruptive technology, but the focus of the theory is what happens in metro regions as a result of disruptive product innovations

Christensen shows why most companies miss "the next great wave." Whether in electronics or retailing, a successful company with established products will get pushed aside unless managers know when to abandon traditional business practices. When the senior executives at large companies in a metro region, like Detroit, miss the next great wave, it is not just the companies that suffer. Thousands of ordinary workers suffer job loss and poor future financial prospects.

Part of the theory explained in this book is based upon a biological metaphor of how new species evolve. It turns out that emerging technologies often find their first applications in new or marginal markets, similar to how a new species originates at the extreme ends of a biological environment

To take advantage of innovation that results from the introduction of a new product, incumbent firms need to learn how to address a new market. Just like existing species need to learn how to compete with the new species.

In Christensen's theories about disruptive technology, his focus is almost entirely on the role of cognitive failures in the senior team as the central explanatory construct. The senior managers somehow failed mentally to understand the threat from the new product.

If senior managers in large corporations had been more competent in following organizational routines, they may have responded differently to the threat. Likewise, the theory explained in this book suggests that leaders in metro regions are sometimes incompetent and fail to react to threats to the local economic environment that arise from their allegiance to the political status quo..

The biggest incompetence in large corporations, according to Christensen, comes from a mental allegiance to the status quo. In much of his work, he explains that large corporations and organizations customarily develop mind-sets and processes that revolve around doing what they already know. Once that pattern becomes established, managers have great difficulty justifying to others or even themselves the need to turn their processes upside down to respond to a barely emergent market change.

By the time the threat is apparent, however, it's usually too late; upstart companies have seized a substantial lead. The same type of allegiance to the status quo in regions affects how regional leaders respond to economic threats. This book explains how and why the leaders fail to respond to threats by placing their behavior in a larger theoretical framework of biological evolution, similar in concept to what Darwin had in mind when he coined the phrase "survival of the fittest."

In this book, regional economies look like environments. Inside the regional environment, there are many species who compete in what looks like networks or alliances. Sometimes the alliances cooperate for short-term advantage with each other, or, with species in other environments. Often, understanding how the networks operate in the region will explain a lot about technological innovation and economic growth.

Each regional environment could be categorized by cultural and political values. Some regional environments could be defined as having a creative culture. In one of his recent books, *Seeing What's Next: Using Theories of Innovation to Predict Industry Change,* Christensen and his co-authors argue that it is possible to predict which companies will win and which will lose in a specific situation.

This book makes a similar argument about predicting the direction of technology in regions. It also makes the same type of claim that Christensen makes about providing advice to senior managers about what to do when they figure out what is going to happen next.

This book directs its advice to ordinary citizens, small business owners, budding entrepreneurs and local elected leaders. The book tries to answer a number of questions readers may have about their own regional economy.

What organizational entity in the region promotes regional knowledge creation?

Part of the problem of finding strategies to promote regional economic growth concerns the fact that regions do not have the same organizational capacity and functionality as private corporations. No organizational entity in the regional economy or society has a mission to create knowledge about technological innovation based upon the region's strategic strengths. Yet, knowledge creation is one of the most important variables in understanding the direction of the economy.

In What Ways Are Regions Like Corporations?

Sarah J. Marsh and Gregory N. Stock, in their article, *Creating Dynamic Capability: The Role of Intertemporal Integration, Knowledge Retention, and Interpretation,* describe how difficult it is for any single corporation to acquire external knowledge or even codify prior internal corporate knowledge.

"Uncertainty about the ability for technological knowledge to be transformed to meet market demands, lack of complementary technologies, the lack of developed markets for a given technical feature, and other types of uncertainty add significant challenges to organizations as they develop products for future markets,"[3] they state.

Regions are like corporations because they have this same set of uncertainty about technological innovation. However, regions do not have senior managers or elected leaders who implement economic strategy on behalf of the citizens in the same way that senior managers implement corporate strategy on behalf of shareholders.

Part of the solution offered by this book is that regions adopt an explicit economic strategy that puts the regional economic interests first, just like the region was a business corporation.

How Can Metro Regions Create and Diffuse Technological Knowledge?

Sometimes, the same source of knowledge for corporations is very useful and would also serve the broader strategic economic interests of the region, if the regional elected leaders actually articulated those interests. As in a biological environment, sometimes there is competition for knowledge where financial interests of corporations are different than the financial interests of ordinary citizens.

As Marsh and Stock point out, "Suppliers, customers, consultants, and the results of benchmarking and reverse engineering all provide sources of external knowledge that may be utilized in the new product development process, as do patent applications, scientific and trade publications, and conferences."

Someone, or some entity, in the region must organize this set of knowledge resources in a way that creates and diffuses technological knowledge so that citizens can take advantage of new market opportunities.

How Can Metro Regions Create a Jobs And Wealth Pipeline In Your Community?

Regional economic development occurs as a result of technical change in production units, generally, manufacturing plants and high technology service units related to information and communication technology. (ICT). Technical change causes relationships between economic, social and political agents within the region to change.

One of the possible outcomes associated with technical change over time is that more wealth and greater per capita incomes are created in the region. There is nothing preordained or certain that this desirable outcome of more wealth or greater income will occur.

There are social, political and economic forces that favor technical change, and there are other forces that inhibit change. Economic development is a contingent outcome of technical change. It occurs in some regions, but not in others.

What Is Technological Change?

Technical change causes new income flows to be created where none had existed before. Part of the new income is a result of increased productivity, meaning that output increases with reduced inputs in the production unit. Part of the new income is in the form of profits related to new goods produced by new production units. Another part of the income is in the form of wages and salaries paid to people who work in the new units.

There is nothing about the relationship between new incomes and new consumer preferences resulting from technical change that would suggest or hint that the relationship between new incomes and new preferences leads, or adjusts, automatically, to full employment at the regional level.

Part of the challenge in creating the jobs and wealth creation pipeline in your community is that most economic theory assumes that the free market will automatically create regional wealth and prosperity. If you and other community leaders rely on existing economic theory to guide you in your policy decisions, your regional economy will probably not experience technical change.

In the region experiencing economic growth caused by technical change, investments made by entrepreneurs in new production units create new inter-industry relationships, and new market relationships that did not exist before. The new ventures produce products whose supply varies, according to the feedback mechanism of consumer preferences.

The new markets created by technical change represent an entirely different economic structure, with its own internal dynamic of growth. The most important ingredient for creating technical change in your regional economy is an economic agent called an "entrepreneur."

The Role of the Entrepreneur.

Pier Saviotti describes why the supply of entrepreneurs is so important to the process of technical change in a region. "The knowledge of engineers, scientists, managers, technicians, etc., involved in the implementation of the technology becomes specialized around the process, technical and service characteristics used. This specialization creates networks of communication and power which reinforce the stability of the artifact dimension of the technology."[4]

In other words, in the region's existing social-business network of skilled individuals, there is a shared specialized knowledge about regional production processes. Within this network, potential entrepreneurs meet with each other and discuss technical problems and how to solve them. Often, the problems cannot be solved within the existing older firms, so the feasibility of starting a new venture is usually a topic of conversation.

Generally, the entrepreneurs discuss new ventures based upon their technical knowledge and their understanding of the potential market for the potential new products that could be produced.

The entrepreneur provides an ingredient to the process of technical change that is absent in the framework of the existing old production unit. According to McAdams in *Paths of Fire,* the entrepreneurs have a "creative vision" in their capacity to "anticipate a new convergence of consumer preferences and technological possibilities."[5]

Peter Temin makes this same point in his article, *"Entrepreneurs and Managers."* He states that "...entrepreneurs are the agents of change, ...(they) see new opportunities, invent new machines, discover new markets, ...(they) perform a different function from that of the manager, who works within a known technology, organization, and market."[6]

The entrepreneur is the agent that links the unknown future of consumer preferences to technological possibilities, the result of which is economic growth.

In making the distinction between unknown costs and risks of the future, and the known costs and risks in the existing old production unit, Temin and McAdams hit upon the single greatest economic contribution that entrepreneurs make to the evolution of technical change.

Entrepreneurs perform the economic function of creating the future markets by imagining how that market will work. They provide the guesses of prices and profits, and how technological change in production units will interact with, as yet unseen, consumer preferences. In contrast, the existing firm does not create a future market, it adjusts itself to the prices and profits of the status quo market.

The Role of Technological Knowledge Diffusion as a Social Process of Learning.

Diffusion of knowledge is a social process of learning that occurs in a region's network of relationships. Technology is often defined as a body of knowledge about how things work.

In *"Technical Change as Cultural Evolution,"* Richard Nelson states that "...technology needs to be understood as consisting of both a set of specific designs and practices, and a generic knowledge that surrounds these and provides an understanding of how things work, the key variables affecting performance, the nature of currently binding constraints and promising approaches to pushing these constraints back."[7]

Nelson identifies the two key components of technology as the learning component and the knowledge component. Learning about technology generally occurs as a result of social processes characterized by *learning by doing.*

Learning by using, and *inter-industry learning,* results when suppliers, vendors, and customers share knowledge about technology. Each case of learning occurs within a network of regional social-business relationships, some of which occur on the floor of the production unit working with machines.

What happens in the process of learning is that mid-level managers, supervisors, technicians, scientists, engineers, technicians inside the production unit talk with each other every day about how things work, and they also talk with the service technicians, and supply vendors about binding constraints.

Entrepreneurs leave the old production units to create new ventures, using the knowledge they gained about how things work, and with ideas about how to make the new venture more productive than the older units. The new ventures are more productive, and achieve higher overall production output per unit of input.

To the extent that the region has a high rate, or pace of technical learning, and has accumulated technical knowledge, it will have a high rate of technical change in production processes, and consequently, a high rate of economic growth.

The Importance of Regional Industrial Clusters of Industries and Knowledge.

Technological knowledge is not distributed uniformly across regions. Saviotti notes that innovative firms "...tend to cluster in those (areas) that were already innovating countries...this specificity can not be explained by factor endowments, but is more likely to be caused by specific institutional configurations, and by the cumulative, local and specific character of the knowledge that the institutions possess."[8]

Some regions have clusters of technological innovating firms and supportive social networks and some do not. The accumulation of technological knowledge and the pace of technical change are contingent outcomes of the social and political institutional structure of a region. For technological progress to occur, according to Mokyr, "...it must be born into a socially sympathetic environment."[9]

Whether the region has a sympathetic environment for technical change explains much about why economic growth occurs in some regions and not in others.

The Role of Regional Sources of Venture Capital.

In his historical review of technology, Robert McAdams noted that historians share a widely-held belief about the origins of venture capital in the eighteenth century. McAdams wrote "...all of the sources are in agreement that considerable increases in disposable wealth came into the hands of a substantial elite during the later part of the eighteenth century. Perhaps it is not so much their diversified and growing desires as consumers that quickened the pace of technological advance (during that era) but rather the increasing supply of potential venture capital for which this elite was beginning more aggressively to seek new avenues for profitable investment."[10]

McAdams highlights two important factors about the origin and disposition of venture capital. First, he describes venture capital in the hands of the financial and political elite as "disposable wealth," not disposable income.

In the case of venture capitalists, the general source of wealth is the capital gain they achieve on the sale of their ventures.

Second, McAdams noted that the elites in the eighteenth century were looking for new ventures to invest their wealth. The elites were venture capitalists, not commercial bankers, but sometimes in economic literature, the role of venture capitalist is used interchangeably with the role of commercial banker. If, and when, the elite decide to invest in new ventures, they contribute to technical change.

The creation of a supply of venture capital at the regional level is correlated with the supply of entrepreneurs. In this case, Says Law may be working, in that supply seems to be related to demand. Bruno and Tyebjee identified the supply of venture capital as one of the top three factors that seemed to explain where entrepreneurs came from before the became entrepreneurs.[11]

The supply or absence of venture capital in a region seems to be a matter of historical contingency. Unlike the existing set of factor endowments a region may start economic history with, the creation of a pool of venture capital is determined by human history. No region is initially born with venture capital, but some regions, as a result of history, are lucky enough to create a supply of it.

As Herman Minsky points out, regional economic development is a "social process," which is influenced by what social actors, like venture capitalists, decide to do with their wealth.

The Ultimate Goal is Self-Sustaining Regional Economic Growth.

If a new pool of regional venture capital is created, and if that supply of potential new disposable wealth is then re-invested into subsequent new equipment and machinery, then the conditions for self-generating regional economic growth for future periods will have been established.

The pool of capital that becomes available for reinvestment does not depend on cash flow from old production units, nor is it related to the conventional loans made by commercial bankers. The potential pool of capital is created by profits on exit events made by the venture capitalists.

The reinvestment decision depends on what the venture capitalists in the region decide to do with the disposable wealth that is created by the forces of technical change. If the regional economy is dynamic in the creation of new investment opportunities, and if the venture capitalists decide to make a second generation investment in new technology, then there is a chance that a second round of new innovative ventures will be created.

Saviotti states that innovating firms are not uniformly distributed across geographical territory. Innovative firms tend to be located near other innovative firms. This tendency of firms to concentrate in a region contributes to the development of a regional macrotechnology.

The reason one region develops a macrotechnology as opposed to any other region is related to the "...specific institutional configurations and by the cumulative, local, and specific character of the knowledge that the institutions possess."[12]

The good news in Saviotti's insight is that the specific technological institutional configuration is something that citizens in a region can deliberately choose to create. Charles Kindleberger, in *World Economic Primacy,* noted how a certain set of cultural values tended to favor an attitude towards technical innovation. He characterized this attitude as the "...capability and will of individuals, companies and governments to break free of existing habits, perceptions, institutions, and task allocations, in order to revise them in light of constantly changing circumstances and developments."[13]

However, nothing about the process of creating a regional technological structure can be explained by reference to natural laws of supply and demand that tends to suggest that the economy adjusts to some point of equilibrium based upon quantity or price competition.

Technical change is a social phenomenon caused by the interaction of humans engaged in social/business relationships in a specific area. Elected leaders in a region are participants in these relationships and can either contribute to technical change or act to inhibit it. How they choose to respond has much to do with their concept of promoting the public purpose and whether the region will experience self-sustaining economic growth.

If elected leaders in the metro region choose to promote technical change, they can create the new venture financial and business infrastructure in a matter of months. The theory in this book predicts that from that time of the creation of the new infrastructure, it will take about 3 years before the new jobs and new incomes start coming out the other end of your new job and wealth creation pipeline.

Chapter I

From Clocks to Genetics: The Need To Modify Existing Economic and Marketing Theory to Explain the Trajectory of Technology and the Evolution of the Economy

In 1957, an economist named Robert Solow, used conventional economic theory to analyze the U. S. economic performance from 1909 to 1947. At that time, and continuing to current times, conventional economic theory relied on two variables, capital and labor, to explain changes in economic conditions.

Most of the theory suggested that very slight changes in the use of capital or labor in the production of goods and services created price signals in the marketplace that would lead economic agents to a unique supply and demand equilibrium point.

Solow's results indicated that gross output per man-hour of labor doubled over this period of time, indicating a great increase in productivity. In other words, holding the input of a unit of labor constant, the unit of output doubled, meaning that the use of capital and labor resources in production had become much more efficient. Some non-economists may refer to this increase in productivity as "getting more bang for the buck."

However, Solow found that about 87% of the total increase in productivity could not be explained by changes in the allocation of either labor or capital. Some other factor was responsible for causing the increase in productivity, but conventional theory, limited only to the variables of capital and labor, could not explain how this other "factor" was related to the conventional explanation of increased productivity and economic growth.[14]

The basic argument of this book is that the evolutionary model of biological population genetics provides a better scientific model for explaining economic relationships than the general equilibrium theory used by Solow in his analysis.

Technology, the economic factor that Solow could not account for, is too important a variable to be left out of a general theory of the economy. Economics, as a science, needs to move from a metaphor of clocks, which is based on explaining how very small changes in labor and capital, always returns the economy to an equilibrium position, to the science of biological genetics, which describes how the economy evolves.

Predicting Technology

An important part of the modification of existing economic theory is the recognition that after the passage of about 7 years, the natural forces of supply and demand in a free market may not end up in equilibrium. The telos (from the Greek word for "end", "purpose" or "goal") of a market economy may be equilibrium for a brief period of time, after which the future direction of the economy is better explained by adopting some other philosophical end point.

Part of the purpose of this book is to explain when the existing theory is useful and when equilibrium theory, as in the case of Solow's analysis, leaves many important causes of economic growth unexplained.

Technology, as a economic factor, "causes" the market forces of supply and demand to change, and often, the effect brought about by technology on capital and labor are irrevocable, meaning that the past points of equilibrium do not contain any philosophical meaning for predicting future economic positions.

This book describes a theory, which can be used by scientists and engineers to predict the trajectory of technology in specific metropolitan economic regions. In addition to describing a new economic theory, the book provides a practical business application process to help product developers and potential entrepreneurs assess the market prospects of the innovative products they are developing, both for the current generation of products, and future technological iterations of the product.

The key to understanding economic evolution is to understand how an initial distribution of income changes over time. While the relationships between income and technological evolution are complicated by feed-forward and feedback information flows, the essential outcome of the new theory is that without changing income distributions, new technological innovations will not have market demand from buyers.

And, without technological innovation, new markets do not emerge. Stated another way, new markets will not emerge based upon maintenance of the status quo distribution of income. Evolutionary population genetics can explain how new market demand arises in future markets as a result of the relationships between incomes and technology better than the neoclassical economic explanation, which is based upon the explanation of a theoretical return to equilibrium.

Products evolve technologically when new technology is incorporated into existing products in a process similar to genetic mutation. Consumers select either existing products or new technologically superior products. The buying patterns of consumers affects income flows in the regional economic environment, both in a current time period, and contingently, in the future time period.

Existing firms either adapt their existing products to compete with new products or the firms die, based upon what products consumers select. Sometimes, the adaptation of existing firms is based upon dropping the price of their existing good, and sometimes the adaptation is to make marginal technical changes to the existing good so that its usefulness matches some of the attributes of the new good. That type of marginal technological adaptation is a naturally occurring response to competition, and the new theory would describe that adaptation as non-disruptive technology, or more specifically, "asexual" technological mutation.

Clayton Christensen, in his book, *The Innovator's Dilemma*, calls this type of asexual innovation a sustaining technology, which means for him, improved product performance.[15] The main question Christensen is asking is "How can a manager of a large, successful company deal with these realities of size and growth when confronted by disruptive change."[16]

In contrast to Christensen, this book's use of the concept of asexual mutation is aimed at placing technological change within the broader theoretical context of regional economic growth. Asexual technological innovation is a competitive response that involves either a manufacturing process improvement for existing products, which tends to drop the market price of the earlier generation of a product, or it involves making minor technological adjustments that improves the functionality of the earlier version.

Conventional neoclassical theory captures this part of economic behavior associated with declining prices in existing markets for existing goods. But, as demonstrated by Solow's results, the appearance of new technology causes economic changes that conventional theory does not explain very well because technology is not a price-based labor or capital market phenomena.

The deficiency in neoclassical theory becomes severe when the theory is used to predict how new market demand emerges. New markets emerge as a result of the appearance of "disruptive technologies." Marketing professionals and product development engineers are handicapped from the start, if they rely on neoclassical theory to help them understand future market opportunities or when to anticipate the appearance of a "disruptive technology."

In the existing markets for goods and services, economic agents called venture capitalists procreate the new ventures, which produce technologically superior new products.

As a result of new ventures being born, new products may hasten the creation of markets with new final demand relationships that evolve from existing markets. The market demand relationships in the new markets create income flows that did not exist in the previous time horizons. As a result of changing market demands, the distribution of income within the region slowly changes, which modifies the regional economic environment.

Given a new distribution of income, the effects of technological innovation on market relationships in the regional economy can be assessed for predictions about the economy's future pathway during the next seven-year period of time.

If new technologically superior products do not create new markets, then regional income distribution will not change. Without the appearance of new markets, regional markets, which produce existing goods and services, may then experience the long run decline in demand for existing products, which would be analogous to a biological process described as Mueller's Ratchet of genetic inbreeding.

Once the decline in demand for existing technologically obsolete products occurs, it becomes very difficult to re-generate market demand for regional products. The declining markets kill the channels of information flows within the region, which are essential for the process of knowledge creation and diffusion.

Knowledge, as a regional asset, is an essential precursor for product evolution. Existing neoclassical theory does not do a very good job of incorporating knowledge as a prime variable in explaining economic growth because knowledge is not usually a variable that has a market price attached to it.

While equilibrium theory can describe how regional supply and demand relationships of labor and capital may result in equilibrium in any seven-year time horizon, the theory is not very good at explaining how knowledge is related to technological economic obsolescence and regional economic decline.

In other words, from the perspective of existing theory, the resource allocation for existing products may be efficient and in competitive price equilibrium over a period of time when prices are declining to the end point of zero market demand. The regional economic decline may be better explained as a result of technological obsolescence and knowledge deterioration than to prices. Nor does the contemporary theory provide very good policy advice on what elected leaders and business leaders should do to reverse regional economic decline.

Economic behavior of economic agents in a regional economy follows a certain logical sequence of events in time, which can be explained by adopting a biological evolutionary model of population genetics as applied to the birth and death rates of firms and the evolution of technology in products.

But, it is not a perfect fit between biology and economics, and Darwin's notion of natural selection and random variation must be modified for a better fit to economic evolution in a regional environment. The schematic of Diagram 1. describes relationships of the logical sequence economic evolutionary events described in this book

The emergence of future market environments, after the appearance of a disruptive technology, is contingent upon a certain evolutionary sequence of events taking place. If another sequence of events takes place, income distribution will not change and new markets will not emerge.

Rather, the firms in the regional economy will probably die, especially if the regional market is deprived of technological diversity, the analogue to genetic diversity. The primary forms of technological and market competition in the creation of future markets are not primarily priced-based in the Walrasian system of factor supply and demand equilibrium, but are based upon how existing firms in an existing market compete for technical innovation when other new firms introduce technologically disruptive products.

The most important contingent variable is how consumers react when they first "see" the new product, and then "imagine" how the new product may "fit" with their expectations of the future. Much of contemporary marketing theory does not do a very good job incorporating this "seeing" and "imagining" behavior of consumers in predicting a product's market demand.

The seeing and imaging part of the explanation is a biological function that occurs in the brains of each consumer, and marketing theory would be better if it incorporated more about the human brain's biological response to novelty in a marketing environment.

Another part of the needed modification of marketing theory is to understand what parts of the economic system, such as knowledge, fall outside of price relationships in existing markets. Marketing theory, as a science, is adequate for describing how exchanges and transactions, or as Wroe Alderson called them, transvections, based upon prices affects market demand in any seven year period of time.[17]

But, many variables in the market environment are not price-based, and the deficiency in existing marketing theory is very great for products that do not currently exist or do not have any price history. In other words, if potential new products do not have prices attached to them, existing marketing theory loses its most important explanatory variable related to future market demand.

Current marketing theory can describe, for instance, why technologically obsolete products in existing markets lose market share. However, marketing theory is not so good at describing why existing firms, as a result of producing

17

inferior products, often turn to the political process to maintain their market positions favoring the status quo technology. Rent-seeking behavior, via the political process, to maintain the existing distribution of income, is usually considered to be outside the parameters of either economic general equilibrium or current marketing theory.

But, understanding the political forces that desire to maintain the existing distribution of income equilibrium is essential to understanding the dynamics of new market demand emergence and technological evolution.

The primary form of long-term market competition between existing firms and new ventures is based upon commercialization of technology. The short-term competition is based upon prices for existing products, but the sequence of events that underlie the emergence of new markets is based on how technical knowledge is created and diffused within a regional industrial cluster, which is a social network phenomenon.

The market selection process involving what happens when consumers first see the technologically superior products are based upon how the human brain processes decisions involving novelty, and the functioning of imagination in human brains is only remotely connected to changes in market prices in existing markets.

Market demand describes relationships between humans, and much of the description of a regional economic environment entails an analysis of how the structure of production relationships in the economic environment are changing in response to changes in market relationships.

The structure of interindustry relationships in the regional economy serves a double duty of describing both the production technology of the region and the institutional social class structure of market relationships in the region's industrial cluster. Social, political and legal relationships, which define the way markets facilitate transactions, are not generally price-based, but power based. Depending on how the social class structure functions, the process of diffusing technical knowledge can either help or hinder the rate of new venture creation.

The social class structure also affects the birth rate and death rate of ventures because cultural values, like adherence to social rules, trust and loyalty, determines the amount of risk associated with producing a new product. In the absence or the presence of a certain configuration of social and cultural values, the risk associated with a future appropriation of profit from a capital gain exit event changes.

Cultural values are geographically specific, and each region must be treated differently from a market analysis perspective. If venture capitalists and entrepreneurs in a specific metro region cannot appropriate their profits from an investment in a new firm, they have no logical reason to make investments in that region.

Without a high rate of regional capital investments in new firms today, future markets in a specific metro region will not emerge, yet cultural values are not price sensitive, and fall outside the current theoretical framework of marketing. Marketing theory would be more useful in explaining how future markets emerge if the theory incorporated more about how cultural values influence market behavior and the propensity of venture capitalists to make investments in potentially disruptive technology.

One of the interesting dynamics of the analysis of regional economic environments is that social and cultural values that occur in social relationships change more slowly than either economic relationships in existing markets or changes in income distribution.

In other words, prices for existing products change much faster than incomes, creating a complex interplay between the historical forces that favor the status quo arrangement of power in regional social and political relationships and alternative forces that favor a new arrangement of interindustry technological relationships, via new venture creation.

Stated another way, cultural values associated with new venture creation must remain relatively stable over a longer period of time to reward investments made in an earlier time, whereas cultural values involving current prices do not require long term stability in order to facilitate current market transactions.

This complex historical interplay can be seen in the process of how new ventures are born when venture capitalists decide to fund them. The decision to fund a new venture is not dependent on operating cash flows of an existing business, but depends on the expectations of a future capital gain from a transaction called an "exit event" by the capitalists. Venture capitalists do not generally concern themselves with operating cash flow from existing firms.

Operating cash flow, however, is an issue of great concern for commercial bankers who lend money to existing firms, and who tend to shun the type of equity investments in new ventures that are favored by venture capitalists. The commercial bankers in a regional economy act as a financial interest favoring the political status quo arrangement of power because the stability in cash flows allows the interest and principal on the commercial loans to be repaid.

The financial and political interests of venture capitalists and commercial bankers are different, and so are their respective sources of capital, a point glossed over by neoclassical equilibrium analysis. Much of the contemporary economic theory considers all capital as ubiquitous and homogeneous and tends to view all capitalists, whether they are commercial bankers or venture capitalists, as the same agent all of whom have the same welfare function.

Contemporary economic analysis will often describe capital as homogeneous "units." For commercial bankers, the value of the units of capital is calculated on the steady repayment of interest and principal. The introduction of new products and new markets tends to upset the steady flow of the units of capital for debt repayment favored by the commercial bankers.

For venture capitalists, the source of the units of capital is profits based upon capital gains from the exit event. The units of capital associated with exit events are not related to production prices in the existing market. The valuation of the units of capital for venture capitalists are not based upon the rate of savings from existing firms, retained from operating cash flows, nor are they based upon the interest rates applied to the repayment of debt from loans made by commercial bankers.

The value of the units of capital in the business model of the venture capitalists and the value of the units of capital for commercial bankers are entirely independent and nothing in current equilibrium theory can tie them together in a logical framework.

The capital gain profits, viewed as sources of capital for venture capital investments, fall outside of the analytical framework of production prices that are the essential causal variable in existing general equilibrium economic theory. Yet, their ability to obtain those future rewards depends on stability in cultural values involving trust and honesty, and reward based upon risk taking that aims at creating new flows of income.

Those cultural values are not the same set of cultural values that under gird the commercial banker's ability to obtain interest payments on debt which aims at maintaining the status quo distribution of income, at least long enough to have the current debts repaid.

Venture capitalists, not commercial bankers, are, to borrow a phrase from Schumpeter, the Ephors of the new e-economy when they invest in new ventures. What they decide to with their form of capital gain profits can be explained when it is linked to a biological metaphor that explains what consumers do when they first see the new product. The new product's market acceptance can be predicted with the help of a concept called "genetic technological crossover."

If the genetic crossover between two technologies eventually has a great rate of market acceptance, it may create a whole host of complementary products and new ventures within the region in the future time period. Some economists refer to this new set of complementary firms as an "industrial cluster."

Genetic technological crossover, in this book is called two-parent sexual reproduction and is equivalent to the birth of a "disruptive product technology," because the new technology of the new product in an existing industrial cluster completely disrupts market demand relationships in older industrial clusters and existing markets.

Clayton Christensen uses the term "disruptive technology" as seen from the perspective of senior managers in multi-national corporations. For those managers, a disruptive technology, whether it originates in their own corporate organization, or from some outside organization, tends to disrupt the existing market demand of their existing products.

The techniques of market analysis taught by graduate business management schools that emphasize statistical trend analysis and economic modeling, fail to predict when or how a disruptive technology may occur or what to do about one, if it does appear on their radar screen. "The techniques that worked so extraordinarily well when applied to sustaining technologies, however, clearly failed badly when applied to markets or applications that did not yet exist."[18]

While the term "disruptive" as used in this book is in agreement with Christensen on the idea that a disruptive technology must be analyzed as if the market does not yet exist, the term is placed in a different theoretical context of regional economic growth and decline. This change in theoretical context for understanding the use of the term disruptive technologies leads to different conclusions from those reached by Christensen.

In his case, a disruptive technology results in worse product performance, and is cheaper than products that are based upon sustaining technologies. In the use of the term in this book, a disruptive technology is normally much higher priced than the existing products, and performs much better, for the very small niche market which is willing to pay the higher price for the improved functionality, when users first see and imagine how the new product will "fit" into their welfare functions.

When the technological crossover for a new product first occurs, however, the market demand for it is usually very small. It is very difficult to predict if the market demand for a new product will grow, and much of the future growth depends on the growth of demand in future markets that are related to the new product.

If consumers accept a sufficient threshold of new complementary ventures, which are related to the new technologically disruptive product,, then a unique type of market event called a "micro market bifurcation" may occur in a specific regional economy.

The micro market bifurcation described in this book is based upon a concept called a "Hopf Bifurcation," by biologists. The metaphor is between partial changes in the genetic technology of the environment, which signals the position of intermediate points along a region's technological trajectory. These intermediate points suggest the future direction for the emergence of new industrial clusters.

The use of the Hopf Bifurcation gives marketing professionals a clue on where to look for the creation and emergence of a new market that had not previously existed. In the logical sequence of events surrounding technological crossover, the two parent technological reproduction occurs first, meaning that technology between two clusters is crossed, and then, subsequently, and contingently, a new market demand for the new technology may emerge.

The main question that marketing agents should ask when they try to analyze a new market is "what kind of consumer would use this new technology?"

They would not be investigating an existing market of consumers, and they certainly would not be looking for a very big market. Philosophically, what they are asking themselves is what the consumer for this new product would look like, if market demand for it were to develop? Clayton Christensen describes these types of consumers as "nonconsumers."[19]

The concept of the Hopf Bifurcation suggests where to look. They would begin their search for the potential new market at the intersection between the technologies of the two parents. Part of the market demand is probably located with the technology of one parent, and part of the future potential market demand is located in the market of the second parent.

Consumers in either of the two parent's markets may not be able to verbally articulate their desire for new technological functionality, but they generally know a good thing when they first see it. In other words, marketing professionals would look for a small niche in the existing environment, which would be environmentally sympathetic to the appearance of a new species.

As a result of the two-parent genetic crossover of technology, that creates a potentially disruptive technological offspring, the market demand for the new product may come into focus. But, like all biological processes, this new market demand for the new product emerges slowly, and sometimes, the new product dies because the existing species in the market are able to kill it.

The new market will often be a small niche of consumers within the bigger regional environment who are receptive to the technological functionality of the new genetic product species. However, it is also likely that the environment for the emergence of a new market in a given regional economy may not be sympathetic.

The new product technology is not fully functional nor fully self-sufficient, when it first appears, and potential users in the market niche may not know how to use the new product. The market demand for the new product is generally nascent, and from an empirical scientific methodological perspective, the emergence of the new market would have been unknowable, based upon ordinary statistical methods of regression and correlation analysis of past prices in existing product markets.

If a series of micro market bifurcations occur in a regional economy, over a 30-year period of time, the regional economic environment may change both its technological structure and contingently, its market structure entirely, much like a larvae shedding its earlier form. There is a small window of opportunity through which a regional economy could pass, called a macro economic bifurcation.

The distribution of income that comes after the economy passes through the window is entirely different, in terms of regional market demand relationships, than what occurred in the earlier period. The pattern of events to look for in predicting this long range economic outcome are technology crossover, market emergence, and then, changes in income distribution.

Each micro bifurcation point provides a hint, or a clue, in a Bayesian way, about the future trajectory of the economy and where the market may next emerge in the future.

The region's future is related to its past in variables like laws and cultural values, but the future market, just like the butterfly, is different in shape and function, than the larvae. As a result of passing through the macro bifurcation window, final and intermediate demand relationships in the regional economy have changed forever, and consequently, the regional economic environment is different.

The future has become the present. The prior environment created the conditions of evolution for technologically new products, yet the emergent relationships in the market created by the new products have caused the environment to change.

Passing through a macro market bifurcation point is not automatic, nor is it "natural" in the sense that Darwin used the term. If the future market is different than the current market, there is no logical way for neoclassical theory to explain how the economy has "returned to an equilibrium" because the economic structure of the former period of time, including all of the prices for products that are now technologically obsolete, have become philosophically irrelevant.

Nor is there anything that looks like "pre-determined" growth stages or naturally-occurring patterns of economic growth that characterize the stages regional economic growth from the early primitive resource extraction period to the later appearance of high technology economies.

The process through which new regional markets emerge is more like a biological evolutionary process based upon either asexual or sexual technological mutation, than it is an a historical process of general equilibrium economics based upon prices and the telos of equilibrium. Predictions about the future of a regional economy can be more accurate if the regional economy is viewed as a biological environment where species grow, adapt, evolve and die.

And die, they do. Regional economies are either growing or they are dying. From any hypothesized point of time within a seven year steady-state equilibrium, the regional economy is either tracing out an upward sloping curve towards the macro bifurcation window, or tracing out a downward sloping sigmoid pattern of decline.

The difference in the two slopes is that on the downward slide, micro market bifurcation points are irreversible. Just like the ageing process of brains that lose nerve endings and the resulting loss of memory, regional economies on the downward slide lose the ability to generate new technology and commercialize new ideas.

It is a cumulative process accurately described by Gunnar Myrdal, Alvin Hansen and Evsey Domar as cumulative causation; with the additional insight by Mueller that downward micro bifurcations represent a ratchet as the knowledge base of the region is destroyed.

The upward or downward slope of the regional economy can be described by the technological coefficients of a regional input output model of the regional economy between two points in time. From any point in time, the economy will either continue its upward trajectory to the next micro bifurcation point, or slide into equilibrium conditions. Equilibrium conditions set the stage for future environmental decline through loss of technological diversity.

Rather than hypothesizing equilibrium as a positive ideal end state telos to which an economy returns after a perturbation, a biological metaphor sets up equilibrium as an end state to be avoided. A regional economy returning to "equilibrium" of a former time period is an economy on a pathway to economic decline.

In modifying Darwin's theory of natural selection to better-fit regional economic evolution, a set of better descriptive concepts need to be applied to the evolutionary processes.

First, regional economic evolution is contingent. The process of product heredity and technological mutation depends on certain types of selection behavior by consumers in a prior generation that causes an economic effect in a future generation. What consumers do, in terms of selection, when they first see a new disruptive product is a contingent event, that depends both on social and cultural factors specific to a region and on human biological responses in the brain.

Second, regional economic evolution is selective and positive in terms of choices and decisions made by consumers when they first see a new product. In Darwin's model, the evolutionary genetic processes occur randomly, with the survival of the fittest arising from successful genetic environmental selection.

Third, most technological mutation for an existing product within a generation is based upon asexual behavior within an existing regional technological envelope. This very slow asexual technological mutation looks much like what Kimura describes as nearly neutral genetic drift.[20] Because the slow technological asexual mutation process allows the appearance and technical characteristics of the new product to look like the old product, consumers are more likely to buy the slightly different product, because it looks like something they have seen and used before.

Only in the case of sexual reproduction, when technology from two different technological frontiers combines genetic material, in a type of genetic technological crossover, are the conditions for new evolutionary trajectories created. When these new, or novel environmental conditions occur, existing organisms in the regional environment are confronted with choices about how to adapt and survive.

Senior executives in existing firms, for example, when confronted with new market entrants or superior products, do not sit around trying to figure out a market strategy for maximizing profits. Rather, the senior decision makers in the firm are trying to figure out how to stay alive and survive as long as possible, just like any other living organism that fights for survival when the routine environment changes.

This book calls the set of new evolutionary economic descriptive concepts "Structural Evolutionary Regional Economic Theory" or SERET. The telos of SERET is an explanation of where the regional economy is headed next and how consumers relate dynamic changes in a regional economic structure over time to technological innovation in products and market selection.

Diagram 1.1 describes how existing neoclassical general equilibrium theory can be modified to accommodate the biological metaphor of evolution. Part of the modification involves the inclusion of variables, like political power and cultural values, that traditional economic theory usually does not incorporate.

Another part of the modification is the inclusion of the passage of time and the use of history as important variables to describe what may happen next when a new disruptive product technology first appears in the regional economic environment.

Predicting Technology

Diagram 1.1. The Logical Sequence of Events Underlying Regional Economic Evolution.

Elapse of Time	Social/Political Setting	Structure of production relationships	Intermediate/Final Demand Relationships
Antecedent Historical Conditions Of Production Technology	**Institutional networks of knowledge creation.** **Initial distribution of income.** **Cultural values regarding property.**	**Regional input-output technical coefficients.** **Population size of region.** **Regional industrial clusters.**	**Historical rates of consumer selection of products.** **Social income classes.** **Market demand for regional products.**

Direction of causation

	Social/Political environment	Production transformation matrix	Exchange markets equilibrium
Current 7 Year Time Horizon Of Production Technology	**Institutional networks of knowledge diffusion.** **Allegiance to status quo.** **Birth/Death rate of firms.**	**Addition or deletion of rows or columns in regional I-O transaction matrix.** **Rate of product or process technological obsolescence.** **Relationship between regional production and global production units.**	**Regional intermediate demand markets.** **Final demand markets.** **Labor markets.** **Debt capital markets.** **Equity capital markets.**

Evolutionary Trajectory of Production Technology	Social/Political Change/Stasis	Future Production Technical Coefficients Matrix	Exchange Markets tendency to micro bifurcation
	Distribution of income. **Distribution of political decision making.** **Allocation of capital surplus.**	**New firms with technologically different products in industrial clusters.** **Change in income/employment multipliers.** **Technological trajectory of regional eigenvalue.**	**Adaption/selection of consumers of new products.** **Selection of venture capitalists for new ventures.** **Death rate of existing firms within regional industrial clusters.**

Leading to Potential Micro Market Bifurcation

Contingent Emergence of New Markets/New Distribution of Income

Creation of complementary future supply and demand markets to support new technology.

Creation of new income flows where none had previously existed.

Rate of profit reinvestment from "exit" events back into regional industrial cluster.

Modification in regional occupation/skill matrix.

Leading to Potential Macro Economic Bifurcation

Information feedforward and feedback between markets and income distributions

26

Chapter 2

How Equilibrium Economic Theory Serves As The Foundation For an Evolutionary Theory That Predicts Technology

If the supply and demand forces in the real world of economics behaved as if they were in the idealized perfectly competitive world of perfect competition, how would the real world forces behave?

In other words, starting with a given hypothetical model of ideal perfect competition as the reference point, how do the forces in the real world compare to the ideal world? Contemporary economic analysis begins with the ideal point of reference and then proceeds to investigate real world forces as if the real world acted just like the perfect ideal world.

Part of this analysis is useful for understanding short term trends in technology because the theory seems to accurately describe economic behavior in the short term that leads buyers and sellers to a point of equilibrium, based upon prices. From a philosophical point of view, building a new theory about technology and economics should probably start from what currently exists in the way of theory, and see if the current theory can act as a starting point, or philosophical bridge, to the new theory.

Part of the problem with much of the marketing theory and product technology theory today is that it is not connected, philosophically, to the heredity of general equilibrium theory, and consequently much of the writing appears as general conceptual speculation that occurs in the absence of a theoretical framework.[21] This chapter is designed to incorporate conventional theory into both marketing theory and the new evolutionary economic theory.

The starting philosophical assumption in contemporary economics is that the real world economic forces are always in a continuous, timeless movement towards the ideal. Much of the analysis is conducted as if the state of equilibrium has already been achieved, and end-state economic models, mostly based upon the second derivative of many simultaneous differential equations reaching zero at the same moment in time, usually show how the real world ends up at the end-state of perfect harmony.

Sometimes, however, it is convenient for economists to assume that the economy is just starting out on its pathway to perfection or has somehow gotten away from the idealized end state. There is an unusual duality in the treatment of time in the application of economic theory that is not disclosed adequately at the beginning of most contemporary analysis.

If the continuous, timeless movement toward equilibrium is disturbed, or to use a phrase from economic discourse, "perturbed," the theory predicts that economic forces will always return to the perfect adjustment pathway, after the perturbation.

This part of the contemporary theory would be a good starting point for the new theory if the end state of equilibrium were modified by the assumption that the economy will not return to the telos of equilibrium. Technology could be seen as a factor that changes the economy's movement towards the ideal end point.

The two most important concepts of supply and demand in economic analysis are ubiquitous. The concepts apply to any element in the economic world that could potentially be supplied, or demanded, be it factors of production, land, profits, money, labor, capital, finished goods, or semi-finished goods.

The agents who supply whatever it is and the agents who demand it are called sellers and buyers, and no matter where they meet, in whatever market, all supply and all demand forces everywhere in the ideal economy reach equilibrium at precisely the same moment at the end state of all adjustments.

If some element can be supplied, and that same element can be demanded, then the hypothetical conditions exist for a market exchange based upon prices voluntarily agreed upon by buyers and sellers that ultimately ends up in harmony.

Buyers and sellers meet each other in hypothetical markets, and when they meet each other, in whatever market it happens to be, the quantities of supplies exchanged and the quantities of demand that are bought are based upon the concept of prices. The mechanism that adjusts supply and demand in the market is price, and no buyer and no seller in an ideal market can affect or control the price in whatever market is under investigation.

As a result of the exchange in the market, at the market price, each buyer and each seller achieves a fleeting moment of "bliss" right after the exchange. The moment of harmony, or bliss, in a single exchange is added up in the economic theory, all over the economy in every exchange, and the cumulative total amount of bliss, or utility resulting from the exchanges in every single market is called "equilibrium."

Two of the most important social outcomes resulting from the exchanges based upon prices are that there is "efficiency" in the deployment of resources used in production, and that social welfare can not be made better by improving the bliss for any single individual without decreasing the amount of bliss enjoyed by another individual.

Part of the good moral outcomes assumed by contemporary theory is that the exchanges are based upon voluntary choices, made without coercion. Since they are free choices, the outcomes of the free market exchange are considered to be morally superior because some deity or government official is not imposing an outside moral judgment on the exchanges.

Economists call this second desirable social outcome "Pareto optimality." What it means is that at the social bliss point of equilibrium, no single individual's welfare can be made better off if, at that same moment in time, some other individual's welfare will be made worse off.

This is the implied end-state promise of a perfectly competitive free enterprise economy towards which the free market system is always directed. The implied promise in economic theory has the characteristics of a social contract between all parties who freely agree to enter into exchange transactions in the free enterprise economy.

The contractual promise of perfect competition in free enterprise goes something like this: *If the real economy operates like the ideal economy, we promise each other that no one will be made better off if, at the same moment, someone else is made worse off.*

According to John Locke, citizens freely entered the implied social contract of free enterprise when they tacitly agreed to use money as the medium of exchange. The social contract, according to Locke, once entered, is irrevocable and irreversible.

Within any fixed time horizon of about 7 years, with an assumption of fixed capital equipment on the plant floor, fixed production functions that have certain desirable characteristics regarding how inputs are turned into outputs, fixed supplies of labor, etc., in other words, holding all technological variables in the real world constant, observed economic reality seems to conform to the ideal.

During that fixed period of time, for the purposes of developing a new economic theory, the existing conditions of technology within a geographic region can be described with the assistance of price movements as they are used in contemporary economic theory.

Current economic theory describes price movements with the assistance of graphs that show how supply and demand curves interact as prices change. The standard treatment is shown in Diagram 2.1. Part A. Perhaps a better way of describing the idealized intersection of supply and demand at equilibrium would be to show how supply and demand slowly approaches equilibrium over a fixed time period.

An improved graphical representation of equilibrium would show economic oscillations, in a seven-year period of time, circling around the idealized point of equilibrium, with the amplitude of each oscillation becoming smaller as the real economy got ever closer to the ideal. This modification of the standard graphical treatment of equilibrium is shown in Diagram 2.1. Part B.

In the standard treatment of equilibrium, as the price goes up on the vertical axis, the amount demanded decreases, along the horizontal axis. The idea conforms to observed reality that buyers tend to buy less if the price goes up, and would probably buy more if the price goes down. Also, as price goes up, sellers and suppliers would likely supply more, while if prices are lower, they would probably supply less, of whatever it is they are supplying.

At the end state of perfect competition, as the graph in Part A shows, the standard treatment of demand must be shown as a horizontal line, because in perfect competition, after all adjustments have been made between supply and demand, no single consumer or single producer can affect market prices.

This condition is the preordained outcome, or telos of the theory and the graph shows the duality of the treatment of time in neoclassical theory. As depicted by the graph, the standard treatment shows the end state of adjustments, after all forces in the economy had reacted to price changes.

The proposed modification could be drawn with several inwardly directed arrows, each of which represents the price trajectories of various markets under investigation. At equilibrium, all arrows converge upon the center point that equates supply forces with demand forces.

If, for example, the supply and demand relationship begins in the upper right hand corner of the diagram, the force of price competition will cause the direction and the amplitude of the trajectory to swing down along the narrower lower band of the cycle, and inwardly towards the center point.

The proposed modification introduces the concept of dynamic price adjustments in time between the forces of supply and demand, and this concept of dynamic adjustment is needed to incorporate technology into the analysis. The introduction of time and technology is useful to describe how economic transactions in an earlier period of time are related to changes in the economic environment in later periods of time.

Diagram 2.1. Modification of the Graphical Representation of Supply and Demand Equilibrium.

Part A. Standard Treatment of Equilibrium.

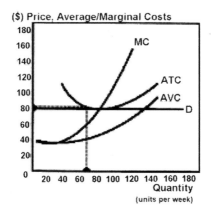

Part B. Proposed Modification of Equilibirum

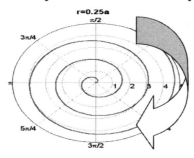

At any moment in time, technological conditions may be changing and the new analytical framework would allow the analyst to ask: Given the conditions of equilibrium in the current economic environment, and applying an evolutionary model of technology to the environment, what type of economic environment is likely to emerge in future time periods?

31

Diagram 2.2. describes how the proposed modification of supply and demand relationships could address future time periods. If the original modification of an Archimedean spiral of supply and demand in perfect competitive equilibrium is laid on its side, like a slinky toy, and expanded, the spirals could either be visualized as opening up, with the amplitudes getting bigger, or the cycles could be seen as continuing to collapse towards the center.

The logarithmic spiral, for example, shows an economy breaking away from equilibrium on an economic growth trajectory towards a new future equilibrium. The hyperbolic spiral, in contrast, is useful in depicting the idea that the economy is collapsing towards equilibrium of lower economic activity.

On the upward spiral of growth, the center points of each oscillation could be determined and connected as a line through those center points. Even though the amplitude of the oscillations are growing, the center points would be tracing out a logarithmic curve whose rate of change would be approaching zero at some future point in time.

The curve is logarithmic to show the idea of cumulative causation. Each initial increment of growth, as the economy breaks away from the old equilibrium, adds a large amount of exchanges between supply and demand to the cycle of growth. Later increments of growth add to the cycle, but at a diminishing marginal rate.

The hypothesized future point of equilibrium, where the rate of change is close to zero, would represent the economy's next equilibrium point.

As the new forces of supply and demand replaced the old forces, the economy could be visualized as passing through a micro bifurcation point where the future exchange relationships in supply and demand no longer looked precisely like those of the immediate past.

On the downward spiral of economic decline, the amplitudes of each cycle become smaller, representing the idea that the overall economic activity of exchange transactions is diminishing. The rate of change in economic activity is depicted as a curved line that connects the midpoints of each oscillation.

Diagram 2.2. Proposed Modification of Graphical Representation of Supply and Demand at End of Seven-Year Period of Time.

Logarithmic Growth Spiral of Supply and Demand As Economy Breaks Away From Equilibrium. Amplitudes Increasing.

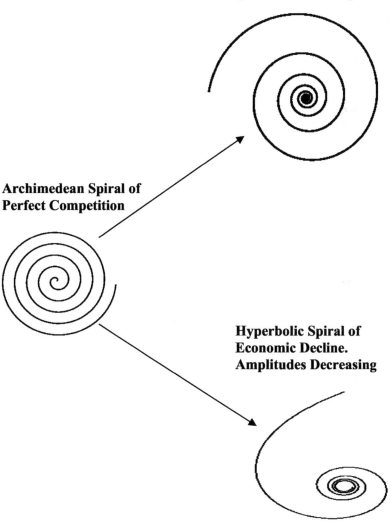

Archimedean Spiral of Perfect Competition

Hyperbolic Spiral of Economic Decline. Amplitudes Decreasing

The line traces out a sigmoid pattern to describe negative cumulative causation. If various parts of the economy become dysfunctional, other parts of the economy are affected, and may no longer function as they did before. If one element of the economy in equilibrium is connected to something else by price adjustments, and the first element dies, than the death of that one thing may mean that other parts of the economic environment may also die.

For example, if a hypothetical buyer can no longer find his former supplier because the seller has died and gone out of business, then the buyer's welfare may also be negatively affected, potentially causing the buyer to go out of business. In this case, a previously existing exchange relationship between supplier and demander has been extinguished, and the future level of economic activity is therefore diminished, depicted graphically as a smaller oscillation.

The regional economy, as it loses its vitality, can be visualized as passing through micro bifurcation points, from which the return to the earlier points of equilibrium are impossible. One may imagine how this graphical representation of the economy would apply to a small mill town where all the buildings along the main street are shut and the windows are all boarded up with plywood.

The mill closed, and all the workers lost their jobs, which caused the other businesses in the town to close. The economic structure of the town has changed, and the graph captures this downward shift in economic activity as a micro bifurcation point.

Diagram 2.3. shows how the dynamic supply and demand relationships would look from a three dimensional representation over a 7 year period of time as it approaches equilibrium from either a preceding growth phase or from a point of economic decline. The center points of each spiral represent the current pathway of the interim attractor points to equilibrium, which the economy is slowly approaching.

The economy in the future time period could be described as either tracing out a trajectory of growth or a trajectory of decline. Economic growth would appear, graphically, as a logarithmic upward sloping curve, passing through a bifurcation point. The amplitudes increase to describe the relationship between supply and demand in an economic growth cycle.

New demand for new factors or new goods in the growth cycle calls forth abundant supply, which is deployed in increasing rates of production and exchange.

Diagram 2.3. Three Dimensional Representation of An Economy Approaching Equilibrium. Amplitude of Oscillations Decreasing to Reflect Stable Exchanges Between Supply and Demand Based Upon Prices.

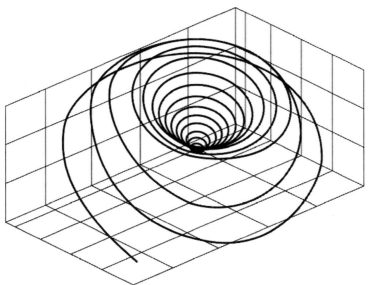

At some upper limit of growth, the trajectory of the economy flattens, and supply and demand relationships, at that bifurcation point, could settle into a static relationship for the next seven-year time horizon. From that static point of hypothesized static equilibrium, the economy can either grow or decline.

As the economy approaches equilibrium, the economy may come to rest at that point. The task for the new theory is to explain what may happen next in the next iteration of time after the economy reaches equilibrium.

It is at this stage in economic analysis that existing contemporary theory needs to be modified by changing the telos that the economy will always end up in a timeless, a historical equilibrium.

In order to better explain what may happen next, the contemporary must be placed into a framework population genetics. It would be helpful, in terms of modifying neoclassical analysis to fit evolutionary concepts, if some of the evolutionary units of analysis came from within the existing philosophical tradition of contemporary theory, to act as bridge concepts between the old and the new method of inquiry.

In other words, the task of this chapter is to explain how the philosophical offspring, evolutionary economics, somehow looks like its equilibrium parent, and not be seen by economic scholars as some sort of genetically-modified alien philosophical branch radically grafted upon the existing roots of equilibrium analysis.

Part of the bridge concept from equilibrium to evolutionary theory can be derived from Diagram 2.1. Part A, showing the standard treatment of a firm in equilibrium. The firm is depicted as a "price-taker" meaning that it enters the market and accepts whatever price had been established for whatever product the firm is selling.

Neoclassical economic theory is based upon the bedrock assumption about human behavior that the firm attempts to maximize profits, no matter what the price happens to be, or wherever the economy happens to be at that moment in time. For all of time, and in every market, the representative firm's behavior, as described in Diagram 2.1. represents the behavior of all firms everywhere.

For example, in the diagram, the firm is shown as it produces its quantity of goods precisely at the point of the tangent intersection between the firm's marginal cost of production and the firm's average total cost of production. In this case, the firm produces 80 units and sells at $80 per unit.

This graphical representation is an example of how the theory shows that the end state has been reached. At that precise end state, the profit-maximizing firm would produce 80 units and sell each unit at $80. Prior to that end state being achieved, the forces in the economy were directing the firm to that optimum point.

The most interesting feature of the equilibrium treatment as it may apply to the transition to evolutionary economics is that at the precise point of equilibrium, the "representative" firm earns zero profits.

From whenever and wherever the representative firm happens to start in the neoclassical analysis, it is always on a cosmic pathway to zero profits as a result of the competitive forces in the economy. At the ideal end state of equilibrium, after all the second derivatives of all differential equations have reached zero, any surplus profits associated with the representative firm have been completely eliminated as a result of competition between firms.

In other words, if the new theory assumes that firms compete with each other in defined product markets, in specific geographical places, and after some period of time, earn zero profits, then this concept of profits may be akin to biological economic death of the firm.

From an evolutionary perspective, the competition is between a population of existing firms, who initially are assumed to make a profit, and potential new firms, not yet born, who would like to make the profits, but to do so, must be born and then enter the market in order to take away the profits currently being made by the existing firm. The new theory assumes that it takes the new firms about 7 years to erode the profits of the older firms, which is called the period of short-term price competition.

At the beginning of any 7-year period of price competition, the regional economic environment is assumed to possess certain conditions:

1. **There are many firms in the regional industrial sectors of the market under consideration.**
2. **There are no barriers to entry or exit into the industrial sectors of the market under consideration.**
3. **The products offered by the firms are perfectly homogenous and perfect substitutes for each other.**

These initial environmental conditions, in existing economic theory, tend to possess certain desired mathematical properties regarding the outcome of zero profits at the end of the period of time under analysis. The new theory incorporates the initial conditions of the old theory, in order to act as bridge concepts.

Given that both the representative firm and the individual buyer enter the market that possesses these starting conditions and see exactly the same set of market prices at exactly the same moment in time, and holding all other variables constant, the new theory would ask: how long does it take for the exchanges in the initial period of time to lead to zero profits?

The existing theory about profit maximization is based upon the behavior of the "representative" firm, whose behavior is the surrogate for all firms. The senior managers in the representative firm apply a type of rational decision-making logic about how to maximize profits which is rooted in the mathematical properties of the initial conditions.

In the actual real world application of the theory, the managers of the representative firm can achieve optimum profits by manipulating the quantity of labor used in the production process.

Recall from Solow's analysis of economic growth in America, that there are only two variables, capital and labor, that can be manipulated, and in equilibrium theory, it is convenient to hold capital constant, in order to see what happens if labor is "varied."

In order to determine the right amount of labor, the senior management of the firm makes a decision based upon the following neoclassical economic chain of logic.

1. The marginal product of labor is equal to the wage divided by the price. $MPL = w/P$

2. Profits are equal to wages divided by the marginal product of labor.
   $P = w/MPL$

3. Marginal costs in production are the change in variable costs divided by the change in output.
   $MC = \text{variable Costs}/\Delta X$

4. Marginal costs equal wages divided by marginal product of labor.
   $MC = w/MPL$

5. Profit maximization occurs at the point where prices equal marginal costs.
   $P = MC$

Since all firms in perfect competition are price takers, the price of the good X, is set by the interaction of competitive supply and demand forces of the buyers and sellers when they meet each other in the market. If the profit maximization level of output for any single representative firm results in a profit (prices are above the firm's average total costs) then new firms will "see" those profits.

In the case of the new theory, many of the new firms that "see" the profits are not yet born. As soon as other firms "see" the profits, those firms will enter the market. As the new firms enter the market, factors of production, including labor, are shifted from their prior uses towards the production of the good that is now producing a profit.

The market entry of new firms leads to an outward shift in the supply of good X, creating a surplus of production for good X because demand is being held constant for the sake of conducting the analysis. As the supply curve shifts outward, the price of good X goes down. As the price goes down, the profits associated with good X for the initial firm are eroded. This process of price reduction and profit elimination continues until equilibrium is established between supply and demand.

For the initial representative firm, the new equilibrium for the level of output will be where the price for good X equals the marginal cost for the firm of producing good X, which now becomes the minimum value of the average total cost to produce good X.

In Diagram 2.1. Part A, this point can be seen as the intersection of the marginal cost curve with the average total cost curve. According to the diagram, the firm produces 80 units of X and sells each X for $80. If for some reason, prices for the representative firm continue to drop, say for example, if new firms continue to enter the market and then produce the product even more cheaply, prices may fall below the initial firm's average variable cost.

When prices fall below average variable costs, the representative firm cannot survive, without subsidies from the government. Their price for X is below their fixed costs to produce good X.

The basic inference from this analysis is that prices, in an economy that is in the process of reaching competitive equilibrium, generally fall as a result of new firms entering the market. New firms enter the market wherever and whenever they see profits being made by other existing firms.

As prices fall, profits erode for existing firms, and as a result, the typical existing firm, under competition earns no profits on its output, which generally takes about seven years for any specific good X.

Zero profits, in the end state of equilibrium, are the desired mathematical result obtained and preordained from the beginning of the analysis. This inference can be transitioned to the biological metaphor of economic evolution. Existing firms, with fixed production on the plant floor and fixed inputs, are on a pathway to extinction because, in perfect competition, new firms, with new production equipment, and less labor used in production, produce the good more cheaply and sell at a cheaper price, a sequence of events which continually eats the profits of the existing firm.

The observed evidence of declining prices, in the new theory, is used to predict how much longer existing firms will live, if nothing else changes.

The effect of reduced prices on the existing firm can be seen with the aid of a graphic representation depicting the technological conditions of production over the time period that prices are dropping. Diagram 2.4. Part A, shows a normal distribution of production technology associated with all firms in a region that are producing good X in at the beginning of time period T.

Some existing firms, in this initial time period, are new, and some firms are older, and have older production equipment on the plant floor and employ more labor than the newer firms. If the production technology of all firms was analyzed for age and production efficiency, some measure of the region's "average" production technology could be determined. This average technology is shown as the middle of the bell curve, and is described as Aij in the diagram.

Diagram 2.4. Part A. Graphical Representation of Average Production Technology, Aij, to Produce Unit of X at Beginning of Time Period T.

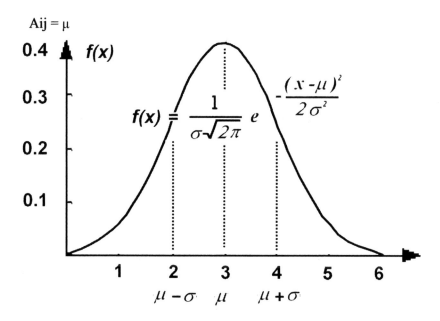

Aij $= \mu$

At the moment that the new firm enters the market, their production technology to produce good X represents the very best, least cost method of production.

In Diagram 2.4. Part B, the next period of time is described for the new entrant at $\mu + \sigma$. The new firm's production technology becomes the new competitor to beat, in terms of costs, and acts as an attractor, or reference point, for all other firms. Some firms, whose technology of production is in the area under the curve from μ to $\mu + \sigma$ are close enough in terms of technology to catch up to the new best practice, and senior management may choose to invest operating cash flow to upgrade plant equipment.

Or, alternatively, in order to compete with the best practice, managers of firms in this area under the graph may choose to cut variable costs, the most likely candidate being labor costs.

Other firms, with older production technology, in the area under the curve $\mu - \sigma$ may not be able to catch up, technologically, with the new best practice. The senior management in those firms may choose to cut costs down to average total costs, so that they can at least cover their variable costs as they cope with their declining sales and declining profits.

In order to cut costs, the senior managers will most likely cut variable costs, eliminating any factor of production not completely essential to stay in business in the new harsher environment brought about by price competition. Since plant equipment on the plant floor represents a fixed cost of capital, the most likely candidate for cost cutting is labor.

In neoclassical equilibrium analysis, there are only two factors of production under consideration, labor and capital, and one of these two variables in time period $T + 1$ must to be cut by the older firm in order to stay in business.

For other existing firms, more than 1 standard deviation from the average production technology, the prospects for survival are grim. They have experienced a steady erosion of profits, so they are not good candidates for commercial bank loans to upgrade their equipment.

With the declining prices, their positive operating cash flow has just about reached zero, so they can not finance new capital equipment internally. And, because they are in mature product markets, they do not look like good candidates for a venture capital investment to inject new capital into the production process.

The senior managers in these firms are not sitting around contemplating how to maximize profits, they are thinking about what they are going to do in their next career after their firms go out of business.

Applying the biological metaphor, those firms are going to soon be extinct, and their rate of death is an important piece of data for understanding how technological trends affect the regional economy.

These older firms are probably going to die within the seven-year period of time. They could not compete in the new harsher environment with the newer firms. The newer firms were born, or created, because entrepreneurs "saw" some profits being made in firms producing good X, and they thought to themselves: "Hey, we can make X better, cheaper, faster than those other firms, and if we do it, we can eat their profits."

Diagram 2.5. Part B. Graphical Representation of New Firm Entering Market With New "Best Practice" Production Technology, Aij2 to Produce Identical Good X, at Time Period T +1.

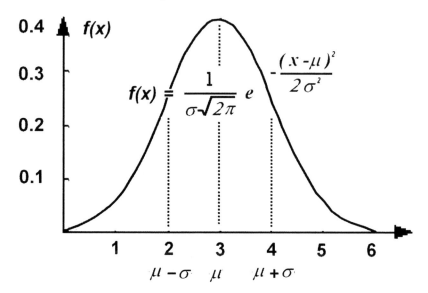

New Best Practice Production Technology Aij2 = μ + σ. Represents production costs about 66% lower, or about one standard deviation from the costs associated with the average regional production technology. Price for Good X drops in Time Period T + 1.

Part of their decision to enter the market for good X is influenced by the level of profits being made, and part of the decision is influenced by how long good X has been on the market, without experiencing technological change or innovation.

If good X has been on the market for several years without innovation, it probably has a limited product life cycle remaining, and it may not make sense, economically, for the entrepreneurs to invest capital to build the new plant to produce a good with a limited life horizon.

The type of decisions existing managers make about how to compete with the new entrants who are causing prices to drop, has ramifications for the region's economic environment. If managers decide to make investments in capital equipment and manufacturing process improvements, those new investments in T + 1 may push the region's production possibilities frontier outward, away from the existing hypothetical point of equilibrium.

If a supply of capital for new investment is available in the region, and if managers can obtain that supply of capital to make the new investments, then those investments may, contingently, create new future aggregate demand in the region.

However, if the managers of existing firms, as a group, do not make the right decision about the level and rate of regional investment, or alternatively if they cannot obtain capital, then negative cumulative causation may occur in the region.

According to Kalecki, "once declining investment has reached the point where it no longer covers current replacement (depreciation of the existing machinery) the mechanism goes into reverse and a cumulative depression sets in until the decline in the rate of profit is halted."[22]

From within the neoclassical tradition, it becomes very important to determine what influences the supply and demand for investment capital in order to determine whether new firms will be born in the region that will compete with existing firms.

If new firms are not born or created because they can not obtain investment capital, then existing firms may not go out of business as fast as they might have if new firms, with better production technology had been created. In neoclassical tradition, the regional savings must equal the regional investment at equilibrium.

As Keynes noted in his 1930 work *Treatise on Money*, the relation between the amount saved out of income and the amount subsequently devoted by entrepreneurs to investment, as additions to real capital, was the primary cause of tendencies to expansion or contraction in the economy via the effect of this savings/investment relation on prices and profits.[23]

Part of the supply of regional investment capital in neoclassical tradition is related to profits from existing firms. Those profits act like a beacon of light in attracting potential entrepreneurs. If the entrepreneurs "see" or discover that profits are being made, according to neoclassical tradition, they will immediately enter the market.

The profits that they see, however, are owned by existing firms, and one may wonder why the owners of existing firms would share their profits, as the source of investment capital, with potential competitors to help them get a new firm started?

J. S. Mill solved part of this conundrum for neoclassical analysis when he explained that profits depend on the cost of production in the past, on tools, materials, and buildings. In other words, according to Mill, something in the former economic environment is related to something happening in the current and future economic environment.[24]

Mill modified David Ricardo's labor theory of value by adding the term "abstinence" in relation to profits. In Mill's treatment, the hypothetical person who owns the firm that produces good X is exactly the same person who determines whether to make an investment in the new firm that would compete with good X. Mill modified Ricardo's use of the word "labor" with the word wages, and said that profits resulted from "abstinence" in remuneration for all classes of labor who may have helped produce good X in the past.

In other words, according to Mill, profit was the part left over from wages not actually paid out to labor. Profits, according to Mill, were always on a pathway to some minimum level at which they would just barely remunerate "abstinence." The ultimate outcome of this pathway towards zero profits, according to Mill, was a stationary state of equilibrium, at which point there would be no further inducement for investment.

If there are zero profits in the regional economic environment, then there will be no savings in the economic environment. If there are no savings, as a result of firms practicing "abstinence," there can be no investment, because in neoclassical tradition, savings must automatically equal investment at equilibrium. If there is no investment in new firms, the entire economy will ratchet down to a lower level of economic equilibrium in the next seven year time period.

From the evolutionary biological perspective of the new theory, the rate of savings in a former seven-year period of time must be invested during that seven-year period of time in order for the economy to grow in the next seven-year period of time. Just to maintain equilibrium in the future, a certain required threshold level of investment is required today.

As Domar noted, "It shows that it is not sufficient, in Keynesian terms, that savings of yesterday be invested today, or, as is often expressed, that investment offset savings. Investment of today must always exceed savings of yesterday…The economy must continually expand."[25]

Perhaps a more evolutionarily descriptive statement would be to say that a regional economy is either growing or dieing, and that in order for the regional economy to grow, new firms must continually be born, using profit from existing firms today as the source of investment capital for new ventures in the next seven year time horizon. This economic growth is the only form of growth possible, as viewed from the traditional equilibrium theory.

Clayton Christensen has noted that these same phenomena of economic growth or death seems to apply to large companies, and suggests that the evidence of death appears in the form of declining stock prices. "Probably the most daunting challenge in delivering growth," states Christensen, "is that if you once fail to deliver it, the odds that you will ever be able to deliver it in the future are very low."

Of the 172 companies cited by Christensen, 95% reached a point where their growth in sales stalled to rates at or below the rate of growth in the GNP. After the period of time that the growth rate stalled, "only 4% were able to successfully reignite their growth even to a rate of 1% above GNP growth."[26]

Christensen shows how the stock market price declined for companies whose growth rates stalled. In some cases, the decline in stock price represented 75% of their previous market capitalization. While not a part of Christensen's analysis, the time horizon prior to the period of stalled growth rates, from the new theoretical evolutionary model, could have been predicted to be about 7 years.

The economy "may" grow if investments in new firms, after some time lag, expand productive capacity in the existing markets of the regional economy. If investments in new firms increase productive capacity, for example, in the market for good X, those investments will increase the supply of good X, and therefore tend to drop the price of good X, sufficient to keep the demand for good X resulting from the introduction of the new production capacity in balance with the new supply.

This type of economic growth is like running in place. From the perspective of Diagram 1.1. Part B, this investment just keeps the regional economy oscillating around the hypothetical point of equilibrium.

In order for the new investment in new firms to move the economy along a new trajectory, new exchange transactions must arise. According to Kalecki, "The system cannot break the impasse of fluctuations around a static position unless economic growth is generated by the impact of semi-exogenous factors such as the effect of innovations upon investments…Semi-exogenous factors, such as innovations, enable the capitalist system to break an impasse of the stationary state and to expand at a rate dependent on the importance of these factors."[27]

In terms of modifying neoclassical theory to accommodate a newer evolutionary economic theory, Kalecki's point must be expanded.

First, contrary to the neoclassical theory of Walras, everything in economics is not connected by prices to everything. Some things, like technological innovations, are exogenous to prices, and are not explained by notions of equilibrium.

Second, new firms which enter the market to compete with existing firms in existing markets, with new technological production capacity, do not contribute either immediately or automatically to economic growth.

Kalecki's introduction of the term "innovation" relates to an exogenous factor outside the price system. That factor, innovation, is not always a production improvement resulting from new capital equipment on the plant floor in an existing market. In other words, productivity improvements in production processes are not necessarily a factor that contributes to future economic growth. Productivity improvements allow the regional economy to "run-in-place" around an existing hypothetical equilibrium point.

This slight deviation from conventional economic wisdom about the goodness of productivity improvements flies in the face of most current economic conjectures about the effect of technology. Michael Porter, for example, of Harvard University, has made an astounding public relations impact with his notion that sustained productivity growth is the essential measure of a nation's economic competitiveness.[28] For Porter, the improvement in productivity is directly related to technological innovation.

From the perspective of the new theory, however, productivity improvements are something to be viewed with an eye towards how fast the regional economy is headed for zero profits. The factor that causes future economic growth, on a contingent basis, is technological innovation in good X, which is not necessarily related to the concept of productivity.

Nicholas Kaldor stated that the rate of economic growth depends on the "technical dynamism" of entrepreneurs in their will and ability to foster innovation. However, Kaldor stayed within the framework of neoclassical theory, preferring to cast technological innovation in terms of productivity improvements.[29]

From the perspective of the new theory, the technical dynamism that creates growth in future time periods is not based upon productivity improvements in existing firms which allows a firm to produce good X better, faster, cheaper for existing markets at existing price relationships.

Future economic growth is based upon the birth of new firms who introduce technologically different products than existing products, and which create new exchange relationships. Productivity improvements do not necessarily lead to new markets, and it is new markets, with new income distributions, that cause economic growth.

If, as a matter of contingent evolutionary process, these new technologically different products create new income flows, and if those new income flows modify the initial distribution of income in the region, then future economic growth may occur. It is not automatic, however, that growth will occur, even if income distribution changes.

Kalecki, Kaldor, Solow, and Keynes were asking a slightly different question involving economic growth than the major preoccupation of most conventional theory, which is the attainment of equilibrium based upon price adjustments. The question about growth, though, is the right question to ask if economic analysis is to shift to a more evolutionary model of the population genetics related to the birth and death rates of firms in a region.

While economic growth has not been the predominant concern in the economic community in the past 250 years, the question of economic growth, along with the metaphor of evolution, has made enough appearances to provide a conceptual bridge from conventional inquiry based to the newer evolutionary economic inquiry.

Following the advice of Keynes, it would be a wise philosophical decision to include these premises of the neoclassical sources as part of the philosophical foundation of the new theory.

In 1841, Friedrich List, in his work, *The National System of Political Economy*, stated that economic growth depended heavily on the social and cultural resources accumulated by a nation. List noted the difficulty most nations faced in assimilating technical knowledge from other nations into the native cultural fabric and the complexity involved in transferring technical ideas into commercial products.[30]

Commenting on List's contribution, Archibugi and Michie noted, "The route which leads each nation to build its technological competence is highly path-dependent...nations which fail to exploit innovation can find themselves in an underdevelopment trap."[31]

List's use of the variables of national knowledge, culture and technology, all factors outside the price system, and the further extension by Archibugi and Michie, that something that happens in the area of technology in a prior period influences the path of economic growth in a later period of time are useful examples to include as bridge concepts.

Archibugi and Michie use the term "path-dependent" to describe how the past is related the future, and if this sequence of events in time is "law-like" in the sense of being repeatable, then methods of scientific inquiry, based upon a natural science analogy, can be used to understand the scientific laws involved that link the past to the future. In addition, if the future economic condition is characterized as a "development trap," then scientific laws of inquiry may be able to explain how and why that trap exists.

Prices for factors of production in the seven-year time horizon affect the choice of production technology, according to Paul David. Those production technology decisions consequently influence the path of technical change in production technology within a specific geographical region.

According to David, "...a localized learning-by-doing in which decisions concerning techniques influence the later learning process...choices among techniques...set in motion a long-run, evolutionary process linking factor prices, the choice of techniques and the direction of technical change."[32] David ties cultural values and learning processes at the local level, which are environmental factors outside the price system, to decisions about production technology, which are factors influenced by the relative factor prices which arise in a specific period of time.

From a neoclassical equilibrium perspective, a decision about new production technology in a specific period of time is based upon existing prices, as shown in Diagram 1.4. Part B. The new production technology has the effect of reducing costs to produce a good X. Economists call this cost reduction "declining marginal costs of production."

As Rosenberg notes, "When, through accumulated improvements, the costs are eventually reduced and become roughly equivalent to those prevailing under the old technology, even a small further reduction (in marginal costs of production) may then lead to a widespread adoption...there is a threshold level at which the costs of the new technology become competitive with the old."[33]

While it may become financially wise for existing firms to adopt the new production technology at that threshold, their ability to obtain capital to implement the new production technology, at that moment in time is contingent upon many factors, some of which are outside the price system. At this point, contemporary theory is silent, relying upon the telos of equilibrium that everything will work out for the best.

From an evolutionary perspective, there are a limited number of the total firms in the region that have the technological and financial ability to make the desired adjustments to their existing production technology.

As seen from Diagram 2.4. Part B, it is likely that firms in the area under the curve more than one standard deviation from the average production technology may not be able to make the technological leap to the new technological production process. If they do not make the leap at that moment in time, those firms are probably going to go out of business as a result of the declining prices of good X, and the resulting decline in profits associated with selling good X.

Part of the existing firm's decision to make the new investment in capital equipment is based upon their assessment of the likely future demand for good X. From a neoclassical perspective, a production technology improvement in the process of manufacturing good X causes a cost reduction.

The cost reduction causes a price reduction, which is shown in neoclassical graphs as a downward shift in supply. That shift in supply may cause existing buyers to buy more of good X, as the price drops. But, the declining marginal costs of production to produce good X does not necessarily open up a new market for good X for buyers who had been satisfying their need for good X with some cheaper alternative, rather than buying good X.

A demand curve shift for good X would involve bringing entirely new buyers into the market for good X, and the decision to invest in new production equipment partially depends on whether existing firms think new buyers will enter the market because of the reduced costs and reduced prices associated with good X.

Clayton Christensen and Michael Raynor address this potential new market in terms of "new market nonconsumers," who would buy the new product if it were to exist and solve a "job" that the nonconsumers need done.[34]

In terms of applying the evolutionary metaphor, product X starts out life at the top of the income class food chain, with high prices targeted to high-income classes, generally in very small market niches. As product X evolves in terms of production improvements, the price of good X drops, and it becomes available to lower income classes.

The market widens but the profits, per unit of good X, are declining. Finally, as a dominant design is reached across all global production locations, good X becomes so cheap to build and distribute that it enters the mass, standardized global market. From an evolutionary perspective, the entrance of good X into the global mass market is the point in time that marks the end of the life cycle for good X. This entire sequence of events can be captured and described by neoclassical theory.

However, the next part of the story, which is the development of a new market, cannot be explained by contemporary theory. The decision to invest or upgrade existing production equipment for existing firms, from a neoclassical perspective, depends therefore on the ability to obtain capital, a process outside the price system, and on the expected future demand for good X, a variable determined by changes in the technological desirability of good X compared to new and improved substitutes for good X that appear in the market.

From a neoclassical perspective, as Rosenberg has concluded "Continuous rapid growth thus requires the development of new products...low long term income and price elasticity of demand for old final consumer goods will have limited impact on growth."[35] In other words, economic growth does not automatically come exclusively from productivity improvements in existing production processes for existing goods, like good X.

The senior management in existing firms understand this element of markets and when confronted with a choice about improving the existing production technology of good X would probably base their decision on how long they think good X will survive in the market before good X is made technologically obsolete by the introduction of a new and better good X, or more likely, the introduction of good Y, that combines technology from good X and some other good A that satisfies buyers even better than good X alone.

From an evolutionary perspective, the introduction of good Y is not priced based in markets for existing goods. The introduction of good Y depends on the birth of a new firm that is producing a slightly different product for consumers in a slightly different market. The success of new good Y, in terms of market demand, is what Christensen and Raynor call nonconsumers, because they do not yet exist.

The biological population analogy for technological innovation is that baby bunnies come from slightly different parent bunnies, and so it is with new products. They are genetically different, in terms of technology, than their parent product.

Most of the time, the evolutionary modification in product technology is very slow, much like a neutral genetic drift. While that slow technological drift is occurring, related market phenomena may, or may not also be occurring at the same time in history. The market phenomena can also be described from a biological evolutionary perspective, and can be linked to certain prior concepts in neoclassical tradition.

David Ricardo thought that profits would decline in an existing period of time. His example concerned the limitation in natural resources, primarily high quality agricultural land that was suitable for growing corn. As the best land in a country was used up, lower quality land would be brought into production of corn. In order to increase overall corn production, less desirable land would be used, and consequently, the labor cost to produce the corn would go up.[36]

In Ricardo's analysis, profits fall because profits, in an existing period of time, say seven years, depend exclusively on wages. Profits are the difference between the value of wages paid to labor, and the value of the product, in this case, corn, that is produced by labor.

The value of wages paid occurs in the sphere of production. The value of the product produced occurs in the final demand market. It was Ricardo's insistence on the exclusive relationship between the value of wages paid to labor and the value of the product of labor, as it was determined in the final demand market place that opens up the historical linkage between neoclassical analysis and potential new markets in evolutionary economics.

For Ricardo, all value created by economic activity is not linked to prices in a single homogeneous market. Ricardo splits the markets into intermediate demand markets, which are akin to factor markets in the neoclassical analysis of production relationships and final demand markets for finished goods. The numeraire of value is the invariable value of labor that Ricardo holds constant in both markets.

Ricardo defines the value of capital in terms of labor value. Ricardo's use of labor value to measure profits did not vary with respect to changes in the ratio of profits to wages. For Ricardo, the entire process of production, from raw materials to finished goods that trade in final markets, constitute a logical sequence of events that occur over time, not instantaneously, as is the case with the Walrasian system.

In this sequence of events, Ricardo sought some standard unit of value that he could use to describe how value increased as a product neared the final demand market. Many years later, Wroe Alderson reclaimed part of Ricardo's analysis in marketing theory by describing the sequence of events as a market "transvection."[37]

The standard unit of value is called "the real wage rate," in Ricardo's analysis. The real wage rate would have the same proportion of production cost in the intermediate stages of production, as the unit of value would have in measuring the value of the finished good that sold in the final demand market place. Ricardo stays true to the neoclassical framework by limiting his variables to labor, capital, and land.

He departs from neoclassical tradition by breaking the production process into discrete units of time, and uses a different unit of value to measure capital. These two departures from neoclassical tradition (explicit recognition of time, and real wage rate) were combined with Ricardo's most controversial departure from neoclassical tradition, namely that the structure of prices in both intermediate and final demand markets depended on the initial distribution of income within the time period and the specific geographical area under analysis of how raw materials are converted into finished products.

In conventional marginal analysis, the entire production process is condensed into a single instantaneous moment that can be described by the mathematical properties of differential equations reaching zero at the same moment. The use of the second derivative of a differential equation as it applies to income distribution tends to suppress the analysis of how income at the beginning unit of time is related to the distribution of income at the end of the period of time, or more importantly for evolutionary economics, over multiple periods of time.

In the case of Ricardo's analysis, initial income distribution determines prices. The economic environment changes for Ricardo, as the tapestry of weaving in the production process unfolds from raw materials to finished good. In the case of Walras, the distribution of income never changes. The distribution of income is held constant in order to answer the predominant question in the minds of neoclassical economists of how an economy reaches equilibrium.

In terms of linking the newer theory to the older theory, asking how the economy evolves is the same thing as asking how the distribution of income changes over time. New products, made by new ventures, create new flows of regional income, where none had existed before.

Income distribution in the regional economic environment slowly changes in response to product technological evolution, as consumers shift their final demand buying habits. Income distribution change is a contingent evolutionary process that can be helped or hindered by the environmental conditions within the region. The environment can either help or hinder new venture creation, new product innovation, and the creation of future complementary markets.

Ricardo's three deviations from conventional neoclassical tradition, taken in total, sets the stage later in history for Keynes to further elaborate on the differences in prices between intermediate and final demand markets. Keynes' analysis on interest rates is based upon the segregation of prices in the two markets.

The distinction in prices, as they relate to movements in interest rates, was later adopted by Kaldor in his "Golden Rule" of neoclassical economic growth. The loose definition of the Golden Rule goes something like this:

Only when ALL profits are invested, and NO profits are devoted to consumption, will the choice of production technology, (within a given period of time), maximize total production output of finished goods. And, furthermore, only if ALL profits are invested in exactly the "best" production technology, will consumption of finished goods allow for a maximum rate of consumption, given the economic growth rate caused by maximum rates of profit re-investment.

Kaldor's Golden Rule of neoclassical economic growth contains two fundamental policy directives:

- The rate of profits should equal the policy target rate of economic growth in order to create maximum consumption of finished goods in the final demand markets.

- Total profit, in a given period of time, say for example, seven years, should be defined as the sum of all investment, plus any profit which may be consumed by capitalists.[38]

Kaldor's two policy directives are logical deductions from his neoclassical equilibrium analysis. His logic goes like this: If all profits are re-invested, then productivity goes up. Productivity improvements cause economic growth to occur. From Kaldor's perspective, and more recently, from Michael Porter's perspective, technological innovation in production processes drives improvements in productivity. Importantly, for the purposes of transitioning to evolutionary economics, technological factors play no role in the determination of wages and profits.

In other words, Kaldor adopts Ricardo's segregation of markets and of prices, and asserts that technology is outside of the Walrasian price mechanism. Kaldor states, "Everything depends on past history, on how the collection of equipment goods that comprise Kt (the measure of capital), has been built up." Economic growth depends on the "technical dynamism," in the economy.[39]

However, Kaldor does not adopt Ricardo's initial assumption that prices depend on the initial distribution of income. Nor does Kaldor break from neoclassical tradition that all capital is ubiquitous and uniform. For Ricardo, profit from production is a different type of capital than profit derived from activities outside the sphere of production.

Profits from within the sphere of production, for Ricardo, still fit within the Walrasian neoclassical price system, and are always declining in a specific period of time. For Kaldor, profits turn into capital when capitalists do not consume profits. Consequently, in Kaldor, economic growth is exclusively related to marginal productivity improvements that result from profits being re-invested in the latest and best production techniques.

Piero Sraffa elaborated on the distinction between Ricardo's two types of capital by describing in more detail the implications of the neoclassical tradition of one ubiquitous type of capital defined solely by prices within the sphere of production. In neoclassical tradition, according to Sraffa, capital is a magnitude, Kt that is imagined by economists to be independent of the income on capital equipment that is generated by the capital equipment.

If the rate of profit generated by an existing set of capital equipment declines, as suggested by Ricardo, then interest rates will also decline. If interest rates decline, then the capital intensity of the existing equipment on a plant floor rises. As capital intensity increases, the marginal cost of production decreases, and therefore, according to neoclassical theory, so will prices.[40]

As prices decrease for the specific goods made by the capital equipment, the markets tend to widen, but profits approach zero for each additional unit sold. As interest rates decline, the exact same set of capital equipment on the plant floor undergoes a transformation from not being capital intensive to being capital intensive, without ever changing its physical form.

The neoclassical riddle on capital contains a vicious logical circle, according to Dmitriev. "Thus, we are apparently enclosed in a vicious circle: to define value one must know the size of profit; and profit itself depends upon the size of value. It would seem that there is no other way out than to make the size of value, or of profit, depend on conditions situated outside the sphere of production."[41]

This is the transition point provided by both Ricardo and Sraffa to the new evolutionary theory. Capital, as profit, must be defined both in terms of activity that occurs within the Walrasian sphere of production, which is useful for analyzing existing production conditions in the current seven year period of time, while capital must also be defined by conditions located outside the sphere of production, which is useful for analyzing where the economy is headed in the next periods of time.

The neoclassical definition of capital that "one-size-fits-all" does not work in an evolutionary economic framework, but does work in a fixed period of time for the analysis of equilibrium. It was Alfred Marshall who made the connection between one-size-fits-all definition and production equilibrium in his *Principles of Economics*.

After 400 pages of how quantity adjustments in both intermediate and final demand markets lead to equilibrium, Marshall gets to his main point: "This is the fundamental difference between those incomes yielded by agents of production which are to be regarded as rents or quasi-rents and those which (after allowing for the replacement of wear and tear and other destruction) may be regarded as interest (or Profits) on current investments...Thus, our central doctrine is that interest on free capital and quasi-rent on an old investment of capital shade into one another gradually."[42]

"Gradually," in Marshall's case, is the period of time capital equipment on the plant floor becomes worn out or technologically obsolete, which would generally be about seven years in his time, probably less time given today's rapid product and production life cycles.

Irving Fisher picks up the implications of Marshall's central doctrine on interest rates by providing the theoretical measure of capital as both a fund and a flow, which allows neoclassical tradition to have it both ways. For Fisher, it is the interest rate in a given existing period of time that links the flow of income from the sale of products derived from a manufacturing process with the fund of capital embodied in the equipment on the plant floor.

The value of the capital equipment on the plant floor, in this treatment, can be measured as the present value of a flow of discounted future incomes obtained from the sale of products produced by the equipment. The capital equipment generates income, but the value of capital reflects the value of future income translated into present values by the interest rate. Fisher as "the impatience to spend income and opportunity to invest it" defines the interest rate.[43]

Capitalists, qua owners of capital equipment, make a decision to either invest more capital in newer equipment when it wears out, or leave their fund of capital in the bank earning interest. The decision is fairly simple, given the prevailing interest rate on Marshall's free capital: does it make more sense to invest in new equipment to produce exactly the same product in the existing final demand market, or would it be wiser just to leave the money in the bank earning interest? If the capitalists leave it in the bank, no productivity improvements take place, a bad outcome for neoclassical economic growth.

This theoretical treatment of Fisher's measurement of capital works for conventional theory as long as the capitalist at the bank and the owner of capital equipment are one and the same person. The great contribution of Joseph Schumpeter, in breaking with the neoclassical tradition, is his insistence that the two functions, production and banking, are separate.

As Schumpeter states in *The Theory of Economic Development*, "By far, the greater part of it (capital) does not come from thrift in the strict sense, that is from abstaining from the consumption of part of one's regular income, but it consists of funds which are themselves the result of successful innovation, and in which we shall see later recognize entrepreneurial profit."[44]

In Schumpeter, commercial bankers perform the function of coordinating savings and investments. The function commercial bankers perform is independent of decisions owners of capital equipment on the plant floor make about technology. The source of investment funds for owners of capital is not their own operational cash flow.

Rather, in Schumpeter, the source of capital is from previously successful entrepreneurial ventures. The profit generated in the "exit" event of those earlier ventures serves as the source of capital for later ventures. Those earlier capital gain events are outside the sphere of neoclassical production and are not explained by the Walrasian price system.

The commercial bankers "...stand between those who wish to form new combinations and the possessors of productive means...(the banker) makes possible the carrying out of new combinations, authorizes people, in the name of society, as it were, to form them. He is the Ephor of the exchange economy."[45]

Schumpeter relied exclusively on the notion of credit, not venture capital, as the source of new capital, and the new evolutionary economic theory described in this book will modify Schumpeter's emphasis on commercial credit to an emphasis on venture capital.

The main point made by Schumpeter, however, is entirely accurate for an evolutionary theory. Profits from earlier ventures are the source of funds for later ventures, and those profits are not, in any way or manner, derived from the price mechanisms in the sphere of production described by neoclassical general equilibrium theory.

Hollis and Nell describe the implications of this definition of capital for the intellectual bridge concept from neoclassical theory to economic evolutionary theory in their book, *Rational Economic Man*. "The neo-classical analogy between the market for factors and the market for final products now breaks down," they state. "In the latter (final demand for finished goods markets), value-equivalents (objects differing in use-value but equal in exchange-value are exchanged; in the former (factor markets in the sphere of production), income is paid to those with property rights in the productive process. Even when capital and labor shift in response to differentials in earnings between industries, there is no exchange between the recipient of net income and the source of income...in the factor market...the payment of income is not an exchange."[46]

From an evolutionary perspective, Hollis and Nell argue that the basic concept in economic inquiry should be the ability of the economic system to "reproduce itself." They never really state clearly what it is that gets "reproduced," preferring to direct their attention to the underlying forces that shape income distribution in a free market.

Applying the work of Schumpeter to Hollis and Nell in order to make the transition to evolutionary economics, what gets reproduced are new firms, some of which produce entirely new products, that are technologically superior to existing products, and some firms which produce older products with very advanced production methods, which has the effect of dropping prices for the older products.

The ability of an economy to reproduce itself means that the economic environment must provide the resources for new firms to reproduce, chief among them capital for creating the new firms. That fund of capital, however, is not derived from price-based exchanges in the sphere of production.

The newly funded ventures are not subsidiaries or divisions of existing production units. In Schumpeter, the new enterprise "...does not grow out of the old, but appears alongside of it, and eliminates it (the old enterprise) competitively, so as to change all the conditions that a special process of adaptation becomes necessary."[47]

Much more will be said later in this book about the biological evolutionary metaphor of new firms eliminating the old firms as a result of taking away markets and profits of the older firms, but for now, the point is to show the transition from neoclassical tradition to a newer evolutionary economic theory.

Schumpeter's work can be placed, in history, beside Irving Fisher and just before Lord Keynes. Applying the biological metaphor, something that was written by Schumpeter at the earlier part of the 20th century is connected to something that occurs, in economic theory, many years later.

Understanding the transition to the newer evolutionary economic theory can be assisted if it is placed in the historical context of Jean Baptiste Say's remark about over-production in a free market. Say's comment tended to be the starting point in history of the predominant concern in neoclassical tradition about equilibrium, as opposed to earlier concerns about just prices and fair rules of exchange.

What Jean Baptiste Say said in his "lois des debouches," was that in a free market economic system, there can never be a situation of over-production or under consumption, because production itself creates its own demand.[48]

As interpreted throughout neoclassical history, Say's law has been abbreviated to "Supply creates its own demand," or in the more contemporary setting, "If you build it, they will come."

Adopting the evolutionary perspective, what Say could have said is that in order for potential demand in the final markets for finished goods to be converted to effective demand, wages and profits from the sphere of production must be entirely spent in the final demand markets.

This is consistent with Kaldor's Golden Rule. The pattern of spending in the final demand markets must, however, be linked to increasing the rate of technological innovation in production processes.

Say's law, in the evolutionary perspective, is a contingent law. Something must happen in a given environment, and if that earlier something causes a second something to occur, then the conditions of supply creating its own demand may arise. The outcome of the contingent law is that increased incomes may occur in the specific economic environment if a certain sequence of events takes place in the earlier economic environment. In the neoclassical perspective, full employment equilibrium is a contingent outcome, not an automatic outcome, a point eloquently made by Lord Keynes.

Schumpeter identified two sources of contingency about future economic growth. The first source concerns the development of future complementary markets that feed into the primary market of final demand as a result of an entrepreneurial investment. Schumpeter described the initial, primary response to investment as the creation of "new combinations," by which he meant, new firms.[49]

These new firms enter the economic fabric at a specific moment in time, and according to Schumpeter, the economic fabric at that moment is seen as a "... circular flow of economic life," that is a closed loop, much like Leontief's closed regional input-output transaction model, where inputs always equal outputs, for purposes of financial accounting. In this closed, input-output economic model, "...sellers of all commodities appear again as buyers in sufficient measure to acquire those goods which will maintain their consumption and their production equipment in the next period at the level so far attained, and vice versa."[50]

What then happens in the economy, after the introduction of the new firm, is a contingent event, a type of Bayesian probability. Given the antecedent conditions in the closed economy, the new theory asks: what the likelihood or probability is that the new firm will create complementary new markets in future time periods?

Economic life in the closed part of Schumpeter's economic system looks very much like a neoclassical economy in equilibrium, slowly revolving around an equilibrium point. His description of how supply and demand forces tend to equalize in the circular flow is very consistent with Say's Law. "The economic system will not change capriciously, on its own initiative," says Schumpeter, "but will at all times be connected with the preceding state of affairs."[51]

It is from the initial conditions of economic stability that the complementary markets may, or may not, arise. Schumpeter was very careful to draw the distinction between the initial closed system, which looks much like an equilibrium system, and the possible future economic system, which resulted from "...a discontinuous change in the channels of the (circular) flow... disturbance of equilibrium, which forever alters and displaces the equilibrium state previously existing...These spontaneous and discontinuous changes in the channel of the circular flow and these disturbances of the center of equilibrium appear in the sphere of industrial and commercial life, not in the sphere of the wants of the consumers of the final product."[52]

In other words, the contingent changes take place first in the sphere of production relationships and then, after some passage of time, and contingently, in the sphere of the final markets.

Arnold Heertje describes Schumpeter's analysis in terms of technology. "Innovation also covers technological change in the production of commodities already in use, the opening up of new markets or of new sources of supply," states Heertje. "Economic evolution is characterized by upward-moving neighborhoods of equilibrium that are separated from one another by two distinct phases."[53]

The two distinct phases Heertje is describing concern markets, which develop on a contingent basis, based upon what consumers do when they first "see the product," and based upon whether complementary markets form around the initial technological innovation.

The first market is the existing market for goods and services, which is adequately described by Walrasian price relationships of supply and demand. The second, future market cannot be described by prices, because the future complementary markets do not yet exist. The "separation" between phases that Heertje describes could easily be translated into the newer evolutionary theory if they are recast as micro bifurcation points.

The second force identified by Schumpeter that has a contingent effect on future economic growth is allegiance to the status quo held by powerful economic and political interests who benefit from the initial distribution of income. This force appears to be a naturally occurring human trait of resisting change, especially if the change implies a loss of income or benefits for powerful people and organizations.

The allegiance to the status quo and resistance to technological change, in the neoclassical setting, are captured by Keynes when he said that "prices are sticky."

In other words, the economy can adjust to a lower equilibrium point and stay there because rent-seeking and political manipulation of prices keeps it at the status quo equilibrium point. Neoclassical equilibrium models based upon price adjustments do not work well with variables like cultural values or political power because the cultural variables are not easily translated into prices.

On the other hand, an evolutionary economic theory may be able to better incorporate these types of variables, if they can be shown to influence either the birth rate of new firms, or the technological evolution of new products.

In bridging the concepts from conventional theory to the evolutionary perspective, it would be useful to find some trace of mention of how the variables of cultural values and political power affect price adjustments found in the world of neoclassical tradition. If those earlier theoretical statements can be used as a bridge to the newer theory, then perhaps the evolutionary bridge can be better appreciated by current neoclassical economists.

In *Regional Development Theories and Their Application*, Benjamin Higgins and Donald Savoie provide a convenient opening for making this transition by describing some of the predominant cultural values in the period of time around 1600. Martin Luther's notion of "the calling," and Calvin's notion of "the chosen," and much later, Veblen's equation of the market with the jungle, are precursors to Schumpeter's insistence that entrepreneurship depends on the ambient social and cultural values of a region.

For Schumpeter, the entrepreneur is an agent of social change who acts in an unconventional manner by breaking free of standard operating procedures in social and economic affairs. Along these same lines of thought, Veblen described economic progress as a conflict between technological progress and the irrational, magical and ceremonial resistance to technological change.[54]

In this conflict between entrepreneurs, who favor a break from the tradition of the status quo, and existing producers who benefit from the status quo, political appeals to non-priced-based values occur. Harrod's theory of increasing underemployment in advanced market economies can be fit into this model.

In Harrod's analysis of economic growth, if the growth rate of income, (Gw), exceeds the natural (italics added), growth rate of income, (Gn), which occurs when population declines or technology changes, the economic growth rate will lie below the growth rate of income. The economic growth rate requires investment to be at the same percentage rate as the rate of growth in national income, which in Harrod's analysis, is equal to the marginal propensity to save.[55]

The marginal propensity to save depends on what capitalists do with their incomes, obtained from cash flow from existing enterprises. If the capitalists do not save enough, so that the marginal propensity to save is either zero or negative, the economy will enter into a cumulative downward spiral because the rate of investment is deficient to support future economic growth.

Harrod, and later Domar, do not describe why capitalists would choose to increase savings from existing cash flow operations, but a reasonable assumption is that capitalists may be interested in hanging on to the status quo arrangement of power and income for as long as possible, and thus would thwart new investments that would upset the status quo.

The concept of the cumulative downward spiral of economic activity described by the Harrod-Domar economic theory, can be extended to evolutionary theory if it is placed within the context of micro bifurcation points which represent ratchets that prohibit economic activity from returning to the prior rates of growth.[56]

Schumpeter described, prior to the development of the Harrod-Domar economic growth theory, the problem of "detaching productive means from the circular flow." The "detached" funds for investments, in Schumpeter, do not come from operating cash flow from existing enterprises, but from credit issued by commercial bankers. The credit has the effect, in Schumpeter, of creating future final demand for the new products made by the new enterprises.[57]

It is the bankers who constitute the "selection" committee on what new enterprises get funded, and consequently, the direction of the economy. Yet, the social conflict, as described by Schumpeter, is that bankers depend on stable flows of revenue to repay their loans, and thus, choose only to fund the most cautious and stable of enterprises that come before the selection committee. The repayment of loans to commercial bankers tends to establish the prevailing rate of interest for the commercial bankers, based upon their assessment of risk.

This same rate of interest is what capitalists look at and compare with the rate of profit that they could potentially make, if they invested in more capital machinery. As Marshall noted, "...interest on free capital (profits that have been saved, and are now in the hands of commercial bankers), and quasi-rent on an old investment of capital (derived from operating cash flow) shade into one another gradually."[58]

Both the bankers, and the capitalists who own existing enterprises, have a dependency relationship tied to maintaining the status quo of income distribution that is intermediated by the rate of interest obtained by bankers on commercial loans. Everyone depends on economic and political stability in order to continue to get paid, and nothing in this system benefits from an entrepreneurial change to the status quo arrangement of political power.

Allegiance to the status quo distribution of income, and consequently to the existing technology of production and products is an example of what Keynes meant when he described "sticky prices." The automatic price adjustment mechanism envisioned by Walras does not work well in an economic environment characterized by sticky prices.

Allegiance to the status quo, therefore, affects the pricing mechanism in free markets, but neoclassical equilibrium theory has no explanation for how or why allegiance to the status quo affects prices.

With a little tweaking, neoclassical general equilibrium theory can serve as the parent theory to a newer evolutionary theory. It is not a perfect fit, nor a perfect bridge from the old to the new, but the incorporation of the old seems like a necessary philosophical task for all who would like to invoke Schumpeter's name when they casually mention evolutionary economics and its relation to technological innovation.

Chapter III

Equilibrium As Non-Disruptive Asexual Technological Evolution

The idea of a naturally occurring "equilibrium" is an intellectually attractive concept. Many scientific disciplines incorporate the idea that natural biological or economic or philosophical forces direct the natural environment towards some point of harmony.

In many scientific disciplines, the idea extends to a return to equilibrium if the natural environment should experience disharmony or disequilibrium. The naturally-occurring forces are considered so overwhelming that the return to equilibrium is accepted as a naturally-occurring end point, or telos, of nature.

Little scientific or philosophical attention has been directed at the alternative idea that an even more powerful force would be required to knock the natural system out of equilibrium and move the system to some other end point. In this sense, "breaking away from equilibrium" would be a discipline in its own right with the goal of understanding where the natural system is headed once the initial equilibrium had been overcome.

John Maynard Smith describes one of the reasons why "breaking away from equilibrium" may be worthy of scientific inquiry, at least from a genetics point of view. "Information can pass from DNA to DNA, and from DNA to protein," said Smith. "But, information can not pass from protein to DNA – information being passed specifies the amino-acid sequence of proteins...if a protein with a new amino acid sequence is present in a cell, the protein can not cause the production of a DNA molecule with the corresponding base sequence."

Smith provides an electronic technological metaphor to help readers better understand what he is describing. "You can not make a new record by singing into the speakers of a stereo."[59]

If the genetic information flow is one-way, then the biological equilibrium of one time period would not exactly be like the equilibrium of the ensuing time period. In genetics, for example, the introduction of new information, in the form of a new molecule, would alter the protein structure, possibly resulting in a new genotype.

The new genotype, given the right environmental conditions, could possibly result, in an evolutionary way, a new phenotype. It would be interesting both from a genetics point of view, and from an economics point of view, to understand how the forces of novel information, in genetics or economics, creates a one-way flow of genetic or technological information whose end result is not a return to the prior equilibrium.

Part of the complexity of understanding the effect of a one-way flow of new genetic information is that the effect depends on the environmental conditions at the moment the new information is introduced. The effect on species in an asexual reproducing environment will be different than the effect in an environment where there is sexual reproduction, which may lead to the introduction of entirely new species.

The natural forces of transmission, selection, and genetic variation operate differently, both at the genotype and phenotype level in each environment. In the case of an asexual reproducing environment, for example, the natural forces of evolution lead to stasis and decline because the forces of equilibrium overwhelm the forces that resist equilibrium. In this case, "breaking away from equilibrium" would not be expected.

Austin Hughes describes this asexual process as adaptive evolution. "Thus, a process of "hitchhiking" occurs," says Hughes, "whereby a certain portion of the chromosome on which the mutation originated is carried along with it…linked nucleotide sites are "swept" to fixation along with a linked favorable mutual called "selective sweep." "At the population level," adds Hughes, "this process will have the effect of reducing variation at sites linked to the locus under selection."[60]

This process of asexual mutation almost fits as the biological metaphor for Darwinian evolution as it applies to general equilibrium economics. In Darwinian evolution, there is intense adaptive competition in a specific geographical region among species who do not interbreed. Carl Woese describes this vertical gene transfer, and contrasts the asexual process with "horizontal" gene transfer.

In horizontal gene transfer, according to Woese, the sharing of genes between unrelated species is prevalent. The horizontal gene sharing allows for new genetic information to be shared so that "clever chemical tricks and catalytic processes invented by one creature could be inherited by all creatures."[61]

In the pre-Darwinian evolutionary period, characterized by horizontal, or sexual reproduction among unrelated species, the basic biochemical machinery of life evolves very rapidly. In the Darwinian period, characterized by asexual, non-interbreeding species, evolution occurs very slowly "because individual species, once established, evolve very little. Darwinian evolution requires species to become extinct so that new species can replace them."[62]

In addition to intense competition between species, in the case of asexual product evolution, there is intense competition within the product species between older versions and the most recent technologically advanced version. The intra-species competition, both for resources to eat, and for market selection to reproduce, hastens the time to product extinction.

Freeman Dyson speculates that modern contemporary times resemble an evolutionary end to species competition and the beginning of "cultural evolution," which replaces Darwinian evolution. Cultural evolution is based upon the spread of information in a horizontal process. New ideas or technologically new information, that ends up in the form of new products, for example, would result in the appearance of a new species, akin to the earlier pre-Darwinian era of horizontal biological evolution.

Old or existing products, like existing species, evolve very little, and the evolution is primarily adaptive, as a result of process improvements in their manufacture. In cultural evolution, the horizontal flow of genetic information opens up the possibility of sexual cross-species breeding.

Like old or existing species, old products are on an evolutionary pathway to extinction, and potentially could be replaced, in a Darwinian way, by entirely new species, if the environment allows new information to flow horizontally and freely. In asexual, adaptive Darwinian evolution, it is very difficult for an environment to break away from equilibrium, whether it is population genetics or regional economics that is under consideration.

In the vertical, or constrained flow of new information, the environment would not be expected to break away from equilibrium. Thus, part of the general equilibrium economic explanation based upon price and quantity adjustments leading to an equilibrium between supply and demand is accurate, from a biological evolutionary perspective. Prices, as an information flow, in a market system, lead the economy to a point of equilibrium, which is very difficult to escape.

The metaphor for this part of biological evolution is described by Austin Hughes as "mutation during redundancy." As he applies the term, mutation is an inheritable change in the genetic material. In the case of products, a mutation would be an inheritable change in the technological features of the product, acquired from the parent, in an asexual process.

While product mutation is adaptive and directional within an existing market environment, called the regional technological envelope, the bigger piece of evolution, called market evolution is a contingent and rare event.

The repertoire of genes within an existing technological possibilities frontier is based upon prior flows of information. Some of the genes are expressed in the current product/current market environment, while other genes are latent, but able to replace or substitute for current genes, given the right set of environmental or information conditions.

Mutation during redundancy serves two functions. The non-expressed genes serve as the supply of genes in the adaptive evolution of products, and also serve to set up a potential stage for a new market. The existing market "calls forth" the non-expressed gene as the forces of adaptive competition change in an existing period of time. As the genes are called forth, they are expressed in the form of product mutation that is asexual, adaptive and directional.

The genes called forth and selected by the market demand conditions are inherited in the next generation of products, but once called forth, due to the one-way direction of information in genetics (singing into the speakers), they contribute to the sweep towards genetic fixation. Fixation, used in this context, is analogous to equilibrium, as it is used in economics.

The mutations that disrupt the existing environment the least are the most likely to be selected, and passed on, genetically. The greater the rate of mutation that disrupts the existing environment, the less likely the rate of selection, but if selected, the greater the rate of market mutation and bifurcation.

To return to Motoo Kimura's theory of nearly neutral evolution, "...in protein evolution, amino acids which are similar in structure and chemical properties are substituted more frequently than dissimilar ones...(there is) a positive correlation between amino acid similarity and the frequency of evolutionary substitution...amino acid substitutions which are accompanied by small chemical changes occur much more frequently in evolution than those accompanied by large ones."

Applying the biological metaphor from Kimura, "the smaller the difference between two amino acids, the higher the probability that they are selectively equivalent."[63] Or, alternatively, when consumers see a new advanced product that looks similar to the old product, but performs somewhat better, technologically, they are more likely to "select" that product than a product that is radically dissimilar.

The product selected has the greatest probability of passing its genes along to the next generation product, in an asexual, adaptive and directional pattern of heredity.

The selection process in economics, unlike Darwinian evolution, is not natural or random, it is positive and directional, based upon what consumers do when the first see the new product mutation. Market selection in economics is not neutral, as Kimura suggests it is for genetics. A new product that actually gets selected by consumers, however, is influenced by the genetic pattern of interaction in the technological procreation of the product.

As Kimura points out, in genetics "proximity," not size, is what matters. In this case, close counts. "Probably, what determines the pattern of interaction between amino acids in evolution, says Kimura, "is their physical proximity or direct contact within the folded protein."[64]

Proximity matters both for small adaptive changes, which consumers select, and for the closeness in the one-way information flows in technological innovation that occurs in distinct geographical settings. Technological closeness in products for regional economics is analogous to closeness in amino acids in the DNA structure of the folded proteins.

The added caveat for economics is that for genetic technological diversity to occur, the one-way information flows must be horizontal and free, not vertical and constrained by forces which inhibit the free flow of technological information. When information is not horizontal and free, the economy can not break away from equilibrium.

Species evolution slows down because product species change very little, and without technological genetics being stirred up by sexual interbreeding between different species, the existing products are on a pathway to extinction.

Doucet and Sloep suggest a mathematical model for biology that can be applied to regional economics that describes the "stability" of the forces of equilibrium around an attractor point, or equivalently, a Nash equilibrium at a specific period of time. Stability used in this sense is analogous to how economists refer to the ability of the economy to return to equilibrium after it has been perturbed. The return to stability is a canon of faith for neoclassical general equilibrium economists.

From another scientific perspective, stability would indicate the strength of allegiance by political elites to maintain the existing distribution of benefits by limiting the horizontal flows of information. Part of the "breaking away from equilibrium" in an economic philosophical sense involves a shift from a preoccupation of stability of an equilibrium to an investigation of conditions that would allow the economy to break away from equilibrium so that the economy can evolve.

"Asymptotic stability," writes Doucet and Sloep, "asks whether a change or perturbation in the initial conditions will produce a solution that converges to the original solution when (t) time, becomes very large. If a neighborhood around $X_{(0)}$ exists such that all perturbed solutions starting within that neighborhood converge to the original solutions, then the original solution is called asymptotically stable."[65]

The same type of question could be asked in economics of how strong the political allegiance to the status quo arrangement of power via maintenance of vertical flows of information, when new technological information is first introduced into the regional environment.

New technological information, applying the biological metaphor, serves as food or energy, for firms. Some food gets eaten, some food gets stored for later use, and some food may spill over, accidentally to the plates of firms which had never eaten that kind of food before.

The reason that economic evolution is positive, haploid and directional is that political elites want to direct who or what firm gets to eat the food, in a vertical or constrained way. The discussion and scientific inquiry that political forces may affect the distribution of information makes neoclassical economists very nervous because the discussion would not be "value-free."

In the mathematical model created by Doucet and Sloep, the exponent λ is the variable that describes the rate of technological information creation. Their model describes an oscillation around X_0, and if the rate of technological knowledge creation has a negative real part, meaning that the rate of technological information creation is declining, their model suggests that the system under investigation is trending toward asymptotic stability.

"A linear system is asymptotically stable, if and only if, all of its poles, (eigenvalues) have negative real parts."[66] The convergence to a stable limit cycle, they suggest, is neither chaotic, nor deterministic. It is a contingent stability cycle which could lead either to stasis, or given the right environmental conditions, could lead to a bifurcation, where the system that emerges is different than the system that preceded it.

Applying their biological model to economics, the goal of the scientific inquiry of economics is to determine and explain when and where these bifurcation points arise in market environments. The key variable is not price, it is the exponent λ, the one-way flow of technological information in either vertical or horizontal pathways.

John Nightingale explains how this interpretation of biology as it is applied to economics needs to be modified from the traditional Darwinian evolutionary model. "Darwin saw the generation of variety as independent of environment, a natural process of excessive creativity pouring potential variation of organisms and of speciation into the pre-existing environment. The environment selected those varieties that were adaptive...Darwin was a selectionist...genetical variants appear randomly and are selected."[67]

In contrast to Darwin, in economics, the creation of technological variety is not a randomly occurring event, it is a reasoned and strategic outcome and is based upon human imagination of the future. In the logical chronology of the passage of time, after technological variety has been created, the selection process in the marketplace by consumers is not purely adaptive.

Individual humans, as the unit of economic analysis, affect their environment through their imagination and creation of technological variety, and are in turn, affected by the environment in which they happen to be living by what other humans do when the other humans first see the new technology.

"Human adaptations," writes Nightingale, "are virtually entirely directed. But, the direction (of causation) is from the fertile and experimental creativity of the human mind's imagining new possibilities (to applications that may work in their environment)."[68]

Like the analogy of singing into speakers to make a new record, the direction of causation in the genetics of technological information, as it applies to economic evolution, is a one-way flow from human imagination of technology to market selection. Consumers in a market cannot sing into the speakers of technological variety to produce the new products that they desire.

What actually happens economically depends on whether the new genetic/technological information flow is horizontal, in which case inter-species breeding may occur and new species may arise, setting off a new market bifurcation, or whether the information flow is vertical and controlled, leading to stasis and economic decline.

And, to complicate matters scientifically, part of the economic reality of marginal price movements in general equilibrium economics describes the biological equivalent of a steady state environment characterized by asexual vertical information flows.

In biology, the process described as "mutation-induced speciation by recombination," (MISR), would apply to an economy on its trajectory to a steady state. Hans-Georg Beyer sets up the MISR initial conditions by stating that "Physical mutations are transformed into genetic variety by dominant recombination, which produces a more or less stable population distributed in search space...there seems to be an "invisible confinement" keeping the individuals together without any selection pressure."[69]

In biology, states Beyer, "All individuals (in this confined space) are more or less crowded around the average type...The population first shrinks and some kind of clustering occurs (around this average type), but finally the population is catched in a cloud. This cloud has a certain stability. From time to time, there are random bursts driving some individuals away from the cloud, however, on average they are driven back to the cloud."[70]

In an asexual product innovation process, it would be difficult for products to break away from the regional steady state economy. Products within the regional industrial cluster would possess the average technological coefficients of their parents.

There may be some occasional bursts of intellectual diversity and creativity in this environment, that potentially could lead to genetic bifurcation, as opposed to genetic recombination, but mostly the evolutionary process is for one generation of products to look pretty much like the parent's generation.

The consumer selection process in this type of market would not be generating much demand for radical new products, and events would pretty much be headed for a steady state. Marginal equilibrium analysis can describe this part of economic reality, but is not very good at describing what happens next, from an evolutionary point of view.

In the case of asexual heredity, for example, Oster and Guckenheimen offer a model for populations with overlapping generations. "If the population breeds continuously, so that generations overlap, then the appropriate model is ordinary differential equations."[71]

Oster and Guckenheimen continue with the application of their model to a Lotka-Volterra predator-prey population. The Lotka-Volterra model is based upon food that is eaten in a defined geographical territory. As they point out, "virtually all of the models for predator-prey systems possess either a stable equilibrium or a stable limit cycle.

In their model, the limit cycle oscillations are directed inward due to the finite population limitations. They suggest that the predator, in the absence of prey, dies out exponentially, the hypothesis, which they test with their model.

In their case of overlapping population generations, with limits on food, they very reasonably predict that the population of predators would reach some stable equilibrium. However, for certain types of initial conditions in the environment, for example an environment that contained 3 or more species, the possibility exists for higher order bifurcations. "Successive bifurcations beyond the first occur when the eigenvalues of the Poincare map passes outside the unit circle, headed towards a contingent vague or strange attractor."[72]

This strange attractor, in the application of the biological metaphor, would be the potential new Nash equilibrium, the point to which the regional economy may be headed, if the regional environment had obtained, somehow, miraculously, a new supply of food, in this case, a new supply of technological knowledge.

Which begs the scientific question, "by what miracle does the new food of knowledge get introduced into the economic environment?"

Following the suggestion of Fred Hoyle, the introduction of new technological food results from a combination of genetic pressure with chance environmental fluctuations. "Whenever genetic pressure forces down the number of individuals possessing a particular property below a certain level," suggests Hoyle, it is then an adverse environmental fluctuation that delivers the final blow to survival."[73]

Applying the biological metaphor, there are two adverse environmental fluctuations at work in any regional economy. First, existing products, in existing markets are experiencing their own rate of technological obsolescence as a result of the asexual process of technological evolution, as the repertoire of non-expressed genes in the regional technological possibilities frontier are used up, as they are "called forth."

Plus, in the final demand marketplace, the rate of product obsolescence is hastened by competitive price pressures which are dropping the marginal rate of profits to zero. The final blow to survival is the chance introduction of technology that eliminates the product from the environment and sets the economic trajectory on the pathway to extinction.

What the eigenvalue describes is the rate of technological transformation in the regional economic structure from one time period to the next. Given a certain rate of technological knowledge creation, the regional economic trajectory could be either upward, towards a new strange attractor, or downward to economic decline.

One of the reasons why Jane Jacobs' work on diverse metro clusters is correct, from a biological metaphor point of view, is that multiple initial clusters of technology, for example clusters producing 3 or more product species, have the greatest chance of cross fertilization in inter-species breeding.

As Hoyle points out in the case of biology, "Most species are limited to a geographical area, with good adaptation to the conditions inside the area, but with less and less good adaptations towards its boundaries...species stay obstinately fixed, disappearing as the limits of their habitats are reached."[74]

The environmental conditions for breaking away from equilibrium, therefore, depend both on genetic pressure, caused by firms seeking new sources of technological food, and environmental chance, in the form of initial technological conditions that allow for inter-species product breeding, within a defined geographical region.

Christian Forst describes the three process involved with understanding how an economy can break away from equilibrium. First, within the product sequence space, technological genotypes must be mapped in both the asexual and sexual heredity space.

Second, in the product phenotype space, technological selection must be mapped from product to market selection. Third, in the geographical space, the topology of the technological intersections between industrial clusters within the region must be mapped, in order to understand how technological genotypes in one cluster end up in phenotypes in a new cluster.[75]

The first process is characterized by a one-way flow of genetic information. The second process contingently involves a two way flow of horizontal or vertical information, which affects the third process, which itself can feedback, via political manipulation of the environment, and affect the first flow of information.

From a biological point of view, the chance environmental conditions, coupled with genetic pressure in all three processes, that would create the conditions for breaking away from equilibrium would be rare, and dependent on just the right mix of events to push the evolutionary process to the strange attractor point that looked entirely different than the current state of equilibrium.

It is remarkable, from a scientific biological perspective that economic evolution of product species ever occurs. Declining markets seem like the most likely outcome of ordinary economic interaction. Thomas Nagle provides an accurate description of what happens in a "declining market."

"When production costs are largely fixed and sunk because capital is specialized to the particular market, the effects of market decline are more onerous…The goal of (pricing) strategy in market decline is not to win anything; for some it is to exit with minimum losses through retrenchment, harvesting, or consolidation."[76]

To return to John Maynard Smith's metaphor, once prices come out of the speakers as music, they do not immediately go back and stand in line at the front of the stereo to create a new CD. The prices explain the music produced on that CD, made at a specific period of time, under unique environmental conditions, and selected by consumers for a very short period of time.

In *Rethinking Economics* Ulrich Witt asks, "Why does everybody not acquire the new information instantaneously?", speaking about the diffusion of new ideas in an economy. He answers his own question with reference to the fact that industrial clusters, which affect how new technology, is turned into knowledge, bound the channels of communication. Each individuals' decision depends on how many other members of the population have already made a particular choice."[77]

Witt identifies emergence and dissemination of novelty, "…new information is created and diffused throughout the economy and induces new kinds of action…" without ever breaking free of the equilibrium price model. Evolution, as an idea, used inside the neoclassical tradition, does not work because it is not a price-based phenomenon. The metaphor of evolution, as it applies to economics, must come from a scientific tradition that incorporates genetics, heredity and bifurcation.

To answer Witt's question about the timing of the arrival of new information, an economy in decline is killing off the channels of information and communication, which destroys creation and diffusion of knowledge. In biology, an organism that is dying is killing off nerve cells in the brain, which distribute mental images.

In an economy, once mental images, called imagination, are killed off, the food of knowledge is destroyed and the economy will die. This is not a price-based phenomenon that returns the economy to the prior equilibrium steady state.

Farmer and Mathews identify cultural values and the rule of law as important variables to explain the emergence of new technology, but are at a loss to link cultural values to the movement of prices. When an individual imagines a new technological solution, the ability to implement the new idea, according to them, is "…based upon culturally embedded cognitive frameworks and subjective expectations about future states of the world."[78]

If mental imagination is not a price-based activity, then imagination, as an economic variable, cannot be used by conventional economic theory. The better question for Farmer and Mathews to ask is why humans developed the mental capacity to imagine different futures, and what cultural conditions are required to allow imaginations about future states of the economy to be realized.

Brian Arthur shows how price-based equilibrium theory can be modified and extended by incorporating elements of how both prices and expectations can fit into a larger biological evolutionary theory. He begins by making a distinction between homogeneous expectations about prices and dividends, and heterogeneous expectations about prices and dividends.

Applying the biological metaphor, homogeneity in expectations looks something like an economy with little genetic variety in a short period of time. Homogeneity could be translated into the idea that many mental images in both the production side of the market and on the consumer side of the market are the same.

Everyone is thinking alike. Homogeneity in expectations fits within the existing neoclassical tradition for explaining how an economy, in a short period of time, leads to an equilibrium outcome. As long as the behavior being explained is for exactly the same set of consumers, the same products and the same price expectations. As economists like to say at the beginning of each scholarly article: ceteris paribus.

Under conditions of heterogeneity, says Arthur, "unknown price expectations merely lead to the repeated iteration of subjective expectations of subjective expectations, an infinite regress in subjectivity."[79]

The heterogeneity in price expectations performs same type of function as genetic variety performs in evolutionary theory. Heterogeneity in expectations is a way of introducing mental imagination about the future into neoclassical analysis.

Arthur calls his homogeneous economy a non-complex economy, and his heterogeneous economy a complex economy. Changing the mathematical formulas somewhat from linear to dynamic non-linear equations would allow the iterations to be viewed as spirals that reflect either inward regressions toward extinction, or outward regressions toward some strange new attractor point.

A trajectory towards some strange new attractor point would be interpreted, from a neoclassical perspective, as an economy breaking away from a stable equilibrium.

From the biological metaphor perspective, heterogeneity in expectations reflects the appearance of new technological knowledge. Everyone is not thinking alike as a result of this new technical knowledge. Different minds are imagining different futures with different technologies and different prices.

If their imaginations about the different prices are realized, they can imagine how their incomes would change for the better. In the case of changing incomes, brought about by changing technology and new prices, the environmental conditions would be ripe for technological bifurcation that is caused by horizontal gene transfer among phenotypes.

Johansson and Andersson describe how the production technique for existing products that has become routine over time means that a growing number of firms in many geographical areas are able to supply the standardized product to an existing market. "As market demand expands for the new product, production techniques (for the new product) improves, which moves the regional technology set frontier outward."[80]

They link knowledge creation to the introduction of new products, which cause the technological possibilities to change. "Along a product cycle path," they write, "the knowledge intensity is high when a product is non-standardized and the process is non-routine."[81]

From the biological metaphor perspective, they could have added that knowledge intensity is highest along the technological border between two genetically different products that share some production techniques in common.

"Standardization and routinisation," they note, "means reduced knowledge intensity." If the new products should, by chance, or by marketing efforts, meet consumers "...the stronger the prerequisites for substitutions between the (old) product and the (new) product...as a result of price changes and learning among customers."[82]

They make the connection, from a biological evolutionary perspective that the regional economic trajectory, without new technological knowledge, is on a pathway of decline. "The trajectory of an ordinary product cycle portrays sales growth during a product's formative years, with an *inevitable* (emphasis added) slowdown as the product matures."

The pathway of the regional economy that produces new products however is very uncertain and risky, because they state, "...new product success depends on formation of both future markets (complementary markets that support the new product) and customer demand."[83]

The initial environmental conditions for the creation of new technological knowledge are heterogeneous expectations, genetic diversity in technology, and horizontal information flows. If all of those conditions are present in a regional economy, then a new product, born from sexual breeding between two phenotypes, may lead to future economic growth, if consumers can learn about the new product and choose to buy it.

The choice of consumers however, is only one necessary condition for market bifurcation in demand from the old patterns of demand. As Johansson and Andersson correctly note, the bifurcation in market demand depends on the creation of complementary markets, which support the new product, while at the same time, the complementary markets speed up the rate of technological knowledge creation, via brand new horizontal information flows.

In their new product cycle theory, "the speed of change of technology depends on the level of new investment that creates new ventures."[84]

In order to analyze how an economy breaks away from equilibrium, neoclassical theory would be required to incorporate several component of sociological theory about the role of capital that is not price-based. "By capital," says George Homans in Social Behavior, "I mean anything that allows them (investors) to postpone actions leading to some immediate reward in order to undertake other actions whose rewards, though potentially greater, are both uncertain and deferred...it (capital) may take the form of a moral code, especially a code supporting trust and confidence between men; a well-founded belief that they (investors) will not always let you down in favor of their private, short-term gain."[85]

Moral codes, while important to understanding the formation of capital, are not price-based variables. If the moral codes do not transfer from generation to generation in a process akin to cultural heredity, investors will not be able to reap their deferred rewards.

If they do not reap their rewards, complementary markets will not be created, and the conditions for horizontal gene transfer will not be established, thus killing off the source of creation of technological knowledge. In which case, equilibrium will be re-established, that leads to a period of fast economic decline.

Market exchanges for products based upon prices reflect temporary relationships between buyers and sellers that do not require long-term trust and honesty in order for the exchange to occur.

Investments are based upon long-term moral codes of honesty and truthfulness in order for the investors to appropriate the profits that have been deferred.

From an evolutionary perspective, a regional economy that featured a social structure based upon trust and honesty would be hypothesized to lead to the greatest rates of economic growth because investments were creating the conditions for faster rates of knowledge creation from complementary markets, which could lead to market bifurcations.

The existence of moral codes are, for Arthur's analysis, the variables that lead neoclassical theory out of the infinite regress of subjectivity when there is heterogeneity in future expectations. The subjective probabilities converge to a strange future attractor point of an objective probability, given a Bayesian analysis of the prior distributions of the subjective expectations.

Knowledge creation is not a price-based activity, but is dependent upon the economic structure of interindustry relationships that exist in a regional economy. To the extent that the temporary price-based relationships in the regional economic input-output structure are characterized by forward linkages from intermediate demand to final demand, and backward linkages, from final demand to intermediate demand, the rate of technological knowledge creation should be greater.

To the extent that the regional input output structure features both vertical flows of production technology information, up and down column coefficients, and horizontal flows of information of demand information, along row coefficients, the rate of technological knowledge creation should be greater.

Part of the new evolutionary understanding for economics is that technological innovation, as it is described by genetic bifurcations between different product species, constitutes a one-way flow of information, while prices in the economy, for short periods of time, constitute a two-way flow of information.

The causes of the information flows are different, and the effects are different, but both types of information flows complement each other, and together, determine the evolutionary pathway of the regional economy that is breaking away from equilibrium.

In order to describe an economy breaking away from equilibrium, which Schumpeter called "economic development," he first identified the source of capital for investments in new ventures. "Capital," says Schumpeter, "is a concept of development to which nothing in the circular flow (traditional neoclassical analysis) corresponds...By far, the greater part of it (capital for new ventures) does not come from thrift in the strict sense, that is from abstaining from the consumption part of one's regular income, but it consists of funds which are themselves the result of successful innovation, and in which we shall later recognize as entrepreneurial profit." The profits from the earlier investments were destined, in a subsequent period of time, for investment in the "...founding of new businesses."[86]

In other words, for Schumpeter, the source of capital for investments in new ventures is derived from the loans made by commercial bankers on prior successful investments, whci he called entrepreneurial profits. "It (entrepreneurial profit) attaches to the creation of new things, to the realization of the future value system...Without (entrepreneurial) development, there is no (entrepreneurial) profit, and without profit, no (economic) development...without (entrepreneurial) profit there would be no accumulation of wealth."[87]

In order to have economic development, capital from the earlier loans would automatically be invested in new businesses. The dynamic of time enters Schumpeter's theory of economic development from a logical chronology of events. In an earlier time period, profitable investments took place in a new business. In a later time period, the profit would be invested in the next generation of new enterprises.

The process of making capital investments over several time periods, for Schumpeter, allows both economic development to occur, in the form of new demand for new products, and allows for an accumulation of wealth, in the hands of the new business owner.

The process of making capital investments over extended periods of time could not occur if cultural values of trust and honesty were not inherited from generation to generation.

Schumpeter makes two points that are important to making a philosophical transition from equilibrium theory to evolutionary economic theory. First, he notes that one effect of new investments is to cause new distributions of wealth among society.

Second, the prices in the second time period associated with capital equipment are determined by the distribution patterns of wealth and incomes in an earlier period of time. For Schumpeter, as in Ricardo, income distribution in the earlier time period explains, or determines, prices in the later time period for both capital equipment and the products that the capital equipment produces.

"It is not essential," says Schumpeter, "that the new combinations should be carried out by the same people who control the production or commercial process...new combinations mean the competitive elimination of the old...It (the investment process in new firms) explains on the one hand the process by which individuals and families rise and fall economically and socially...In a non-exchange economy, for example, a socialist one...the social consequences (of the investment process) would be wholly absent."[88]

The profits from the earlier investments are re-invested in the second time period, according to Schumpeter, and the effect of the investment in time period two, is to create new income and wealth in time period three. The investment process in new firms creates new income in the future, which Schumpeter called "purchasing power," at the same time that it eliminates the existing firms.

"The entrepreneur needs capital...to serve as a fund out of which productive goods can be paid for...it is a fund of (future) purchasing power." The banker, on the other hand, which has obtained the profits from the earlier exit events, is continually looking for new firms in time period two to invest in. The new firms, for Schumpeter, represent the demand for capital, while the banker represents the supply of capital.

The reason that the banker is always searching for new ventures, or from the evolutionary perspective, new technological food, is that the source of food, new technological knowledge, in the Lotka-Volterra sense is being depleted.

"For what business yields interest permanently?" asks Schumpeter. "The return (from operational profits) of every business ceases after a time, every business, if it remains unchanged, soon falls into insignificance...According to our view, the capitalist would first have to lend his capital to one entrepreneur, and after a certain time period to another, since the first cannot be permanently in the position to pay interest."[89]

Schumpeter got part of the picture right regarding the capital investment process that created new future income, and new future demand, but also got part of it wrong, because he continued to rely on the equilibrium concept of the circular flow that the capital supply that came out of the economy allowed marginal assets to be deployed in more (marginally) productive processes.

Schumpeter wrote, "The (new) demand...causes a rise in the prices of productive services. From this (rise in prices) ensues the withdrawal of good from their previous use...the newly created purchasing power (new incomes) is squeezed out at the cost of previously existing purchasing power..." [90]

In his model, the commercial bankers loaned capital to new firms. The alternative model is that profits from the exit events are re-invested in new technologically advanced firms in the form of equity investments, not loans. The future wealth and income from the investment creates the future conditions for the future exit event if consumers switch their buying habits from old firms and existing products to the new firms.

The source of capital for the new firms is derived from exit events, which create capital gains, not capital that is created from the repayment of interest and principal on loans. The motivation for making the investment is to create future incomes, which compete with the existing distribution of income.

Modifying Schumpeter's model somewhat, breaking away from equilibrium requires three fundamental conditions to happen in a logical time sequence.

First, cultural values of trust and honesty must be inherited from generation to generation in order for the venture capitalist to reap his reward, and appropriate his hard-earned capital gain profit from an earlier risky investment.

Second, knowledge creation and diffusion must occur in the earlier time period so that the venture capitalist can find new firms to invest in.

Third, the investment process in time period two "must" create new income flows in time period three, in other words new future final demand for finished goods, to be sufficient for the capitalist to reap his rewards a second time from the exit event.

The profits from exit events in the future are not explained by price-based returns to marginal productivities in time period one. The future profits depend on the creation of new future wealth in time period two.

The investment process in technologically advanced firms creates, contingently, new future income distributions. The competition in time period one that is relevant for understanding how an economy breaks away from equilibrium is not the price-based competition of products of neoclassical theory, it is the income competition between those families and social forces that derive income from the status quo arrangement of power and the venture capitalists and owners of the firms they invest in that are motivated to increase their income.

The new firms destroy the old firm's source of income, and if you happen to be an owner of an old firm, your logical response is to deny the new firm entry to the market.

Income competition, as Schumpeter correctly noted is based upon political control. "Every individual loan transaction is a real exchange...the exchange of present for future purchasing power...the *control* (italics added for emphasis) of present purchasing power means more future purchasing power (more income) to the borrower."[91]

In the neoclassical equilibrium perspective of the "circular flow," capital assets released in one productive enterprise can only create wealth when used in a more productive enterprise, which is called productivity growth. But, productivity growth never allows an economy in equilibrium to create entirely new sources of income or new future demand. And, to paraphrase Schumpeter, what existing firm stays profitable infinitely?

In the closed circular neoclassical model where the forces of equilibrium reign, "the possibility of profit, therefore, and with it the potential effective demand have no definite limit...the demand (for loans) with interest at zero, would always be greater than the supply (of capital)"[92]

The economic growth that comes about from technological innovation is a force that is external to the price-based system of marginal analysis, or as Schumpeter said about capital, it is a concept of development "to which nothing in the circular flow corresponds."

The competition for income between existing firms and new firms, that produce new technologically-advanced products, affects the supply and demand curves for investment capital in a given fixed period of time, if all other factors, especially the prices for goods, remain constant. The logical implication of stable income equilibrium, from an evolutionary perspective, of course, is economic extinction.

Without new dynamic flows of income, and new variations in the distribution of wealth, which creates future demand, which creates entirely new market relationships, a regional economy could never break away from the Nash equilibrium point, in that limited period of time.

In a regional economic environment that is experiencing a high rate of new firm creation, there is an increased likelihood of genetic crossover between product species. The analytical economic framework to evaluate the probability of genetic crossover would look like a regional input output transaction matrix, modified to show technological closeness between species.

If a genetic crossover happens to occur, then there is a second likelihood that the new species may alter the environment through the creation of a new market. The creation of a new market would have the appearance of a regional economy breaking away from equilibrium.

However, the creation of a new market depends on a selection process that is distinct from the genetic crossover process. New phenotypes (product species) contain different assortments of genotypes, which differ in their market "fitness" attributes.

A market transition algorithm could suggest the probability that a certain configuration of genotypes could lead to a "fitness" that would be selected by the market environment. The market fitness algorithm contains an irony with respect to describing how a regional economy could break away from equilibrium. The irony involves an element of human psychology and the mental attributes of how the brain processes images when it first confronts novelty.

To the extent that the new phenotype has an assortment of technological genotypes that looks like existing products, consumers in the market are more likely to select the new phenotype. The greater rate of market acceptance is based upon the brain's search and sort mechanism for solving novel situations.

Consumers may have seen a product that looked like and acted like the new product. Consumers can imagine how the new product may "fit" with their existing assortment of products, and can imagine how to use the new product in their existing daily routines. However, the greater the technological affinity the new product has with existing products, the less likely the new phenotype will lead to an economy breaking away from equilibrium.

A phenotype created from an asexual heredity process has a limited chance of breaking away from the stable local attractor point.[93]

New product phenotypes with a unique assortment of genotypes create the conditions of an unstable equilibrium. The more the new product is different genetically, the less likely consumers are to select it because their brains are searching for how the novel situation "fits" with the prior experience.

The likelihood of selection of the new product goes up in a market environment where consumers are confronted with the appearance of new product phenotypes that are slightly different than the products that they have already seen. The probability of selection goes down if the consumer has never seen the technological attributes of the new product.

Part of the consumer's risk of selecting the new product can be decreased however, depending on the environmental conditions surrounding the selection. In a genetically diverse environment, with high rates of new firm creation, and high rates of genetic crossover, an individual consumer is more likely to take a "risk" on selecting the new product with an unproven technological track record.

The environmental conditions of genetic product diversity supplement the individual consumer's own mental reluctance to select something new. The consumer's willingness to select a new product is based upon a social environmental condition that concerns the level of income in the genetically diverse environment.

Wealthy regions with higher incomes are associated with willingness to take a risk because the higher incomes cushion the downside risk that the new product, which is introduced to the market at a higher price than existing competitor products, may not fit.

Poor regions, desperate for growth, are generally populated by consumers with limited experience in selecting genetically new products, and are risk-averse and status quo oriented. The likelihood of selection of a radical new phenotype goes down, but especially so in a poor region, because consumers can not imagine how the new product "fits" and are not willing to take a risk that the product may not work.

The greater the historical rate of market selection of new product phenotypes that are radically different than existing phenotypes, the greater the probability that the regional economy will break away from equilibrium to a new local attractor point.

Regions with high incomes, populated by consumers who have greater experience in selecting new products, are therefore expected to have higher rates of economic growth.

There are environmental factors in high income and genetically diverse regions, which inhibit the rates of consumer selection of new products. Mancur Olsen describes the emergence of social resistance to further innovation because the existing status quo distribution of income satisfies the most recent generation of product innovators.

New knowledge on the part of consumers to understand how new products may fit, and new firms, which may divert income from the existing distribution of income, threaten the status quo local attractor point stability.

Technological change in the form of new phenotypes, born from sexual genotype crossover, leads to substantial risk of income loss by those who derive the greatest amount of income from the continuation of the status quo.[94]

As Mokyr suggests, the "causal chain could thus run from technological success to income and from there, to institutional change, rather than from institutional change to technological change."[95] "Technological progress," says Mokyr, "has run into an even more powerful foe: the purposeful self-interested resistance to new technology...Without an understanding of the political economy of technological change, then, the historical development of economic growth will remain a mystery."[96]

Investments made today in new technological products can cause income distribution to change in the future, if consumers select the new products. If consumers select a new product, new complementary markets may be created to service and support the new product that consumers have chosen to select.

If these new complementary market are created, the regional economic environment may change, and entirely new patterns of income and what Schumpeter called "purchasing power" may arise, and displace old products and the status quo distribution of income.

Resistance to the investment by powerful social forces is a LaMarckian adaptation to maintaining the status quo, which leads, ultimately to regional economic decline, because, as Schumpeter noted, "what firm stays profitable infinitely?" The more that technological innovations can be directed to small genetic changes, which are more likely selected by consumers, the less likely the regional economy will be to break away from equilibrium. The social forces that resist technology and investments in new products, thus have a evolutionary reason to control the direction of technological innovation by keeping it channeled into very specific genetic varieties.

Existing firms, and existing commercial bankers who may have loaned money to those firms, have a motivation to control the direction of technology in order to maintain their incomes.

"Research and development is directed towards shaping and refining knowledge in very specific ways," states Peter Hall. "Research and development is worth doing only if it generates a product or process of commercial value...which both fits with the firm's existing capabilities and meets market requirements (of existing consumers).[97]

As a point of reference, the idea expressed by Hall is the same idea expressed by Clayton Christensen when he describes sustaining innovations. "Sustaining innovations," states Christensen, "are what move companies along established improvement trajectories. They are improvements to existing products on dimensions historically valued by customers."[98]

The social resistance to technological innovation that could possibly lead to new markets contains the most ironic outcome associated with the application of the biological metaphor to regional economic evolution.

By manipulating the free horizontal flow of information and attempting to impose asexual technological innovation, the short term stable attractor point is maintained, leading to a faster slide to evolutionary extinction, with fewer varieties of genetics left in the regional technological possibilities frontier to re-generate economic growth in the future.

Given the rare set of circumstances that must coalesce in a chronological sequence of time, it is remarkable that economic evolution that leads to economic growth occurs at all. As Mokyr observed, it just so happened in the modern history of economics, that one country would first experience technological innovation, then economic growth and subsequently experienced economic decline, only to be replaced by some other country that was experiencing technological innovation.

The alternative explanation of why one country replaced another country with faster rates of economic growth, for relatively short periods of time focuses on the environmental conditions that allow technological knowledge to be created, commercialized via investments in new firms, which disrupt income and wealth in the future, and contingently creates a new market environment.

Chapter IV

How Economic Equilibrium Leads to Economic and Political Inbreeding

Michael Storper, in 1997, surmised that neoclassical product cycle theory did not provide adequate insights into the "how, why, and where," of the initial geographical agglomeration of industrial sectors. His criticism of neoclassical economic theory was based on the absence of history and politics as useful explanations of how economic development occurred in the global market.[99]

More recently, Joel Mokyr has highlighted the debate between Eric Jones and David Landes. Jones believes that culture and history are largely secondary and endogenous factors in the explanation of economic growth. These variables should be subordinated to the larger explanatory variable of price movements that lead an economy to equilibrium.

Mokyr contrasts Jones' concept of economic growth with the thoughts of David Landes, who believes that cultural values are critical variables for understanding economic growth in one region versus another.[100]

In contrasting the debate, Mokyr asks why, in the history of economics, it appears as if the economic growth benefits for a region related to technological innovation seem so fleeting in time.

He answers his own question by reference to "Cardwell's Law" that suggests that most societies that have been technologically creative have been so for relatively short periods, but that almost miraculously, there was at least one other nation that was technologically creative, and that the others would follow.[101]

To better understand the origin of the initial institutional conditions for moving from one point in economic time to another point in time, the work of George Homans in *Social Behavior*, is useful.

Homans developed a theory to explain how social behavior, in this case economic behavior in markets, gives rise to relatively enduring social structures. As he notes, "Without repeated social actions, there are no enduring social structures."[102]

In the case of economics, it is the regularities and uniformities in behavior exhibited by the "units of analysis" as they imagine and anticipate the behavior of others in the social institutional environment called a "market."

What motivates human behavior in markets, Homans suggests, is the expectation of rewards and the incentives provided by the institutional structure to obtain the rewards in the market. "What a man expects to get by way of reward or punishment under a given set of circumstances," says Homans, "is what he has in fact received, observed, or was told that others had received, under similar circumstances in the past."[103]

In an institutional market structure characterized by the rule of law, individual expectations for reward could be met, as long as everyone followed the rules, and rewards were granted based upon individual merit and individual effort.

On the other hand, in a market characterized by lawlessness, reward based upon merit would not be obtained because the rewards in prior periods were not characterized by certain outcomes in the market if one obeyed the rules.

"The past history of men makes a big difference to their present behavior, and not just the recent past, but often the past of long ago. A man's past history of success, of stimulation, of the acquisition of values all affect the way he behaves now," states Homans.[104]

Homans describes this part of social interaction as a contrast between "distributive injustice," and "distributive justice," which is where reward is based upon merit.

An injustice occurs when a person does not get the amount of reward he had expected to get based both upon what he had seen rewarded in the earlier period, and what he gets in comparison to the reward another person gets in the same time period.

Injustice, in this case, is legitimate expectations denied unfairly because the rule of law and the application of the rule of law is unequally tilted to the most powerful agents, who have captured control over the use of the police power of the state.

As Homans points out, capital is not just money used for investment. "Capital may take the form of a moral code, especially a code supporting trust and confidence between men; a well-founded belief that they will not always let you down in favor of their private short-term gain."[105]

Contemporary economists call this type of capital "social capital," whose effects usually extend about 50 miles from the center of a metro regional economy. Granovetter has called this effect the "moral economy." In his concept, the moral economy is the "...degree to which a group's operations presuppose a moral community in which trustworthy behavior can be expected, normative standards understood, and opportunism foregone."[106]

Adherence to the standards of behavior in the moral economy is equivalent to the allegiance to the rule of law, not in the strict judicial application of the law, but in the civil norms and values that guide everyday behavior. To the extent that many brains are processing and filtering images of the future, based upon a common perspective that other brains will follow the rules, then current investments can be expected to obtain future reward and the more likely that the expected future market will actually materialize as it slowly comes into focus based upon common expectations.

Robert Cialdini mentions two of the most important civil rules of behavior that under gird the more formal "rule of law" in society that allow brains to filter common images and expectations about another person's behavior. His two important rules of behavior are reciprocation and personal responsibility.[107]

The moral code of reciprocation means that one person in an exchange who absorbs a future obligation to another person actually performs the obligation. The common language term for this rule is trust, and a person who follows the moral code of reciprocation is often called "trustworthy." The civil rule of personal responsibility means that the person who is obligated to reciprocate in the future maintains his behavior over an extended period of time in order to discharge his moral obligation.

As Homans points out, most of neoclassical theory simply overlooks the importance of these two rules of civil behavior as essential institutional structures that make the marginal analysis of neoclassical math work. "Economics," states Homans, "can explain many features of behavior provided that it takes certain things called institutions, the market itself...as simply given...economics disregards the relatively permanent relationships between individuals or between groups, which form social structures."[108]

When the market, as an institution, is placed in the metaphor of population genetics, and the civil rules of law are examined as a part of the ambient environment for their effect on evolution, it becomes apparent that a region characterized by the rule of law would have a different economic trajectory than a region that did not have a moral economy.

Further, an economy that once possessed the rule of law and then had lapsed into lawlessness, based upon special interest manipulation of the rules, would be expected to experience economic decline associated with biological political inbreeding which comes from killing off the multiple diverse sources of knowledge.

Inbreeding causes a loss of genetic diversity, and in the case of economics, the loss of diversity destroys the gene pool of regional knowledge.

This hypothesis follows the insights of Darwin about the loss of genetic diversity via the process of genetic inheritance. Darwin believed that the blending process of inheritance would produce uniformity in phenotypes, and the uniformity would eventually destroy variation.[109]

In the application of the biological metaphor, products serve as phenotypes. Based upon the mathematical modeling provided by Burger, the estimated loss of variation would require that one half the heritable variation in the population would have to arise anew in each generation.

In the case of product life cycle, the relevant time of a generation would be about 7 years, and the entire generation of a specific product technology would probably have a genetic technological life span of about 28 years.

In order to avoid the Nash equilibrium, a regional economy would need to generate entirely new technological knowledge about every 15 years. In any given regional economy, once a Nash equilibrium point had been reached, it would probably take about 20 to 25 years of no knowledge creation to begin the regional economic slide towards extinction.

To amplify on Mokyr's application of Cardwell's Law, the fleeting period in history for regional technological leadership would be about 25 years, if all institutional and political things remain constant, and the regional knowledge frontier does not expand outward.

Unlike the loss of genetic variation in Darwin, which is a random naturally occurring event, the regional product technological inheritance is not random but positive and purposeful, and based upon the "fitness" selection process made by consumers.

In economics, the "fitness" of the product phenotype is analogous to adaptation in biology, and adaptation is the economic equivalent of market competition. The product selection of consumers leads to or "causes" variation in technology to decline as a result of consumers selecting existing products because they do not have radical new products to choose, as an alternative. They have no new products to choose because of political manipulation of the rules that have the effect of eliminating the rate of investment in new products.

The expected loss of heterozygosity is empirically verified and tracked by the expected decline in profits for a mass produced standardized product, which looks like Darwin's insights about "uniformity" as it is applied to product phenotypes.

As products become more standardized in their technological features and more uniform in their production process, their marginal profit is headed to zero, and as the profit heads to zero, the political manipulation of the rules becomes more pronounced as income competition regarding maintenance of the status quo intensifies. The fighting over the existing income pie, which is growing smaller is getting more vicious. The greater the level of political inbreeding, the less likely the regional economy will produce new knowledge.

Without new knowledge to eat, regional firms experience a decline in the available diversity of technology. All knowledge, in the political inbred regional economy, must look like the old knowledge because new knowledge, which could manifest itself in new investments, may jeopardize the status quo distribution of income.

The political manipulation of the rules has the effect of eroding "trust" and, without the regional asset of trust, the expected future returns on new investments made today become less certain. With less certain future returns from investments made today, the more rational behavior is to intensify the manipulation of rules to obtain more of the static income in the current period.

The population genetics of products in this case is called positive haploid asexual selection based upon inheritance of technological features from the parent product's technology. Competition occurs around the local attractor point, which serves as the target of performance in both production and manufacturing of intermediate markets and as the target for the kinds of products to produce in the final demand market for finished goods.

As adaptation among firms in the region becomes progressively better, the regional economic economy can be visualized as circling around the Nash equilibrium attractor point. The circles, or loops could be depicted as inward spirals whose amplitudes are decreasing as the economy gets closer to the equilibrium point.

In the case of asexual haploid product evolution, new vintage production technology, without radically new technological features being added to the parent product technology, hastens the time to obsolescence because it speeds up the rate to zero profits. This economic condition would be the norm for most of the regional economies in America based upon the research conducted by F. M. Scherer.

In his work on the flows of inter-industry technology, he estimated that about 75% of all research and development by firms was directed to adding on technological features to existing products that served to improve the performance of the parent product.[110]

This type of asexual product technological mutation, commonly called product innovation, or sustaining innovation, does not generally create environmental conditions for genetic crossover, and but does tend to intensify political manipulation of the rules regarding income distribution.

The reason for the effect on political manipulation and inbreeding is related to the difficulty of a firm to "appropriate" or obtain the profit from the investment in a short-enough time horizon, as the economy is headed to the Nash equilibrium point.

"Both behavioral and measurement considerations," stated Scherer, "lead us to believe that performing industries will secure, at best, only a modest fraction of the productivity benefits from their product research and development."[111] Eventually, the time to obsolescence becomes so short that no new investments in product technological features are made, which is equivalent to the Nash equilibrium point being attained. The empirical evidence in the environment that would be observed are firms going bankrupt and high rates of unemployment, with an increase in what James Buchanan calls "rent-seeking."

Other regional economists have characterized this stage of regional economic development as exhibiting "lock-in," or path dependency. Peter Hall, for example, suggests that as the rate of adaptation by regional firms increases, the more likely other firms will be forced to adapt.

The environmental conditions associated with this last stage of the Nash equilibrium are cost reductions in the production process, increased imitation, adoption and copying of the latest production process as a result of learning-by-doing, and increased market externalities associated with common production technology in distinct industrial clusters.

The set of environment conditions cause three economic outcomes associated with lock-in, at this stage of regional economic evolution. First, Hall cites the fact that learning by doing in each firm becomes detached from external learning in the environment because the regional environment is not generating new knowledge.

Second, the cost of searching and the risk of commercializing new knowledge from outside the region becomes very high for the firm, given the very short time to gain a return on the investment.

Third, and related to political inbreeding, as the income pie is shrinking, the complementary relationships in production, that in an earlier time period had facilitated new knowledge creation, become deleterious to new knowledge creation. Hall states that the complementary relationships have become "too embedded," which is another way of saying that the allegiance to the status quo has become dominant.[112]

Once a regional economy has entered the final few loops around the attractor point, the gravitational pull towards the equilibrium point becomes irreversible. Cardwell's Law becomes absolute and irreversible for a regional economy as a result of the political inbreeding.

Applying Burger's model, when the product technology for finished goods in the final demand market has become standardized and the regional manufacturing process is uniform in the industrial cluster, "...detrimental mutations may accumulate and eventually become fixed..." (in the language of economics, locked-in).

When the product technology in the region becomes fixed, and the regional political structure is inbred, the regional economy experiences an increased rate of fitness decline that results in population extinction.

At this stage, suggests Burger, "if no back mutation occurs, (and no genetic crossover occurs) this class of individuals (meaning product phenotypes) cannot be reconstituted in an asexual population because in the absence of recombination, offspring cannot carry less mutation than their parents. Thus, the class (of most recent vintage product) with one more mutation (innovation without crossover) will be the new least-loaded class, and after some time, suffer the same fate (as the parent product)."[113]

Burger states that the final phase of mutational meltdown is very short. "The mean time to (product) extinction is primarily determined by the length of the phase (product life-cycle) during which the mutations accumulate (product innovation based upon the parent's genetic technology), because the final phase of the mutational meltdown is very short...The mean time to extinction decreases with the increasing rate of selection (of the mass produced, standardized product in the final demand market).[114]

The last few inward spiral loops around the Nash equilibrium point, usually around the 20th or so years of regional economic evolution, are very fast, and each loop has the appearance of Mueller's Ratchet. In North Carolina, for example, the last few inward spirals for textiles, tobacco and furniture occurred in a 10 year period from 1992 to 2002.

As the competition over legacy income distribution in the dying economy intensifies during the economic meltdown to the Nash equilibrium, the institutional structure of the region undergoes a profound transformation. In the once, vibrant, open and diverse environment that previously had created and diffused knowledge, income had been growing and distributed according to merit.

The regional economy could be characterized as being on a trajectory of endogenous growth, based upon self-generated knowledge and technological innovation, which was commercialized in the form of new ventures. The risk associated with creating the new ventures was diminished as a result of "trust" and the adherence to the rule of law.

As the region loses its ability to create new ventures, the political inbred elites, who are fighting over the shreds of legacy income, seek political alliances with multi-national corporations, who act as gateways to the global final demand market for finished goods. Regional tax incentives and other inducements are used by the regional political elites to attract external sources of economic growth as a substitute for the previously internally generated growth.

The use of tax incentives has the effect of political lock-in with control over the sovereignty of the region ceded over to the multi-national corporations who are using the region in a global production and marketing strategy.[115]

As long as the last shreds of income in the region can be politically directed to the inbred elites in the region, the past distribution of income can be maintained for some limited period of time into the future. Mueller's Ratchet in genetics has a counterpart in the world of politics and each turn of the political ratchet means that greater public resources must be directed to external sources of economic growth to extract the last vestiges of income.

In the case of North Carolina, for example, at the beginning of the period of economic decline, around 1990, political elites could attract global corporations with modest tax grants of $1 million, per project. By 2004, the ratchet had turned up to $300 million in tax incentives to recruit a Dell computer assembly plant, to make a mass produced, standardized, finished good in the global final demand market that had an extremely limited time to obsolescence.

In the politically inbred system of North Carolina, the elites who benefited from this use of public funds were the local elites who owned the 189 acres where the plant was to be built. According to press reports about the Dell deal, "Leaders with Winston-Salem Business Inc., particularly board chairman and auto magnate Don Flow, have been aggressively promoting this site to Dell, while also developing a package of local tax incentives that might apply to Dell and its suppliers alike.

The site is owned by the Winston-Salem Alliance, made up of the city's largest corporations, who may also play a role in offering incentives. Dell would enable the Alliance to brand the new park nationally as a location for high-tech manufacturing."[116]

With its very limited connections to the rest of the regional interindustrial infrastructure in North Carolina, the Dell plant will not create any long-lasting economic benefit, but it will reward the local elites for a few more years on the profits from the real estate transaction.

The Dell plant and personal computer it manufactures are on a trajectory to obsolescence and zero profits, and the location of the plant in North Carolina will not add to technological diversity or the creation of new knowledge because the plant will not add genetic technological diversity and because the social and institutional infrastructure had already entered the final loops to the Nash equilibrium.

Predicting Technology

At this stage of economic development, the product technology of the computer is fixed, and the regional political structure is inbred, leading to a faster rate of economic decline and "fitness" that will result in evolutionary economic extinction in North Carolina, much like the same set of circumstances lead to economic decline in Northern England at the turn of the 20th Century.

The appearance of new knowledge at this stage would potentially upset the status quo distribution of legacy income, if the knowledge were to result in new investments in new products. For that reason, the politically inbred elites must gain political control over the sources of venture capital and commercial banking functions to maintain control over the direction of the economy.

The rule of law, and the role of trust gives way to the rule by the elites and secret dealings over the use of public resources to benefit private individuals. The effects of political inbreeding are to destroy the functions and operational capacity of free markets, which, in a regional economy, perform the socially valuable role of creating and diffusing knowledge.

Each completed inward loop on the spiral towards the Nash equilibrium attractor point can be graphically depicted as a ratchet, to represent the idea that the trajectory is irreversible in time. The ratchet is describing the outcome of inbreeding in both product genetics and in politics.

While the attractor point can be considered an "equilibrium" point, in the same sense as the term is used in neoclassical economics, it is an equilibrium for a specific period of economic time, and once that point in time is past, the economy will never return to that equilibrium again. The prices that are adjusting supply and demand for that period of time are unique and specific to the products and the income distributions relevant at that historical period.

The interest rates, for example, during the 1970s, are not relevant to supply and demand for investment capital in the early part of the 21st Century.

The idea behind Mueller's Ratchet in population genetics is that important genes are lost when the genes are transmitted from generation to generation via "vertical" sexual heredity. As applied to economics, and the heredity of product phenotypes, the parent's genes are transmitted in an asexual, single-parent, process of heredity. In population genetics, the deleterious mutations accumulate and usually end up as lethal to the organism.

As a result of the asexual process associated with deleterious mutations, the phenotype's offspring do not obtain "good" genes. Consumers, who are selecting the product phenotypes based upon the "fitness" of the product, select, if they have the choice, products with superior genes. The deleterious mutations in the product accumulate, (in economics, this means they become obsolete) and once they are obsolete, they never come back.

In contrast to the asexual genetic inbreeding process, sexual reproduction allows "good" genes from both parents to be mixed via a process called crossover. Genetic crossover, in economics occurs when the genetic technology of a product in a regional industrial cluster crosses over into the genetic technology of another product in a geographically close cluster.

The new product has two parents. In population genetics, if one phenotype has an accumulation of deleterious mutations, and mates with a phenotype that does not have copies of the bad genes, then the offspring have advantageous mutations without obtaining the deleterious mutations. Thus, in population genetics, a bad set of genes can be overcome, in an evolutionary process that allows the lethal trajectory to be reversed.

Political inbreeding causes rule manipulation, which erodes the rule of law, while at the same time, the inbreeding destroys the diversity of knowledge. Both effects of political inbreeding are usually irreversible. The reversal of the ratchet and the inward spirals towards the Nash equilibrium occur in the very rare economic case where genetic product technology occurs and consumers select the new product because it "fits" better.

The more usual evolutionary process is for political inbreeding, which is analogous to destroying genetic diversity, to force deleterious mutations to accumulate and try to overcome the workings of the free market. What actually happens in each regional economy is based upon the historical and political facts and circumstances, unique to each region.

In this case, political inbreeding not only destroys the institutional structure of the final demand market, but also destroys the socially-beneficial effect of knowledge diversity and knowledge diffusion that occurs in the regional interindustrial input-output relations for semi-finished goods.

Diagram 4.1 graphically depicts the regional economy on the inward spiral towards the local Nash equilibrium attractor point. A region which started out the evolutionary period with a production possibilities frontier of technology would have some large, but finite, genetic recombination product potential.

If all of the genetic mutations and combinations were tried out in products, starting with the first generation of the parent product in the region, there could be some large, but finite number of products that could be produced in the region.

As explained by Melanie Mitchell, "If the genes for these traits are already in the population (in the regional technology frontier) although not expressed or frequent in normal environments (existing markets) they can fairly quickly be expressed in the changed environment. A gene is said to be "expressed" if the trait it encodes actually appears in the phenotype (product).[117] (parenthesis added for explanation).

Predicting Technology

Each product would have some finite life cycle, based upon the selections consumers make between the older parent product, and the newer, more technologically advanced offspring. In the absence of any other genetic crossover from one phenotype to another phenotype, the regional economy would be on a pathway to the local attractor point.

Each turn of the spiral represents a turn of Mueller's Ratchet as products use up the genetic mutation of the previous generation and become obsolete as consumers select the most recent version, which has declining costs to produce and, therefore, declining marginal profits.

Over the period of time the economy is tracing out its inward spiral trajectory to the Nash equilibrium attractor point, genetic product technology is being used up in various product configurations. The product innovations are matched, in time, by production process improvements, as firms in the regional economy mimic and imitate each other in competitive adaptation in production techniques. Production costs are dropping, even as the product is improving and becoming standardized, technologically.

Diagram 4. 1. Regional Economy Trajectory to Equilibrium Attractor Point.

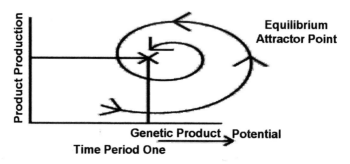

As the production costs drop, the price drops, and lower income consumers begin buying the product, that had been priced out of their reach in the earlier period. The market widens, but the marginal profits on each additional unit sold are dropping towards zero. The regional economy is headed to the Nash equilibrium, where elites are engaging in political rule manipulation to hang on to legacy income, which destroys trust and adherence to the rule of law.

At the Nash equilibrium point, the regional economy does not simply stall and remain frozen in time. What happens next is not described by neoclassical economics, but can be explained with the help of Mueller's Ratchet, as it is applied to economic theory. It is primarily the manipulation of rules in the political structure that causes each turn of the ratchet to be irreversible.

Political inbreeding kills knowledge creation, which is an irreversible evolutionary effect on economic growth.

During this period of time, as long as the declining marginal profits can cover the variable costs of production, slight product innovations will occur in the existing legacy production and manufacturing plants in the region.

The slight technological innovations, in the asexual heredity, however, do not create new knowledge. The economy traces out a trajectory to the next Nash equilibrium at a much lower level of economic activity in the regional economy. The mid points in each spiral loop trace out the trajectory over time, which would probably not be a straight line.

Diagram 4.2 describes the next stage of regional economic evolution as the economy reaches the Nash equilibrium point.

Diagram 4.2. Regional Economy Trajectory to Next Attractor Point.

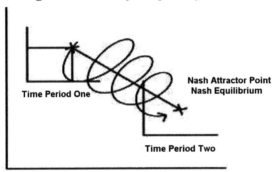

The likely trajectory would be more curved and logistic, to depict the idea expressed by Burger that in the initial stages of evolutionary collapse more genetic material is lost, and in the later stages, there is less genetic material available in the environment. When the trajectory crosses the zero point of genetic product potential on the x-axis, the final consequences of Mueller's Ratchet have been achieved.

There is no economic life left in the regional environment, which would empirically be observed by an absence of market transactions. In most cases, this stage of evolution would probably be characterized by extremely high rates of unemployment, high crime rates, and a collapse of civil rules of procedure. The regional economy would operate according to the Darwinian rules of the jungle and not by the rule of law.

The mid points of each loop in the spiral could be modeled and predicted as eigenvalues, using Bayesian statistical analysis. Given a prior set of observations in the regional economy, and based upon the history of the region, the future mid point in the next time period could be analyzed.

The exact location of the mid points would not necessarily be realized over time, in reality, but could be estimated as a stochastic probability around a potential future Nash attractor point.

The Bayesian analysis allows for scientists to predict a contingent outcome in the future. It would be contingent because nothing about evolution is certain. Other outcomes could easily occur, and what happened in the past economic history could easily have been something else, genetically, if certain types of genetic bifurcation and crossover combinations had occurred.

What is absolute and irreversible, in an evolutionary sense, is the effect that political inbreeding has on knowledge creation and diffusion, which is analogous to food, in the biological metaphor.

One of the very few social and political forces strong enough to break free from the inward spiral of Mueller's Ratchet is the force of knowledge as it is applied to economic markets. The exact trajectory of where the regional economy goes when new knowledge is unleashed is impossible to predict, but, like the downward trajectory, potential future attractor points can be estimated from about two product generations out as a stochastic probability.

As the future attractor point comes into focus, it would have the appearance of a moving trajectory slipping through a slight opening in time, much like the price of a futures contract brings into focus the current market price of the underlying commodity.

In an irony associated with evolutionary economic theory, the knowledge must be both diverse in its base, in other words, genetically rich, and must be widely distributed within the regional population, in order for it to have its potential affect the economic trajectory of the region.

In other words, knowledge, as a regional asset, cannot be subjected to political manipulation and political control, and if control is attempted, knowledge, as an asset, erodes. This is an application of the Golden Goose rule in economic theory, with knowledge being the goose that lays golden eggs, unless something like political manipulation kills it.

New mental images in the brains of individuals, in other words, imagination, which is the basis of knowledge, is not amenable to external political control. Human brains are always spinning out new alternatives and new ideas about how to make life better and have more control over individual destiny.

More will be written about the conditions for future economic growth in the next chapter, but Diagram 4.3 provides a preview of the theoretical concept of how knowledge escapes the inward gravitational force of Mueller's Ratchet of economic decline.

Starting from an existing base of knowledge in time period one, and given prior conditions of the rule of law and a diverse regional interindustrial input-output social structure to diffuse knowledge, many new product ideas may be tried out, genetically.

The loops of the spiral at the Nash equilibrium at time period one are therefore depicted as wider than later time periods. Using the modified Feser method of technological correlation coefficients as the prior conditions in a Bayesian analysis, future locations of potential attractors could be analyzed. There are many contingencies associated with moving through time towards this future attractor point, which could become the next Nash equilibrium.

The greatest uncertainty, of course, is whether high income consumers would buy genetically new products, that had been procreated by two product parents as opposed to continuing to buy versions of the older product that had been procreated in an asexual technological process.

Diagram 4.3. Regional Economy Breaking Away From Equilibrium

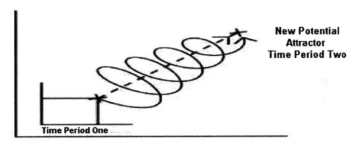

Even if consumers bought the new product, the major contingency in the future is whether the new product had the potential to create new complementary products in the input output supply chain in intermediate demand markets, which is analogous to asking if the new product had the future potential to create and diffuse knowledge.

The social and political barriers and obstacles to economic growth are much more severe than the more ordinary allegiance to the status quo, as visualized by the Nash equilibrium point. From an evolutionary perspective, the economists in history who predicted that free markets had a tendency to collapse, as a result of inadequate final demand were probably right.

Around the vicinity of the local attractor point, which can be viewed in geographic terms as a regional economy characterized by close interindustrial relations, the occurrence of product genetic crossover would be called a micro product bifurcation. As described by Frenken, Saviotti, and Trommetter, each product has a set of technological characteristics that make up the design code of the product, "...analogous to the genotype of an organism."[118]

In terms of micro product bifurcations, the closer the location of the a_{ij}, of the two products, the more likely the genetic crossover is. However, in an irony associated with evolutionary economics, the more the two genetic codes are similar, in a sexual crossover, the less diversity created in the regional market.

The greater the span in technology the product micro bifurcation, the greater the diversity created in knowledge, but conversely, the less likely consumers are likely to select the radical new product.

As Frenken puts it, "The rise in the number of market niches relates to the rising number of characteristics (in products) in which firms compete...the increase in variety (of new firms) is both a result of increased differentiation between market niches (industrial sectors within the regional industrial clusters) and within market niches (of firms located in the same sectors within the cluster)...The greater the span (of genetic technology within the cluster, when it begins) the greater the number of niches that can be created within it."[119]

This begins to answer Storper's question about adequate theoretical insights into the "how, why, and where," of the initial geographical agglomeration of industrial sectors.

Given a certain kind of history, and specific political institutions, a region that begins with a rich genetic heritage can be predicted to move to the next higher level of economic growth. Multiple product bifurcations could potentially lead to even bigger market bifurcations, if market selection by high income consumers favor the genetically different products than the older products that are based upon asexual mutation.

Concomitantly, the increase in diversity constitutes a greater political threat maintaining the status quo distribution of income in the region.

Political and financial elites who benefit from the existing status quo distribution of existing products and markets can therefore be expected to engage in rent-seeking, which destroys the genetic diversity of knowledge in the region.

The greater the span of genetic technology in product mutation, the greater the risk associated with what consumers will do when they see the new product in the market for the first time. Greater risk, all other things being equal, requires greater level of trust, and greater allegiance to the rule of law so that risks taken in period one can lead to appropriation of income in period two.

The equilibrium associated with the Nash attractor point, and the productivity improvements associated with mass produced standardized products do not lead to economic growth in the next period. These factors lead to greater levels of conflict in the existing time period between elites who desire to maintain their incomes.

The operation of free markets affects the political institutional structure, and the elites then obtain political control over incomes in order to control the direction of the market. The early casualties are trust and the rule of law, while the later victims are non-elites in the future time period who suffer reduced levels of income and wealth as a result of the political inbreeding.

One consequence of the political inbreeding at the Nash equilibrium is a loss of sovereignty and control or the regional dynamics of economic growth. In an open, diverse political environment, the functioning and operations of the free market, free of political control over the distribution of income, a regional economy could be expected to trace out a trajectory to a higher welfare point at a potential attractor.

The new attractor point logically implies a new distribution of income which results from consumers selecting new technological products that did not exist in the earlier time period.

The buying patterns of consumers for new products creates complementary purchasing patterns which contribute to new income patterns. There is nothing automatic about an economy achieving this new, higher level of economic welfare. Reaching the new higher level is contingent on many factors, including the maintenance of the rule of law in the region over a considerable length of time.

In a politically inbred region, the elites manipulate political rules to obtain legacy income associated with their prior capital investments, thus killing the food supply of knowledge that fuels endogenous regional economic growth.

As a substitute economic policy to endogenous economic growth that comes from commercialization of knowledge, in the form of new ventures, the elites seek political alliances with multi-national corporations to provide the exogenous sources of economic growth that comes from transactions in the global market for finished goods.

The transactions of the multi-national corporations in the global final demand market for finished goods create income flows for the corporations that are easily directed to "rent-seeking" political elites in a selected region. The economic consequence of this regional-global political arrangement is to accelerate Mueller's Ratchet, which further hastens the rate of economic decline in the region.

Peter Blair and Andrew Wyckoff studied the structural interindustrial changes from 1972 to 1984 in the U. S. economy resulting from more open global trading patterns. They state, "A principal implication of this structural realignment is that the economy as a whole has become more specialized – contracted out, out-sourced. However, the service sectors that gain from this development produce products that have few connections with the rest of the economy."[120]

The global corporation's use the assets of the region to serve the strategic corporate interests in the global marketing and production of the corporation's products and services. The strategic financial interests of the corporation are different than the long-term economic growth interests of the region because long-term economic growth is based upon endogenous assets of knowledge.

The location of a branch operation of a multinational corporation in a region that has "...few connections with the rest of the economy..." is not contributing to the regional interindustrial structure that serves as the institutional structure that creates and diffuses knowledge.

The location of the branch operations of the multinational corporation serves to kill knowledge by destroying the environment, much like application of salt and acids destroys a farmer's soil. The only entities in the region who benefit financially from this setup are the very small group of inbred political elites who have obtained political control over the economic direction of the economy.

The elites benefit because their legacy production facilities and real estate operations are the landlords for the multinational tenants who are attracted to the region with the use of public tax incentives and tax rebates.

This gives a new interpretation to Buchanan's use of the term "rent-seeking." The rents the inbred elites seek are rental payments from multinational corporations who need the regional location for a limited period of time to serve the corporation's financial interests.

The economic outcomes and changes in the structure of the U. S. economy that Blair and Wyckoff between 1972 and 1984 included less use of raw resources in a value-added production chain, less output in both intermediate and final demand output from domestic producers, and more use of professional financial advisory services, such as insurance, commercial real estate and legal services.[121]

In other words, as the outsourcing and contracting out process associated with the movement to the global market continued for the period of time under study, the sources of knowledge were eliminated. Regional economic growth became a function of serving multinational corporate needs, with regional elites ceding local political control over the region's destiny to the 1500 largest corporations in the world.

The standardized, mass produced goods that are sold by the corporations in the global market for finished goods are all on a pathway to zero profits, and do not require special skills or new knowledge to produce. Neither do they require a political system based upon trust and the rule of domestic law. International law and global trade agreements become much more important than domestic civil law.

Hyman Minsky described the process associated with the changes in the U. S. economy as "managed money capitalism." He asked, "How technological dynamism is to be sustained in a world where the natural risk aversion of business and finances is amplified by liability structures that pledge a major part of cash flows (derived from the legacy production and income systems) is a question that the growth of managed capitalism opens."[122]

The ultimate use of the cash flows that are mortgaged and pledged as security in the global system is the reason why Storper's criticism of neoclassical theory is valid. Legacy cash flows in the managed global corporate capitalism derived in one period are not used as a source for investment in regional new ventures that would create endogenous economic growth in the next period. Such investments would jeopardize both the inbred political elites ability to extract legacy income, and would serve to create potential sources of product competition from genetically new products.

As Tichy accurately observes, "...in the early life (of a regional industrial cluster) the production process is not yet standardized and can afford the specialized skill of the region...the more the production process becomes standardized, the less necessary are specialized worker, their skills and the sophisticated information networks...One can observe that new products which substitute for old ones are usually developed and produced by new firms."[123]

New firms will not be created, regional heterogeneity in technology will not be enhanced, and new knowledge will not be created if capital from cash flows is not invested in new firms which commercialize technology from genetic crossover between industrial clusters in a specific geographical environment.

And, even if new investments create new ventures, there is no guarantee that consumers will buy the genetically new products when they see them for the first time. If consumers do not select the new products, then new income flows will not be created, which is the political outcome sought by the inbred political elites who are manipulating the rules of appropriation and reward in the regional political environment.

Following Burger's analysis, "Natural selection acts in many different ways on the phenotype of the organism...In principle, selection can be described by a fitness function that relates fitness of individuals to the (quantitative) traits under selection."[124]

As the biological metaphor is applied here, products are phenotypes with certain technological genetic characteristics that are selected by consumers based upon the fitness function between the consumer's mental image of how the product will "fit" given the technological characteristics and traits of the product.

Selection, following Leven's biological model, "operates separately within each local deme in a density-dependent manner: the fraction of adults in every deme is fixed...Nonrandom assortment of genotypes into demes, however, and certain spatial structures may easily lead to the maintenance of stable polymorphisms...(where) detrimental mutations may accumulate and eventually become fixed, thus leading to a progressive fitness decline that can result in population extinction."[125]

Political manipulation and political inbreeding leads to a stable polymorphic economic system based exclusively asexual technological innovation process in the regional industrial cluster deme, ultimately leading to, in a biological evolutionary way, to economic extinction, based upon the application of Mueller's Ratchet.[126] The stability is not a market-derived phenomena that is based upon price adjustments, it is derived from political manipulation of laws and rules.

The greater the rate of selection of mass produced, standardized products in the global managed capital system, the greater the rate of product obsolescence and regional economic extinction.

Put another way, the more the offspring product, in an asexual genetic process looks like the parent product, the less likely genetic crossover will occur because of the greater likelihood that consumers will select the product that is slightly better than the old parent product, but not radically different.

This pattern of consumer selection fits the needs of the inbred elites just fine, because it continues the extraction of their legacy income flows from their old product investments. As long as they can eliminate new technological knowledge as a competitive threat, they can use the regional assets of knowledge to derive future income.

As profits on the standardized products head to zero, the elites make marginal adjustments in product technology, and, concomitantly, apply greater rates of political repression of genetic diversity to control the emergence of genetically new products and, even worse, from their financial point of view, the emergence of entirely new markets.

The asexual product innovations usually show up in slight variations of technological characteristics of the parent product technology, and in slight improvements in the manufacturing process, as the multinational corporations seek out regional advantages associated with tax incentives and skills that complement the corporate core technology. Neo classical theory captures this activity as "productivity" gains, and the advocates of the theory imply that productivity gains are associated with economic growth.

Applying the alternative biological metaphor, the productivity gains around a local Nash equilibrium are indicators describing an economy headed for decline. As described by Ulrich Witt, "New ideas that are entirely unrelated to earlier interpretations and problems are unlikely to occur..." when "...no newly detected possibility of action is considered relevant unless it solves a given problem."[127]

Technological commercialization and new venture creation depend upon an underlying market structure that creates and disseminates knowledge. The initial conditions, to pick back up on Storper's initial criticism, within any given regional economy, are based upon a culturally embedded framework that enforce rules and norms about "how things get done around here," and "who gets paid when things get done."

Within any given regional economy, the units of analysis must learn over time who to trust, given the risk associated with starting a new venture which will not pay-off until some future point in time. Rules, laws, and trust must be in place long enough for the unit of analysis that creates the venture to obtain the future reward.

To answer Storper, the working hypothesis of evolutionary economic growth theory is that regions that start out with technological "closeness" in industrial clusters, that have open and diverse political environments, would be expected to have higher rates of technological knowledge creation and diffusion than regions that did not possess these attributes.

The knowledge creation and diffusion are an essential precursor condition that allows entrepreneurs to take a risk on starting a new venture. A region that had once possessed this type of institutional structure, rules, laws and trust, could easily slip into the orbit of a Nash attractor point and experience the effects of Mueller's Ratchet of economic decline.

The economic inbreeding in technology has an analogue biological process in politics that involves political inbreeding. Both evolutionary processes of genetic inbreeding follow their own internal forces, but both reinforce and complement each other at various times in history.

As William Baumol observes, "entrepreneurs are economic animals... variations in reward structures determines the impact of new venture creation." When the politically-inbred elites capture the police power of the state, they direct legacy incomes and rewards to themselves.

Baumol explains that, "It is easy to imagine how the reward structure which benefits the governing elite might be perpetuated by that elite, with the simultaneous effect of discouraging disruptions which might threaten their power."[128] It is politics, not prices, that determines the direction of the regional economy, and the competition is not about products and utilities, it is about incomes.

Chapter V

Income Competition As The Basis of Disruptive Technological Innovation

"Whose magic wand," asked Maurice Dobb, "decreed that every increase of bank or savings deposits would be forthwith matched by increased investment by business?"[129] In the ideal world of neoclassical economics, savings always equals investments at equilibrium because it makes the math associated with the equilibrium outcome work, not because the equilibrium outcome explains economic reality.

It is only as a result of shifting incomes, that create new markets for new goods, that allows for an explanation of economic growth. Future consumer preferences and future income distribution are linked to present investments, which affect both present and future markets, but in different ways.

As long as neoclassical theory holds income distribution as a constant in order to evaluate how prices today affect supply and demand today, the question asked by Dobb will remain unexamined. It is an important issue though, and some of the earlier attempts to explain the relationship between incomes and future markets under different institutional relationships, is valuable.

As Charles Wilbur pointed out in 1973, "Public ownership in the Soviet Union allowed for former luxury consumption from property income to be converted into savings for investment purposes...which permitted the Soviet Union to channel savings and those resources into the most productive purposes..."[130]

Wilbur did not mention from whose perspective, consumers or politburo members, the definition of "productive purposes" was derived. Presumably, he did not have a consumer sovereignty model in mind given the Soviet's huge expenditures on productive nuclear weapons based upon slave labor in the Gulag.

Wilbur's analysis indicated that "Current investment changes both productive capacity and employment and thus exercises an important influence upon market prices by changing relative scarcities. Accordingly, the present structure of market prices cannot be used as a sure measure of the future structure of prices, or therefore of what will be the return on any particular investment."[131]

This is the same conclusion that Clayton Christensen reaches in his investigation of innovation in large corporations. He states that current prices do not provide a reliable guide for investment decisions based upon an evaluation of likely return on investment.

Wilbur continues "A market rate of interest would emerge from the particular configuration of time preferences. The market determined rate of interest would be the rate at which the marginal productivity of investment equals the market rate of discount that emerges from the interplay of unilateral decisions of savors and investors."[132]

We are back to Dobb's magic wand, because the math of neoclassical theory of equilibrium only works with one precise rate of interest, for a specific and fixed distribution of income. Given the prerequisite first assumption about a fixed distribution of income, the neoclassical model can generate the precise rate of interest that solves the system of differential equations in supply and demand between savings and investments that lead to equilibrium, in today's capital market.

As Wilbur, then points out, "…there is a particular time preference configuration for every possible income distribution. If the income distribution changes between the present and the future, then ceteris paribus, the investment rate will also change."[133]

In other words, if future income distributions are allowed to vary, neoclassical theory's single perfect interest rate is useful for explaining the pattern of investment that works with the existing pattern of income distribution, as if it was also the future income distribution.

Coincidentally, there are powerful financial and economic interests who favor this status quo distribution of income as the defining the "right" target level of investment today, just as the communist economists favored the "right" level of investment that yielded their "fair" distribution of income.

The political allegiance to the existing status quo distribution of income by the very same set of savors and investors who are supposed to be guided in their investment decisions by this mythical rate of interest is assumed to be non-consequential in neoclassical tradition because their starting assumption is always that income distribution is held constant.

Whose magic wand, to paraphrase Dobb, gets the savors and investors to deny their own time preferences for income in order to perform the socially-valuable task of investing their hard won profits today at a rate sufficient to create economic growth in the future, if making that investment today means their future incomes will be sacrificed by changing distributions of income?

There are not two different units of analysis, business savors, and business investors, as imagined by the neoclassical model. The same people who make profits in production of goods, as business owners, also make investment decisions about where to invest their profits as business investors. They do not meet themselves every day in an imaginary capital market, with a split personality, and ask themselves how they will invest if they other side of their personality shows up.

As Hollis and Nell pointed out, "The neoclassical analogy between the market for factors and the market for final products now breaks down. In the latter (market of final demand for finished goods) value-equivalents are exchanged." (goods that differ in use value but are equal to their market-price exchange value).

In other words, consumers choose between finished goods and equate marginal utility with marginal price, and the neoclassical math of the second derivative behaves because the consumers actually choose the cheapest good that satisfies their preferences, at their existing level of income.

"In the former (factor market of intermediate demand for semi-finished goods), income is paid to those with property rights in the productive process. Even when capital and labor shift in response to differentials in earnings between industries, there is no (market) exchange between the recipient of net income and the source of income (the wealthy folks who own the factory)…the "factor" market (where goods get produced) differs essentially from the market for goods, in that the payment of net income, (in the factor market) is not an exchange (that is equivalent to the market exchange based upon prices in the finished goods final demand market.)[134]

In other words, the distribution of income, as Ricardo pointed out, is outside the system of production and is derived from political factors associated with the cultural and constitutional values of property rights in each society.

The single, unified market exchange mechanism conceived by Walras, based upon prices that clear supply and demand in all markets, both present and future, final and intermediate, and product and capital, can not explain economic growth.

The interest rate does not work as a price exchange mechanism in capital markets the same way as prices in either the intermediate demand market finished goods markets.

Walras' math only works for a specific geographical market in the finished goods market at one precise interest rate that clears savings supply with investment demand, but at only for one precise existing distribution of income. The math only works by assuming that the society being investigated has property rights, which are constitutionally under-girded by the rule of law and where owners of capital can legally appropriate profits.

Which is why Hernando DeSoto states that the economic model of North American capitalism does not work in most of the world.[135]

Once product evolution occurs, prices in the existing market that reflect competition between old products and newer technological versions of that same product are not in any theoretical way connected to consumer preferences in future markets for genetically superior different products that have no prices.

Existing firms are adapting, products are evolving, and markets are emerging that are not tied in a causal explanation to existing prices in today's markets.

Eating new knowledge is the Lotka-Volterra economic process through which firms generate genetic technological diversity in new products. Free markets are either growing and evolving because the consumers "select" technologically new products or they are dying, based upon the diminishing supply of their food source.

"Somehow," states Berten Martens, "a method has to be found to account for the emergence of *ex nihilo* preference arguments for new goods."[136] Martens envisions a market economy that represents "...a third tier of evolution above Darwinian survival and Lamarckian learned adaptation." Martens correctly identifies the process by which evolutionary theory can be applied to economic theory when products are viewed from the perspective of product "heuristics."

According to Martens, heuristics represent the utility that consumers obtain from consumption of the specific properties and characteristics of goods. Martens' use of the term "heuristics" has the same meaning as "technological characteristics" as it was used earlier in this book in the context of applying the biological metaphor of genetics to economics.

"A new or innovative good will be preferred if its total characteristics vector yields a higher level of consumer satisfaction for the same budget outlay...new goods provide an original recombination of product characteristics."[137]

Martens suggests that the potential shift in consumer preference from existing older products to newer technological versions of that older product can be analyzed with the use of Bayesian statistical probability theory which would indicate the shift in consumer demand as new products emerge which contain properties and characteristics of old products, only better.

The process that Martens is describing for product evolution is evolutionary heredity based upon genetic technological mutation, which is usually called product innovation. "Innovation builds on existing preferences for characteristics and provides only an original or enhanced (re) combination of a bundle of characteristics."[138]

Martens analysis has a close accommodation to the concepts of Lancaster about product life-cycles.[139] Product life cycle theory raises the important economic issue of the role of free markets in diffusing technological innovation.

"Markets are the central organizing institutions in an economy with known resources, preferences and technologies...all economic agents (in the existing market) play extremely passive roles in that situation," wrote Sherwin Rosen, in his description of entrepreneurial behavior.[140]

"Therefore," continued, Rosen, "entrepreneurial activities must involve the organization of resources that are initially outside the existing market system. That is, they are activities that, in effect, create new markets, new forms of organization that did not exist before."[141]

It is in these new forms of organization that did not exist before that must account for the emergence of Martens' *ex nihilo* preference arguments for new products.

"The market mechanism (of prices in the existing market) does not contain within it any means of extending itself and creating new markets; as it were... Entrepreneurial projects are risky precisely because they take place outside the established market mechanism and therefore involve unknown and perhaps unknowable elements," added Rosen.

What makes the risky capital investment projects feasible is not prices and interest rates in today's market, but the element of trust and joint expectations, in other words, joint and common beliefs about the future, in a society characterized by the rule of law.

"One must conclude that social institutions and cultural frameworks have something fundamental to do with the entrepreneurial motive. Religious beliefs and ethical precepts might, indeed, be as important to entrepreneurial activity as science and technology," said Modecai Keaz.[142]

Markets based upon the rule of law, coincidentally, create an environment most conducive for the creation and diffusion of knowledge.

The diffusion of knowledge is not random, as the Darwinian notion of evolution posits, but Lamarkian, in the sense that the search for knowledge is purposeful and results in behavior adaptations of the "units of analysis" that affect genetics in the immediate time period following the adaptation. The behavior that adapts is human behavior not the behavior of inanimate prices.

Martens highlighted this trait of adaptation in trading systems associated with market economies by noting that, "Societies that allow specialization and trading systems to emerge thus have an evolutionary advantage over those that do not...Communication and trading systems require only the reproduction of a small set of a "parents" behavioral algorithm into a material carrier that transfers this (knowledge) to any other recipients."[143]

Predicting Technology

Martens based much of his analysis on Coase's theorem, which identified the costs of transactions as an impediment on the market's ability to solve problems. Coase thought that the emergence of norms, rules of behavior, and public laws regarding market transactions, reduced transaction costs, and therefore stimulated greater economic growth.

The emphasis on trading systems is key to understanding that transactions in the intermediate demand market for semi-finished goods effect adaptation in existing markets, and contingently creates the basis for the emergence of new markets. Prices in the existing intermediate markets affects the process of behavior adaptations and product innovations of technologically similar products, which share a parent technology, or a common technological heredity.

In the existing markets, with existing prices, at the beginning of a product's life cycle, improvements in both manufacturing processes and in product innovation leads to marginal increases in profits, as correctly predicted by neoclassical theory. In general, the time horizon covered by this period would be about 3 years.

The logic behind the theory depends upon a price elasticity of demand for the most recent version of the product that is greater than one. A representative firm's total revenue goes up with both productivity improvements on the plant floor and product improvements, as long as the elasticity of demand is above this critical threshold value.

As Hermann Schnell points out, "Further cost improvements (in the production process) combined with the shifting consumer preferences for new products (with better technological characteristics than the older versions of the same product) will accelerate the process of decay in existing firms... once the borderline threshold elasticity of demand falls below one, the firm is doomed."[144]

As described earlier, from a biological evolutionary perspective, process innovations in manufacturing shift supply curves downward, reflecting that production costs are going down, and concomitantly, as profits are eroding, the market environment, and all the existing units of analysis are dying.

After about 3 years of a product's life cycle, it becomes irrational to make further investments in either process improvements or product improvements because the time horizon of market demand for the product is not sufficient to reward the investment.

The "units of analysis" making that investment decision happen to be the owners of the firms making the product, not the commercial bankers who finance production operations through revolver lines of credit secured by inventory and accounts receivables, and who have a great financial interest in maintaining the status quo.

As Schnell correctly diagnoses, "There is only one kind of innovation that is able to reverse the above process of downward evolution: generic innovation (as distinct from incremental innovation in an existing product's technological characteristics). Generic or radical innovation in the first place is product innovation that creates new markets and thus new demand...which brings about the onset of high-price elasticities (for the radical new product)."[145]

As opposed to the "incremental" product innovation as characterized by Martens and Schnell, the radical product introduction into the market represents an evolutionary "genetic bifurcation." Products undergo technological genetic bifurcation, and, sometimes, contingently, that radical product bifurcation leads to a market bifurcation, where the future final demand in the finished goods market place is completely different than the market demand in the previous time period. The final demand markets bifurcate when the structural relationships between firms in the intermediate demand markets change to accommodate production requirements for the radically new product.

This type of intermediate market demand change occurs in geographically specific market environments, usually in metro economic regions which have extensive interindustrial trading relationships in "complementary" markets. Economists also refer to these complementary market relationships as the regional economic structure, as described by technical coefficients in a regional input-output transaction matrix.

Regional economic environments initially characterized by diversity, variety and complexity in interindustrial relationships have a competitive, evolutionary advantage over regional economies that do not possess these starting characteristics, or regional "assets."

Further, regional economic environments characterized by the rule of law and private property rights in the transfer of title to both real estate and units of ownership in business enterprises would have a competitive evolutionary advantage in the creation of new future markets than regional economies that did not initially have the rule of law under-girding the exchange mechanism in the market.

"Mainstream economics focuses on decision-making within given structures; it confines the concept of structure to indicate the composition of production and the configuration of institutional arrangements...to show how economic actors deal with changes within the structure, not of the structure," stated Jan Lambooy and Ron Boschma, as they explained the difference between neoclassical theory and evolutionary economic theory.

"Evolutionary economics opens the way to investigate the interrelations between the structure and the actors as a feedback mechanism...Key concepts in evolutionary thinking such as routines, path dependency and selection suggest that new variety is shaped and formed by its surrounding environment."[146]

Their emphasis on the feedback mechanism is important because it helps to explain how *ex nihilo* preference functions in future markets attach to radically new products and feedback information to the intermediate demand market of semi-finished goods.

Nicholas Kaldor had part of this theory exactly right when he stated, "the growth rate depends on what is termed the "technological dynamism" of the economy...the prime mover in the process of economic growth is the readiness to absorb technical change combined with the willingness to invest capital in business ventures."[147]

Unfortunately, for the evolutionary transition of economic theory from neoclassical to evolutionary theory, Kaldor failed to mention exactly who or what entity or units of analysis had to display the "willingness" and "readiness" to absorb technical change and make the investments.

Following Saffra, what neoclassical theory can explain is a sequence of logical events related to price movements in production that leads to economic stagnation. As profit rates decline, interest rates decline, and capital intensity of existing machinery therefore increases.

Marginal costs of production go down, prices for finished goods decline, even as markets widen, profits are approaching zero. Operating cash flow from existing enterprises can not be the source, therefore, of capital for new investment.

At one rate of interest, associated with one rate of profit, neoclassical analysis explains supply and demand relationships in capital markets, but as interest rates change, this same analysis shows another, equally valid set of supply and demand relationship associated with the existing set of capital equipment that produces the goods.

As the interest rates switch and as the profit rates are tending to zero, and operational cash flows from existing enterprises are not sufficient to provide the source of capital for the level of investment that achieves maximum future consumption.

As Dobb finally concludes: "We are led to conclude that price ratios are determined by the technological conditions of production...the proper conclusion is that the rate of profit is not successfully determined by the Walrasian theories from consideration of production coefficients, utility functions and so forth..."[148]

And, to answer Dobbs' question of where capital comes from for investing in genetically new products, it comes from outside the system of production from "units of analysis" motivated to obtain future income, by changing the existing distribution of income.

In other words, the capital comes from venture capitalists, who obtained profits from capital gain exit events on prior investments, not from operational cash flows on existing enterprises. The venture capitalists are not the same "units of analysis" as owners of factories, nor are they the commercial bankers, who finance manufacturing operations, as identified by Schumpeter.

Leontief described the venture capital source of capital for investing in genetically new products as a combination of "entrepreneurial returns, monopolistic revenues and windfall profits resulting from appreciation of commodity stocks on hand."

In order to describe how the economy was a circular flow, his method of input output analysis required that this source of capital be lumped together with net revenues from operations, which is the traditional source of profits in neoclassical marginal analysis.

Leontief pointed out that the entire combination of capital, called "undistributed surplus," plays a double role for the firm. "On the one hand, it represents the values of materials, additional pay rolls, and other cost elements, on which, it usually is spent in the process of new investment."[149]

According to Leontief, the venture capital profits represent "on the other hand, the productive services of capital and entrepreneurship."[150] This source of capital for investment in technological genetically new products, just like wages, is outside the neoclassical system of production and prices.

"It would seem," said Dmitriev, that there is no other way out than to make the size of value, or of profit, depend on conditions situated outside the sphere of production."[151]

Dmitriev had both types of profits in mind that are outside the price system of production. However, in order to explain economic growth, the decisions about how to invest the part of the profits made by the venture capitalists, via feedback information flows from guesses they make about the future market demand for radical new products, is how *ex nihilo* consumer preferences attach to new products, which do not have prices in the current finished goods final demand markets.

The guesses made by the VCs are often wrong, and therefore do not affect the economic trend to economic stagnation. The wrong guesses lead sometimes to wild excesses in supply and demand, and sometimes do not create future demand at all, and thus contribute to the free markets natural trend of economic stagnation.

Further, VCs usually only fund about 2% of the projects that they review each year, raising the same question Lord Keynes raised about inadequate aggregate final demand. Keynes correctly stated that the proportion of profits to national income depended on the rate of investments in prior periods.

Prior period profits that are used for investments, according to Keynes, must create future final demand. If there is no investment today, there will be no final demand tomorrow.

Even if there is investment today, it may not create demand tomorrow, as all the barren investments in internet-based enterprises in the mid-1990's demonstrated.

Investments in technologically radical new products today must perform the essential task of creating future markets, which, contingently, creates new distributions of income, as the VCs take their profits from selling their shares in the new ventures, only to mull over again how *ex nihilo* consumer preferences can be created in future markets.

Martens' idea is that *ex nihilo* preferences are a result of product "heuristics." The technological properties of a new product links to the consumer preferences via product heuristics in the final demand market for finished goods. This linkage is not a priced-based activity, it is a mental-guess-based activity, with the guesses of venture capitalists, who have capital to invest in the new technological product heuristics, matching their guesses with consumers, who are making guesses about how the new technological characteristics of the product will meet their preferences, or what economists call, utility or satisfaction.

This guessing activity is in contrast to behavior in existing markets with older versions of the product. In existing markets, the neoclassical marginal equivalencies of Walras' theory work for the brief periods of time that consumer preferences can be linked with prices in the final demand marketplace.

As noted by Brian Arthur, "...the equilibrium approach does not describe the mechanism whereby the state of the economy changes over time...(nor) for the emergence of new kinds of relevant state variables, new entities, new patterns and new structures."[152]

The equilibrium approach does provide an explanation and description of how prices for existing finished goods in the final demand market leads to adjustments in supply and demand within any short period of time.

Guessing about future demand and future prices for new products however, is not priced-based, and guessing does not automatically, or naturally, lead to equilibrium in all markets. It sometimes, however, leads to the emergence of entirely new final demand marketplace, with a new distribution of income. An evolutionary explanation describes how capital markets today create final demand markets for finished goods in the future that do not currently exist.

Ex nihilo consumer preferences for new products are created when the guesses of venture capitalists in one time period match the guesses in a later time period of consumers about how a new technological product fits into their utility function.

New markets are created when the mental activity of guessing about the future via the insight-imagination process creates the future markets as the present market. Future markets come slowly into the present through a slight opening in time when guesses about the future between consumers and investors are confirmed.

As Arthur notes, "...agent's expectations are formed on the basis of their anticipations of other agent's expectations...traders in a market continually hypothesize (about the future)...the traders are coming up with appropriate hypothetical models to act upon, strengthening confidence in those that are validated, and discarding those that are not..."[153]

When the future markets arrive, mutually reinforcing beliefs and expectations are confirmed in reality. Under-standing how future markets are created is based upon an evolutionary understanding of how the human brain makes guesses about the behavior of other humans.

In complex economies, characterized by high rates of knowledge creation, venture capitalists make investments in new ventures today based upon their expectations both of what other investors are likely to do, and how consumers are likely to respond when they see a new product for the first time.

The knowledge creation and adaptive learning in the complex economy creates new markets when current expectations about the future based upon individual guesses are confirmed by collective expectations in future markets. The new ventures that the venture capitalists create act as a market signaling device, in an information feedback system in the intermediate demand markets that function to coordinate mutually reinforcing expectations between the investors and the consumers.

In an adaptive economic system, a future market becomes the present market based upon evolutionary mechanisms of asexual product technological inheritance and technological variation in product improvements, linked by consumer selection of the newer, better products.

In an adaptive system, product heuristics mutate, in a process of product innovation, and consumers and capitalists modify their behavior by improving strategies in a constrained maximization environment by buying the new and better goods that are produced at lower costs than existing goods and are sold at prices that yield a slightly higher (marginal) profit for a brief period of time.

In the absence of new income flows and new technological products, the adaptive economic system eventually dies in a biological process described as Mueller's Ratchet.

In an evolutionary economic system, new future markets are created when products bifurcate via two parent sexual genetic crossover. The bifurcation creates a novel event for humans to adapt to, and like all novel events, the human brain sorts and selects based upon prior memories and new mental images, trying to obtain quantum coherence in how to respond to the novel event.

Bifurcation of product technology is analogous to the appearance of a new species that upsets the existing environmental status quo. Other species, in this case, humans, have to figure out what the appearance of the new species means for their survival.

Their decisions are not random but purposeful, and consequently would not be modeled based upon Darwin's theory of evolution. The consumer's response to the appearance of the novel event determines if *ex nihilo* preferences are created in the as-yet-to-be created future market, which may contingently be created if a sufficient level of market demand for the higher priced novel product materializes.

Thomas Nagle reports that empirical studies "...indicate that demand does not begin to accelerate until the first 2 to 5 percent of potential buyers adopt the product."[154]

In other words, if the guesses about the future made by the venture capitalists match up and are confirmed by the guesses made by consumers when they first see the new product in the market, then a new future final demand market for finished goods may be created.

In this rare case, product bifurcation in genetic technology may lead to an even bigger evolutionary event, called macro market bifurcation, where income distributions change, costs of production change, prices on existing older goods decline at a faster rate, and new target rates of return on venture capitalist's investment criteria change.

The new product heuristics, based upon genetic bifurcation in technology, would then have created new market heuristics where the pattern of final demand, and the flows of income are radically different than those in the immediate preceding period of time.

In the existing final demand markets for finished goods, there are two types of searching activities being conducted by the units of analysis in a specific regional environment.

According to Wroe Alderson, "Suppliers and consumers are engaged in a double search and each is providing the other with clues to guide their search. Consumers specify their needs or, in the case of shopping for goods, partially specify their needs in advance of entering the market. Suppliers identify their products and invite consumers to buy them to see whether the products meet the specified needs."[155]

For existing products with existing prices, consumers can search for the price that equates their marginal utility of consumption of the last unit consumed with their marginal cost curve, in order to derive maximum rational utility at their exact level of income.

Alderson notes that in the real world, "consumers are frequently heard to remark that they did not get their money's worth out of a given purchase. Hesitation about buying a product in the first place undoubtedly means that they are trying to estimate this expected value."[156]

In other words, it is not just the single consumption at an immediate point in time that the consumer is evaluating in making the decision to buy. Something is causing Alderson's imaginary consumer to hesitate. The search function, in Alderson's scenario, seems to be a separate activity from the selection function.

Which raises an interesting question of what the suppliers in the Wroe Alderson double search scenario, are searching for? Alderson suggests the more plausible explanation that the suppliers are searching for customers, who "customarily" buy from the supplier.

For Alderson, the unit of analysis of "customer" denotes a continuing relationship between the consumer and the supplier, and this on-going relationship over time presents a theoretical issue for neoclassical analysis because the instantaneous act of search and consumption in Walras' is based upon a price in a single isolated act in the ubiquitous autonomous market.

As Alderson notes, "If strongly motivated problem-solvers (i.e. searchers) face each other in a discrepant market, it can never be cleared but only moves in the direction of that equilibrium state...Traditional economics has no place for marketing effort because saleable products were sold simply by raising or lowering the price to equate supply with effective demand."[157]

Suppliers are searching for customers who will buy their newer, improved, second generation product at a price higher than the first generation product, which is on its pathway to technological obsolescence and extinction.

The supplier search is somewhat urgent, in the sense that the supplier's cost of production for the first generation product are declining, the prices are declining, and profits are headed to zero. They know they had better come up with something new and improved that they can sell at a slightly higher profit, or they too, will soon be extinct. They are searching for customers for their second-generation product in order to survive.

Applying the biological evolutionary metaphor, the activity of "marketing" in both existing markets and future markets is the process through which the double-search of consumers and suppliers gain information about each other in the searching and sorting of mental images.

Suppliers use the tools and techniques of marketing to influence the imaginations of consumers to help them "see" into the future about how a new product may fit into their utility function, both with the older competitor products and new complementary products that may not yet be in existence.

Consumers use information obtained from marketing and send marketing feedback signals to suppliers about innovative products, in the adaptive scenario, or radically new products, in the genetic bifurcation scenario.

Broadly speaking, marketing is how *ex nihilo* preferences are created in a regional economic environment, usually denoted as a regional marketplace as a result of human brains searching and sorting images about the future.

Sometimes, consumers may have seen a combination of innovative product heuristics before, and the utility of the product could be more easily imagined as a result of the market search activity.

Sometimes, in more rare cases, such as the appearance of a new drug like Viagra, the insight-imagination process associated with marketing is more extensive because consumers have a harder time imagining how a radical new product fits into their utility function.

As a result of the double search marketing activity, the new drug's potential benefits create *ex nihilo* preferences, in this case based upon the heuristics of genetic product bifurcation, as opposed to the more common product adaptation of product genetic mutation.

The technology of the products evolve, and markets may, contingently, emerge, depending on what consumers and suppliers do when they first "see" the radically new product and start imagining how the product fits with their mental image of themselves.

A better explanation of how consumers make decisions about products based upon their search of product characteristics, and how suppliers also, at the same time, make decisions about their search, is based upon the use of evolutionary algorithms. The algorithms are mathematical models which replicate a natural environment, in this case, a regional economic environment.

In *Spatial Evolutionary Modeling*, Krzanowski and Raper set up the initial conditions of their evolutionary algorithm with products possessing information contained in "genes." The genes in this algorithm are similar to product heuristics in Marten's model. A gene is responsible for one feature of the product, called a characteristic.[158]

As they search for products, consumer behavior can be modeled by use of a "fitness operator," which calculates the fitness score that each product has for satisfying the utility function of the consumer.

In any defined geographical setting, a "fitness landscape" of all possible configurations of genetic material for all existing products could be hypothesized. This fitness landscape is similar to a regional production possibilities frontier, whose outer concave curve expresses the maximum number of combinations of genes that could be expressed in all possible product combinations as a result of "chromosomal mutation." The mutation "rearranges blocks of genes on the chromosomes, which carry genetic hereditary information."[159]

The complete set of genetic material in any specific product would be called that product's genotype, and the entire population of similar genotypes would be called a phenotype. According to Krzanowski and Raper, "The theory states that under the specific environmental conditions, organisms with particular combinations of features suited for these conditions become dominant in the population…features become more pronounced, and the accumulation of these small changes in the organisms features may produce a completely new species."[160]

In order for a product to mutate, the chromosomes must be located close to each other on DNA strands, as would be expected in any regional industrial cluster. The evolutionary algorithms are searching rules that guide the search for solutions among a set of possible solutions in a specific region being conducted simultaneously by both consumers and suppliers of goods.

The algorithms represent an extension of Alderson's double search model by placing the searching activity into an evolutionary biological model and incorporates the work of Ed Feser in his description of regional industrial clusters that share certain technological features in their production technology.

The searching algorithms are distinct from the "selection" algorithms, as Alderson correctly stated. Consumers spend a considerable time searching for the right product, even when they may have already purchased that product in the final demand market.

Part of the consumer search is based upon scanning the horizon for newer, improved products, and part of the search is based upon price. The more the newer improved product "looks" like the older version of the parent technology, the less time the consumer searches, and the greater the probability that the consumer will select the newer, improved version of the product that is slightly different.

The "fitness" value of the product, as it is translated from biology to economics, is the monetary value of sales made of the product in a particular period of time. The fitness operator is the algorithm that calculates the likely fitness score a new product would obtain, compared to close competitors, when the new and improved product first enters the final demand market.

The fitness of the slightly different innovative product can be better, or it may be worse, than the existing versions of the product. However, the fitness of the new product also influences the fitness of the older products, sometimes by hastening the trend of product obsolescence.

As the new, higher priced product enters the market, the older versions of the product are forced to drop their prices in order to compete. Dropping the prices drops the profits, which creates the conditions for Mueller's Ratchet for the older versions of the product.

The more rare event is two parent genetic crossover where genetic material from two distinct regional industrial clusters who share a common production technology combine in a micro bifurcation. The technological features, or heuristics, of the offspring differ from the features of the parents. In genetic crossover, the new product has two parents and the biological equivalent is diploid sexual reproduction.

In mutation, the newer versions of the product are based upon the single parent's genetics in asexual reproduction. The more the newer product differs from any other existing product on the market, the longer consumers will search and evaluate before buying, and the less likely they are to buy the radically new product because they can not "see" how it fits into their utility function.

The more radical the product, the greater the effort to create *ex nihilo* preferences via marketing so that consumers can see how the product fits, even at the higher initial prices compared to any other product on the market.

Diagram 5.1 provides a graphical depiction of the relationship between the market search algorithm and the market selection algorithm for existing first generation asexual products in the final demand marketplace. The diagram describes the idea that higher income customers have a different search algorithm than lower income customers. The genetic search algorithm for each income class is shown as C, with the subscript denoting income class.

Producers are searching for customers who will buy the most recent version of product X_1, which contains the highest assortment of product characteristics available from the regional production possibilities frontier of production, called the fitness landscape.

Producers use the information from their search to set the price of X_1 at the highest level possible when it first enters the market, knowing that the most recent version will become obsolete soon. Producers store this information about the price and sales of the most recent version in their Product Fitness Operator Algorithm.

The producer's product fitness operator algorithm guides the guesses about what consumers are likely to do when the first see the second generation of product X_{12}, which contains the most recent assortment of genetic technology.

The product fitness operator algorithm guides the producer in decisions about how much marketing information is required, given the searching algorithm of the highest income class. The marketing information creates consumer preferences, sorted by income class.

The most recent product generation, which contains the highest assortment of technological characteristics, is aimed at the highest income class for as long as possible to derive profits on that version, before the product becomes obsolete, and profits start dropping to zero.

Before the first generation product becomes obsolete for the highest income class, lower income classes are using a different search algorithm to search the production fitness landscape. They are guided in their search by prices and by the assortment of technology most likely to satisfy their utility function.

Diagram 5.1. Relationship Between Dual Market Genetic Search and Consumer Market Genetic Selection Over Two Generations of Products.

Dual Market Search	Market Genetic Selection	Genetic Search
First Generation Occurs	First Generation	Second Generation
In Product Technology	**Product Fitness Operator**	**Product Technology Fitness**
Landscape		

By Consumers	By Producers	Price of first generation product drops
Searching for	Searching For	
Product Fit	Consumers	

Sorted by Income	Sorted by Vintage of	Prices	Customers
Class	Product Technology		

C_1	X_1	G_1	X highest	Sales X_1	$X_{12 \text{ second}}$ generation
C_2	X_2	G_2		Sales X_2	$X_{22 \text{ second}}$ generation
			X		
C_3	X_3	G_3		Sales X_3	$X_{32 \text{ second}}$ generation
			X lowest		

C = Income Class
G = Product Generation

As the consumers buy the older versions of the product at the lower prices, producers store the data in their product fitness operator, and use the data to guide decisions about the length of time the older versions of the product are likely to remain viable before reaching zero profit.

The basic evolutionary functions being described are Search, Select, Marketing, and then Search again.

The select function occurs in the same period of time of economic evolution that existing firms and existing consumers are adapting their behavior to the existing assortment of products in the regional economic environment.

Predicting Technology

Firms and consumers adapt over time through a mental imagination process of solving problems as novel situation arise in their environment. As producers make guesses about the future, venture capitalists are making guesses and searching for what technology may create the greatest capital gain event and are deploying their capital with producers whose product fitness operator shows the greatest Bayesian probability of success.

If new versions of product X_{12} look promising to the venture capitalists, that product may receive capital investments for new production technology that creates the newer improved version of the product. The investment in new machines and equipment to produce X_{12} drops the cost of production, making the price of the product competitive with the earlier generations.

For a brief evolutionary moment, the profits on X_{12} are greater than the earlier generations, which hastens the decline in profits in these older products.

If, in a rare event, product X_1 is being produced in close geographical proximity to product Y_1, then genetic crossover may occur as a result of the venture capitalist investment in X_{12}. This is in an unlikely event that X and Y share a common production technology and are located close to each other.

It is also an unlikely event because it is so risky from a marketing perspective. The selection function for the new product in the marketplace would require greater marketing effort to create the *ex nihilo* preferences in the search algorithms of the highest income classes.

It is less risky for the venture capitalists to just maintain the status quo on newer versions of existing products via product mutation/innovation, for as long as possible, and not worry about what consumers are likely to do when they see a radically new product technology for the first time.

The evolutionary processes of searching and selecting in the market on the part of consumers, producers and venture capitalists takes place over a considerable length of time. There are a number of discrete mental processes that are taking place in the brains of each unit of analysis.

Enis and Mokiva have attempted to break all the different mental processes into a scientific taxonomy, which is useful for placing the search and selection process into an analysis that would fit with the use of an evolutionary algorithm that included the lapse of time as a variable.

In their set of marketing functions for consumers of finished goods in the final demand market, they posit seeking, matching, programming, consummating and auditing as mental functions involved in the search and select process. The end goal, for the consumer, they suggest, is "..defined in terms of product benefits that customers expect" over a considerable length of time.[161]

The one part of this entire process that is captured by neoclassical economics occurs in the "consummation" of the transaction, which involves an exchange in the final demand market based upon price. But, as Alderson's paradigm of marketing suggests, the historical conditions prior to the act of consummation and the period of time after the exchange are generating information flows, both forward and backward, to other units of analysis.

One of the most important pieces of information in terms of explaining the search and select process are the negative feedback effects when exchange after the search process does not occur because of the introduction of a newer version of the older product.

The evolutionary algorithms attempt to capture this element of information flows over a period of time by evaluating how old product X compares with a newer version of the product X, and potentially, to an entirely new technological product A.

The solutions with high "fitness" are progressively chosen, while the less fit solutions are deleted from the population of solutions, just like less fit products are eventually deleted from the marketplace by the choices consumers make.

The basic processes of this economic evolutionary algorithm are:

- **Initialize the regional population in terms of consumers and producers.**

- **Evaluate the initial population in terms of existing market choices and existing interindustrial relationships.**

- **Perform a competitive iteration given the technological trajectory of the regional economy.**

- **Evaluate the possible solutions of the iteration.**

- **Project the technological trajectory of the regional economy.**

In the initial condition, the "technological closeness" of production of X_1 and Y_1 is described by Feser's matrix of coefficients in his modified input-output transaction table.[162] The extent of closeness in the intermediate demand markets determines the flow in information within the geographical region, and is related to the regional capacity to create new knowledge and transmit knowledge.

The greater the closeness, the more likely that the marketing effort to create *ex nihilo* preferences will be successful, as the upper income consumers absorb the knowledge in their search function and consider modifying their purchasing decisions in their selection function.

Further, in an evolutionary way, after upper income consumers have gone through the experience of buying new products, they gain experience in dealing with novel circumstances, in other words, they "learn-by-doing" in buying products they have never seen before, but can only "imagine" how they may fit. This is the forward linkage process from intermediate demand markets to final demand markets that are not yet created.

The ability to imagine how the radical new product may fit into the consumer's utility function is based upon the brain's ability to search and sort images, some of which is based upon memory and some of which is provided by the marketing effort.

The brain's learn-by-doing experience is a geographically bounded phenomena, with the brains in some regions being more "sympathetic" to new ideas, new products, and new ways of doing things, than the brains in other regions.

From a biological perspective, the regional assortment of technology is nonrandom. Certain spatial structures, notes Burger, "...may easily lead to the maintenance of stable polymorphisms." The stability of the regional technological assortment may not be ultimately beneficial to the emergence of new genetics.

"In a finite, asexual population," states Burger, "detrimental mutations may accumulate and eventually become fixed, thus leading to a progressive fitness decline that can result in population extinction."[163]

Without the region's ability to create new knowledge, and in the absence of an initial assortment of technology in production phenotypes that are closely related, the regional economy will die based exclusively upon adaptation and product mutation.

"In the absence of recombination," Burger continues, "offspring cannot carry less mutation than their parents...the mean time to extinction is primarily determined by the length of the phase (product life cycle in this case of economics) during which mutations accumulate, because the final phase of the mutational meltdown is very short."[164]

This is the biological equivalent of saying that once a product has reached mass standardized production in the global final demand market for finished goods, it has entered the final last gasps of life.

"The mean time to extinction," says Burger, "decreases with increasing rates of selection." In other words, as the product works its way down the income class chain, at progressively lower prices, it is headed toward extinction, and unless the regional technological assortment has come up with new products, based upon genetic crossover between product X and product Y, the regional economy will also become extinct.

This is the evolutionary process of how guesses made by consumers and producers in an existing time period create the environmental conditions of the future markets. It would be considered a more purposeful LaMarkian evolution than random Darwinian evolution. This is another case where there is not a perfect fit between Darwin's theory and evolutionary economic theory.

The economic evolutionary algorithm allows the processes of search, select, and mutate to be modeled in a more realistic treatment of time. The search function is based upon the available options confronting consumers and producers.

The selection function determines which products are the most "fit" in terms of technological genetic characteristics and the mutation function describes what type of genetic mixing and technological innovations may occur as a result of geographical proximity and knowledge flows.

The mixing of genetics is a competitive adaptation process that allows an existing product to evolve, based upon the parent's genetics. For long periods of time, this evolutionary adaptation process is based upon asexual technological reproduction of the single parent product.

The parent product's "genetic code" represents the input recipe of intermediate goods and services that went into the making the product. The entire regional repertoire of genetic possibilities is analogous to the production possibilities frontier at the beginning period of time of the evolutionary analysis.

The search, select, and adapt algorithm is defined by a logical set of rules designed to mimic the flows of information, both forward and backwards, based upon the solutions being chosen by consumers and producers in the final demand market for finished goods. In the existing model of competitive adaptation, the newer generation of products replace the "less fit" parent products, which are deleted from the product selection repertoire.

Existing products and existing consumers are described by adapting to each other through final demand market interaction as the market itself is changing. Sometimes, this interaction favors the selection of "less fit" technological solutions, based upon the application of political rules and customs associated with allegiance to the status quo in an asexual technological reproduction economy.

The set of logical rules, therefore for each region would be different, for each regional algorithm, as would the specification of the initial populations of consumers and producers. The initial specification would also describe an important asset of venture capital profits available in the regional economy from earlier capital gain exit events obtained by the venture capitalists.

Regions which possessed both venture capital and regional rules that favor novelty and innovation would have an evolutionary advantage over regions that did not possess these assets because sympathy to new ideas and products in regional rules is how sexual technological reproduction, via genetic crossover, occurs.

The algorithm itself could describe what happens in a regional economic evolutionary scenario if political rules, and laws change. Initially, rules and laws that are sympathetic to innovation could be shown as changing over time, consequently leading the economy to getting "stuck" at inferior solutions, where further evolutionary innovation via adaptation ends. This type of condition was described by Nash as a circumstance where the units of analysis have no incentive or motivation to deviate from the status quo.[165]

Getting "stuck" in a Nash Equilibrium is the biological economic equivalent of consumers and producers having no ability to break out of the equilibrium conditions associated with economic decline because their food source of knowledge has been destroyed.

Without the food of new knowledge entering the economic environment, there is no possibility of new genetic diversity being created. Without an institutional social structure that facilitates information flows, the new knowledge will not be transmitted throughout the economy.

The Nash equilibrium becomes fixed, or stuck at an inferior point, setting up the conditions for Mueller's Ratchet of regional economic decline.

Once that evolutionary dead end had been modeled, a new, different set of rules could be applied to the algorithm to describe how the regional economy could move away from the dead end associated with a Nash equilibrium.

The analysis being described is the science of markets, which involves an understanding of how *ex nihilo* preferences are created, given an existing set of technological conditions and rules associated with a region's final demand marketplace for finished goods.

The geographically-bounded spatial diffusion of knowledge is based on the concept of technological closeness in production technology. Feser's modified input-output transaction table can describe the degree of "diffusity" of the intermediate demand market for semi-finished goods.

As described in *Nonlinear Dynamics,* if the "diffusity" of a medium, in this case an environment experiencing an infection of a disease, exceeds some threshold value of susceptibility, an epidemic wavefront of infection propagates through the medium.[166]

Applying the biological metaphor, if a regional economy with an existing industrial cluster reaches some threshold value of closeness in interindustrial relationships, a new idea or new technology would propagate or rapidly diffuse through the regional intermediate demand market.

The diffusity of the regional intermediate demand market is a surrogate for the social and business communication networks and information flows within the region. The interpretation of the degree of diffusity relates to the social institutional structure.

By itself, this structure would not necessarily indicate whether a new idea rapidly diffused through the regional market, nor would it describe if the new idea became commercialized in the form of a new venture.

The rate of diffusion and the rate of new venture creation are more dependent on the social and cultural values in the region, which determine if new ideas, new knowledge and new venture are all born into an environment that is sympathetic to new ideas.

In other words, the rate of diffusion depends on what happens next when the "boundary-spanner" returns to his work place with a new idea. If the communication networks do not exist in the first place, the boundary-spanner is not likely to find any new technological ideas in the social structure of the regional economy

The diffusity of the regional intermediate demand market affects both the rate of social learning and knowledge flows, as well as the rate of adaptation of the units of analysis as slightly new, improved products enter the regional final demand market.

Given a certain initial level of diffusity in the regional industrial cluster, Epstein applies a method of analysis to derive the speed of propagation of the disease through the regional economy as:

$$C = 2[D \ (r\S_0 - \lambda]^{1/2}$$

where D is the degree of diffusity

where r is the rate of infection

Where λ is the rate of removal of individuals who were infected, have recovered and are now immune, and therefore removed from the rate of infection.[167]

The metaphor that the spread of a disease is like spread of knowledge is captured in the idea that once a person learned and adapted to new knowledge, in other words, once the individual's brain had formed new mental images, they would not be candidates for learning that piece of knowledge again.

They would have "gotten" it. Sometimes, the brain gets it on the first go around, and sometimes, in later rounds. The brains of consumers and producers that get it in the earlier rounds have a higher rate of adaptation to the changing environment, and their individual response in adaptation serves to hasten the regional economy's movement towards the Nash equilibrium.

Epstein speculates that there is a theoretical upper boundary or constraint on how fast any disease would propagate through a population. His rate of propagation is affected by how many people had been infected and are now immune, and removed from the analysis of the rate of infection.

Applying the biological metaphor, a region's upper bound is defined by the number of scientists, engineers, technicians and information technology workers working within the regional intermediate demand market for semi-finished goods.

This cluster of workers share a common language of technology, in other words, are susceptible to infection because their brains receive and transmit technological knowledge in the form of new mental images.

The rate of diffusion can be defined by a logistic function, given the initial antecedent conditions, as specified by the technological closeness of Feser's modified input output tables.

$$I(t) = \underline{c\,I_0}\,r\,I_0 + (c - r\,I_0)\,e^{-ct}$$

But, this is a contingent logistic function, meaning that the environment described by the intermediate demand market may contain the structural conditions to propagate new knowledge, without actually transmitting or diffusing new knowledge.

Further, the secondary effects described by the contingent logistic function associated with the creation of new commercial ventures that are descendents of the existing products and technological production processes, in other words the adaptation/mutation process, depends on information feedback effects coming from the behavior of consumers when they first see a newly improved product in the final demand market for finished goods. Those feedback effects take a considerable length of time to feedback to the intermediate demand market.

In the case of graphically depicting the regional intermediate demand market, the slow time dynamic associated with feedback and feed forward effects can be seen as a spiral sink, whose slow oscillations around the Nash equilibrium get smaller and smaller.

Diagram 5.2 describes this relationship. The biological equivalent depicted in this diagram is the Lotka-Volterra predator-prey model in a defined geographical territory where predators are the existing firms with the existing set of scientists, engineers and technical workers, and the prey is knowledge.

Diagram 5.2. Depiction of Regional Economy Adapting to Mutational Changes in the Intermediate Demand Market for Semi-Finished Goods.

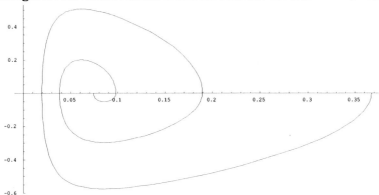

Each distinct industrial cluster in a regional interindustrial intermediate demand cluster, as defined by Feser's method, would have its own inward spiral sink oscillation, all on a seven year cycle towards the theoretical Nash regional economic equilibrium.

The inward spiral is based on the concept that product innovation, or mutation, is derived directly out of the experience of intermediate market production. This linkage between product mutation/innovation and intermediate demand markets is described by Philippe Aghion and Peter Howitt as "secondary innovations."[168]

In their concept of endogenous economic growth, radical new products, based upon fundamental research and development is "...more forward-looking, compared to Learning-By-Doing, because R & D is aimed at capturing rents from future products."[169]

This forward looking search for profits depends on the creation and diffusion of knowledge within the region, which is prompted by information flows from the final demand market to the intermediate demand market.

The product mutation/innovation process is based upon learning by doing with existing products, which are undergoing a slow evolution, as firms adapt to the changing economic environment of declining profits on existing goods. They introduce their concept of "vintage of a good," which both Schumpeter and Leontief had described using different language.

The vintage of a good is based upon the heredity of the good which is defined both by the date at which the good was introduced to the market, and the date of the line of descent, or the heredity of the good traced from the parent product.

The production workers and the skilled scientific workers in the intermediate demand markets are the units of analysis who influence the rate of knowledge creation and rate of knowledge diffusion when the "boundary-spanner" returns to the firm with knowledge from another production technology.

During the production of an existing good, the production workers encounter problems or they come up with ideas on how to improve the product, and they try out new ideas. They overcome problems and make product innovations based upon the trial and error process of what may work.

Their brains are forming new mental images, and they are imagining the future of how a product may fit both in their existing production process and in the future final demand market for finished goods.

Aghion and Howitt derive a model that describes the arrival rate of new intermediate demand products based upon the vintage of the parent good. The arrival rate of new intermediate demand products is based upon the product obsolescence cycle and the urgency associated with production workers whose skills are also becoming obsolete working on the same production technology associated with vintage products who are on the pathway of extinction.

This evolutionary process occurs over seven years, and as Aghion and Howitt point out "Incumbent, existing firms are not automatically leap-frogged by their rivals." Rather, a more gradual technological evolution of products is occurring

They speculate that there is a brief period of time of increasing rates of profit for a firm that introduces a innovation to an existing product, but then profits decrease. "This implies," they note, "that the intermediate firm will necessarily become insolvent if it never innovates after a (certain) date...there exists a maximum date at which the firm's cumulative profits just cover the adoption cost of the new technology"[170]

In other words, in the existing intermediate demand market for semi-finished goods, a firm either adapts to the declining profits of existing products with a new mutation, or it misses the small window of opportunity to adapt. If it fails to adapt, it goes extinct, unless it can get the life-support of government subsidies to keep it alive artificially.

The basic piece of empirical evidence regarding the movement towards the Nash equilibrium within the regional intermediate market is found in Feser's modified transaction table. The piece of evidence being sought is the slow movement of the region's average technological coefficient, the a_{ij}, in a time period, towards the best practice a_{ij}, which occurs from the most recent vintage of production.

The adaptation evolutionary process in the intermediate demand market is much slower than the rates of consumer adaptation in the final demand market for finished goods. This slower rate of evolutionary adaptation acts as a cushion for market risk for introducing innovations in the semi-finished goods intermediate demand market.

While the rates of adaptation are slower, the risks of failure are also less because firms within the regional intermediate demand market in the industrial cluster provide a more stable source of revenue and demand than the unpredictable demand in the consumer final demand market.

The more stable demand in the regional cluster is based upon social and business values and "close" relationships between producers in the information networks which are based upon trust and not upon price, as the conventional economic theory would posit.

A portion of the reduction in risk associated with the intermediate demand market for semi-finished goods is based upon a relationship between large multinational corporations, which may be located in the regional environment and the indigenous firms, which supply semi-finished goods to the multinational corporation.

Cappellin describes this relationship as "constellation of subcontractors and specialized suppliers around a "leader" firm."[171] From a biological metaphor perspective, the multinational firm brings back information from the global final demand market for finished goods, and provides that information to the smaller firms, which are not capable of selling their goods in the global market. This is a feedback information flow from the final demand market for finished goods to the regional intermediate demand market for semi-finished goods.

The delivery of information is not an automatic, or naturally occurring event, and just because a multinational corporation happens to be located in a region does not imply that it is serving this biological information feedback function.

If the constellation of relationships exists between the multinational firm and regional firms, then in some cases, according to Cappelin, the larger firm's information ends up helping workers in the semi finished goods market to create a new venture, and provides a built-in demand for the new firm's products, thus reducing the risk that new firms face in creating a market for their new, slightly improved product.

A regional economy experiencing what Aghion and Howitt describe as "endogenous" growth would be expected to have a continual movement, over any 28 year period of time, from an average production technology to a continually improving best production technology in this intermediate demand market.

As they state, "Each time an innovation (in an existing product) occurs in sector it, (the innovation) creates a new generation of intermediate good i."[172]

Predicting Technology

On that day that the new intermediate good enters the production process, the new intermediate i becomes leading edge technology, or the best practice a_{ij}, the target technological coefficient that all other average technological coefficients are competing with.

When the best practice a_{ij} stops improving, that would be empirical evidence that the Nash equilibrium has been reached for that specific regional industrial cluster, and that the part of the intermediate demand regional economy that depended on that cluster for creating the conditions of economic growth was at the stage of extinction.

During that 28 year period of time, unless some new knowledge had been created, diffused, and commercialized in the form of new ventures, producing new semi-finished goods for a newly emerging industrial cluster, the regional economy will also die.

The key piece of observable empirical data for this analysis is the birth rate of new venture creation within the intermediate demand regional cluster over a 28-year period of time. Alternatively, applying the biological metaphor, the rate of death of firms that fail to make the adaptations, in other words, who fail to make the investments in production to move towards the best practice production technology is evidence of economic death.

As Aghion and Howitt put it, the firms that fail to make the leap through the small window of opportunity become "insolvent." Without some new source of endogenous growth, given a high death rate of firms in the intermediate demand market, the regional economy will also die because there is no longer any "market" environment that sustains viability of the units of analysis.

The changes in technical coefficients occur over a long period of time because it takes the owners of firms in the regional environment a long period of time to process the information feeding back to them from the product innovations occurring in the final demand market for finished goods. The rate of adaptation of firms is based upon the structure, or information networks that exist within a particular regional economy, and depends on the social and cultural values of the region.

Each regional environment, therefore, is going to be different, in its rate of adaptation, and its rate of new venture creation. Each regional economy is also different in its intermediate demand structures, as characterized by the Feser method, because the column coefficients of his modified transaction table reflect the region's unique product mix showing correlation coefficients between industrial clusters.

"The fact is," said Fontela and Pulido, "that the column structures depend on the product mix, and this product mix is extremely different in each country."[173]

The important empirical evidence from an evolutionary perspective is the rate of change and the direction of change of the existing technical coefficients because that evidence suggests how firms in the regional environment are adapting to the changing environment.

An equally important piece of information can be gleaned from this analysis, which is the addition of new technological coefficients in the modified transaction table.

The addition of new coefficients provides an insight into genetic crossover which indicates that somewhere in the regional economy, radical new species are being introduced, meaning that the conditions for genetic bifurcation leading to the emergence of entirely new final demand markets may be positive.

Marten's concern about *ex nihilo* preference creation and Alderson's emphasis on consumers who rely on their past experiences to conduct their search activities, raises the point that evolutionary economics based upon the metaphor of biological evolution of population genetics requires that economics, as a science, is best understood when placed in the context of history. The biological metaphor of evolution requires an understanding of what happened in the past, and so does economics.

The behavior of humans in a market can be described and understood if the human behavior is based upon some historical philosophy that helps scientists understand what motivates humans over long periods of time.

In contrast, equilibrium economics is based upon instantaneous transactions based exclusively on market prices, any single exchange of which is independent of any other exchange, and where the utility functions of the buyers and sellers are imagined to be completely independent.

Understanding and explaining how future markets emerge from current environmental conditions which themselves are undergoing evolutionary changes, requires that the historical conditions that led to the current conditions be incorporated in the fuller understanding of human behavior in a distinct geographically specific regional economy.

Peter Allen, in his explanation of evolutionary economic theory, makes the point that "People can only grow and develop within the framework which they inherit, using the paths and levers that exist, and building on what went before. They cannot start from a clear slate, and formulate their ideal choices...(regional) structure is locked into perceptions and values, as well as into organizations and the changing circumstances due to new technology and new desires stress (threaten) these stable entities."[174]

A single exchange in the final demand market based upon price does not start from a clear slate, and the social/institutional structure of the market in which the exchange occurs is unique to that specific geographical region. As Allen points out "People cannot consume what is not produced...demands and preferences are shaped by the supply that actually occurs."[175]

From an *ex nihilo* preference creation point of view, demands and preferences are based on the historical circumstances in the market, and the future markets that emerge are "caused" by the new preferences creating new income flows. Income competition is therefore, the single greatest source of conflict in the historical context of technological innovation.

Piore and Sabel pointed out in 1984, that what really mattered was understanding the history of cultural values within a bounded geographical region. "What may matter the most is not proximity per se, but whether or not social relations are such that they lead to trust, loyalty, and tacit understandings and whether these outcomes enhance a firm's willingness to make risky deals and to share their resources."[176]

The historical perspective that explains how humans respond in a market environment that is evolving must incorporate both the elements of biological evolution as it applies to technology and history as it applies to the historical circumstances the humans find themselves in unique geographical settings.

A region characterized by close technological correlation coefficients and which have a history of social/business relationships based on trust would be expected to generate a higher rate of risky new venture creation, and thus have an evolutionary advantage in regional economic growth over regions which did not possess these characteristics.

The explanation and causal linkage between cultural values and regional economic growth was described by Udo Staber as a three step chain of logic between knowledge flows in a tightly-knit regional market, that also possessed the cultural values of trust in business relationships. The two regional assets, combined, were useful in stimulating economic growth, and one asset, without the other asset, was not sufficient for sustained economic growth.

As stated by Staber, the intermediate market of producers provides for the mechanism that allows "...exchange and flow of information about the needs, techniques and technology among buyers, suppliers, and related industries."[177]

The second element in Staber's chain of logic relates to the effect that close communication flows have on the units of analysis in the regional industrial cluster. "Co-location gives firms incentives to act in a trustworthy manner...trust is a key resource for holding district networks together."[178]

In other words, being in close proximity to each other, and having social networks that transmit knowledge, tends to create the cultural value of trust in business relationships.

From a biological perspective, the close geographical proximity of units of analysis allows their brains to process mental images and imagine the future with common perspectives. Common mental images and common imagination leads to the creation of common expectations about the future based upon trust in human dealings.

As Staber points out, "Mutual trust, social expectations, and the force of tradition and history, may be powerful mechanisms for blunting opportunistic motives and preventing the breakdown of cooperative relations."[179]

The historical circumstances related to trustful business relationships, sustained over a long period of time, leads to the creation of an economic environment that is sympathetic to new venture creation because the socialization of the risk is reduced by shared values of trust. Staber describes this third element "an external scale economy."

From an economic perspective, the shared value of trust reduces the risk of innovation for a single individual, and, in certain specific geographical settings, the risk is socialized, or collectivized, across the entire interindustrial production cluster.

In other words, the historical circumstances related to trust in the region is an explanatory variable for reducing risk of new venture creation, because the risk of a single investment are socialized to the entire regional environment, and thus the environmental conditions are favorable for the creation of more new ventures.

Some historical philosophy is needed to tie human behavior in markets to the development of trustful business relationships in distinct geographic regions. The marketing part of this historical equation comes from the empirical evidence about what happens when consumers see a higher priced product in the final demand market for the first time.

The evidence from Nagle suggests that "...a higher price in relation to the competition is no deterrent if a strong sales effort can communicate that the product is worth the price."[180]

The "worthiness" of the product is communicated to the consumer via marketing messages that describe how the product fits with the consumer's vision of the future. Trustful business relations are built when those marketing messages are confirmed by the expectations of the consumer.

Borrowing an insight from human psychology, Nagle suggests that "...it should be easier to sell something if its price can be presented as an opportunity foregone rather than as an outright loss." The factor related to human psychology is that consumers view paying the higher price today as a less painful experience than missing out on the opportunity foregone by not buying the newer version of the higher priced product.

The "missing out" of a future opportunity, while useful for understanding marketing messages for newer higher priced products does not complete the picture of how history explains this behavior over long periods of time. To make that connection, it is necessary to apply Hegel's interpretation of history as understanding the role of human reason in achieving a life goal.

According to Hegel, "...the real meaning is the ever-increasing realization of human freedom,...in the sense of ability to exercise human potential fully..."[181]

The "worthiness" of the newer, higher priced product is judged by the capacity of human reason to imagine how the product attains control over the human's own destiny. In other words, the product must fit with the human desire for freedom from coercion and manipulation by others, an enduring human characteristic that explains human behavior over long periods of time.

Within any distinct geographical market environment, there are social institutions that provide the framework for individual humans seeking to establish control over their destiny. Some regions, characterized by the rule of law and trustworthy business dealings, would be expected to provide a greater level of freedom for individuals than regions which did not possess these social institutional attributes.

In other words, a region that allowed individuals to gain individual freedom would be characterized by Kant's moral imperative that each "unit of analysis" is a moral end, in and of themselves.

These types of regions would be expected, applying the biological metaphor, to have greater rates of product innovation and endogenous economic growth, than regions that did not have these attributes, leading to an evolutionary economic advantage.

The same human motivation in history of seeking control over one's destiny that affects the "search and select" function in final demand markets for finished goods, naturally, affects human behavior in the intermediate demand market via the creation of new risky ventures.

Darwin's struggle for existence is modified by Hegel's struggle for individual freedom and control over one's destiny. Buying the higher priced product is understandable when placed in the historical context that the consumer is attempting to avoid an "opportunity foregone" that may affect the individual's control over destiny, if the newer, slightly improved product is not bought, even at a slightly higher price.

Selecting the higher priced product, when it is not tested or has not been used before, depends on morality and trust that the marketing message is truthful.

When the final demand markets for finished goods "feeds back" the information of what consumers are doing to the intermediate demand markets for semi-finished goods, individuals in the intermediate market use the information to start new ventures, if the regional economic environment is "sympathetic" to that activity.

The success of the new ventures is enhanced, and the risk associated with starting the new ventures is reduced, if the regional environment is characterized by trust and truthful dealings.

The individual impulse for freedom and control is enhanced by a social framework that supports individual freedom to start risky new ventures, some of which have built-in starting demand for their new products as a result of being born into a regional industrial cluster that needs their new intermediate product to produce the slightly innovative product.

If the cultural values of trust and truth are strong enough in a region, than structural changes in the intermediate demand market may occur, and the regional economic environment may evolve into a new type of environment.

The technology of production, and the technology of new goods are historical factors which vary, while the human impulse for freedom remains a constant. Hegel's interpretation of history, as it applies to economic evolution, is the struggle between the social and political forces that accommodate technological change, and those forces which favor the status quo. In the balance hangs both the fate of individual freedom and regional economic growth.

Placing the analysis market heuristics into the context of history allows scientists to better understand the relationship between social/political institutional configurations in distinct geographic regions and rates of economic growth. As Alexander Rosenberg points out, "…social arrangements can put us at the risk of others using us as a means, and rational agents will want strong protections against doing so…"[182]

The same interindustrial institutional framework that diffuses knowledge and information in a regional environment serves as the institutional arrangement through which individuals seek control over their destiny. The framework, by itself, however, is not sufficient to explain the birth rates and death rates of new ventures in the region. The explanation of economic growth also requires an understanding of how cultural values and rules affect individual freedom and choice.

Applying the biological metaphor, human evolution is best understood from the perspective of the rational pursuit of self-interest, and economics must incorporate the history of the pursuit of self interest to understand human behavior in markets.

Regional economic environments that allow individuals to select social and political rules for the rational pursuit of self interest, according to

Rosenberg, would have an evolutionary advantage over those cultures that did not allow for this selection.

"The locus of selection," notes Rosenberg, "is the individual organism, not larger groups in which individuals participate...individual members maximize fitness."[183]

Individuals, not collectivistic entities, are also the units of analysis to study, for understanding the forces which oppose technological innovation in a distinct geographical setting. Those powerful individuals, whether in a capitalist setting, or socialist setting, are motivated to direct the benefits of technology to themselves, based upon the same human motivation of self-interest as other individuals who are seeking freedom and control over their destiny.

Placing market heuristics into the historical setting allows scientists to answer the irony in history of why the wealthy owners of capital equipment would ever voluntarily make investments which would seem to upset the status quo of income distribution.

It is not the investment in new production equipment, per se, that defines the rate of technological innovation. It is the market selections made by upper income individuals who have both the higher marginal propensity to consume and the higher discretionary income to buy the higher priced products that feeds back information from the final demand market to the intermediate demand market about what kinds of new ventures may work.

The wealthy individuals possess a higher marginal utility for innovative products with a greater propensity for taking a risk on the untried product when it first hits the market, because they also possess a greater loss associated with opportunities foregone, if they do not buy the higher priced good. They combine the ability to take the risk of loss with the ability to spend the money, without facing financial catastrophe, as lower income consumers would, for a new higher priced product.

When this evolutionary self interest of the wealthy consumers is placed into a geographical setting that has close interindustrial relationships and social/political rules that maximize freedom of choice and selection, the wealthy individuals can be seen as fulfilling part of Adam Smith's dictum about the workings of free markets.

When moral rules are selected by the wealthy that allow maximum freedom for individuals to consume higher priced new technology goods, the rules are based upon the rational pursuit of self interest for both the wealthy and the non-wealthy.

The rules freely adopted, as if in a state of nature, would be chosen as if the wealthy imagined the tables turned, and they found themselves at the bottom of the heap. Choosing moral rules maximizes the rational pursuit of self interest, and following the moral rules leads to better outcomes for all.

In the case of moral rules being created and obeyed, technological innovation occurs, new ventures are created, and the distribution of incomes undergoes a slow change.

Sometimes, if the moral rules and laws continue to favor individual freedom, the slow changes in the distributions of income may lead to an even bigger evolutionary economic event called a market bifurcation.

The innovation in technology in new venture A stimulates demand for supplies and products in new ventures B and C. More new ventures means greater technological diversity, increasing the slight chance that technology from one venture may slip over into the DNA of another product. An entirely new complementary set of industrial clusters may be born which creates a set of final demands that did not exist before in an earlier evolutionary time.

Sometimes, however, the wealthy consumers who have the political power to direct the benefits of technological innovation to themselves, also gain the political power to set civil law and establish cultural norms that limit new venture creation in a distinct geographical region.

If they also obtain financial control over the process of venture capital investments or the flow of funds to start new ventures, then the social and political environment becomes coercive and manipulative.

In this case, wealthy people are using non-wealthy people as a means to an end, their end, so to speak, and their selfish behavior undermines technological evolution and future regional economic growth. In this scenario, the trend would be set for technological obsolescence, economic decline, and increasing political limits on individual freedom via the coercive use of government control to maintain the status quo as the economy began its slow spiral to death.

An economic theory that purported to explain economic growth would want the scientific ability to explain the difference between these two types of market environments without having to resort to the use of Dobb's magic wand.

Markets change when income distribution changes, and incomes will not change without technological innovation.

Chapter VI

Applying the Biological Metaphor of Population Genetics to Economic and Marketing Theory

In their book about predicting technological change, entitled *Seeing What's Next,* Clayton Christensen and his colleagues suggest, "…countries whose economic systems facilitate and motivate disruption have better long term growth prospects."[184]

Their book purports to be about a theory of technological evolution, but their main focus is on how technology affects large companies. Their description of the geographical conditions that lead to "economic systems that facilitate and motivate disruption" is not germane to their main focus, and the section contains few intellectual nuggets, other than to offer "… our belief is that a cluster of firms grouped around new market disruptions could be a real growth engine."

There is a more substantive theoretical connection between geographical industrial clusters and technological innovation that Christensen could have discussed, but the theoretical framework for explaining this relationship does not reside in either contemporary management school or in equilibrium tradition.

This chapter begins the process of applying the model of biological population genetics to the model of regional economic evolution. This application of a metaphor follows the 1962 suggestion by Max Black, that scientific metaphors, "…cause a profound reconception of the subject matter."[185]

In this case, the re-conceptualization is from an understanding of economics as a Platonic ideal system that always seeks "equilibrium," to an understanding of economics as an evolutionary system. The power of the re-conceptualization is that it allows the new theory to accommodate a range of facts and observations about the real world that the prior theory could not address.

Black said that the metaphor works by applying to the principal subject, in this case, the regional economy, a system of "associated implications," or characteristics, of the subsidiary, or source theory, in this case, population genetics. The target of the explanation is the regional economy, whose functions and trajectory, have certain underlying regularities and uniformities that seem to follow principles associated with biological evolution.

Biological theory, prior to Darwin, was also framed by the philosophy of Platonic idealism, as the source theory. Prior to Darwin, the notion of the biological "ideal" was the standard to which real world biological events were compared. The failure of real world biological events to conform to the ideal was taken by scientists as a "measure of imperfection of nature."[186]

After Darwin, biological evolutionary theory could be reconceptualized in a way that allowed it to accommodate new ideas, like molecular genetics, and new scientific methods and processes like proteomics.

In the application of the biological metaphor, evolution, as a theory or explanation, provides a means of transferring inferences from the source theory of biology to inferences for the target theory. The mechanisms of genetic processes, at both the molecular and phenotypic level, are used to explain the mechanisms of economic processes.

In the metaphor, certain rules about human nature, the functioning of the human brain, rules of genetics, and rules of civil society, are called upon to explain how the regional economy came to the existing position, and offers the prediction of what may happen next, in time, as the economy evolves.

The basic metaphor raises the question: How is regional economic evolution like biological evolution? As mentioned in the Introduction, Darwin's theory of natural selection is not a perfect fit for economics, and part of the task of this chapter is to explain where the metaphor does not fit.

The chapter begins with an overview of the scope of the metaphor, in order to delimit the parameters of the theory of regional economic evolution. The chapter then describes the basic, elementary biological processes that can be applied to economic evolution. The chapter ends by making a transition from biology to economics, by describing how technology in economics is like genetics in biology. The metaphor works well as long as technology is equivalent to genetics.

Most of regional economic evolution could be described in biological terms as being asexual, directed, positive, and haploid, based upon the heredity of technology embodied in products.

Most of the selection processes in regional economic evolution are market-based contingent events, not random nor chaotic, and the market selection processes usually exhibit pre-selective biases. While the emergence of new economic environments is not random or chaotic, neither is it deterministic.

Much like biological evolution, what comes next in economics could very easily have been something else. Starting at any point of time in history, it is very difficult to predict the exact course of the either the biological or economic evolutionary trajectory. However, hindsight, based

141

upon equilibrium theory, can be used to see where the economy has been, and predictive theory, based upon genetics, and the notion of bifurcations, allows for an analysis of the likely next course of the economy, with the help of Bayesian probability methods.

For long periods of time, in economic evolution, not much changes in the regional economic structure that is readily observable or apparent. During these long periods of time, a certain type of biological metaphor is better at describing economic structure than Darwin's theory.

This theoretical metaphor is called, neutral genetic drift, and its primary proponent is Motoo Kimura.[187] The essence of this theory is that at the level of molecular evolution, evolutionary changes are mainly due to very small mutations whose effects on the selection/adaptation process are nearly neutral.

This nearly neutral effect is in contrast to Darwin's view that organisms positively and progressively adapt to their environment by accumulating beneficial mutations. Kimura's theory is particularly useful for analyzing the period of time most contemporary economists call "equilibrium."

In its application to regional economic evolution, Kimura's theory means that technological inter-dependencies in the regional production relationships are very slow to change. Part of the slowness is related to the technology of production, and part of the slowness relates to a feedback relationship between market demand selection and the technology embodied in finished goods, which are akin to phenotypes in biology.

Like the parallel processes in biological evolution at the molecular and phenotypic level, economic evolution has parallel market processes that are undergoing evolution, and the processes in the market, while distinct, have feed-forward and feedback effects on technological processes.

The two processes in economics are in the technology of products and the evolution of consumer demand for finished goods in the final demand market. And, for long durations of time, the relationship between the two processes is better explained by Kimura that by Darwin.

The scope of regional economic evolutionary theory in this book, however, follows the scope laid out by Darwin. In Darwin's theory, it is primarily phenotypes, or individual products, within a unique environmental setting that evolve. Among individual populations of different species, Darwin found enough diversity, and enough blind variation, to sustain an evolutionarily adaptive selection process. In his theory, there are three major objects of inquiry.

First, entities within the population must multiply and reproduce, based upon some observable, logical, and natural scientific explanation, in his case heredity. Second, the entities must be subject to categorization by how they vary among themselves and between species. The phenotypes are subjected to a selection process associated with the unique environment, and, over time, certain species adapt to the demands of the environment, and pass the selected traits, through heredity, to their offspring.

Darwin's theory is most useful for describing the processes involved with a regional economy breaking away from equilibrium, either on an upward trajectory of growth, or on a downward trajectory of economic decline.

The emphasis on Darwin, as opposed to Kimura, as the basis for delineating the scope of the metaphor is that Darwin's theory allows for an explanation of how the future economic environment is derived from the existing and past environment. In other words, Darwin's theory can accommodate two important economic concepts about how the future economic structure may evolve, given a set of antecedent conditions, while Kimura's theory is useful for explaining the existing economic environment, especially as it relates to the concept of equilibrium during a fixed or certain period of time, for example, seven years.

The explanation of how the future comes into existence is important because it can be extended to an explanation of how unknown future markets may emerge from buy and sell relationships in the existing final demand market for finished goods. The "emergence" of the future market is a contingent event, which requires the application of Bayesian statistical analysis that assesses the probability of emergence, given prior conditions.

Diagram 6.1 describes the scope of the metaphor between the source theory of evolutionary population genetics and the reference theory of structural regional economic evolution (SERET). In Darwin's theory, the basic unit of analysis is the phenotype. The phenotype is the scientific unit of observation that adapts to the environment over many generations, as a result of heredity.

In regional economics, it would be fair to ask: what unit of analysis is like a phenotype that that inherits genes from a parent in order to adapt to the changing economic environment? The selection of the correct unit of analysis goes to the very heart of the difference between Platonic idealism and the metaphor of scientific evolution.

The analogy to Darwin's phenotype in economics is the product, which is produced by a firm, and its owners, who make decisions about the firm. There are three major units of analysis in evolutionary theory and one important unit of analysis in regional economics is the product.

Another important unit of analysis are owners of firms, who bear the capacity to learn and adapt to changing economic circumstances. The firm produces, or procreates products. Firms, which make products that look alike, in the biological metaphor, are species.

Some products, like some children, do well, once they are procreated, and are successful in the existing environment. Sometimes, the owners of firms do not learn lessons from the existing environment, and the owners make bad decisions about products, which do not sell well in the existing economic environment.

Sometimes, the products produced for a particular market are technologically obsolete, causing declining sales, declining profits, and death to the product. Without the life source of revenues from products, the firm, itself, will eventually die.

Sometimes, the economic environment becomes so hostile that all the species of a particular type die. The key factor of product viability in the market is how consumers select technology, and the technology of product characteristics, in economics, looks like genotypes in population biology.

In neoclassical economics, the firm is lumped together with other components and entities under the heading of "capital." In this aggregation of capital, it is difficult to apply the biological metaphor because the agent which bears "learning" is aggregated into a concept of capital, which has no mental capacity to learn. The individual human owner, who has a brain, is capable of learning. Capital, as an entity, or unit of observation, has no brain, and can not "bear" or possess the capacity to "learn" or "adapt."

In regional economics, the product is the same thing as the phenotype that evolves in Darwin's theory. In the classification scheme of economics, products are categorized by firms who share certain characteristics in common. Firms are born, firms grow, firms die. Some firms do extremely well in a short period of evolutionary time, and the owners are rewarded by high rates of profits. If, during this period of high profits, these successful firms procreate new products, which produce new streams of revenue, the firms may continue to enjoy success in future periods of time.

Of course, if the market environment changes, and their products become less successful, the firms may not continue to be successful. Understanding and predicting the reasons for the difference between successful firms and non-successful firms is one of the objects of inquiry in regional evolutionary economics.

The owners of firms follow a biologically observable behavior when they make decisions about how to adapt their firm to the changing economic environment. Their behavior in making decisions can be modeled or observed and may contain certain uniformities or regularities. In other words, given a certain set of environmental conditions, the science of regional economics asks what decisions would make the most sense, from the perspective of the owner?

The uniformity or regularities in behavior are drawn from Darwin's theory. They are based upon the notion of the "rational pursuit of self interest," as perceived in the brain of the individual making the decision. The correct scientific method in this case is something called "methodological individualism" as it applies to owners of firms. The correct way to apply methodological individualism is to understand how the human brain processes information that leads to decisions.

The conclusions drawn from observing behavior in terms of regularities and uniformities comes from comparing what an individual owner decided in a certain environment, to what similarly situated owners, or peer groups, did in the same environment. This process of comparing behavior is like the scientific method of intersubjective verification of reality, where a person reasons through a problem by asking himself, "Well…what would most people do in this situation?"

In the case of regional economics, the question would be, "well, given this set of economic circumstances, what do most owner's of firms do?" When enough observations are built up from watching individual behavior, a type of law-like conclusion may be reached that would suggest what most owners would do in the future, if they are confronted with this same set of environmental conditions.

The value of Darwin's approach is that it allows the economist to ask, "Given a change in the environment, and given the law-like conclusions of behavior drawn from the previous environment, what type of decisions are owners likely to make in the new environment?"

In Darwin's theory, the biological evolutionary analysis is a two step process.[188] First, scientists observe variation in the phenotypes that exist in a specific geographical area in a specific population. Biologists apply a very detailed classification system to describe the variation of phenotypes in the population, just as economists have a detailed classification system of variation of firms in an area classified by the products that they produce and by the other firms within the geographic environment that they rely upon to produce the products.

In regional economics, this classification scheme is generally based upon a government classification system called Standard Industrial Classification. Using the SIC code of a company allows the company to be placed in an economic phyla and fauna table called, "a regional input-output transactions" table.

Diagram 6.1. Scope of the Metaphor Between Evolutionary Population Genetics and Structural Evolutionary Regional Economic Theory (SERET).

Biology Units of Analysis	Basic Rules/ Algorithms	Antecedent Conditions	Existing Environment	Future Environment
Genetic molecules DNA Demes Genotypes Phenotypes	Units must multiply Units must vary Variation is heredity Adaptation Selection Survival of fittest	Initial population Birth rates/death rates Inbreeding	Current advantaged phenotypes Current rates of genetic evolution	Heterozygosity leads to new species VS. Mueller's Ratchet of inbreeding

Logical Progression of Thought and Time Chronology of Analysis

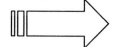

Biology Units of Analysis	Basic Rules/ Algorithms	Antecedent Conditions	Existing Environment	Future Environment
Humans Products Firms Markets	Diversity Variation Selection Adaptation Obsolescence Civil rules Social rules Moral rules	Initial population History Culture Existing infrastructure Industrial clusters, skills Technological envelope	Birth/Death rates of firms Rate of technological product innovation Local attractor points Regional economic structure [A] Final demand market selection Intermediate demand market selection	Bifurcation growth points Bifurcation decline points Future economic structure [A'] Eigenvalue from [A] to [A']

Bayesian statistical analysis

Second, biologists look for the "fittest" members of the population in the geographical area of analysis and try to determine what "selective" advantage exists for these fit phenotypes, in order to predict and explain the probability that the fit phenotypes will transmit their genes (technology in the case of products), to the next generation.

The metaphor for economics is that some firms produce products with certain technical characteristics, which are "selected" in the market environment, and if the selection process was fully understood, economists may be able to explain and predict which genes, or technological characteristics of the products, would likely be passed on to future product generations.

As Stankiewicz notes, in order for the selection/adaptation metaphor to work for economics, the entities under investigation "...must be organized into populations integrated through time by descent." The entities must perform two functions: replication, which means the ability to pass on its structure largely intact in successive replications, and interaction, which means interacting in its geographically-specific environment in such a way as to become differentiated.[189]

In Darwin, the phenotypes in his initial stages of investigation are limited to specific geographical areas. Darwin went to the Galapagos Islands to study the species there because he wanted an isolated geographical region to serve as his natural laboratory.

Darwin was attempting to answer this important question: How do species originate? His general theory, according to R. C. Lewontin, is that "...geographic speciation postulates a multi-stage process, after an initial isolation." [190]

The conclusions Darwin made were that species with the best adaptation to the specific environment were well "...inside the area but with less and less good adaptations towards its boundaries...species stay obstinately fixed, disappearing as the limits of their habitats are reached."[191]

Both the regionally specific geographical areas, especially the reference to "boundaries," and the "obstinately fixed" part of behavior are applicable to the regional economics evolutionary metaphor, but for slightly different reasons than in the biological theory of Darwin.

In the application of the biological metaphor to economics, the main question would be: How do new products originate, and how do new markets emerge from the introduction of new products (phenotypes) in a geographically specific area?

In biology, according to Darwin's theory, in any specific geographical setting, the process of mutations allows the phenotypes within a species to adapt. "Once the range of improvements conferrable by a single base-pair changes have become exhausted, a species cannot evolve further...because the range of genetic adaptation has become exhausted...Only if the genetic system is again stirred up by external incidence, can anything further take place."[192]

As applied to regional economics, a specific economic region starts out with a "technological envelope," or "technological possibilities frontier," which encloses or encompasses all existing and possible future technological mutations given the technology of existing products. Within this geographic technological frontier, in a specific time horizon, once the technological opportunities for mutation have become exhausted, further technological innovation in the product phenotype is limited.

As will be seen in later chapters, it is this technological exhaustion which feeds back into the regional economic decline in a region, as existing companies lose profits from products that have become technologically obsolete. Only when the regional technology is "again stirred up technologically by external incidence," can anything further take place.

And, to add a hint on where this idea is going, the technological stirring up occurs at the "boundary" between two product markets, or in the language of biology, when species interbreed.

Aura Reggiani and Peter Nijkamp discuss the idea of the regional technological envelope in terms of the technological "...environmental carrying capacity as the main limit for the technological system...," within each region.[193] Their idea of environmental carrying capacity can be placed within the context of the biological metaphor with the assistance of the insights from Daniel Hartl, in his work, *A Primer On Population Genetics.*

Hartl describes how populations of species live within a "...sufficiently restricted geographical area, such that any member can potentially mate (trade or exchange in the case of economics) with any other member...members of a species are rarely distributed homogenously in space; there is always some sort of clumping or aggregation, some schooling, flocking, herding or colony formation."[194]

In biology, these clumpings, or groupings of species that can mate with each other are called "demes." As Hartl notes, local inbreeding units in geographically structured populations are the units of analysis for population genetics, because it is within the demes that local units evolve.

In Hartl's description of evolution, it is "the systematic changes in allele frequency," that is of interest to biologists. In most demes, the process of "positive assortive mating" occurs wherein individual members of the species tend to choose mates that are phenotypically like themselves.

As it is applied to regional economics, the genotypes are the technological characteristics of products, and positive assortive mating between products that look alike or function alike technologically, are called regional industrial clusters. The industrial clusters represent "groupings" of firms by product, and the industrial clusters can be represented in regional input output transactions tables that have been modified by factor analysis to show technological similarities among products.

However, a big difference in the application of the biological metaphor to the economic theory is that most "mating" among members of the regional industrial cluster is "asexual," in the sense that the technology being mated is previously existent in the regional technological envelope.

This asexual, positive assortive mating is consistent with Kimura's nearly neutral genetic drift. Without technology being stirred up, the end result implication of Kimura's theory is regional economic decline, via Mueller's ratchet of inbreeding. The asexual process is more like genetic recombination, where existing alleles are recombined and shuffled in the existing genetic pool, without adding new genetic combinations in a new genetic pool.

As a point of reference, the asexual technological mating is the same type of innovation that Clayton Christensen calls a sustaining innovation. For Christensen, "...sustaining innovations...are what move companies along established improvement trajectories. They are improvements to existing products on dimensions historically valued by customers."[195]

Applying Darwin's theory to regional economics, it is the very rare occurrence of "sexual" mating of product technology that occurs along the geographic technological "boundaries," of the industrial cluster that "stirs up" the technology by introducing new technological alleles into the region. The explanation of the importance of the idea of geographic region to regional economics is very straight forward.

According to Darwin, humans in natural environments are not perfect fitness maximizers, nor are they perfect profit maximizers in economics. "Which behavior is being maximized depends only on the environment which provides parameters fixed independently of which behavior the organism is going to emit.

But, when organisms interact, which behavior one emits may be a function of what the other (organism) is going to do...optimal behavior is one that reflects a strategy which takes account of the prospective behavior of other organisms...fitness maximization becomes a strategy problem."[196]

In other words, fitness maximization in one regional geographic setting may be entirely different that fitness maximization in some other setting. Part of the task of Structural Evolutionary Regional Economic Theory (SERET), is to explain the differences in fitness maximizing behavior of the units of analysis, which in the economic case, are individual humans attempting to maximize their welfare in a specific region at a specific time.

Individual humans, as the unit of observation, "...grow and develop within the framework which they *inherit*, using the paths and levers that exist, and building on what went before. They cannot start from a clear slate, and formulate their ideal choices...(institutional) structure is locked into perceptions and values as well as into organizations and the changing circumstances due to new technology and new desires stress these stable entities."[197]

In economic evolution, just like biological evolution, there is never a tableau rasu, evolution never starts over, but builds from what exists from a regionally specific setting.

To take a more concrete view of the importance of individual humans and technology in a specific region, consider the example provided by Richard Stankiewicz. He notes that "Every engineer is embedded in a particular technological tradition characterizing his profession, the company he works for and the team he is a part of- the technological community...The accumulation and transmission of knowledge occurs in, and through, the formation of technological communities, and is strongly affected by their structure and dynamics."[198]

In the case of SERET, the individual engineer "bears" knowledge, and works for a firm that is producing the range of product phenotypes within a region's industrial cluster, or as Stankiewicz calls it, the "technological community."

What the engineer does with his knowledge, and how the knowledge is diffused within the community, become important elements of the theory of regional economics for explaining which regions grow, and which regions die, economically. The topic of how technical knowledge is created and diffused within a regional technological community is discussed in Chapter Six.

And, to pick back up on the earlier reference to "obstinately fixed" behaviors, it is very difficult for individual humans to break free of their routine daily behavior in their fixed environment. Even if an individual succeeds in breaking free, there are social and political environmental forces that tend to support Kimura's nearly neutral drift hypothesis.

As noted by Stankiewicz, "...technological change undermines the established institutional patterns."[199] Most regional economic behavior can be explained in terms of Kimura's nearly neutral drift because social forces that are committed to the status quo arrangement of power, limit the range of behavior of individual humans, who, if allowed to engage in technologically sexual behavior, would undermine the status quo flow of benefits from existing products which produce revenues in existing markets.

The fitness maximization goal of these social forces that favor the status quo in a specific regional environment is to suppress technological change for as long as possible in order to hang on to their diminishing marginal revenues from products that are growing progressively obsolete. The behavior of powerful social and political forces within the technological community adds a factor of contingency to the theory of regional economic evolution, which is further discussed in Chapter Seven.

The strategies and techniques for maintaining the status quo vary from region to region, and a theory that aims at explaining regional economic evolution must accommodate the contingency of regional variations in human behavior strategies that favor the status quo.

Individual firms, within a region's industrial clusters interact with each other every day, by exchanging technical information and products based upon the store of knowledge in the region's technological possibilities frontier. What the existing firms eat, in a Lotka-Volterra biological metaphor, is technical knowledge. The more technical knowledge they eat, the greater the rate of their asexual product mutation, for their existing set of products, in a positive assortive mating process.

The more technological knowledge that escapes the plate of one firm and ends up on the plate of another firm, called technological spillovers by Edward N. Wolff,[200] the greater the possibility, in a Bayesian way, of positive assortive sexual mating.

If the initial conditions within the specific region allow for both a great number of firms, and a large technological possibilities frontier, which describes the resource of knowledge, then the conditions exist for a contingent economic event called "bifurcation," wherein technology from one product marketplace deme is sexually mated in a crossover of technology from another product deme.

Each regional economic environment is different, with a different history, culture, social rules and set of individual firms. In the face of this regional diversity, the biological metaphor applies universal rules, or algorithms, to explain underlying behavior of the "agents" or units of analysis in each region, just as Darwin found that the universal rules of genetic variation and natural selection could explain much of the evolutionary process in any geographical setting.

In Darwin, in any geographical setting, the population of phenotypes (units of analysis) remains constant (rule). The phenotypes are characterized by variation in their outward characteristics. Variation is a rule applied to how and why the characteristics of phenotypes vary.

The rule of variation is that the pool of genes in each species for each geographical setting is large and blind, and that differences in genes are randomly generated (rule). The fitness selection rule universally applied by Darwin to explain how variations in genetics are matched within the environment, and that those genes that are "selected" (rule), both at the molecular level and at the phenotype level are the species that reproduce.

As a result of reproduction, the rule of heredity applied by Darwin, is that the fit genes are inherited by subsequent generations (rule) of phenotypes.

As applied to humans, Darwin's theory contains a universal rule of human behavior, which Alexander Rosenberg describes as the individual's "rational pursuit of self-interest." "Homo sapiens," states Rosenberg, "have been selected for fitness, and the rational pursuit of self-interest enhances fitness to a considerable degree...natural selection will favor those behavioral strategies that reflect self-interest, regardless of whether these strategies reflect actual occurrent or conscious calculation of costs and benefits on the part of agents."[201]

SERET begins the rule-based explanation of regional economic evolution with the Paradox Algorithm. In any geographical setting, the lower the initial level of genetic technological diversity in new products, the greater the rate of market adoption or selection of products.

In other words, new products, which look and function like old or existing products, have a greater rate of market adoption. On the other hand, the more that new products look like old products, the less likely the introduction of new products will lead to new market demands within the regional markets. New products which inherit technology from old products do so through heredity and mutation, which leads to greater rates of market selection and asexual reproduction.

Regions with a high initial endowment of product technological diversity will have greater rates of new product introduction with products that do not look and function like old products, but the new products will have lower rates of market acceptance, or selection.

Lower rates of market selection sets up the biological metaphor of regional economic decline. Without high rates of market selection of technologically diverse new products, regional rates of profits for existing products will decline, eventually to zero. The paradoxical result is that new products with new technology, obtained through genetic crossover, have a lower rate of market selection, but have the greatest effect on market emergence.

Following John Holland's insights about the role of rules in complex adaptive systems, some rules regarding the relationship of technology to economics could be developed that could help explain this complex paradox. According to Holland, "...rules are simply a convenient way to describe agent strategies...behaviors and strategies of the component system are determined by the stimuli and responses..."[202]

As applied to the technology paradox, Holland's insight would mean that the "agent" or unit of analysis, are individual humans in their capacity as owners of firms. The owners of firms engage in a behavior involving the production of products. As new products are introduced in the regional economy, (stimuli), the agents respond.

The response of owners amounts to a strategy, or a behavior. If there is regularity, or uniformity in the strategy, given a particular configuration of events in the economy, then rules could be associated with the behavior for each configuration.

In other words, if the regional economy has a low rate of product technology innovation, and low rates of new venture creation, the behavior rule, or strategy of firm owners may be to resist changes in the technology of existing products in order to hold on to the benefits from the status quo configuration. The behavior is based upon the bedrock assumption of human behavior that individuals rationally pursue their self-interest.

As Holland states, "For agents in the economy, (firms), the stimuli could be raw materials and money, and the response could be goods produced."[203] Given a certain configuration of technology, raw materials, money and market demand, the rational pursuit of self-interest may be to resist technological change.

As Holland goes on to state, "We talk of the "mobility of capital" where the investors in an industry are distinct from the "locals" so the investors simply reinvest in some other industry when the local industry collapses. The investors do not suffer the consequences of the collapse, at least in the short-run, so they show little concern."[204] Holland is making the point that rules regarding behavior and strategy for owners of firms and for capitalists may be entirely different.

In any regional geographic economic configuration, to extend Holland's point, what is rational from the point of view of firm owners and what is rational from the perspective of the capitalist who makes investments in firms are two different sets of rules. The complexity of regional economics is that each region has a different configuration of assets and market demands, yet the application of rules needs to be uniform across regions in order for the explanation to have the semblance to scientific theory.

In Holland's work involving algorithms, or mathematical explanations of rules for complex systems, the Darwinian concept of adaptation is used as a surrogate concept for behavioral strategy. In Holland, "…adaptations are changes in behavior (rule based), based upon system experience."

Much of the "system experience" in a regional economy is related to what other firms and other humans are doing in the regional market. As Holland notes, "A major part of the (regional) environment of any given adaptive agent consists of other adaptive agents, so that a portion of an agent's effort at adaptation is adapting to the (behavior) of other adaptive agents."[205]

Holland's description of individual behavior comports with common sense notions of how humans learn about and anticipate the behavior of other humans. Applied on a macro economic scale, this reliance on individual behavior is a major theoretical departure from neo classical tradition, which posits adaptive behavior in a system-wide economy that adjusts supply and demand, based on quantity and price movements.

In an existing regional economic environment, the biological metaphor suggests that firms eat technical knowledge. But, unlike fundamental assumptions contained in neo classical tradition, the productivity gains associated with eating technical knowledge are generally non-linear in any 7 year period to time, meaning that a unit input of technical knowledge leads to more than a unit of output.

The more technical knowledge derived from the existing environment, the better the firms' prospects for economic survival, in any seven year period of time. Holland uses a mathematical notation, "r," to describe the rate of transforming technical knowledge into offspring, in this case products.

In SERET, the "r" would be the region's rate of product commercialization. Each new product that is commercialized, following Holland, "…opens up the possibility for further interactions and new niches."[206]

In the regional economic setting, the new interactions caused by new products would be captured and described as the entry of new technical coefficients in a regional input-output transactions table between two points in time, probably about 7 to 10 years.

Holland describes how rules of behavior are derived for explaining how individuals may respond to the new niches by using an analogy to the rules of chess. In chess, a particular new configuration of pieces on the board represents the current economic environment. An owner of a firm, surveying the chess landscape engages in a mental exploration of possible moves, given the rules of chess. "The mental exploration of possible move sequences in chess," says Holland, occurs "prior to moving a piece."[207]

154

The human playing chess anticipates the future events and imagines likely future scenarios and configuration, much like an owner of a firm anticipates the behavior of competitors, by asking himself: If I make this move, my competitor will probably respond with this move."

In the economic setting, the firm's owner imagines how the future economic environment may look, and lives out the future by "trying out" mentally how that future market would be, from a competitive survival rational pursuit of self-interest point of view.

For example, in the case of an entrepreneur who is thinking about creating a new venture, the mental process involves imagining future market demand for his non-existent product. He then anticipates the most likely moves, or responses from competitors if he makes his investment to create the new firm and produce the new product.

The rules which apply to this sequence are much like the moves in a chess game. Given a current configuration of firms and products in the market, and given certain rules about "r," (the rate of technological commercialization), the entrepreneur can "live out the future," by imagining his future rate of profit. Since future prices do not yet exist in this future market, the best data for the entrepreneur to use in imagining the future are current prices, if they apply at all, to his future product.

The social, civil, and business rules in the regional economy establish the institutional setting for entrepreneurial decision making, as noted by Brennan and Buchanan, in *The Reason of Rules*. They note, "There need be no shared objective in sociopolitical rules. Individuals are recognized to possess their own privately determined objectives, their own life plans, and these not be common to all persons.

In this setting, rules have the function of facilitating interactions among persons who may desire quite different things."[208] In the regional economic setting, the rules establish the baseline of stability and security required for an owner of a firm to imagine the future.

As a source of stability in decision-making, social rules tend to support Kimura's nearly neutral drift hypothesis, as it is applied to regional economics because rules establish the status quo conditions of logic. Rules, in conjunction with daily routine decision making by owners of firms, based upon the status quo configuration of firms, are very difficult to modify.

Common language calls this set of circumstances "rules of thumb," which guide decisions and behavior during much of the time. In the case of owners of firms, there are fixed costs of doing business every day, fixed arrangements of capital equipment on the plant floor, and a fixed set of "rules of thumb" about what to do given an ordinary normal configuration of competitive conditions.

Kimura's notion of nearly neutral drift does not work well in explaining what happens when owners of firms confront novel conditions and non-ordinary configurations of firms. In the case of new conditions, Holland suggests that an agent "...combines tested rules to describe novel situations."

Holland describes how the brain decomposes the new situation into familiar parts in order to apply rules of decisions in the past that had been successful in similar situations. The brain is sorting and shuffling mental images, searching for decisions about the solution to the new situation. "When one hypothesis fails, notes Holland, "competing rules are waiting in the wings to be tried."[209]

A novel situation in economics may be the appearance of a new competitor with a slightly different product technology in the existing market of final demand for finished goods. A more dynamic novel situation would be the appearance of a competitor with an entirely new product technology that makes existing product technology obsolete and which also tends to create new market niches that had previously not existed.

The ordinary rules of decision making for an owner of a firm, in the face of a unique or novel situation, requires the owner to go through a mental process to check possible alternatives. Holland's description of how the brain sorts and shuffles alternative mental courses of action is similar to Daniel Dennett's description of how the human brain functions.

In *Consciousness Explained*, Dennett describes this process of image filtering as the "multiple drafts model." He states that information entering the nervous system is always under constant mental editorial revisions. "These editorial processes occur over large fractions of a second, during which time various additions, incorporations, emendations, and overwriting of content can occur, in various orders."[210]

The mental image revisions being filtered at any moment are revised in accordance to memory images or rules of thumb that led to success in the past. The more times the neural circuits fire in a certain sequence and frequency, based upon successful past images, the more traces of chemicals that are released in the vicinity of the brain involved with the sorting process, leading to more permanent, reliable images being created from memory.

This is the chemical/physiological description of the simple common language used by business owners to describe the logic of a decision: "Well, it worked last time we tried it."

Much of the environment of business owners involves decisions about what to do every day, given the existing set of standard problems and fixed resources. When an owner of a firm is confronted with a novel situation, "rules of thumb" about what worked last time may not lead to optimal decisions, which is one of the big philosophical reasons that the profit maximizing assumptions as applied to large corporations are sub-optimal.

What worked last time, as a decision guide, does not lead to profit maximization in novel economic environments. Much of the economic world of business owners involves making predictions of other people's behavior when ordinary circumstances change. The decision rules applied in these novel situations has more to do with something that looks more like what John Holland has in mind, where hidden order is derived as a result of decisions which could easily have been something else.

The mental process of a business owner making a decision in the face of a novel situation is like the mental exploration of possible moves in chess. The move may be optimal or the best one, at that time, but depending on what other humans do, the environment may change radically, and doing what worked last time may turn out to be the end of the firm. The basis of economic decision making in any seven year period of time is not profit maximization, it is self-interest survival satisficing under uncertainty, based upon guesses about what other humans are going to do.

The continual process of asexual innovation in existing products, and the appearance of entirely new products, is an evolutionary response, or adaptation by owners of firms. The innovations themselves are also causing the environment to change. The present market conditions of competition are creating a contingent future market, and in very rare circumstances of technological sexual crossover, a new building block is created that opens a whole range of possibilities for new combinations.

The new possibilities would be captured as data in a regional input-output model that showed increased income and employment multipliers within the regional economy. New industrial clusters in the regional model are equivalent to Holland's new building blocks.

The regional economy is evolving as a result of products evolving technologically. Some type of scientific explanation must be given that describes how the economy moves through time from the present configuration to the future configuration.

Given an existing seven-year period of time, and rules which explain how owners of firms are adapting to the existing environment, the model would suggest, or predict the most likely future economic scenario.

The biological metaphor applied to explain this part of the regional economy is called the "state transition function." The purpose of this function is to describe how a mapping of the current configuration of firms and products within the existing environment, called "U" is transformed or transitions to a future configuration called "X." Getting to "X" depends on understanding the current inputs into "U," and the set of relationships that exists in "U."[211]

The set of variables under investigation in U describe the current state of the regional economy, and u (t) is a function that assumes a time sequence of the variables of U. In understanding how the regional economy moves through time from U to X, an intermediate function, "Y," describes how the conditions in U create, or "cause" the conditions in X to occur.

The current state of the regional economy would be, as described by Doucet and Sloep, "...a strongly condensed resume of past inputs. The state of the system reflects the input history inasmuch as the (existing) state affects future behavior."[212]

Applying the biological metaphor, history is important to economics. Unlike the ahistorical framework of Platonic idealism of neo classical theory, SERET incorporates history and the lapse of time as important intellectual concepts for understanding economics.

The pathway in time from the current economic environment to the future economic environment can be described by a set of two differential equations, based upon the application of some type of "Holland-like" rules. The rules would describe how owners of firms respond to novel situations that require more than the application of "rules of thumb."

If $X_1(t)$ represents the state of the regional economy at time (t), and $X_2(t)$ describes the state of the economy at the future period of time, then the plot of the pair of values $(X_1(t), X_2(t))$, can be thought of as a pathway to a point in time in the future. In the application of certain rules, the pathway may well be a slow oscillation around some attractor point, and in the application of other rules, the pathway may trace out a more linear direction in time.

In stable economic systems, with little technological new knowledge being created or eaten by firms, there would be a very low rate of technological product commercialization or mutation, or "r." In this type of regional economic environment, the time trajectory would be visualized as a slow, periodic oscillation around $(X_1(t), X_2(t))$.

The regional economy, as seen in some seven to ten year period of time, would be in economic "equilibrium." If the time period under consideration is expanded to include a seven year period of time prior to the current period, and some future periods of time, then the trajectory of the stable equilibrium would be seen as slowly collapsing to some low level of economic activity, depicting the dying regional economy.

Biologists call this state of stable equilibrium a "Lyapunov stationary point." Applying the biological metaphor, the regional economic system would be characterized by slow oscillations around the Lyapunov point of equilibrium, with the amplitude of each oscillation decreasing over a long period of time, best visualized over a 28 year period of time.

The point of attraction, to which the economy is collapsing, itself is moving on a slow trajectory downwards in time. The attractor point is called "asymptotically stable," over the seven year period of time.

The stability of the attractor point is derived from the interactions of two forces, the first of which is the rate of "r," and the second of which are the social and political forces within the environment that resist technical change in order to hold on to the status quo arrangements of benefits.

Schumpeter was partially correct about the gales of creative destruction, but a better explanation of economic evolution would have been to set up the dynamic as the conflict between the forces of technological innovation and preservation of the technological status quo.

In the seven-year period of equilibrium, the dynamic between these two forces are strong enough to resist perturbations arising from the introduction of novel technology. There may be product innovation or process innovation, which occur, but the rate of "r," the commercialization of technological innovation into viable ventures, is resisted.

Future economic growth in the region is "contingent" upon counter forces that are strong enough to move the regional economy towards a new attractor point. The element of contingency is created both by the requirement of a strong perturbation, in r, and the creation of strong ensuing complementary effects, which Holland describes as "building blocks."

Without both elements, the solution to the set of differential equations would return to the vicinity of the original attractor point, an evolutionary process much like Kimura's nearly neutral genetic drift.

If a technological genetic crossover should happen to occur that knocks the economy off of its slow periodic equilibrium oscillations, then the condition may exist for one of Holland's new building blocks to emerge.

Doucet and Sloep describes this emergence of the building block in the context of biology. "We want to know whether the solution X*(t), starting at X*(0), is stable (in the context of SERET, whether the forces of the status quo can resist the change), and the conditions to break out from stability[213] (in SERET, called a bifurcation).

They offer an equation for testing the conditions of stability around a local attractor point, or in SERET, the equilibrium point.

$$\lim_{t \to \infty} Ix^*(t) - x^*(t)I = 0$$

159

If a perturbation knocks the system out of equilibrium, the solution would be greater than 0.

Over time, the trajectory of the economic system could be investigated, via another one of their equations:

$$Di(t) = A_{1e}^{-\lambda t}, + A_{2e}^{-\lambda 2t}, + \ldots + A_{ne}^{-\lambda nt}$$

Where each A1,…,An, is specific to each region representing the region's regional input-output transaction table in any seven year period of time.

The exponents, $\lambda_1 \ldots, \lambda n$, are common to each component of time for each single regional configuration of building blocks, or in the case of SERET, industrial clusters. The exponents, λ, originate in the regional economic system's state transition function, and are commonly referred to as "eigenvalues."

It is not necessary to know the precise value of the eigenvalue in order to tell the direction of the regional economic trajectory. The direction is either positive or negative, meaning that the eigenvalue itself is either positive or negative.

Over time, if the eigenvalues are trending toward, or returning toward 0, the regional economy is trending toward a stability point, or in neo classical language, an equilibrium point. Over a 50-year period of analysis, if the trend toward stability continues, the regional economy will stagnate and eventually die. The indicator of economic stagnation is whether the eigenvalue has some negative real part.

A negative real part is a surrogate indicator of the region's rate of technological knowledge creation and knowledge diffusion, precursor indicators to the region's rate of technological commercialization.

Applying the biological metaphor, "If each λ has a negative real part, the system is tending towards stability…A linear system is asymptotically stable if and only if all of its poles (eigenvalues) have negative real parts."[214] In a complex system, such as a regional economy, the system in equilibrium is oscillating around an attractor point, so the form of the function which would describe the system would be:

$E^{at}\sin bt$

which would describe an oscillation around (X_o).

The condition of equilibrium could be described graphically by showing the trajectory of the system in a fixed seven year period of time. This diagram is taken from Chapter 1, and applied in the context of the biological metaphor.

In this graphical depiction of equilibrium, $R_e(\lambda) < 0$. The trajectory is represented by inward oscillations whose amplitudes are decreasing with

160

each oscillation. R is the rate of technological commercialization, and λ, the eigenvalue, has a negative component.

The three state variables under investigation in the economy in equilibrium would be:

The regional intermediate demand market place, as described as the regional transaction matrix that has been subjected to factor analysis in order to show the inter-industrial, intermediate industrial clusters.

The regional capital market, as described by the value-added per unit of regional output matrix.

The regional occupation by industry matrix, describing the regional output per unit of skilled labor input.

Diagram 6.2. Graphical Representation of 7-Year Equilibrium Point.

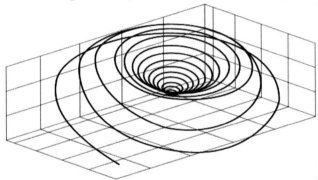

Each state variable is capable of being described, over time, by its own unique eigenvalue. In the logical framework provided by Doucet and Sloep, the state variables are the receiving variables in the economy, which are subject to dynamic input conditions. The input variables change over time, as reflected in the rate of technological commercialization, r, which describes the region's transformation of technology into new regional products.

In the initial state of the economy, characterized in Doucet and Sloep as "U," there exists some ambient level of technological knowledge and technical diversity in the regional environment. Doucet and Sloep posit a hypothetical rule that is associated with this ambient level of technical ability or regional technological possibility frontier.

Applying the biological metaphor, the technological possibilities frontier represents the environment's given state of technology and technological diversity, as represented by the technology of products.

Predicting Technology

At this given state of technology, if all existing potential possibilities for technological mutation were calculated, a hypothetical frontier, or envelope, could be drawn to describe the range of technological innovation, if no other new technical knowledge or product crossovers were to occur.

In any given period of time, around seven years, for example, the given state of regional technology would be represented by the technical coefficients in a regional input-output transaction matrix. The fact that the coefficients are "fixed" mathematically, in the sense that they are based upon historical input patterns in the regional supply chain is actually a benefit for the purposes of the analysis. At this stage of the analysis, it is the fixed, given state of technology under investigation, not the rate of technological transformation of technology into new products and new firms.

At the beginning time period of the analysis, it would seem logical to assume that the larger the initial population of workers and firms in the region, the more likely that the given amount of technological diversity would lead to some rate of product technological mutation greater than the rate of smaller region. It also seems logical to assume that the larger the initial population of people and firms in a regional economy, the greater would be the probability that the rare event of technological crossover would occur, wherein technology from two different species are combined to form a new product.

In either the case of common product mutation, or the rare case of genetic crossover, the rate of "r" the transformation of technical knowledge into products would be expected to be greater in large metro regions than in smaller metro regions.

However, extending the earlier paradox of regional technological evolution, as derived from the biological metaphor of M. L. Rosenzweig, in his 1971 work, "The Paradox of Enrichment," existing firms within a region, no matter how large or small, tend to have a limited geographical radius of influence in terms of absorbing technical knowledge.[215]

Applying Rosenzweig's insight to regional economics, at some critical threshold value of technical knowledge in a region, a substantial number of predators, (firms) can survive. The region's technological possibilities frontier, represented by "K," provide the firms with enough food (technological knowledge) for product mutation to occur.

However, without the addition of new knowledge, within the 50 mile radius of the metro region, the spirals and amplitudes of the regional trajectory will run inwards towards the local attractor point.

If the local, ambient level of "K" is enhanced, there is some probability that the new knowledge may lead to a contingent event of a micro bifurcation, as genetic technological material from one species is mated with different genetic material from another species.

At some point in time, given new products and new investments, these micro bifurcations may lead to a reversal of the spirals, as the trajectory of the economy seeks a new local attractor point. The transformation from one attractor to another attractor point would be described as a micro bifurcation.

And, at some future point in time, after several micro bifurcations, the regional economic structure would no longer look the earlier economic structure. It would have passed through an evolutionary Hophf bifurcation point where a new market had emerged. Passing into that new market is described as a macro bifurcation.

The range of knowledge within the 50 mile radius of the metro region is based upon the range of daily commuting patterns of knowledge workers. Technical knowledge within the region is primarily held in the form of "tacit" knowledge, in the brains of each worker.

Tacit knowledge is different than another type of knowledge known as "codified" knowledge, which is less geographically bounded. This distinction between knowledge will be further explored in the next chapter.

Tacit knowledge within the 50 mile radius is created and diffused through personal communications between knowledge workers about how things get done. A high initial rate of "r" within this radius has two contradictory effects. The high rate of technological transformation increases the rate of technical knowledge creation within the region, which, in a Lotka-Volterra way, increases the rate of predators who are competing for this knowledge.

The paradox is that as the new predators eat the new knowledge and compete with product mutations in the existing time frame of seven years, they are hastening the rate of price competition and profit erosion in the region.

At some critical threshold of initial population, called U, and given an initial endowment of technical knowledge, described by K, the Rosenzweig paradox suggests that a substantial number of predators, all eating the ambient technical knowledge, can survive and compete, economically. The initial size size of "K" determines the maximum rate of "r." Below a minimum level of "r", the spirals around the regional attractor point will run inward.

Following Doucet, "N" describes the initial population size of firms in a regional environment,.[216] At AN(t), there is an existing matrix of firms trading semi-finished goods in a regional intermediate demand market, described by input-output matrix A. At $AN(t_1)$, the next time period, the initial N(t) has been changed by some factor, λ, such that $N(t_1) = \lambda N(t)$.

The factor λ is the eigenvalue associated with matrix A, and the polarity of the eigenvalue describes whether the spirals are inward towards equilibrium and economic death, or outward towards a micro bifurcation point, or new local attractor for the regional economy.

In both biological evolution and economic evolution, the initial population size affects subsequent generations. Following the classification scheme for initial populations provided by Austin Hughes in *Adaptive Evolution of Genes and Genomes*, the processes of technological evolution would initially be placed within an analytical framework that had five features:

- Initially, there is a population of firms and products within the region. The population is either growing or declining from one generation to the next.

- There is non-random, or "directional" asexual mating between products within existing technological industrial clusters.

- Firms and products have overlapping generations, and subsequent generations of products eliminate earlier products via a process of technological obsolescence.

- There are adaptive mutations of existing products, as owners of firms tinker with the outward appearance and inward technological features of the product, within the product's limited life-cycle of technological utility.

- Market final demand is providing the selection force, and final demand forces have both positive and negative feedback mechanisms to both firms and products that tend to "direct" the future contingent pathways of technological evolution.

In his work, *The Genetic Basis of Evolutionary Change,* R. C. Lewontin places the state transformation function idea into a graphic, which, as applied in the biological metaphor, helps depict how the technological genetics of products serve as the basis for economic evolution.

Lewontin's graphic is modified below to adapt it to the regional economic theory, and the similarity between this graphic and the earlier graphic in this chapter, entitled Diagram 6.1 "The Scope of the Metaphor..." "can readily be seen.

Lewontin cites Dobzhensky's (1951), definition of evolution as being "...a change in the genetic composition of populations."[217]

Applied to regional economics, economic evolution can be described as a change in the technological composition of products within a specific geographical setting. Diagram 6.3 below helps describe the application of this metaphor.

The importance of geographic speciation in biology is applied to regional economic specialization. In biology, according to Lewontin, the "general theory of geographic speciation postulates a multi-stage process after an initial geographic isolation."[218]

The two components in economics that are isolated are the genotypes of product technology and the phenotypes of products within the regional industrial cluster, both of which provide the "pre-selective" biases that are extrapolated from individual to collective economic experience.[219]

Some elements of genetic variation in product technology are introduced into a regional population of firms and products from within the region and from outside the region, in a process that looks like biological mutation or recombination. Lewontin posits some basic level of evolutionary rate of mutation, which he calls the "average evolutionary rate."

The key to understanding geographical differences in evolutionary economics, based upon Lewontin's insight, is in understanding the historical sequence of events of how genetic alleles are replaced or introduced into the environment.

As he states, "Thus, two populations that have undergone a long series of fluctuation environments, may have radically different average gene frequencies over their entire history...because the environments occurred in a different order."[220]

The explanation for why one population had a high average rate of gene frequency lies in the historical sequence of introduction of new genetic material, or in the case of economics, new technological combinations.

Diagram 6.3. Adaptation of Lewontin's Graphic to the Biological Metaphor.

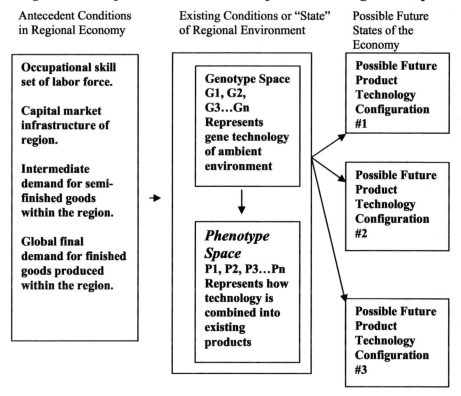

Antecedent Conditions in Regional Economy	Existing Conditions or "State" of Regional Environment	Possible Future States of the Economy
Occupational skill set of labor force. **Capital market infrastructure of region.** **Intermediate demand for semi-finished goods within the region.** **Global final demand for finished goods produced within the region.**	**Genotype Space G1, G2, G3...Gn Represents gene technology of ambient environment** *Phenotype Space* **P1, P2, P3...Pn Represents how technology is combined into existing products**	**Possible Future Product Technology Configuration #1** **Possible Future Product Technology Configuration #2** **Possible Future Product Technology Configuration #3**

In contemporary biology, as in general equilibrium economics, "equilibria annihilates history...the particular history of change is irrelevant, and once the system is at equilibrium, there is no trace of historical evolution."[221]

However, in biological evolution, the major question addressed by Darwin was the origin of the species, as explained by the variation of genetics and the selection by the environment of the most fit species. For Darwin, the historical sequence is essential as an element of understanding the origin of the species.

As applied to regional economics, the history of technology in the region is essential to understanding the main question of evolutionary economics, which is the contingent emergence of new markets.

And, in order to understand and explain the emergence of new markets, the concepts of state transition functions must be linked to the concepts of genetic mutations and genetic crossover, the precursor activity to understanding bifurcations in regional economic demand.

Mutations, recombinations, and crossover of technology are the processes involved in understanding how the state transformation functions describe the scientific logic of how a regional economy evolves.

The concept of how the underlying processes lead from the existing conditions to possible future product technology configurations can be seen by reference to the diagram above. In the diagram, there are three possible configurations, but there could be many more possible outcomes, all of which depend on the underlying processes at work in the existing "state" of technology in the region.

The state transition function most appropriate to describe the exact future path way of the regional economy must be selected by scientific analysis of the rates of mutation and the prior conditions which established the regional technological possibilities frontier. The scientific analysis would focus on determining the dominant processes of recombination, crossover, and fitness.

In the case of the first process, recombination of technology, products within the region "acquire" characteristics from existing product technology in order to better adapt to the regional environment. The market demand within the region is acting to select the most fit product, and owners of firms are continually tinkering with the outward appearance and inside technological features of products to marginally make them more attractive, given an existing level of market demand.

This process of recombination tinkering is an example in economics of Lamarckian acquired inheritance. Christensen has called this process a "sustaining" innovation. In any given year, an existing product may acquire a new outward appearance that consumers seem to prefer over the previous appearance. If the owners determine that the new appearance is marginally profitable, the very next product incarnation may include this acquired characteristic, in addition to some new characteristic.

A mutation via recombination with a very small selective advantage is more likely to be selected by the market because buyers are more familiar with the appearance and use of the product. If no other new technology is incorporated in the existing product, then a slow rate of genetic mutation is occurring in the regional economy.

On the other hand, an asexual recombination with a large market selective advantage will tend to reduce the range of genetic diversity, and hasten the decline towards technological obsolescence. The process of recombination does not add technological (genetic) diversity into product technology, but tends to use up the potential technology within the regional technological possibilities frontier in a process called mutation during redundancy.

Predicting Technology

The "hereditability" of the technological trait or characteristic is both time dependent and geographically specific. As Hartl states, "…hereditability has reference only to a particular population at a particular time in a particular range of environments."[222] It is this feature of time and geographic uniqueness that allows regional economic evolution to differentiate itself from general equilibrium analysis, which is a-historic and geographically ubiquitous in its application.

As Hartl notes, "Given an initial allele frequency of $P_0 = .5$ (as an example for a given region), the average time that a population remains unfixed is about 2.9N."[223]

Each regional economy would be expected to have its own unique rate of mutation, and the telos of regional economic evolution would be to describe and understand how regional technology, given an existing genetic technological envelope, would evolve, compared to other regional configurations of products and firms.

The key explanatory variable would be the time it takes a regional economy to reach its stable and fixed population of products and firms, or as the case described by Hartl, given a frequency of .5, the time to fixation is close to 3 generations. As applied to a product, this biological metaphor would be called the life-cycle of the product before the product becomes obsolete.

Mutation during redundancy describes an evolutionary process that begins in a steady state, or initial condition, of a stable population of species, in the case of economics, a population of products produced by a population of firms within a region. The population of products have characteristics, in this case, technological characteristics, which can be classified into common clusters.

Banzhaf and Reeves describe this initial state of clustering as a "cloud," and the application to economics would be a "technological envelope." As Banzhaf and Reeves describe the process, "From time to time, there are random bursts driving some individuals away from the cloud, however, on average, they are driven back to the cloud…the effect of (individuals crowded around a center) resembles very much the creation of a species."[224]

As applied to economics, the common regional technological cluster itself resembles a species, and it is this common technological cluster which has a trajectory described by the pathway of a regional eigenvalue.

According to Banzhaf and Reeves, "The evolution of the population over successive generations is shrinking, and is finally fixed at a random position."[225] In this description of evolution, there seems to be "an invisible confinement" keeping the individuals together without any selection pressure.[226]

In other words, something is happening within the technological envelope, or regional technology possibilities frontier, of the product phenotypes that is independent of the market demand selection process that is influencing the rate and direction of regional technological evolution.

Austin Hughes describes this phenomenon in his book, *Adaptive Evolution of Genes and Genomes*, as mutation during redundancy. Applying the biological metaphor to regional economics, product mutation via recombination is adaptive, asexual, and directional within an existing regional technological envelope, while market evolution is a contingent and rare event that depends on the dynamics of mutation.

Hughes describes how genes within the initial population may lie redundant, or non-expressed, while maintaining the ability to become functional in the sense of encoding a protein.

The mutant substitutions that are less disruptive to the existing technological genetic structure of the product phenotype, according to Hughes, "occur more frequently in evolution than disruptive ones."[227]

Or, to cite Kimura, "...the smaller the differences between two amino acids, the higher the probability that they are selectively equivalent...the probability of an interchange being selectively neutral is higher between more similar amino acids...what determines the pattern of interaction between amino acids in evolution is their physical proximity or direct contact within the folded protein."[228]

This hypothesis of mutation during redundancy may be truthful and valid for economics as long as the entire regional repertoire of technological possibilities is fixed and given in the initial state of the regional technological envelope, as it is described by a regional input-output transaction matrix at a fixed point in time that is a "snap-shot" of the regional technological coefficients.

If the hypothesis is valid, then the fixed repertoire of genetic technological possibilities will be depleted as they are "called-forth," into commercialization in the absence of sexual mating between two species.

In the case of biology, as Hoyle points out, "...the really crucial matter is that only sexual reproduction with two parents, accompanied by crossover, can positive mutations make headway against the deleterious mutations which occur with far more frequency."[229]

Hoyle cites Haldane's "Single Parent Model," as an example of a mathematical function that describes the rate of mutation for a fixed population of N individuals. As applied to regional economics, the initial state of the regional economy would be described as a fixed population of firms and products, all of which are encompassed within an existing technological envelope, or regional industrial cluster of technology.

Applying Haldane's formula, $(1 - /s/)^{\lambda/s/}$, where the exponent represents the rate of mutation for each product. In the asexual, single parent technology case, the exponent would be negative, reflecting the time to product obsolescence.

Predicting Technology

The obvious implication for regional economics is that if a region has a given and fixed initial technological state of firms and products, then those firms within the region are on a naturally occurring trajectory to extinction. The rate of new venture creation and new technology commercialization must be very high to overcome the natural rate of technological obsolescence that accompanies loss of genetic diversity via mutation during redundancy.

As Hoyle notes, "Once the range of improvements conferrable by single base-pair changes have become exhausted, a species can not evolve further... because the range of genetic adaptation has become exhausted."[230]

In economics, it is both the rate of technological obsolescence and the change in market demand that are working independently, but co-jointly, to reduce technological diversity within the region.

The process that causes a redundant non-expressed gene (technology) to become functional is the positive feedback mechanism of market demand, both final and intermediate demand for semi-finished goods. In this case, market demand, in an existing seven-year time horizon acts to "call-forth" the redundant, non-expressed latent genetic technological characteristic.

As existing market demand conditions change, as a result of declining prices and eroding profits, the genes that are called-forth are expressed in the form of product mutation. The process is asexual, in the sense that the gene is from the existing technological frontier, or envelope, directional, based upon market demand selection, and adaptive, in the sense of being the most fit.

Once the latent, non-expressed genes are "called-forth," they are used up, just like a new car loses value the moment it is driven off the new car lot. As a result of genetic technological inbreeding within the regional technological envelope, the genetic heterozygosity within the region is reduced.

Products produced by mutation during redundancy, given a fixed level of market demand, reach a stable age distribution within the region, without increasing technological diversity, or as in the biological example given by Hartl, in about 3 generations.

The product species cluster around the parent technology, with subsequent superior mutations killing market demand for earlier products, hastening the decline of prices and profits, without creating the basis of technological diversity essential for future economic growth.

At the stage of stable product populations and stable firm populations within the regional economy, the economy is characterized as an environment of the "Living Dead." The firms and products may still be walking around and breathing, but they are soon going to die, without the addition of new genetic technological material.

The general explanation of the Living Dead in biology is called the "Red Queen Hypothesis." Daniel Hartl calls this phenomenon "treadmill evolution," and emphasizes that evolutionary selection/fitness forces work primarily at the phenotypic level.[231] Mutation during redundancy does not produce new genetic material, it produces new genetic combinations of existing genetic material.

New combinations of existing genetic material within a geographically isolated population, such as the Galapagos Islands, allows for a process of allopatric speciation. As applied to regional economics, as a result of product mutation and technological process improvement within a specific geographical setting, costs of production are declining, prices are declining, and profits are declining.

Every species (product phenotype) is subject to a "...deterioration of its environment caused by the adaptive improvement of the other species, and so has to keep running just to stay in place."[232]

In the absence of new genetic technological material, the next generation of products is accomplished in conjunction with a downward twist of Mueller's Ratchet of regional economic decline.[233] In Darwin, the struggle for existence occurred because reproduction capacity exceeded the resources of the environment, leading to a process of the survival of the fittest.

In economics, the struggle for existence occurs because market selection, which is the ability to pass on technological characteristics, acting in conjunction with technological obsolescence, causes profits for existing firms and existing products to drop to zero.

In a regional economic environment of the Living Dead, products may exhibit "fitness" in the sense that they are currently being selected by consumers, without having the potential to pass their characteristics on via technological heredity because the product technology has become obsolete.

Fitness and selection are two independent processes, with fitness being an outcome caused by adaptation and heritable selection within an existing seven-year period of market demand. Fitness, as an outcome of both the process of adaptation (existing market) and selection, (future markets) exhibits "pre-selective bias," in the sense that market demand in one period conditions market demand in the next period of time.

An algorithm of market demand would describe a transition function from existing demand to future demand, with the existing demand establishing the base of data from which the algorithm would begin its iterations. The pathway of market demand could either be upwards, indicating the presence of new genetic material, or downwards, reflecting technological obsolescence.

Understanding the time horizon and sequential pattern of new product mutations is an essential logical component of mutation during redundancy.

Garrish and Lenski describe the process as "clonal interference," where the fate of the original mutation is followed by the appearance of a superior alternative mutation.[234]

As they describe this process, "The beneficial mutant, being competitively superior to the ancestor, slowly displaces the latter until finally reaching fixation at some point of time."[235] Given an initial stable population, they believe that the correct mathematical formula to describe this process is logistic, where the expected number of further beneficial mutations between the time of appearance of the original mutation and its fixation is:

$$u \int_0^{tf} x(t)dt = \frac{u}{s} N \ln N$$

where s is the selection coefficient, derived from market demand based upon the technological characteristics of the subsequent superior product, and

where μ is the rate of beneficial mutation per capita per product generation.

Fitness, according to John Maynard Smith, is a property of a class of individuals, not of a single individual. As Smith states it, "fitness is ascribed to a "genotype" meaning a class of individuals with some genetic characteristic in common."[236] In describing the concept of fitness in biology, Smith defines five essential attributes of the concept.

- Fitness as applied to a class of individuals with some genetic characteristic in common;

- Fitness as specific to an environment;

- Fitness as measured over one generation;

- Fitness as a property pertaining to classes of individuals;

- Fitness as a property of individuals with the biological ability to reproduce, and not a property of "populations" because populations, as a biological entity, do not have the reproduce and are not bounded in time by the concept of one generation.

In an asexual population of individuals, which would apply to the economic case of product mutation during redundancy, Smith estimates that 55% of the asexual population dies selectively each generation. This death occurs, in the case of products, as a result of product life-cycles ending, which is similar to the concept Schumpeter was calling the "gales of destruction."

As described by H. J. Mueller, "...in each generation, there is a chance that, despite their high fitness, all (deleterious mutations) will die without leaving offspring. If so, the optimal class is lost, and can only be reconstituted by back mutation."[237]

In the case of economics, back mutation would occur if market demand remained constant, and consumers went back and selected products from a previous period that had already become technologically obsolete, not perhaps an unheard of, but a very rare, event.

Smith makes another essential point for the application of the biological metaphor to economics. His concept of fitness depends on the relative fitness of a group of interacting individuals within a population in a specific geographical setting. "The fitness of an individual," states Smith, "depends on its own genotype and on the genotypes of the other members of the group. After selection, the surviving individuals re-enter the directed adaptive population where they contribute to the next generation."[238]

As applied to economics, products (phenotypes) within an existing market compete with other products with similar technological characteristics (genotypes). In terms of adaptation (product competition), successful products are selected (mutate) and pass their successful genes to the next generation of products (mutation during redundancy).

The mutation process in economics can be described as asexual, directed, and positive, yet the outcome of the selection process is contingent. In the case of biology, "Any population of entities with the properties of multiplication, variation, and heredity, will evolve in such a way that the component entities will acquire characteristics ensuring their own survival and reproduction."[239]

In other words, there is not a perfect fit between biology and economics because market competition and allegiance to the political status quo intervene in the economic mutation process, causing contingent outcomes which arise outside the scope of technological mutation. There are no economic factors "ensuring" the product's survival and reproduction.

Successful demes of products in economics are linked to existing markets, and the processes of adaptation/competition are occurring in markets with declining marginal profits. The demes themselves are evolving, and the market demand characteristics are also evolving as consumers gradually shift buying preferences towards more technologically advanced products.

Products that are technologically obsolete will not be selected for reproduction, and products whose market demand has declined to some threshold level will not be selected in future product generations, even if they are the most "fit" in a given time horizon.

Selection is a contingent process that generates contingent outcomes, which affects the future pathway of the regional economy. The product evolution sets the stage for a type of forward linkage in time to future markets because product changes affect the current market and the conditions of survival and competition.

The existing market is acting, in a biological way, as the "searching/selection" mechanism for the product mutation/innovation process. Products currently selected in the existing market are more "fit" than those not selected. In order to separate the various processes under investigation, Melanie Mitchell, in *An Introduction to Genetic Algorithms*, breaks the two processes into a "search space," and a "selection space."[240]

The search space refers to some collection of candidate solutions to a problem and some notion of distance between candidate solutions. In the science of biology, her search space is "the collection of all possible (protein) sequences. As applied to economics, her search space would be a region's technological possibilities frontier.

The "fitness landscape," a concept derived from Sewell Wright's work in 1931, is a representation of the space of all possible genotypes along with their fitness. As applied to economics, the fitness landscape would be a representation of market characteristics, such as income classes, along with the technological characteristics of the product, which satisfy consumer preferences.

Following Wright, an organism (product) cannot be assigned a fitness value independent of the other organisms in its environment. As the fitness environment changes, the selection/adaptation process changes for existing products. Product evolution affects the market, and as the market changes, it affects the selection process. As the selection process changes, firms search for new products in the search space of the technological possibilities frontier.

Mitchell develops genetic algorithms based upon 3 basic evolutionary operators to describe the processes:

1. The selection process algorithm selects chromosomes in the population for reproduction, based upon the "fitness" of the chromosome.

2. The "crossover" algorithm, which mimics biological recombination between two single (haploid) chromosome organisms.

3. The mutation process algorithm.

As applied to regional economics, her process would be to start the scientific inquiry with a description of the technological coefficients of existing products. The next step would be to calculate the mean fitness of the products and the best practice technological characteristics of the most recent product innovation.

The third step would be to observe the differences in technology and determine if the most recent innovation is identical in genetic technology to the parent product, or if the new product carries a new chromosome.

If the new product's genetic makeup is identical to the parent technology, even if the phenotype appearance is different, her algorithm would move the product downwards in the market selection/income distribution process. The diagram below shows how the two possible outcomes, based upon whether the most recent innovation is genetically identical to the parent technology.

Diagram 6.4. Existing Market as Described by Income Classes from High Income to Low Income.

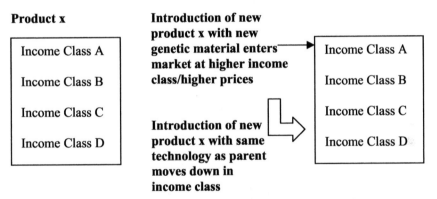

Mitchell's version of the genetic algorithm, as applied to regional economics, would work as follows:

- In each product generation, approximately seven years, a hypothetical set of 100 initial configurations of genetic fitness for a particular region's existing technological envelope is generated by computer simulation.

- A fitness rule is applied to the configurations to derive rates of adaptation and selection. The rules would incorporate measures of allegiance to the status quo arrangement of technology. The rules would contain indicators of product sales, profits, and growth rates.

The application of the fitness rules would generate market demand configuration patterns of the most probable best of class products, which become the template technology for the next generation.

- The technological coefficients of the best of class products would be compared to the regional average technological coefficients.

- A fitness rule is applied to products which are close to the best technology, which then become product candidates for mutation or crossover.

- A fitness rule is applied to products which are far away from the best technology, which are candidates for extinction/obsolescence.

As the products are either selected for mutation or extinction, product technology moves along the trajectory of the region. The trajectory could either be visualized as a cycle or a linear path.

A linear path through time of the trajectory would incorporate a threshold point that represented a micro bifurcation of product technology, which is irreversible. The center points of a cycle would be on a downward trajectory, indicating regional economic collapse.

As Mitchell states, "The computer simulations are microanalytic or "agent based." The algorithms simulate each component of the evolving system and its local interactions; the global dynamics emerge from these simulated local dynamics."[241]

The irony of Mitchell's biological genetic algorithm, as applied to economics, is that in a regional economy with products that are "maximally fit," the genetic algorithms tend to return to a fixed point, indicating the degree of difficulty for an environment to break away from the status quo equilibrium.

Small changes in product mutation would tend to return the economy to the fixed point of attraction in the slow oscillating cycle.[242] The attraction point represents a measure of the mean equilibrium technological fitness in a specific economic region.

The algorithm developed by Mitchell allows for one of the big differences between biological evolution and economic evolution to be explicitly defined. In natural biological systems, selection acts on the phenotypes, which have a potentially infinite number of characteristics, which are correlated in biological function.

As Burger notes, "…it is difficult to disentangle direct effects of selection from indirect effects. In principle, (in natural biological systems) selection can be described by a fitness function that relates fitness of individuals to the (quantitative) traits under selection."[243]

As difficult as it is to disentangle the direct and indirect effects of selection in biologically natural systems, it is even more difficult for economic evolution because of the complexity of the relationships between technology, market demand, and political manipulation of economic technological evolution.

Natural biological systems do not have the element of political manipulation as it applies to allegiance to the status quo arrangement of selection processes.

Burger cites the 1937 work of Haldane's investigation into the effects of recurrent deleterious mutation on the equilibrium mean fitness, and this work can be applied to economic equilibrium.

Haldane's insight was that the loss of fitness of a species (product phenotype) depends on the rate of mutation. Years later Mueller, in 1964, wrote that "detrimental mutations may accumulated and eventually become fixed, thus leading to a progressive fitness decline that can result in population extinction."[244]

Mueller's insight is compatible with the work of Levine, who wrote in 1953, that zygotes or juveniles dispense randomly into local demes and settle. "Selection operates separately within each deme in a density-dependent manner...After selection, all adults from all demes join in a single random mating population to produce the next generation."[245]

While the importance of the geographical local deme of product technology is certainly applicable in the case of regional economic evolution, the big difference between biology and economics is that the selection process is not random in economics, as it is in natural biological systems.

The selection process in economics is positive, adaptive, and directional, while at the same time subject to the contingency associated with political manipulation of technology. Mitchell's genetic algorithm accounts for this degree of contingency in the outcome of the selection process by recognizing the importance of rules that are applied to the underlying rate of mutation and the strength of the local equilibrium attractor point, even after a mutation during redundancy has occurred.

Burger derives a function that can be used to model the results of a local deme which is undergoing overlapping mutations, in which one early generation phenotype exists during the same time period as a later phenotype and competes for local resources: $N_e^{-u/s}$; [246]

Where s = selection process which reduces the relative frequency of individual genomes carrying a k mutation by the factor (1-s),

Where U = genomic rate of mutation, and

Where W = mean technological fitness within the local deme, for N population size of products within the deme, as derived from an algorithm, such as the one created by Mitchell.

The practical application of Burger's function, in the world of biological evolution, is that after a finite number of mutations in a finite number of generations, the earlier mutations will be lost, even though they compete and overlap in time with the newer, more recent mutations. "The mean time to extinction," writes Burger, "is primarily determined by the length of the phase during which mutations accumulate, because the final phase of the mutational meltdown is very short...The mean time to extinction decreases with the increasing rate of selection."[247]

As applied to product evolution and product selection, a product could be "fit" within a generation, and have high rates of consumer selection, but in the absence of genetic crossover, the product is on a short pathway in time to extinction.

As Burger describes it, "...in the absence of recombination, offspring cannot carry less mutation than their parents. Thus, the class with one more mutation will be the new least-loaded class, and, after some time, suffer the same fate (of extinction).[248]

As applied to economics, one of the important parts of the biological metaphor that does fit well is that when an older technological product competes with a new, superior product that is procreated in genetic crossover, the final phase of mutational meltdown for the older product is very short. That final phase of meltdown involves a sequence of events described by the biological process Mueller's ratchet of inbreeding.

In the asexual case of heredity, where a superior product mutation follows in time to the original parent mutation, Garrish and Lenski suggest that the most appropriate function to model the process is logistic. They set up the conditions by assuming that the superior, or "beneficial" mutant, being competitively superior to the ancestor, slowly displaces the ancestor until finally reaching fixation.[249]

In the case where the initial total population size is constant, in economics being the number of firms producing a finite number of products, they suggest that "...the dynamics of the two genotypes are logistic...under a logistic growth, a difference in Mathusian parameters is equivalent to a selection coefficient, when the time unit is generations."[250]

The expected number of further beneficial mutations between the time of appearance of the original mutation and its fixation is given by their concept of the logistic function, cited above.

As applied to regional economic evolution, the implications for fixation in asexual mutation derived from the logistic function provided by Garrish and Lenski are somewhat counter-intuitive at first glance. First, given a larger initial population of firms and products within a region compared to another region, the ambient level of technological genetic diversity in products is greater.

With a greater initial size of population and technological (genetic) diversity, the probability of sexual beneficial mutation based upon genetic crossover in product technology is also higher. However, because of the wide range of diversity in the given conditions, any single beneficial mutation in product genetic crossover in technology has a harder time becoming fixed, should that rare event of crossover occur.

And, to compound the complexity, once a beneficial asexual mutation becomes fixed, meaning that it is the dominant product technological design, the greater rate of asexual product beneficial mutation implies that the dominant design has a greater probability of being displaced by a subsequent offspring mutation.

The practical economic implications of these insights are easy to observe in large metro economic regions over a 25 year period. First, given a high initial rate of technological heterogeneity, the rate of new venture creation and new product innovation is higher than smaller non-metro regions. However, any new product innovation (asexual mutation) in the larger metro region has a very short product lifecycle.

In traditional marginal analysis, economists would say that there is a high rate of product substitution and displacement in the phenotypes product species. In the biological metaphor, the innovation process involves the offspring product displacing the parent product. The first functional relationship to be modeled is the one between initial population size and the rate of asexual beneficial product mutation between parent and offspring products.

The second relationship to be modeled is the rate of product genetic crossover between different product species that share a common technological coefficient production ancestry, but whose "fitness" serves different niches in the consumer environment.

The different products may have some technological genetics in common, at least enough to procreate a new product, but prior to procreation, each of the products serve different markets and "fit" differently in consumer selection algorithms. The sexual crossover mutation rate occurs in the same environment as the asexual mutations and is influenced by the environment associated with a high rate of asexual product substitution, and short product life cycles.

Garrish and Lenski present a functional relationship for biology that can be applied to economics that arises between beneficial asexual product mutation rates, denoted as μ, and the probability of product innovation, given increasing initial sizes of the regional population.

Their relationship depicts a relationship between fixation rates and increasing asexual mutation rates in a product phenotype, which accompany large heterogeneous populations in a distinct geographical region. The probability of any single product technology becoming "fixed" or, in the case of economics, becoming the dominant technological product paradigm, decreases as the size of the population of firms and products within the region increases.

The logic of their relationship is that in a large diverse environment, the span in asexual mutation genetic technology is small, and small spans are more easily recognized and selected by consumers.

However, any product phenotype, while it is in jeopardy of being displaced by its own offspring, has a greater risk of becoming obsolete (extinct) in the rich heterogeneous environment because of the greater likelihood of genetic crossover between product species. They suggest that above a critical threshold of population size, that further increases in genetic diversity "...have surprisingly small effects on substitution rates."[251]

Below this critical population threshold, high rates of asexual mutation may have a functional relationship with increasing rates of fixation. In other words, a smaller region, with a less diverse genetic base, may lead to greater rates of fixation. In large regions, there is a greater probability for the emergence of technological crossover between two product species because asexual beneficial mutation rates have a harder time becoming fixed. The reasons for this outcome are related to the market demand relationships, which form the selection/adaptation environment for genetically new products.

Consumers selecting offspring products rather than taking a risk on genetically new products create stability in market demand in asexual mutations. The consumer selection process and habits create the conditions for equilibrium, which leads to technological stasis, while instability in market demand creates the conditions for technological innovations whose selective advantage could be so great as to create an entirely new set of market demand conditions.

A slight beneficial asexual mutation, whose selection advantage within the existing market demand environment is greater than larger mutations, must compete with many other small mutations in the product species, implying that small mutations are not likely to become fixed.

On the other hand, a large selective advantage inures to a technological genetic crossover, if that crossover product happens to encounter a market environment where a transition from one type of market demand to a new type of market demand occurs.

Under conditions where a product crossover in technology between two species occurs, if consumers favor that product, the probability for market bifurcation exists, where demand characteristics between the two market environments change.

The probability of a crossover leading to a bifurcation in market demand for a new product is contingent, as is an even more rare event, which is the emergence of an entirely new market, which is akin to the creation of a new environment.

Part of the contingency is related to the rate of substitution between older parent product and technologically newer, slightly different offspring products. Substitutions between products appear in time as discrete events related to consumer purchases.

Part of the contingency is related to what happens when consumers see a genetically new product for the first time. Not all new technologically superior products displace market demand of the older products, mostly because of social and political factors, which favor the status quo arrangement of income distribution. Of the new sexual mutations, only a fraction, ε^{-asy}, will be competitively superior to y, the original product.[252]

Of the competitively superior products, only a small fraction, $uR\,\varepsilon^{-asy}$ of the superior mutations, will survive the effects of fixation. In other words, new technological innovations must both be created, commercialized, and then survive the forces of technological fixation.

If these rare events occur, then the conditions arise for what Garrish and Lenski call "Leapfrog" mutation.[253] The implication of "leapfrog" sexual mutation, applying the biological metaphor to economics, is that the process of technological evolution is not smoothly continuous, nor automatic, in the sense that new superior innovations are always uniformly selected.

However, if the new technological innovations are selected, and if they survive the forces associated with asexual product technology fixation, they tend to create a leapfrog effect in technology as they replace the older products.

Predicting Technology

The leapfrog effect occurs when the "best practice" new product genotype is less closely related to the average product genotype than earlier generations of product mutations associated with asexual heredity.

This leapfrog sexual mutation may be very close to what Schumpeter had in mind when he discussed the disruptive effects of product technology, and also why he became pessimistic in his later writings about the forces of monopoly capitalism.

Under monopoly capitalism, the direction and creation of technology is controlled by a small set of corporations, and is politically controlled and manipulated event that displaces the free competitive market environment.

Schumpeter's essential point, as it relates to economic evolution, however, was that product technology evolves as a process of disequilibrium, not equilibrium, and that the evolution itself is also an auto-correlative cause of further disequilibrium.

Schumpeter correctly perceived the relationship between greater rates of technological diversity within an existing market, and greater ensuing rates of economic disequilibrium, which he took as a good thing for society.

The importance of the initial conditions of technological diversity for creating the ensuing conditions of disequilibrium is based upon the notion that product technology evolution is primarily asexual. Citing the work of Maynard Smith, Garrish and Lenski note that there exists a "...speed limit on the rate of adaptive evolution in asexual populations." [254]

The rate of improvement in a population's mean fitness decelerates with rate of beneficial mutation, especially if the rate of beneficial mutation due to clonal interference passes some threshold limit.

The complexity of asexual product technological evolution is partially explained by Hartl and Taubes with their insight that asexual mutations are beneficial in terms of market adaptation and selection, yet, deleterious to existing product technology genotypes. [255]

In other words, the factor which makes the product innovation, via asexual mutation, more attractive to consumers in the market is, at the same time, the factor which makes the product more likely to become both obsolete and technologically extinct as a result of sexual mutation.

This is the same conclusion reached by Woodruff and Thompson, who state, "...asexual reproduction is an evolutionary dead-end because it will lead to deterministic, open-ended mutation accumulation and eventual extinction." [256] The critical factor is the initial size of the technological genetic possibilities frontier.

Consumer demand in the existing market is acting as the selection mechanism, and in the case of product evolution, this would be the case of adaptive, selection-induced mutation. It is positive and directed selection, with genetic technological mutations accumulating in the technological characteristics of products that are being selected by consumers in the existing market, while those products not being selected in the market, in other words, products who are not close to the "best-fit" technology, are deleted from the mutation process.

The fate of the original asexual product mutation is altered and affected by the appearance of a superior mutation, which ultimately replaces the original parent product, technologically, only to be replaced by some future product innovation, until the entire repertoire of technological genetic diversity within the regional economy is used up. Asexual product genetic mutation is an economic dead end.

The notion that regional repertoire of technology can be "used up" may appear, at first glance, unusual to non-economists. Technology, as an input, is no less scarce a resource than energy or capital. Applying the biological metaphor to economics, a more realistic outcome is to target the conditions of economic collapse when technology is used up.

Technology, as an input resource, is subject to both the ultimate scarcity if the evolutionary process stops because of asexual mutation, and is also a renewable resource, given the right level of diversity in regional economic genetics. The pathway of technology, in other words, is contingent.

The contingent pathway of the regional technological trajectory can be captured and analyzed with the help of a regional input-output model. Regional technological coefficients in the transaction matrix vary by economic environment and regional market characteristics.

The types of product technological genotypes that are inherited from one generation to the next depend on the characteristics of the market and in particular to the market selection process that occurs within the specific geographic region under investigation.

As stated by Hartl, "In short, the heritability of a trait has reference only to a particular population at a particular time in a particular range of environments."[257]

The variable under investigation in the regional model is called the "selection differential," by Hartl. It measures, over time, the average deviation from the population mean average technology in a particular product, where the variable, x_i, is the average product phenotypic technology, and where x^* serves as the most recent technological mutation, "best-of-class" product technology.

Predicting Technology

Following Hartl, the pathway or trajectory of technology can be analyzed by reference to the movement over time of three components related to the average and best technology of the regional products:

1. The movement of the mean, u, product technology of all products in the product species class, as defined by the SIC or NAIC code.

2. The movement, over time, from the population mean due to the specific technological genotype of the individual product under investigation for the best-of-class product.

3. A deviation from the population mean due to the specific regional environment characteristics of the market in question.

Hartl sets up a type of "shift-share" analysis to investigate variation among genotype mutations, and the variation in technology that can be traced to regional market environmental factors. As he notes with regard to "exhaustion" or extinction of technological resources, "One of the obvious reasons why a population would eventually reach a plateau is exhaustion of additive genetic variance; all alleles affected the selected trait may have become fixed, lost or have attained stable equilibrium."[258]

The contingency in the outcome, following Hartl, is related to suboptimal resting points of product technology. "Any population on a suboptimal fitness peak is destined to stay there because natural selection will not carry the population down into any of the surrounding valleys and thus, perhaps, into the domain of attraction of a higher fitness peak."[259]

Applying the biological metaphor to economics, the environmental factors for regional best practice product technology may not allow for further evolution. The two primary causes of this outcome are political manipulation of technological evolution, the factor noted by Schumpeter with regard to multi-national corporations, and exhaustion of genetic technological resources in the region's initial technological possibilities frontier.

Technology, as a resource input, is both an input and an output, which allows for further technological evolution. However, unlike biology, there is no "natural" selection process in economics. The primary economic product selection/mutation process is asexual, adaptive, positive, directed, and subject to political manipulation.

John Holland provides the biological interpretation of how and why the technology in the region could reach a plateau and then become used up. According to Holland, an adaptive system must persistently identify, test, and incorporate structured genetic properties, which are imagined to give "better performance."

In this case, the agent doing the imagining and doing the identification of the schemas, is seeking an adaptation in an organism. Holland describes adaptive systems as a tension between "exploration," and "exploitation."[260]

In the case of sub optimal fitness, small mutations in fitness lead the region back to some fixed point. Mutation in asexual product genetic technology is more of a recombination of existing genes than the addition of new genetic material that results from sexual genetic crossover. At some point, recombination of existing genes at a fixed point exhausts the genetic possibilities in the regional environment.

The type of regional population structure that would allow mutation by asexual genetic recombination to proceed the most would be an initially large population, divided into many small partially isolated demes.[261]

The smaller isolated demes provides for a large number of adaptive moves among locally related peaks, while the initial large number of demes provides for a greater rate of shifts from peak to peak.

Applying the biological metaphor to regional economics, the type of regional metropolitan economy that would be expected to have high rates of product innovation would be a large diverse economy characterized by many different partially isolated industrial clusters, probably something that would look like the regional economies of various metro regions of Northern Italy.

Another part of the contingency in the evolution of regional economies is related to the fact that what constitutes "fitness" of a product in any seven year period of time is a moving target. Market fitness is a dynamic concept that is auto-correlated with the underlying processes of new product innovation and new venture creation within the regional economy.

The prices of products that are being adjusted in supply and demand in one period are different than the products of an earlier period, and the conditions for what constitutes equilibrium are different also.

As John Maynard Smith points out, "If a population is under directional selection for a polygenic trait, then genes for high recombination will increase in frequency provided that they are linked to the genes determining the selected trait."[262]

In other words, the value of "fitness" in a seven-year time horizon creates the conditions for adaptive selection, which also creates the conditions for more rapidly using up the region's repertoire of technological genetic recombination.

The further complication in applying the biological metaphor to economics is that as the technology of each product evolves, it alters the regional economic environment of other products, both those within the product deme, (industrial cluster) and those which service and support the product deme, or as economists would say, the regional intermediate demand matrix of products that service the regional industrial cluster.

If the structure of the economy is slowly changing via adaptive selection, then the conditions of equilibrium in one period are not going to be the same conditions of equilibrium in the next period.

Chapter VII

The Disruptive Economic Effect of Knowledge: The Creation, Diffusion and Commercialization of Knowledge

In his book on economic history, Mark Blaug complains that the traditional economic theory of timeless comparative statics fails to provide the "causal" mechanism that would explain economic behavior.[263]

The methodology of neoclassical marginal theory, suggests Blaug, is designed to "...protect theories from those who demand the provision of some sort of causal mechanism, linking the actions of human agents and the operation of social institutions to the outcomes predicted by the theories."[264]

While not exactly promoting Darwinian evolutionary theory as a replacement for the Platonic idealism of marginal analysis, Blaug does suggest a parallel analogy to evolutionary theory that seems relevant as a starting point for understanding the relationship between knowledge and economics.

Blaug suggests that the firms, which currently exist in an economic environment, can not be defined as "perfect profit maximizers," any more than the existing species in an environment could be defined as "perfect" survivors.[265]

Evolution rarely starts over from scratch at the beginning of any period of time, whether it is economics, knowledge, or biology, and what currently exists could easily have been something else. However, the history of how the existing species came to be tells much about what may happen in the next period of time, and the theory of evolution, as it is applied to economics and knowledge, helps to predict the trajectory of each region from the existing period to the next period.

In his review of economic history, Blaug covers the few instances where writers treated the issues of economic growth as the primary idea to investigate. Johan Von Thunen's 1850 work, *The Isolated State*, explains that gains from entrepreneurship were best understood as rewards for risk taking that could not be undertaken by insurance companies.

The gains existed after the entrepreneur deducted ordinary business expenses for the risk taking effort. Insurance companies could not underwrite the risk, thought Von Thunen, because the magnitude of risks of commercializing new ventures or new products was unquantifiable.[266] Von Thunen coined the term "residue" for profits associated with the commercialization of technology.[267]

In contrast to the idea that entrepreneurial profits were a "residue," Joseph Schumpeter wrote that entrepreneurial profit "...attaches to the creation of new things...without (entrepreneurial) development, there is no profit, and without profit, no development...(and) no accumulation of wealth."[268]

According to Schumpeter, the "new thing," created by the entrepreneur is based upon the entrepreneur's application of technology, and comes into the market alongside of the "old thing."

In contrasting the "new thing" with the "old thing," Schumpeter was correctly anticipating, by about 100 years, the use of the biological evolutionary metaphor to economics. He stated, "...the new enterprises either completely eliminate old businesses or else force them to restrict their operations."[269]

The major dynamic of economic evolution for Schumpeter was the Darwinian competition among species, and the elimination of the weaker species by the stronger species.

In both Von Thunen and Schumpeter, the unit of analysis is the entrepreneur and the firm he creates. Applying the biological metaphor, new ideas in economics seem analogous to food, or energy, which gets "eaten" in the Lotka-Volterra biological setting. The units of analysis create new ideas in economics in one geographical setting, and the ideas are "diffused" throughout the environment.

The method of diffusion looks like the spread of a disease or infection throughout a population. Epidemiologists call this diffusion of a disease a contagion, and speculate that the density of the humans, or the "cluster" in which human's habitat influences the rate of contagion.

As the contagion spreads, some of the energy associated with the new idea is "transformed" into new forms of energy. In economics, this transformation function would look like what Schumpeter was calling the commercialization of "new things." New ideas sometimes create new things, but not always.

And, sometimes, the new ideas create new things entirely unrelated to the old thing. Schumpeter thought that this process of new things replacing old things, especially the unanticipated or unexpected replacement of old things, was the key to understanding economic development. He called this process "creative destruction," to capture the element of something new, being creative, and its effect on something old, being extinction.

Writing in the 20-year period before Schumpeter, Alfred Marshall also valued the effect of transforming new ideas into economically useful ventures. For Marshall, the key for understanding the process of transformation involved how much knowledge workers had at their disposal to understand the application of new ideas.

Marshall recommended that young workers be taught how to transform theoretical knowledge into new ventures because it would increase the overall rate of economic growth and prosperity in the region. As he stated it, "...instead of letting him learn only one of these subdivisions (of his trade)...it might be supplemented by a theoretical knowledge of all branches of the trade."

The economic benefit of the broader theoretical training, thought Marshall, would be the unexpected or unanticipated new methods of production or new products that resulted from the worker's ability to imagine new and better ways of doing old things, which would lead to an increase in the productivity of the worker.[270]

J. de V. Graaf made this same point about the broader economic benefit associated with the process of transforming knowledge into new ventures. Graaf stated that "...the ultimate repositories of technical knowledge in any society are the men comprising it, and its is just this knowledge which is effectively summarized in the form of a transformation function...new knowledge, created with perhaps one purpose in mind, but is in fact valuable in a very different context."[271]

Graaf and Marshall capture the element of contingency in the evolution of both knowledge and economics. If knowledge or new ideas are transformed into new ventures, something economically beneficial may occur for the broader economy. The unit of analysis is individual humans, in their capacity as either workers or entrepreneurs, who absorb new ideas and, contingently, transform the ideas into new products, new processes, or new ventures.

However, the process of transforming ideas into new products is not automatic because there are forces which resist change within the economy, and sometimes, as Joel Mokyr has pointed out, the environment is not sympathetic to the new ideas or new ventures.

In 1841, Friedrich List, in *The National System of Political Economy*, anticipated Mokyr's insights by about 150 years. List stated that "...economic growth depended heavily on the social and cultural resources accumulated by a nation...(it) is much more difficult and complex to transfer and assimilate knowledge that to trade in commodities." [272]

Part of the problem List identified in transferring and assimilating knowledge relate to cultural and social values that limit the diffusion or contagion of knowledge.

Knowledge, as an economic variable, may have increasing and cumulative returns. Knowledge, as a variable, may also have multiple forms, as described by Michael Polanyi's works in 1957 and 1967 that distinguished the difference between "tacit" knowledge, which is "embedded" in behavior and routines, and codified knowledge which is embedded in books and documents.

In 1919, Veblen wrote, "...the great body of common place knowledge made use of in an industry is the product and the heritage of the (community) group...a residue of the community experience, past and present...It is a matter of knowledge, usage and habits of thought."[273]

What happens in one regional economic environment, given historical or antecedent conditions, would be entirely different for that region with another set of antecedent social or cultural conditions. The pathway of economic growth for the specific region would be expected to be unique from another region with different historical and cultural values.

The common point of theoretical tangency between neoclassical marginal analysis and the biological metaphor lies right at the beginning of the time period chosen for study of the economy. D.M. Winch has offered a useful framework for understanding how this initial time period can be applied to either marginal analysis or to the evolutionary analysis.

For Winch, the important variable to study at the beginning is the distribution of income in the economy under study.[274] As the analysis by Winch shows, one type of initial distribution of income leads to an entirely different welfare outcome in the regional economy than another distribution of income.

The distribution of income affects prices, the key variable in marginal equilibrium analysis, and, interestingly, the rate of knowledge creation, diffusion and commercial transformation into new ventures, the key variables in the evolutionary metaphor of economics.

The distribution of income in the beginning period of time in both marginal analysis and evolutionary analysis determines the subsequent period's rate of investment. The rate of investment leads to both new prices, new distributions of income, and, contingently, to new complementary markets, if knowledge is transformed into new ventures.

Winch's analysis touches on the value propositions that influence how the initial distribution of income affects knowledge creation and diffusion. In the case of labor, as Locke pointed out, the individual "owns" his own labor, and thus is entitled morally, to income based upon his contribution of labor.

In economic equilibrium, the relationship between the initial distribution of utility of each factor of production (land, labor, capital), and the initial distribution of income could be held constant in order to analyze the rate of investment that would maintain the existing pattern of market demand for goods in the final demand market.

Creation of new market demand relationships depend on the creation of new products that are technologically different than the old products.

The rate of change in technology of products is not a product of the "state of nature." All three variables depend on the laws that govern property rights in a specific society. However, as Winch carefully notes, "We distribute private goods through a market system modified by taxation, and distribute political power through a constitution...If we have one set of ideological values based upon the benefits of private property and market exchange, and a second set of ideological values based upon the egalitarian distribution of voting rights, and these values prevail simultaneously, there is a possibility of conflict between allocation efficiency in production and distributional equity in consumption."[275]

Kenneth Arrow wrote about this problem of the potential conflict between efficiency and equity in the context of a constitutional democratic republic form of government. Arrow noted the problem's logical intractability if the constitution fails to provide the ultimate goal to which the government is directed to pursue and subsequent generations of economists called his characterization of the problem "Arrow's Paradox."

The solution Winch offers is that the price system of free markets be left alone by legislation to determine resource allocation efficiency.[276]

The future markets are contingently created as a result of knowledge evolution. Diagram 7.1 updates Diagram 5.1 by describing how knowledge, as a social process, can be modeled with the assistance of the biological evolutionary metaphor. Knowledge, in its economic context, is created, and is diffused among a regional economic population. In this depiction of knowledge, the units of analysis, following Graaf, are agents who "bear" knowledge.

These agents consume knowledge in order to gain an advantage over other agents, and the pursuit of knowledge becomes an important activity in understanding the behavior of the economic agents, just as the search for food is an important explanation of behavior for what animals do every day.

The pursuit of knowledge creates a dynamic of competition, which involves how the agents deploy or use their knowledge in the marketplace. As the agents use the knowledge, it becomes known to others who also make use of the knowledge for their own pursuits, sometimes in ways unrelated to the earlier use of knowledge.

Knowledge, understood in its capacity as an economic variable, is an asset of the region, and is capable of increasing or decreasing in quantity.

Predicting Technology

Diagram 7.1. Scope of the Metaphor Between Evolutionary Population Genetics and Structural Evolutionary Regional Economic Theory (SERET) With The Addition of Knowledge Creation.

Biology Units of Analysis	Basic Rules/ Algorithms	Antecedent Conditions	Existing Environment	Future Environment
Genetic molecules DNA Demes Genotypes Phenotypes	Units must multiply Units must vary Variation is heredity Adaptation Selection Survival of fittest	Initial population Birth rates/death rates Inbreeding	Current advantaged phenotypes Current rates of genetic evolution	Heterozygosity leads to new species VS. Mueller's Ratchet of inbreeding

Logical Progression of Thought and Time Chronology of Analysis

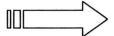

Biology Units of Analysis	Basic Rules/ Algorithms	Antecedent Conditions	Existing Environment	Future Environment
Humans Products Firms Markets	Diversity Variation Selection Adaptation Obsolescence Civil rules Social rules Moral rules	Initial population History Culture Existing infrastructure Industrial clusters, skills Technological envelope	Birth/Death rates of firms Rate of technological product innovation Local attractor points Regional economic structure [A] Final demand market selection Intermediate demand market selection	Bifurcation growth points Bifurcation decline points Future economic structure [A'] Eigenvalue from [A] to [A']

Knowledge Units of Analysis	Basic Rules/ Algorithms	Antecedent Conditions	Existing Environment	Future Environment
Entrepreneurs Scientists Engineers who "bear" technical knowledge	Contagion Clusters Tacit Knowledge Property rights Rates of taxation	Rate of new venture creation. Status Quo Form of government. Rate of investments Historical stock of knowledge	Open or closed society, diversity, Rules, of civil procedure Traditions Educational Attainment Knowledge flows or leaks.	New knowledge. Status Quo. Decline Market bifurcation

Often, in economic literature, knowledge is referred to as a "stock" of knowledge. In this case, at the beginning of the time period, a region would be considered to have a "stock" of knowledge based upon the number of agents in the region who bear knowledge.

At the end of the period, and projecting into future periods, the initial stock of knowledge could either have "flowed" into a greater base of knowledge, or in the case of decline, the stock of knowledge may have "leaked" out of the region.

Sometimes, this phenomenon of knowledge leakage is called "brain drain," to refer to the idea that the agents who bear knowledge have left the region.

The biological evolutionary metaphor can be applied to knowledge because knowledge depends on the biological capacity of the human brain to remember events. "When people meet, they communicate," wrote Ilya Prigogine, and "when they leave, they keep the memory of their encounter. When they meet other people, this communication is propagated to an ever-increasing number of participants."[277]

Knowledge, unlike an autonomous price-based transaction in neoclassical tradition, does not start over from scratch with each new encounter.

Knowledge, like evolution, builds upon what exists in the memory of humans, and knowledge is cumulative, in the sense that it builds upon existing memories. Autonomous prices are one variable in an economic exchange, but the price is only one variable which the agent sees. The more important economic variable is what the agent remembers from the last time he saw the price and what he learned from his last encounter in the exchange.

Predicting Technology

As new products evolve in unexpected ways, new complementary products may be developed, and if a critical threshold of new complementary products are produced and purchased by consumers, an entirely new pattern of market demand may be created that is different than the former demand relationships.

To answer the complaint raised by Blaug about the absence of a causal mechanism in neoclassical theory, the application of the biological metaphor to knowledge creation and diffusion provides one possible "causal" mechanism in economic theory. However, knowledge creation and diffusion, in its capacity as a causal theoretical mechanism, is just one component of a complex social process.

What actually happens in a regional economy in the future is contingent on many other components, in addition to the evolution of knowledge.

In order for knowledge to serve as a causal scientific variable, the concept of "knowledge" must be defined in a way that allows it to be measured. To say, for example, that one region has a greater rate of knowledge creation than another region would mean that knowledge could be measured and compared between two geographical territories and between two points in time.

The theoretical significance of "knowledge" in terms of explaining interesting economic phenomena like rates of innovation would then be subjected to analysis and hypothesis testing, such as the hypothesis that a region with a high rate of knowledge creation is correlated with a high rate of innovation, which leads eventually to greater rates of economic growth.

Part of this needed definitional work has been accomplished in various forms of economic literature that identify knowledge as a regional resource, or as a "stock" or asset of the region. Jonathan Allen, for example, has defined knowledge as an intangible resource.

In his definition, knowledge "...enables new ways of looking at work situations...the ability to investigate the consequences of different courses of action...the skillful creation of new ways of understanding and new programs of action."[278] Allen suggests that knowledge is converted into action by application of the knowledge into solutions.

In order to scientifically measure the concept of knowledge provided by Allen, knowledge could either be measured directly by counting the number of knowledge-bearing units in the region who were capable of looking at work situations in new ways, or indirectly by counting up the number of cases where knowledge had been converted into action, and assuming that the indirect measure of conversions served as a valid indicator of the more direct measure of knowledge.

Allen suggests another indirect measure of knowledge, based upon his hypothesis that conversion of knowledge into action is a "socially-embedded" activity. "A potential user (of novel information)," states Allen, "must participate in a community which helps them interpret the meaning of the information, and thus its applicability to novel situations."[279]

In this case, the indirect measurement of knowledge would count the number of social organizations that constituted a "community" of understanding.

The idea that knowledge is socially embedded means that the regional environment contains some social structure of organizations that allows an individual to work with other individuals in converting knowledge to action. For many researchers in the area of knowledge and innovation, the number and type of firms in the region provide this environmental context of knowledge creation.

The individuals in the firms communicate with individuals in other firms, with other technological associates and attend professional association meetings.

These social organizational networks are the topics of inquiry for researchers interested in understanding how knowledge is created and then converted to action.

Of particular interest is the study of "boundary spanners," who are "… individuals involved in the production, articulation and dissemination of knowledge which potentially can be translated into innovation within their own organization."[280]

To scientifically analyze knowledge in a region, these researchers would measure the structure of inter-industry networks among firms and other social organizations, and come up with statistical measures of how often a "boundary-spanner" communicated with organizations outside of his firm's cluster of ordinary communications.

After observing the communication pattern, the researchers would count up the number of cases where the boundary-spanner or some other individual in the firm converted knowledge obtained by the boundary-spanner into action.

These boundary-spanners have the appearance of biological units who operate along the edges of a genetic cluster, a topic that comes up repeatedly in biological inquiry about how genetic codes are transmitted from one species to another.

Applying the biological metaphor, the region's "stock" of knowledge, or the region's base of knowledge is contained in the structure of firms in the region who have knowledge-bearing workers, and the genetic diversity of the knowledge grows when knowledge from one cluster is added to knowledge in another cluster. Biologically, this would look like bees pollinating flowers.

Edwin Mansfield provided a definition of knowledge that connected both the social structure of firms in a region to the technology of the firms in his book, *Technology Transfer, Productivity, and Economic Policy*. In his definition, "Technology consists of society's *pool of knowledge* (emphasis added), concerning the industrial, agricultural, and medical arts. It is made up of knowledge concerning physical and social phenomena, knowledge regarding the application of basic principles to practical work, knowledge of the rules of thumb of practitioners and craftsmen...*Science is aimed at understanding, whereas technology is aimed at use...*" *(emphasis added).*[281]

This is the same definition given by Schmookler in 1966, who stated that technology was "...a social pool of knowledge of the industrial arts."[282]

Mansfield's distinction between knowledge as understanding something, and technology as the application of knowledge flows through much of the existing literature on knowledge. For the purposes of applying the biological metaphor, the distinction is most important when it is applied to the difference between a technology that improves the manufacturing process, called a "process innovation," and a technology that involves a product innovation (product innovation).

As a sub-category of product innovation, technology can either improve existing products by adding new features, or, in the more interesting case, boundary-spanners can carry back knowledge from another technological cluster, and potentially come up with an entirely new product when that new technology is applied to old technology.

The distinction made by Mansfield often finds its way into economic discourse as the difference between a productivity improvement, where the output of a manufacturing process is held constant while the quantity and value of the inputs decreases. This process innovation is often captured by neoclassical marginal analysis as a gain in productivity, as measured by a decrease in the labor-value of the manufacturing process.

The existing structure of firms in the regional economy provides the base or pool of knowledge because the firms employ knowledge-bearing humans, and that knowledge acts as a resource, if the environment allows for a process of innovation to occur. Innovation is not an automatic event. Innovation, if it occurs at all, can either be process innovation or product innovation.

As Nathan Rosenberg and Stephen Kline have pointed out, "...most innovation is done with the available knowledge already in the heads of the people in the organizations doing the work."[283] If the people doing the work have connections to other parts of the economy, especially parts of the economy outside the routine patterns of communication, then contingently, knowledge may be converted to innovations.

Bengt-Ake Lundvall carefully points out, "…if participants in the exchange (of knowledge) share norms and culturally based systems of interpretation, then interactive learning and innovation will be easier to develop."[284]

Or, to bring Joel Mokyr's point back up, if the environment is sympathetic to new ideas, then the process of innovation may occur. Part of the sympathy is in the form of cultural values that feature individual rights, especially rights that allow the innovator to appropriate the profits from his innovation, and part of the sympathy is in the form of cultural values and laws regarding trust and honesty.

Rinaldo Evangelista builds upon Mansfield's insights about the distinction between knowledge and technology by further describing that the "process of technical change can be conceptualized as a process of generation of new technological knowledge as distinct from the process which leads to its actual use in production…in the form of new or improved machines, technical devices and operating systems."

For Evangelista, technology is a stock of knowledge, that is disembodied, meaning held in the heads of knowledge-bearing humans and not embodied in machines, that features cumulative and increasing returns, and is dependent on the social business structure of the region.

Evangelista states, "While product innovations are usually associated with the creation of new markets or with quality enhancement of existing products, process innovations are introduced for reducing costs, rationalizing or increasing the flexibility and performance of production processes."[285]

When knowledge, as a causal variable, is converted to process innovations, the reduction in costs of production, primarily labor costs, "causes" economic decline, unless the process innovations are accompanied by product innovation, which "causes" economic growth. The variable that provides theoretical linkage between process and product innovation, in the biological metaphor, is knowledge in its capacity as a pool, or stock, or resource of a region.

The knowledge carried around in the brains of the knowledge-bearing units of analysis in a region is often described in economics literature as "tacit" knowledge. The characteristic of tacit knowledge provides the concept with a geographical boundedness.

Hall provides this important insight when he notes that "Technological knowledge has important tacit elements *acquired only in the actual doing of production.* [286](emphasis added). The tacit part of knowledge is an intellectual property gained through experience, or learning by doing.

Karlsson and Manduchi describe tacit knowledge as difficult to codify, or reduce to written or electronic format. They contrast tacit knowledge with "codified" knowledge that means, coded in the form of books or documents. Codified knowledge, like that knowledge gained from books, is easy to manipulate and store.

It is geographically ubiquitous, meaning that a person in Asia can gain codified knowledge as easily as a person in America. As applied in the economic context, the geographical ubiquity of codified knowledge allows automated production techniques, which are based upon codified engineering knowledge, to be replicated in any location in the world, meaning that the cost-cutting dynamic of global markets influences prices in every market.

On the other hand, they state that tacit knowledge is difficult to codify because it is indivisible, meaning that it is carried around in the brains of humans. Being intrinsically indivisible, for Karlsson and Manduchi, means that tacit knowledge is "...difficult to transfer without face to face interaction."[287]

They note that firms use both types of knowledge, but for them, what "...really matters is knowledge about new techniques, new products, new production processes, new competitors, new customers, new business concepts. Without access to the new knowledge created in the marketplace, it seems extremely difficult for firms to stay competitive in dynamic markets."[288]

Applying the biological metaphor, knowledge is a resource that humans gain in a specific geographical territory and they gain the knowledge primarily as a result of seeking it out in face to face communications. In the biological sense, humans that work for firms eat knowledge and the knowledge they like to eat the most, following the logic of Karlsson and Manduchi, is new knowledge.

The new knowledge can either be applied in production processes, that tends to reduce the costs of production, and thus contributes to declining prices, or it can be applied in the form of technologically new products.

Gaining knowledge and applying knowledge is not an automatic function, and the creation and diffusion of knowledge varies by region. If participants in the exchange of knowledge in a region share norms and culturally based systems of interpretation, then interactive learning and innovation will be easier to develop in that region, compared to a region where the social networks are based upon other cultural values or norms of doing business.

All knowledge, therefore, is not equally useful for firms to eat. As Echeverrie-Carroll notes, "High-tech firms depend strongly on both types of knowledge: the kind that can be appropriated (by the firm) and the kind that can not be appropriated.

In contrast, the maquiladoras depend only on *information*. (emphasis added). The difference between information and knowledge is that knowledge leads to innovations, while information (codified knowledge) leads only to more efficient production of the same (old) good."[289]

From a biological metaphor perspective, Echeverrie-Carroll may overstate the case for knowledge leading directly to innovation. Innovation is not an automatic evolutionary outcome of knowledge. Knowledge, as a regional resource, can sit in the brains of individuals, unused, unconverted to action, just like iron ore or some other regional asset that is not mined and commercially deployed.

Innovation is a contingent outcome that depends on a specific type of social structure, and even if knowledge does eventually lead to innovation, the most interesting part of the innovation is new product innovation, not innovation in production processes.

As her case of the maquiladoras shows, cheap production costs along the Mexican border simply leads to declining prices in a global market, which hastens economic decline on a world-wide basis, if the lower costs are not accompanied by product innovation which leads to the emergence of new global markets.

Part of the contingency in converting knowledge to action is based in the type of social structure and communication networks that exist in a regional economy. One region with a great regional base of knowledge may have lower rates of innovation than some other region because the knowledge does not "flow" into channels that converts knowledge to commercially viable products or firms.

Only a particular configuration of social structures, cultural values, and laws regarding market transactions allows for high rates of knowledge conversion. The unit of analysis in comparing rates of knowledge conversion between regions would be the firm, and the analysis would measure how firms in a region converted knowledge, especially knowledge gained from "boundary-spanners."

Ross Thomson summarizes the three different paths of learning that take place within a firm that seem related to the conversion of knowledge into action.[290] His three pathways are:

- Learning by doing, which leads to incremental improvements in the production process.

- Learning by using, which creates knowledge on the commercial capabilities of equipment.

- Learning by selling, which is a market feedback mechanism that makes both existing products and potentially new products more compatible with consumer demand.

In Thomson's schema of learning, the first path, learning by doing, is related to lowering production costs. This type of conversion of knowledge fits nicely into the neoclassical marginal paradigm because the math can model the marginal declining costs of production related to improved efficiency, and the outcome can be measured as a productivity improvement.

Learning by doing, however, does not seem to depend on events, which happen outside the firm in social structures, or communication networks as much as it depends on direct personal experience gained in the application of practice. What the social and environmental conditions create in learning by doing pathway is an environment that allows practice to be converted to action inside of the firm.

In comparing national systems of innovation, Richard Nelson described that technical knowledge could not be characterized a simply a body of practice. In addition to practice and experience, Nelson cited technical knowledge as "...a body of generic understanding about how things work, key variables affecting performance, the nature of major opportunities and currently binding constraints."[291]

The social environment of the firm, said Nelson, "...may be resistant or unresponsive to management commands...the social system of work set norms, enforces them, and resists pressure commands from management that are inconsistent with those norms."[292]

In other words, productivity gains from learning by doing are not automatically obtained just because engineers or production workers gain knowledge through practice. This element of contingency in the application of knowledge cannot be captured by the neoclassical marginal analysis that assumes from the beginning that any and every productivity improvement is immediately and ubiquitously applied throughout the economy.

Applying the biological metaphor to knowledge, the implication for Nelson's insight is that, if knowledge is converted to action through a pathway of learning by doing, then the "...new technology is not simply better than the old technology, in some sense the new evolves from the old...one round of technology lays the foundation for the next round."[293]

In this case of learning by doing, the evolutionary pathway of production technology will not escape the technological boundaries or regional production possibilities frontier, without some source of new knowledge gained from a source outside of the firm being applied in the firm.

And, even if there is some source of new knowledge, the economic and social environment in the firm and the regional economic environment outside the firm must be "sympathetic" to the commercial application of the new knowledge.

If the environment is sympathetic to the application of new knowledge in learning by doing environment, then the actual application will most likely occur in a new firm, and in a much later time horizon.

In other words, there is an element of time elapse from the time an engineer gains knowledge by learning by doing and the application of the knowledge. As Mowery and Rosenberg pointed out in their study of the U. S. national system of innovation, "...engineers and other technically trained personnel served as valuable carriers of scientific knowledge...technically trained engineers moved into positions of industrial leadership...the waves of new product technologies...have been commercialized in large part through the efforts of new firms...The role of small firms in commercializing new technologies in the U. S. ...appears to contrast with the pattern in both Japan and Western Europe."[294]

Expanding on this idea that cultural values in a society affect the rate of knowledge creation, Bertin Martens makes the point that "Societies that allow specialization and trading systems to emerge thus have an evolutionary advantage over those that do not...communication and trading systems require only the reproduction of a small subset of a "parents' behavioral algorithm (in order to transfer knowledge) to any other recipient...which leads to greater diversity and variation."[295]

As Nelson comments, "...best-practice technology was approachable by any nation with requisite resources...With firms all over the world facing a common market for products and inputs, the forces that used to provide the U.S. companies with incentives to get into certain technologies first have largely been eroded."[296]

In other words, the economic gains derived from the application of new production process technology are dissipated rapidly in a global market economy because the knowledge is primarily codified knowledge, once a new plant is built and the capital equipment is placed on the floor of the plant.

Knowledge, in its capacity as a regional resource, is crucial for firms to eat and to apply, but some forms of knowledge seem more important than other forms inside of the firm. Saviotti categorizes the important forms of knowledge for a firm as:

- Scientific knowledge, which is predominantly "eaten" in the research and development departments of a firms.

- Technical knowledge, which is consumed primarily by the production department of a firm.

- Market knowledge, which the marketing and sales department consumes.

In the area of production technology, Saviotti notes that the "knowledge of engineers, scientists, managers, and technicians involved in the implementation of the technology becomes specialized around the process, technical and service characteristics used. This specialization creates networks of communication and power which reinforce the stability of the artifact dimension of the technology."[297]

From a biological perspective, the activity in the firm is contributing to the creation of conditions of sclerosis and homogeneity in genetic production technology, as a result of this allegiance to the regional technological specialization. The networks of communication inside the firm act to limit the application of new technology, even if a boundary-spanner, or some other source of knowledge happened to find its way into the firm.

So, in addition to political allegiance to the status quo by elites who benefit from the current arrangement of power, and in addition to the ubiquitous application of production technology around the world, that immediately drops costs and profits, there is an additional environmental factor inside the firm that "causes" economic decline.

The pathways of communication inside the firm are all loaded against new knowledge being applied in production technology, once a dominant technological paradigm has been established.

The units of analysis themselves are creating the conditions for evolution because the ability to "learn by doing" in a new production technology of the units of analysis has been limited to the existing dominant technology of production. In this case, in any 7 year period of time, learning the "best practice" in the region is equivalent to learning the "only practice" in the region, in other words, learning that "that's the only way we do things around here."

The act of "creation" is defined by the appearance of something new that did not exist before. If knowledge can be defined as a regional asset, or a pool of knowledge, then that pool or asset must be measurable and additions to knowledge must be distinct.

Unlike natural resources, however, like a region's deposits of iron ore, the resource of knowledge can grow, and can also decline. The units of analysis in the measurement of knowledge are the knowledge-bearing humans, who carry knowledge around in their heads.

These knowledge-bearing units gain tacit knowledge from one another in face-to-face communication networks, and they gain codified knowledge by reading books and other documents. They improve their knowledge, and hence the region's base of existing knowledge, by learning by doing, learning by using, and learning by selling.

Sometimes, if the communication networks exist, and if the knowledge bearing units share cultural values, tacit knowledge can be converted to commercial applications. Sometimes the conversion to commercial applications is based on existing knowledge, and in rare cases, it is entirely new knowledge that is commercialized.

In order to measure new knowledge, the "newness" of the knowledge must be distinguished from "old" knowledge or existing knowledge. In the earlier application of the biological metaphor, it was stated that firms "eat" knowledge, which means existing knowledge. Firms also seek new knowledge, just like farmers grow new crops every season to eat, and the pursuit of new knowledge, or knowledge creation, can be better understood from a biological perspective.

Audretsch and Feldman contribute their thoughts on this issue by stating "…firms exist exogenously and then engage in the pursuit of new economic knowledge as an input into the process of generating innovative activity… such knowledge spillovers tend to be geographically bounded within the region where the new economic knowledge was created."[298]

They leave unstated exactly what motivates existing firms, in a biological sense, to pursue the new knowledge, but they do correctly identify who the knowledge-bearing units are, and correctly identify the geographical boundedness of the knowledge creation process.

"New economic knowledge," they state, "embodied in skilled workers tends to raise the propensity for innovative activity to cluster spatially throughout all phases of the industry life cycle."[299]

In other words, they identify skilled workers as the agents who carry around knowledge in their heads, and that the knowledge, both new and existing, tends to affect the "phases" of the industry life cycle. It may also be, that rather than a "cycle" which means coming back to rest at a starting point, that the phase leads to a bifurcation point, where the future does not resemble the past.

Russell Standish takes this same concept of the pursuit of new knowledge and directly applies the Lotka-Volterra metaphor to economics. In this interpretation, the individual behavior of skilled workers in pursuing new knowledge, or creating knowledge, is related to the human urge to avoid risky or uncertain outcomes.

Standish hypothesizes the economy as a "...generalized Lotka-Volterra system of species interaction. The interaction matrix expands as new species are produced by means of mutations and crossovers, and the interactions drive some species to extinction."[300] In his hypothesis, products serve as the species, which interact, and innovation, which is related to new knowledge, acts in the analogy of mutation.

Saviotti also applies the biological metaphor to economics, and identifies the "searching" function in a biological causal explanation of new knowledge. "New knowledge," Saviotti states, "is generated by means of search activities...in order to learn the last unit (of knowledge gained by searching), all of the previously created pieces of knowledge have to be learned.

The more similar the external knowledge is to the existing knowledge base of the firm, the higher the rates of knowledge accumulation, and the higher the barrier (to entry by other firms to the knowledge).[301]

For Saviotti, the biological explanation for searching is linked to competitive survival via competitive advantage in knowledge. The more knowledge a firm gains, the harder it is for other firms to gain entry to the knowledge, which does not necessarily mean a barrier to entry in the market.

As Saviotti further explains, "innovations are forces, which lead to an uneven distribution of the capacity to create and use these innovations...the forces which create innovation occur at the regional level based on unique historical milieux and social institutions and networks. Innovations are operationalized by commercial firms which trade products in markets, and market trade diffuses the innovation."[302]

Like the biological analogy provided by Standish, the appearance of innovations in Saviotti's work are related to product technological genetic diversity which is derived from the application of knowledge. Firms which achieve a competitive advantage in gaining new knowledge are in a competitive position to create, and then commercialize, new products which are technologically, or genetically different than old products.

If, contingently, the new products achieve market acceptance as a result of changing market demand, then the firms which commercialize the new products may survive longer than the firms which do not commercialize new knowledge. Firms and regions which do not promote genetic diversity in products are on a pathway to economic extinction.

An important point raised by Saviotti is the role of the market, both in its capacity of selecting which products become commercially successful, but also, in the biological metaphor, its less well known function of acting as the mechanism of disease contagion, or in this case, diffusing, knowledge.

The market demand characteristics for the new products are entirely different than the market demand for the old products, although the emergence of new demand characteristics depend on evolutionary mechanisms. This evolutionary scenario begs the question: what exactly does new knowledge look like?

Paul Krugman suggests we will never know because knowledge leaves no paper trail. This conclusion seems somehow unsatisfactory.

New knowledge is created in a mental "insight-imagination" process when the brain encounters a novel circumstance. As the image of the novel condition is filtered and processed by hundreds and thousands of neural synapse firings, the brain is searching and sorting for the right fit between the external image and the internal model of the image. The main goal of the sorting and searching, from a biological perspective, is quantum coherence in a course of action or behavior to seek advantage or seek survival.

As the thousands of images are sorted, the neural networks tend to line up and fire in sequence, which is a condition called "making up your mind." Often, the brain is calling upon memory circuits of something that looked liked the novel circumstance, and combining those memories with new internal images to come up with the right fit and the right course of action.

Humans are confronted with novel circumstances primarily in their dealings with other humans. Evolution of the brain has allowed humans to anticipate the response of other humans, and imagine the future as if it had in fact occurred.

This process is called "imagination." The future that is imagined is tried out mentally, thousands of times a second in an individual's brain as it sorts and searches for the truthful reality of what may happen if a sequence of events occurs. The truthful reality confirmation process is aimed at confirming the beliefs associated with the mental images. New knowledge is created as a result of the confirmed beliefs associated with an individual's internal and external images lining up together.

In its application to economics, Ulrich Witt has noted, "Novelty takes the form of new mental constructs. The creation of those constructs may also be considered as a recombination (of prior mental images). More basic cognitive configurations stored in memory are recombined, possibly compounded by incoming perceptions, so that they merge into a new pattern."

Ulrich raises again the criticism of neoclassical economic theory in its inability to include this memory-based mental attribute of economic behavior. "The (neoclassical) "everything is given" interpretation excludes from the theory of economic behavior the dimension in which the individual uses his imaginative power to create possibilities of action that have not been there before."[303]

As the insight-imagination process continues in the brain of an individual, the individual's confirmation of reality is either confirmed or not confirmed, by other humans. This is usually called "inter-subjective verification of reality" where another person sees the same reality and confirms the beliefs. Social, tacit knowledge is confirmed beliefs about reality held by more than one person.

Often, in an economic setting, the confirmed beliefs become the cultural rules and norms about how things work. The rules and cultural values tend to become entrenched in the form of laws and then become hard to change. The creation and diffusion of new knowledge is not a routine event, which is one reason why new product creation is so risky.

"What constrains the choices of players," (in an economy), states Douglass North, is a belief system reflecting the past- the cultural heritage of a society…current experiences as filtered/interpreted by that belief system, which is why path dependence exists."[304]

From an evolutionary perspective, what North means by "path dependence" is that the past history of the regional economy constrains the choices of technology and the choices of people to pursue new opportunities. A regional economy becomes "locked" into a pathway because the old ways of doing things become entrenched, and new knowledge, new ideas, new ways of doing things are not allowed.

In economics, this condition would be called constrained maximization within a production possibilities frontier that can never change. The only outcome is increased production efficiency, which leads to reduced costs, reduced profits, and ultimately, economic extinction.

The political defense of the status quo, however, is not based upon what is good for avoiding extinction, but what is good for keeping the arrangement of power that continues the existing flow of benefits from the current relationships, or stated differently, the current state of confirmed beliefs.

New knowledge is dangerous to the existing distribution of income because it upsets the status quo way of doing things. Individuals that create new knowledge are often shunned in society, and given unflattering names, like "entrepreneurs," which has its root meaning in the ability to see new things.

James Juniper suggests that the new knowledge distilled in the minds of entrepreneurs can be modeled in a Bayesian sort of way, and it is this insight that allows the criticism of Krugman that new knowledge leaves no paper trail to be dealt with.

Juniper suggests that the new knowledge created in the minds of entrepreneurs about uncertain economic events is eventually tested and improved, in the mind of the entrepreneur, to the point where the new knowledge becomes objective reality.[305]

The internal subjective probabilities associated with the images being sorted in the brains of the entrepreneur become confirmed by external events. The confirmed beliefs do not reduce the risk of the uncertain outcomes, but establish a minimum threshold risk that is acceptable to the entrepreneur to "try out" the idea.

The mental images leave no paper trail, but the "trying out" part of the act leaves a trail definitely empirical in nature. The Bayesian expectations about the future tend to create the future markets. The units of analysis that carry knowledge around in their heads are testing the images, looking for ways to try out their ideas. When the mental images move from testing in the brain to being confirmed beliefs by others, something tangible occurs.

The agents shape the future market environment while at the same time, the current market environment shapes the agent, by either constraining his choices or allowing the agent to implement the idea.

The act of trying out the idea is captured in a moment in time in an economic accounting system by the appearance of a new coefficient in an input-output transaction matrix. The appearance of a new coefficient in the matrix is, biologically, just like the appearance of a new neural synapse in the brain resulting from an insight/imagination that became new knowledge.

The new coefficient shows linkages between cells that allow transfers and exchanges, further confirming the beliefs. In both cases, the linkage is a result of something new occurring, and, in both cases, that new thing is new knowledge based upon shared insights and imaginations.

The new knowledge is created as the agents form their expectations abut the future in anticipation about what other humans are going to do. Applied to economics, as noted by Brian Arthur, "...traders (in a market) continually hypothesize (about the future). The more uncertainty and risk associated with the future, the less likely that individual expectations will be realized but the more likely it is that new knowledge will be created.

On the other hand, and in a paradox, the more standardized and stable the environment, in other words, the more the current economy looks like equilibrium, the less imagination and insight is needed to gauge the behavior of other humans.

The implication of this is that equilibrium, as an outcome in economics, is more amenable to the rational expectations model associated with marginal analysis, while the more dynamic and diverse the economy, the less applicable rational expectations analysis is for understanding the economy. An economy in equilibrium is not an economy generating much new knowledge because the behavior of other humans has become routine.

Following Melanie Mitchell's work in *An Introduction to Genetic Algorithms*, the human process of knowledge creation, in its biological evolutionary context, is amenable to replication in a mathematical model. Her algorithm breaks the knowledge creation process into a "search space," and a "selection space."[306]

The search space refers to some collection of candidate solutions to a problem and some notion of distance between candidate solutions. In the science of biology, her search space is the collection of all possible (protein) sequences.

As applied to economics, her search space would be a region's technological possibilities frontier that contained all possible technological sequences, both applied and latent. In economics, as in biology, the greater the range of genetic diversity to begin with, the greater the potential rate of genetic mutation and knowledge creation.

If knowledge can be defined as a regional asset, or a pool of knowledge, then that pool or asset must be measurable and additions to knowledge must be distinct. Unlike natural resources, however, like a region's deposits of iron ore, the resource of knowledge can grow, and can also decline.

As Lancaster hinted at in 1966, what firms are "searching" for are new goods with new technological characteristics, some of which come from an act of genetic recombination, and some of which come from bolting together genetic material not previously combined.[307]

To the extent that the firms find new products, new knowledge is being created in the region, and the empirical evidence, to answer Krugman, shows up in the transaction matrix as new coefficients. When coefficients show up in the transaction matrix, new knowledge is being created, and the regional economy is growing.

Mitchell's algorithm, as applied to knowledge, contains both the search space, which occurs in the region's technological possibilities frontier, and the "selection" space. Selection, in economics, in the production space is a discrete event in time involving a "lumpy" irrevocable investment choice of which equipment to use in the new production process.

In making the investment decision about what type of capital equipment to put in which pattern on the plant floor, owners of firms "guess" at the future about production costs and "guess" at the future about what products consumers may buy at what price. Their guesses involve the mental images derived in their brains' selection/sorting activity.

Their guesses about the future become either confirmed by what consumers do, and therefore become truthful reality, or their guesses are not confirmed. So, there are two distinct types of selection processes under consideration in knowledge diffusion: production guesses by owners of firms and market selection guesses by consumers about the "utility" of new products versus old products.

As the selection choices are made, one of which occurs in a discrete moment in time, and the other of which occurs over an extended period of time, the information about the choices feed forward and feed back into the region's social network, causing knowledge to be diffused.

This opens the question of how new knowledge in new products are "selected" by consumers who previously had not known about the new products. Consumers are also "guessing" about the future of how the new product compares to the old product. A consumer "guess" today, is followed tomorrow by another guess.

Consumers make many guesses about new products, and one potential economic outcome of these guesses, over a 28-year period of time, is whether the initial distribution of income changes in the region.

The consumer demand side of the equation, in terms of knowledge evolution is also better suited to the biological metaphor than the current marginal theory. As Saviotti has stated, the market acts both as the disease contagion mechanism in diffusing the knowledge and the knowledge selection mechanism in fulfilling the market demand function.

It is in the market demand selection function that initial and changing income distributions become related to knowledge creation and diffusion. Market selection by consumers happens over a long period of time, and if over a long period of time, consumers select new products instead of old products, then income distribution may change.

From a logical passage of time chronology however, new knowledge is first created, then diffused, and, contingently commercialized in the form of new products. After new products first appear in the market, consumers either "select" the new product or continue to buy the old product.

There is both a feed forward effect from the production side, and a feed back effect in knowledge diffusion from the market demand side, and in this sense, knowledge diffusion exhibits a certain type of "LaMarkian" characteristic. Existing firms can modify, in a marginal way, both production and products, on the fly, within the technological parameters established by the region's production possibilities frontier.

Christopher Freeman summarized the research findings on this two-way diffusion process by noting, "Rosenberg, Gold (1981), and several other economists who have studied the diffusion process in depth have emphasized very strongly that the product or process which is diffusing through the adopter population often bears little resemblance at the end of the diffusion to the one that started the whole process."[308]

In terms of knowledge creation and diffusion, the social networks that exist within the region serve as the units of investigation to determine if an initial stock or pool of knowledge is either growing or dying. Within this social network, the units of analysis who bear knowledge engage in the biological activity of searching and selecting knowledge for gaining advantage or for survival.

Their external behavior, which is observable, is guided by their internal mental activity of sorting mental images and imagining the future, which is not an observable activity, yet. The guesses, or beliefs about the future are either confirmed or not confirmed by other humans.

When others confirm the internal beliefs as truthful reality, new knowledge is created. The schematic flows of information in Diagram 7.2 suggests that the model of the social networks that diffuse knowledge can be represented by the traditional transaction matrix of a regional input-output table.

The diagram gives a rough approximation of this idea of feed forward from the networks, and feedback to the market selection processes in the consumer networks.

The traditional matrix has been modified by factor analysis to describe correlations between industrial clusters which share technological characteristics in production.

Stan Czamanski was the pioneer in applying correlation coefficients to transaction tables that he developed to study the regional economy of Nova Scotia.[309] Czamanski's early work has been considerably extended and refined by Edward Feser, who developed the technique of applying factor analysis to investigate the degree of strength of underlying associations between industrial clusters.

Feser's basic hypothesis is that "co-located businesses that are in the same production chain, share similarities in intermediate input consumption, technology or worker skill mix and are related through other intermediary institutions or informal means."[310]

Feser's method is to create the traditional input-output transaction matrix, where:

X_{ij} represents intermediate good purchased by sector j from sector i, as a proportion of j's total intermediate goods purchases.

Y_{ij} represents intermediate good sales from i to j as a proportion of i's total intermediate good sales.

Diagram 7.2. Feedforward and Feedback Flows of Knowledge.

Initial Conditions of
Technological
Diversity In Production
Possibilities Frontier

Cultural Values Related
to The Status Quo

Knowledge Creation. Guesses and Imagination About What Other Humans Will Do.	Social Structure of Networks For Diffusion of Knowledge. Regional Input-Output Transaction Matrix modified by "Czamanski Correlation Coefficients" to describe industrial cluster value chains	Knowledge Confirmation In Consumer Marketplace via Market "Selection."

New Knowledge Feeds
Forward Through Social Structure
as diffusion/contagion

Confirmation of knowledge
feeds back to affect
social structure. Income
distribution either changes or
does not change, based
upon consumer market

In Feser's method, the columns of the matrix are initially set up to represent the intermediate input purchasing pattern of each industry, j. The rows of the matrix are set up to represent the intermediate output sales pattern of each industry i. Thus, in setting up his transaction matrix, prior to the application of his next step of using pairwise correlation analysis and then using factor analysis on the correlations, he establishes both the production side of the institutional networks, and the market demand side, as it exists in intermediate industrial flows.

This addition of the market demand side in the initial set up of the transaction matrix allows the ensuing matrices to be linked to the final demand for finished goods marketplace, which allows his model to show

how consumer feedback information flows back into the social structure of networks, and perhaps how final demand affects the distribution of income.

In his second step of the method, Feser develops the correlation coefficients that group industries with common technology in production and common intermediate demand markets. Next, he applies factor analysis to uncover the relative strength of the relationships between certain variables associated with production technology and the factors which explain how the sectors are linked.

As Feser explains, "By grouping those firms that are most likely to interact with each other, both directly and indirectly, the clusters reveal relative specializations in the economy in terms of extended product chains (buyer-supplier, import replacement, and entrepreneurship based strategies) as well as technology deployment and cross firm networking initiatives."[311]

The clusters that are uncovered by Feser's method are surrogates for social networks which allow new knowledge to flow within the regional economy.

Given an initial configuration institutional networks in Feser's clusters in a region, it would be possible to project both the knowledge creation potential of the region, based upon conditions of heterogeneity in genetic technology, and to predict how new knowledge would be diffused within the region, based upon the "density" or closeness in technology between clusters.

The higher the density in the cluster, the faster the rate of contagion, as the disease of new knowledge rapidly infects those knowledge-bearing units closest to the outbreak.

In his assessment of the method's usefulness, Feser modestly notes, "... the clusters represent distinct technological groupings of sectors or product chains...Although the conduits of interdependence between firms extend well beyond supplier linkages, input-output flows provide the single best uniform means of identifying which firms and industries are most likely to interact through a myriad of interrelated formal and informal channels."[312]

The predictions about the potential of a region to create knowledge, and the hypothesis that the technological "closeness" of firms in their value-chain relationships all hinge on the underlying assumption that economic activity is not distributed uniformly over the geography of the world. There is both a geographic dimension to the clustering of firms, and a technological/knowledge creation dimension to the creation and diffusion of knowledge.

As Saviotti notes, in a subtle criticism of neoclassical theory, the geographic dimension of the clustering of firms "...cannot be explained by factor endowments."[313] The initial factor endowments of land, labor and capital, however, are the only explanatory variables that make the math work in marginal analysis.

Saviotti goes on to explain that the innovative potential of the region is more likely caused "...by the specific institutional configurations and by the cumulative local and specific character of the knowledge that the institutions possess."[314]

Feser's work provides the analytical framework for investigating the region's knowledge creation and diffusion of new knowledge. Using his analytical framework means that sociological theory about institutional networks is applied to an economic theory of economic growth in order to understand the evolution of knowledge in a region.

His analytical framework of a regional input-output model, modified by factor analysis can describe how both the feed forward and the feedback forces of new knowledge affect the institutional structure of networks.

One benefit of the Feser methodology is that it opens the investigation of knowledge to a better understanding of how knowledge, as a pool, factor endowment, or asset of the region, can also erode over time.

In his study of technological systems in Sweden, for example, Bo Carlsson used an analytical model like Feser's to describe how a certain institutional configuration of firms would lead to negative cumulative feedback effects in knowledge.

Carlsson noted that "...there may be self-reinforcing mechanisms at work (in the existing industries). A vicious circle, in which industry chooses not to become involved in an expanding technology, influencing universities and government policies to make the same choice."[315]

In other words, Feser's framework allows for an explicit political dimension to be added to the economic and institutional dimensions to address how allegiance to the status quo ways of doing things leads to knowledge extinction by destroying the environment's ability to create and diffuse new knowledge. The allegiance to the status quo is a LaMarkian effect in terms of evolution, but in a negative kind of way.

In the biological metaphor, it would be called genetic inbreeding. Economists sometimes call the outcome of genetic inbreeding in regional economics "technological lock-in". The same effect is also called "technological trajectory or pathway," by others.

The process of genetic inbreeding, which occurs in the process of knowledge creation/diffusion, is further strengthened by macro global forces related to international flows of codified knowledge, which tends to diffuse among large global corporations much more rapidly than tacit knowledge.

Carlsson's study, for example, focused on just 4 multi-national corporations, and the deleterious effect just these four corporations had on knowledge creation/diffusion in Sweden.

Krugman has also linked technological lock-in in regional economies to international trade. For Krugman, "Lock-in, refers to the inefficient but entrenched arrangement of the keys on the keyboard...once a pattern of specialization (in regional production process technology) is established, it tends to become locked-in because (business social networks favor the status quo) of the cumulative gains made by international trade."[316]

More will be said about the political power of multi-national corporations to force knowledge creation and knowledge diffusion in a regional economy to serve proprietary financial interests of private corporations that benefit from maintaining the status quo of global markets. For now, the important point is to raise the issue that the exercise of political power affects the regional environment's evolutionary path in a LaMarkian way.

There is nothing "natural" or biological about the exercise of this political power, but the application of power determines the evolutionary pathway of the region by exerting political control over how knowledge is created, diffused, and ultimately, commercialized. The value of the biological metaphor as applied to regional economics is that the application of power can be modeled and captured in the analytical framework provided by Feser.

In order to deploy Feser's method in an evolutionary context, the analytical tool of input-output analysis must be seen in a new light, or used in a new way, that is different than the traditional way the tool has been used by economists for the past 50 years. The proposed use of input-output analysis may have been the method Leontief was developing right before his death.[317]

Leontief stated that his new application "...describes the structural relationships that governs the successive states of the economic systems from the beginning to the end of a particular stretch of historical time... Past relationships (among firms) suggest the technological trajectory of the region."[318]

One of Leontief's associates, Faye Dutchin, has extended this new way of looking at input-output analysis. In her work, she states that the use of structural economic analysis allows "each scenario about the future to be viewed as a hypothesis or an experiment."[319]

Resistance from the status quo community of economists, both to the traditional use and the new use of input-output analysis is to be expected, according to Duchin. "It is not that the coefficients do not change (that neoclassical economists dislike) but more specifically that physical structures do not respond automatically to changes in prices...Elasticities of substitution are not built into the conceptual framework of input-output economics."[320]

In contrast to the conventional use of input-output analysis, where all transactions end up describing how prices adjust the economy to equilibrium, the proposed new use of input-output analysis in the biological metaphor would describe how the economy is evolving. In this new perspective, the interindustry matrix, as it changes over time, is a reflection of how new knowledge is created, diffused and, contingently, commercialized.

Anne Carter, in her early work on the use of input-output analysis, made this same point about the ability of the method to describe technological change. She stated, "For it is in the composition of interindustry sales that mirrors most directly the effects of changing technology and the organization of production...As methods of production change, more of one kind of input will be required and less of another."[321]

For Carter, it was the use of new capital equipment on the plant floor that provided the key insights into the changing technological structure of the regional economy. "New types of capital goods are at the core of technical change and are of prime importance in explaining current account structural change as well as stock requirements...capital stock coefficients show total value of fixed capital per unit of capacity for each sector."[322]

Carter's emphasis on capital equipment foreshadowed Feser's use of the method in the newer application because Carter linked investment decisions about capital equipment to changing final demand, which is caused by changing income patterns, as consumers make their decisions to buy either the old products or the newer products made with the new capital equipment.

Carter's suggestion that increased volume of intermediate inputs means the regional economy is on a trajectory to "specialization," allows for a new interpretation of specialization. From the neoclassical perspective, starting with Adam Smith, the notion has persisted that the specialization in the labor market was a good thing and depended on the "extent of the market."

For Smith, the extent of the market was important because it defined how much income small nations could create from domestic markets.

An alternative explanation, from the biological metaphor, is that specialization shows a loss of genetic heterogeneity in technology, which means a loss in the region's ability to create knowledge, which ultimately means extinction. A regional economy that is on a pathway of "specialization" is on the pathway to economic decline from genetic inbreeding, if there are no other forces in the economy creating technological diversity.

Genetic technological diversity comes from knowledge creation and diffusion, which is contingently commercialized, in new products. Specialization is merely genetic substitution in the existing environment's genetic technological possibilities envelope. It is a reshuffling of the DNA along the region's production curve that produces greater production efficiency, but no mutation.

Specialization in both economics and biology is a form of inbreeding that leaves the species vulnerable to rapid extinction when a new species or new disease is introduced into the environment.

Perhaps this biological metaphor of economic technological homogeneity provides a better way to understand what happened to the heavily specialized manufacturing regions of Northern England when the global economy changed at the beginning of the 20th century, and to North Carolina's economy at the end of the 20th century. When these overspecialized inbred economies were subjected to the new disease of global trade, they promptly died.

In the traditional neoclassical view of input-output analysis, the method was applied with the starting assumption that fixed proportions of inputs, called factors of production, existed in all production processes everywhere, and at the exact same moment in time. The traditional view could not accommodate the idea that there may be many different techniques of production, even many techniques within a specific regional economy.[323]

The importance of Carter's insights about the technological coefficients being updated as a result of capital investments in new capital equipment is that it provided a conceptual opening to break away from the traditional view of fixed proportions at a fixed unit of time.

Carter's "best practice" technology of the newly installed capital equipment allowed estimates to be made about technical change in specific industrial sectors in specific economic regions. The new technological coefficients reflected the best process within the region's production envelope at that time.

The technological change described by the timely introduction of "best practice coefficients" provides a surrogate indicator of knowledge flows and knowledge commercialization, using the regional input-output transaction table as an institutional model of the structure of information networks in the regional society.

The best practice coefficients could then be compared to the region's "average practice," in order to analyze how new knowledge was being imitated or, to borrow a phrase from biological evolution, how firms were "adapting" to the new best practice. This was the method being developed by Leontief right before his death.

The scientific value of deploying input-output analysis in the new evolutionary way is that it allows the interindustry matrix, modified by Feser's correlation coefficients, to clearly show how technological closeness, and "boundary-spanners" work to diffuse knowledge. Saviotti described how certain institutional arrangements and social structures create and diffuse different types of knowledge.

As Saviotti stated, "different types of knowledge are often created and transmitted by different types of institutions and are combined in the production of final outputs...the extent of correlation can be measured by the span of the particular piece of knowledge...the smaller the *span* (italics added), the more local the knowledge."[324]

Translating Saviotti's insight into the biological metaphor, the closer the technological "span" in coefficients in each regional matrix, (the R^2 described by Feser's method), the more local (tacit) the knowledge is, the faster the rate of knowledge contagion (diffusion) when new knowledge appears in the regional economy.

One regional social/institutional matrix would be completely different than another matrix, a point not captured by the way input-output analysis is deployed by neoclassical ubiquitous equilibrium method. Storper noted that firms that master that non-codifiable tacit knowledge are tied into various kinds of "networks and organizations through localized input-output relations, especially knowledge spillovers..."[325].

The value of the proposed use of the input-output method is that the localized knowledge networks can be made explicit and the technological closeness of the networks can be examined. Missing from the metaphor, though, is the issue of what motivates the behavior of the "boundary-spanner," the agent that goes from one industrial cluster to another, carrying the nectar of tacit knowledge.

In the biological metaphor, the boundary-spanners are seeking the food of market and technical knowledge in their regional environment. Everett Rogers explained how this search function was related to the closeness of the firm to other firms in terms of technology and geography.

"Information about innovation," said Rogers, "is sought from near-peers...This information exchange about a new idea occurs through a convergence process involving interpersonal networks...essentially a social process in which subjectively perceived information about a new idea is communicated."[326]

For Rogers, the diffusion of knowledge through a regional economic environment entails a social process of communication and influence whereby potential users of technology become informed. To the extent that a boundary-spanner can bring back knowledge, the adoption of that knowledge, in other words, the diffusion from firm to firm, depends on whether the firm has knowledge-bearing agents who can mentally form new images in their brains in order to understand the knowledge.

Unlike neoclassical economics, which always assumes that a new production technique is instantaneously communicated and immediately implemented, the biological metaphor allows for contingent outcomes in the knowledge diffusion process, by raising the question: what happens if the boundary-spanner gets back with new knowledge, and the units of analysis in the firm says "that's not the way we do things around here."

The application of the regional input-output model, in the new biological metaphor allows this question of contingency to be evaluated. As Nelson and Winter have suggested, "A searching firm draws on a random distribution of technological coefficients in the neighborhood of its current techniques (the average a_{ij} in Carter's method), and compares the cost of the alternative techniques it finds with costs associated with the status quo (compares average a_{ij} to Carter's best practice coefficients).[327]

For existing firms, in existing markets of existing goods, with real prices, neoclassical analysis can explain the behavior of what happens next by reliance on the price mechanism. Neoclassical economics calls this next step the "elasticity of substitution."

From the biological perspective, the elasticity of substitution explains how price competition in existing markets is leading the economy toward zero profits and economic extinction. Nelson and Winter make this distinction by pointing out that if the search for information ends up in the firm "imitating" the best practice, then the pathway to extinction may be faster because the diffusion of knowledge would be faster among firms that are bound more closely.

In this case, the disease of knowledge is rapidly diffusing in a tightly-knit community. They raise the possibility of the region's natural technological trajectory, where the searching activity occurs along the region's "technological regime."[328] This regime is the beliefs about what is feasible or at least worth attempting" when the boundary-spanner gets back with the food.

Translating to the biological metaphor, if the boundary-spanner gets back, and if the firm "imitates" the best practice, the firm is "adapting" in the new environment. But, this adaptation to the new knowledge about manufacturing processes in an existing market merely hastens the extinction of the firm.

The more interesting story, from an evolutionary perspective, is what happens if the knowledge brought back by the boundary-spanner is about how technology can create a new product, and the knowledge-bearing agents actually change their mental images to accommodate the new knowledge.

In other words, what happens if the units of analysis at the firm begin "imagining" how the new product may fit into the future market. If the new product were subsequently produced and delivered to the market, this type of situation would be represented by a new coefficient in the regional matrix where none had been before, signaling the entry of a new product. The new coefficient would arise if, in Carter's method, an investment in new capital equipment had been directed to a new product.

The key variable is an investment in capital directed to a new product, not new capital directed to existing products. In this situation, Nelson and Winter scratch their heads in wonderment, and note "It is surprising, therefore, that the relationship between innovation and investment has hardly been studied empirically at all...Presumably, a successful innovation yields both profits and attracts demand."[329]

In order to address the relationship between investment and innovation in new products, there would need to be a conceptual link between future market demand, which Nelson and Winter highlight above, and investments that serve to create new products in the current time period that are destined to be consumed in a future period of time.

Making that conceptual linkage depends on making explicit and observable the underlying process of how income distributions change as consumers shift from buying old goods to new goods.

The explanation of how new knowledge leads to new income distributions is not a direct causal path and the effect of knowledge on income distribution is not instantaneous. There are feed forward effects from knowledge creation to the finished goods market of final demand, and complicated feed back effects from the final demand market to the social networks that allow new knowledge to diffuse among the "knowledge-bearing" units.

Edwin Mansfield investigated the time lags associated with new technical knowledge, and estimated that it took about 5 to 10 years, on average, before one half of the major firms in an industry begin using an important innovation.[330]

Mansfield was primarily addressing how global corporations adapt new knowledge about manufacturing production technology. That would be an investigation based more on how "codified" knowledge in a global market diffuses than on how tacit knowledge is diffused in a regional economy.

Codified knowledge tends to diffuse more rapidly, but even codified knowledge exhibits time lags. "Even when a firm begins using a new technique," said Mansfield, "this does not mean that the diffusion process is over for this firm. It generally takes a number of years before a firm completes the substitution of the new technique for the old."[331]

The lag in time in adapting new manufacturing production techniques is associated with "learning-by-doing," and resistance by knowledge-bearing units of having to learn new routines about "how things are done."

Part of the resistance can be explained by an easy to understand biological evolutionary metaphor that the economic effect of implementing new production techniques means that workers on the old plant floor are likely to lose their jobs in the newly automated factory. The behavioral response of resistance by the knowledge-bearing units could be called a "survival" strategy.

However, Mansfield hits upon the correct mathematical formula that can explain both knowledge diffusion in new products, as well as diffusion in new production techniques. "In general, the growth in the number of users of an innovation can be approximated by a logistic curve. And, there is definite evidence that more profitable innovations and ones requiring small investments had higher rates of imitation."[332]

In identifying the logistic curve as the right mathematical tool to study diffusion, Mansfield anticipated the biological metaphor of disease contagion in a defined population as a model for knowledge diffusion. He also touched upon one of the complex paradoxes about knowledge creation and knowledge commercialization.

The smaller the gap, or "span" of knowledge between the old technology and the new technology in manufacturing innovation, the greater the probability of diffusion and adoption in production processes, but the smaller the effect on future knowledge creation.

On the other hand, a greater span between old knowledge and new knowledge in new products that are actually adopted by consumers, the greater the effect on changing the economic structure.

However, radical new products face a smaller probability of adoption of the new product by consumers in the finished goods, final demand market. The major point is that process innovation has a different economic effect than product innovation, with the more radical product having the hardest road to commercialization but the greatest effect on changing the economic structure.

While new products have the potential to be delivered to the market, consumers need time to learn about how the new products compare to the old ones, and the bigger the gap in their knowledge, the less likely the adoption by consumers. And, in the absence of switching their purchasing patterns from the old to the new, the feed back effect on new knowledge, and ultimately on changing income distributions will not occur.

Income distributions change when consumers buy the radically new and disruptive products, and the economic structure changes when all of the complementary service and support industries grow up to complement the new product.

Feser's regional input output transaction table, with the newly added correlation coefficients in the intermediate sales matrix, allows for this complementary market development to be tracked and investigated. The development of the intermediate market, as evidenced by new coefficients, is a surrogate model of how knowledge creation and diffusion is proceeding in the institutional networks of a specific regional economy.

Mansfield also identified the relationship between the number of knowledge-bearing units in the firm when the boundary-spanner returns with new knowledge as a key variable in understanding knowledge diffusion. In his case, he was investigating what happened in 140 firms, spread over ten industrial sectors, with geographical operations around the globe.

In other words, the universe of firms studied by Mansfield contained multinational corporations primarily involved in obtaining codified knowledge about innovative production process technology related to computer controlled machine tools, not tacit knowledge about new products.

He found that firms that had high research and development expenditures had high levels of "technically competent personnel, who are likely to be better able to evaluate new technologies of any sort, and…tend to be less resistant to change."[333]

When the boundary-spanners got back to the 140 firms with the new knowledge about the production efficiency of the new computer controlled machines, the knowledge-bearing units at the firms formed new mental images in their brains. New knowledge was created. New knowledge was diffused.

And, the new knowledge had a better chance at commercialization, because the knowledge-bearing units were not resistant to changing the production process on the plant floor.

All of which improved production efficiency without adding genetic technological diversity in new products, which had the evolutionary effect of hastening the arrival of economic extinction resulting from global price competition and declining profits. As the price comes down, more consumers buy the good, saturating the market, and feeding the profit decline on each unit sold.

Mansfield estimated that the process of adopting the new production technology took place over a 10 year period. Another academic, Baruch Lev, has studied the time lag of adoption of new technology from a slightly different perspective. Lev studied the relationship between a firm's expenditures in research and development and the intellectual assets of the firm. Lev calls these assets "intangibles," which are mostly associated with intellectual property, brand names, customer loyalty, and "organizational capital."

As firms succumb to the price declines in global markets resulting from production efficiencies, they tend to cut back on expenditures on the firm's intellectual assets, the knowledge-bearing units who form new mental images when the boundary-spanner returns.

"In other words, the company turns its products into commodities, and margins decline. As the cycle continues, the stock price descends further, pressuring the company to reduce investment in intangibles still more. A company spiraling down like this can lose the core of its competitive advantage without anyone's being aware that there was any alternative."[334]

The straight-forward explanation for how a company could lose its' competitive advantage "without anyone's being aware," is that the knowledge-bearing units, who would have been aware to form the new mental images, had all been outsourced and restructured. Firms facing profit declines usually outsource all of their organizational intellectual capital.

Lev found that it takes about 7 years before an investment in intellectual intangible assets returns a profit. But, in the era of declining profits, resulting from earlier investments in process efficiencies, the firm can no longer take the risk that an investment in research will pan out over the seven years.

Mansfield found in his studies on the diffusion of industrial innovation that "...it is reasonably clear that firms where the expected returns from the innovation are the lowest tend to be the slowest to introduce the innovation."[335]

From about year 4 to year 7 after the introduction of a process innovation, neoclassical marginal analysis can effectively be deployed to describe the firm on its marginal pathway to extinction because the decline is observable as both existing prices in an existing market and as the absence of capital investment in process equipment.

The knowledge diffusion process is not amenable to investigation by neoclassical theory because the diffusion process is not based on prices and is much slower than the instantaneous and ubiquitous outcomes reflected in the differential calculus of marginal analysis. And, additionally, the outcome of the diffusion process is contingent, not automatic, as the marginal analysis requires.

It takes time for the knowledge-bearing units in firms to search their near-peers for new ideas, and it takes time to form the mental images that translate imaginations into new knowledge. Rosenberg pointed out, in 1976, that the starting point for the search for new ideas begins "...within the framework of the existing technological horizon, along a range of options that been successful in the past."[336]

If the CEOs search within the existing technological production possibilities frontier of the regional economy reveals knowledge about production processes, this type of knowledge would not generally be a source of genetic technological diversity for new products, a distinction often overlooked by conventional economic analysis.

The act of imitating the "best" production practice, by placing a new machine on the plant floor, changes the existing technological coefficient in the input-output matrix, but does not add a new coefficient. New coefficients show up in the matrix when new products are created with new technology, and eventually, are complemented by more new coefficients reflecting new intermediate markets.

New products, created by new knowledge, represent new species, that are mutations of old genetic technology. As Evangelista correctly points out, "The general process of technological change can be conceptualized as a process of generation of new technological knowledge as distinct from the process which leads to its actual use in production...in the form of new or improved machines, technical devices and operating systems."[337]

The slow diffusion of knowledge, as distinct from the more rapid rate of price declines resulting from adaptation of new production equipment, is best captured by a mathematical model that shows a slow rate of diffusion when the new idea first appears, then increases rapidly, as more brains get the idea, and then declines, as the population becomes saturated with the knowledge, as just about every one "gets it."

The best model for describing this diffusion is the disease contagion model, which is a logistic function, with the added twist of an oscillation around the logistical path, which decreases in amplitude as it approaches the end point of population saturation.[338]

The oscillation around the logistical path describes the social phenomena that some folks just never get it. They resist change and resist new ideas. The common language of resistance that they use is "that's not the way we do things around here."

If it so happens that these very same units of analysis are in political control of what new ideas get diffused, then they become powerful forces to limit the creation and diffusion of knowledge, which, in the evolutionary metaphor, means controlling the distribution of income.

It would be a case of genetic inbreeding in knowledge leading to the evolutionary demise that comes from the absence of genetic diversity. If everyone thinks the same thing, and believes the same thing, no new knowledge will be created, and the distribution of incomes will not change.

In the sphere of knowledge related to production processes, the rate of adoption/imitation is affected by the closeness of the correlation coefficients in the transactions matrix. In a specialized, tightly bound regional economy, the most efficient "best practice" technology in the region evolves rapidly to the point of zero profits as more and more firms imitate the best manufacturing practice. The disease of new tacit knowledge spreads quickly.

At some point within the 7 year imitation process, it does not make sense for firms to imitate or adopt the new production technology because the time horizon to zero profits is so short. The declining costs of production lead to declining prices, which leads to declining profits.

The incumbent firms want to hold on to their legacy declining profits for as long as possible, and so do their bankers, whose interest payments on the lines of working capital extended to the firms depend on revenues generated on old products produced by the old equipment.

The Ephors of the status quo regional economy would then become hostile to new ideas and new knowledge which upsets the status quo way of doing things and would seek extra-market limits on the introduction of new products which, contingently, could lead to new distributions of income.

As Eliasson and Taymaz correctly point out, "Our proposition is that incumbent firms have only limited possibilities of reorganizing production in the very long run compared to the range of flexibility through new entry (of new firms)…Eventually, without entry (of new firms) the economy will start contracting…without entry, the industry will start contracting."[339]

At the point where the incumbents can limit new firms from introducing new products, they have shifted from behavior explained by prices to the behavior that James Buchanan calls political rent seeking. Incumbent firms aiming to limit the creation and diffusion of knowledge portray part of the rent seeking behavior. Commercial bankers, aiming at limiting entry of new firms to the market by restricting access to credit, portray part of the other side of this behavior.

Schumpeter diagnosed this second behavior as early as 1911. The coefficients in the regional input output table, as a result of the rent seeking behavior, would remain fixed over time, until they started disappearing, as in the case of the Chicago economic structure.

The social networks in the regional economy reflect the set of knowledge-bearing units who interact with each other, and transmit information. The strength of the correlation coefficients reflect the strength of their connections with each other. The pattern of their interactions, if subjected to factor analysis, would reveal the underlying industrial clusters within the region.

"In this sense, the particular networks within a social system at a given point in time represent its structure," writes Saviotti. "The networks indicates a combination of actors and links…relationships between actors in these processes are not impersonal, and display both persistence and structure formation."[340]

The social networks can be analyzed from the perspective of the biological evolutionary metaphor, which incorporates the application of political power that limits the evolution of the regional economic structure.

As Saviotti notes, the application of this political power is not "impersonal," and it is not priced-based, either.

As early as 1961, Benjamin Chinitz was making a break with traditional price-based neoclassical tradition by raising the possibility that the local market structure interacted with other factors to limit or promote the advantages of proximity.

Part of the advantage of proximity is the ability of knowledge bearing units to obtain tacit knowledge from boundary-spanners. The ability to gain knowledge, however, is not automatic, and there are political forces within the local market structure that are motivated to limit knowledge or to direct the flow of knowledge to their own private proprietary advantage.

This is a type of LaMarkian behavior, but in reverse. Instead of the usual acquired characteristics showing up from one generation to the next, this type of behavior imposes genetic inbreeding in knowledge to the detriment of genetic diversity from knowledge creation and diffusion.

As Chinitz noted, "...in competitively organized places, the potential for nurturing new, dynamic, and innovative businesses is much greater than in those places where oligopolistic industries predominate...the entrepreneurial supply curve is also a function of certain traditions and elements of social structure which are heavily influenced by the character of the area's historic specialization."[341]

A better scientific approach to understanding how knowledge creation affects economic evolution would have been to build upon Chinitz's work by linking the regional input-output model of social structure to a Bayesian time series analysis to provide predictions about the future economic structure. The coefficients in Feser's modified regional transaction matrix provide the posterior distribution of the parameters of the social structure.

From an analysis of the transaction matrix, primarily the auto regression and correlation coefficients, predictions about the future social structure could be made.[342]

As Leontief noted, "the past (I-O) relationships suggest the technological trajectory of the region. The trajectory is used for manufacturing engineering estimates on the next period inputs."[343] The shape and slope of the trajectory that Leontief was describing would be defined by the Bayesian time series analysis.

Part of the prior distributions about knowledge would be obtained from an analysis of the biological survival of new knowledge in a given local environment. This analysis would be the scientific side of determining whether a regional social structure was sympathetic, in Mokyr's use of the term, to new ideas. In other words, if the boundary-spanner gets back with new ideas, and the knowledge-bearing units in the firm start forming new images in their brains.

The survival probability of new ideas is best modeled by a stochastic model provided by Greiner and Kugler.[344] While they apply their model to the survival of a new production process, the same model applies to the survival of new knowledge about products, given the social structure contained in Feser's model.

The reason for using a stochastic model in conjunction with the Bayesian time series analysis is that the lags in time for diffusion of knowledge are different for a production innovation than for a product innovation based upon technological genetic diversity. In addition, the evolutionary effects on economic structure are different as a production process innovation builds upon its success via learning by doing.

Enos found that the first production process innovation attempted in a plant often dropped the cost of production by 1.5% per year following its introduction. Subsequent improvements in the initial innovation yielded greater cost reductions, amounting to 4.5% per year, as engineers and technicians learned how to use the new equipment.[345]

As the engineers get better at dropping the costs of production in a single plant, the other competitor plants in the regional industrial cluster are faced with an evolutionary dilemma either to imitate or die.

For competitor firms, it is both cheaper and quicker to imitate than to innovate. This type of imitation is the evolutionary equivalent of lemmings adapting to their environment by jumping off the cliff together. Mansfield found that, "On average, the ratio of the imitation cost to the innovation cost was about .65, and the ration of the imitation time to the innovation time was about .7"[346]

At some point in the 7-year horizon, following the introduction of a process innovation, some percentage of competitors move from the average a_{ij} to the "best practice" a_{ij}. The ones who make the leap, so to speak, help drop costs, which drop prices, which eliminate profits, and ultimately lead to economic extinction.

The ones who do not make the leap hang around at the edge of the cliff, hoping that their rent seeking political behavior can modify the competitive environment through price subsidies or government protection. In either case, innovations in production processes are examples of LaMarkian adaptation in reverse.

Creation and diffusion of knowledge can either lead to genetic technological bifurcations in economic structure or, alternatively, new knowledge can lead to equilibrium. The difference in the two outcomes concerns whether capital investments in the existing 7 year time horizon are directed to existing products and existing manufacturing processes or to new product mutations.

As Evangelista points after conducting his analysis, "...the evidence provided in this book shows that investments in fixed capital remain the fundamental channel through which knowledge is diffused and used throughout the economy...Activities consisting of the adoption and diffusion of new technologies through investment in fixed productive capital should be considered a central component of the overall process of technological change."[347]

However most of the investment in fixed capital is directed to marginal changes, or tinkering with existing products or tinkering with existing manufacturing processes. Audretsch and Feldman estimate that about 87% of all product improvements consists of "modest improvements designed to update an existing product."[348]

These findings are similar to Archibugi, who estimated that "96.9% of the innovations fall into the gray zone of (either) products or processes, according to the type of definition adopted."[349]

These type of modest, or marginal, improvements would show up in the regional transaction matrix as changes in the existing coefficients, not in the addition of new coefficients, which would indicate new technological knowledge being applied to new products, which are creating new intermediate supply chain relationships within an emerging regional industrial cluster.

The investments in existing products or processes would show up in a neoclassical study of marginal analysis of price movements as improvements in productivity, which hastens economic obsolescence, if it is not accompanied by new genetic technological diversity somewhere in the regional social milieux of knowledge creation and diffusion.

John Rees had it partially right in his assessment of the relationship between technological knowledge and productivity, but got it wrong about the effect on regional economic development. Rees said, "...technology is the prime "motor" for understanding the process of regional development... technology is the primary determinant of productivity, (true) and therefore regional economic growth (false)...productivity is what kills ventures (true for existing ventures).[350]

The process of regional economic development begins with the creation and diffusion of knowledge, which sometimes is translated into commercially-viable products. The process of commercialization involves the creation of new ventures.

As the case of Route 128 in New England demonstrates, a regional economy can experience the creation and diffusion of technology, without experiencing economic growth. The key factor is the type of social institutional relationships that diffuse knowledge and the cultural values associated with individual freedom to create new ventures and appropriate profits from the commercialization of the knowledge.

As Anna Lee Saxenian found, "Route 128 is characterized by autarkic corporations that internalize productive activities...authority is centralized and information flows vertically...Focused inward and lacking dynamic start-ups from which to draw innovative technologies and organizational models, the region's large minicomputer firms adjusted very slowly to the new market conditions."[351]

Just like the dinosaurs who responded slowly to the changing environment, those New England dinosaurs are mostly extinct. The environment changed, and yet not many new ventures were created in New England because of the control over knowledge flows exerted by the autarkic corporations.

The difference in the biological metaphor is that the dinosaurs did not create their own environment, while in the LaMarkian case of autarkic New England corporations, they did. The big autarkic corporations seek out regions which have dynamic, diverse, and open systems of knowledge creation and diffusion, in order to "...avoid being caught off guard by unanticipated breakthroughs."[352]

The big corporations are the desired targets of industrial recruitment efforts of local commercial real estate and commercial bankers, who use tax dollars to lure them to the region. The large corporations, once located in a region, seek to turn the creation and diffusion of knowledge to their own private proprietary advantage, thus distorting the social basis of knowledge creation that existed prior to their location in the region.

Once the large corporations locate a branch operation in a region, they tend to disrupt the ability of the region to create knowledge via new venture creation, in other words, they destroy the environment.

As Danson and Whittam discovered in their analysis of the economy of Scotland, "The role of branch plants in diminishing the ability of entrepreneurs to set up their own business was noted frequently as more unexpectedly was the skepticism and obstruction of the business development and academic establishments."

They conclude from their study that "...Without a countervailing, long-term sustainable development of indigenous companies, it is recognized that such peripheral economies will progressively lose further control over their destinies."[353]

The loss of control over future economic growth in the region is made worse because the large corporations leave the region to seek out knowledge in some other region.

Once they leave, the region has neither the ability to create new knowledge nor the minimum threshold of indigenous firms in the regional intermediate sales matrix to diffuse knowledge. The knowledge-bearing units and their social structure have been destroyed. This is an example of LaMarkian adaptation, but in a reverse, and economically perverse sort of way.

In the evolutionary metaphor, "...product innovations are usually associated with the creation of new markets or with quality enhancements of existing products, while process innovations are introduced for reducing costs, rationalizing or increasing the flexibility and performance of production processes."[354] Once the regional asset of knowledge creation is destroyed, the regional economy's ability to create new products is destroyed.

It takes many generations to restore the region's knowledge creating ability, as the case of Northern England's economy amply demonstrates. The engine of economic development is not productivity improvements in global autarkic corporations, but the birth of a great number of small firms "...whose innovative activities consist of using and adopting new vintages of capital."[355]

In order for the knowledge-bearing units in small firms to create new products, they need 2-way knowledge flows. They need the knowledge that comes from the production side of the economy, which is technical knowledge about how to make products, and they need knowledge from the consumer side of the economy, about consumer preferences for potential new products.

The regional interindustry intermdiate sales matrix is the social institutional structure through which this 2-way knowledge flow informs the knowledge-bearing units.

Lundvall notes in his study of innovation that it is necessary to "...focus upon the capability of an economy to produce and diffuse use values with new characteristics – innovations based upon knowledge about the needs of potential users...a new product's use value characteristics are transmitted (both to end user consumers) and back to producers."[356]

It is both a feed-forward of knowledge and a feedback of knowledge mechanism that is captured by Feser's modified input-output matrix.

The regional asset of knowledge, and the regional social institutional infrastructure of knowledge flows, are different for each region, and can not be explained by the neoclassical theory of initial factor endowments and price movements along supply and demand curves.

Niles Hansen cites the empirical work of Rigby and Esolitzbichler (1997), which showed that within the entire U. S. manufacturing sectors, "… there are substantial long-run variations in regional techniques of production that cannot be explained by industry mix or business cycles. (Regional) technology tends to move along different trajectories conditioned by local learning processes."[357]

If the transmission pathways for price movements of supply and demand are different in each region, then prices in each region are not transmitted along a single ubiquitous market pathway that connects markets in all regions. A price equilibrium in one region would be completely different than the marginal equivalencies required by the conventional theory in some other region.

Even if the minimum conditions of knowledge creation and diffusion are met in a regional economy, there are major forces at work to prohibit the commercialization of knowledge, which are not accounted for by the traditional theory's exclusive reliance on the price mechanism for the universal explanation of economic behavior.

Clayton Christensen hinted at the outlines of how this evolutionary economic theory would describe innovation. "After a technology takes root in new markets," said Christensen, "and after new growth is created, disruption can invade the established market and destroy its leading firms."[358]

In the evolutionary metaphor, the leading firms are phenotypes who compete for resources with other species, in a biological competition over knowledge. Except in this competition, the new species do not have the political and social power to invade the territory of the incumbent firms directly.

The new species usually seek niches along the edges or the borders of the territory in the environment. They target "…customers at the low end of a market who don't need all the functionality of current products and allow the innovator to earn attractive returns at discount prices unattractive to the incumbents."[359]

The universal human behavior that explains the action of the incumbent firms is self-interest and self-preservation, which constitute the images the brain is continually sorting. The brains of executives of incumbent firms are searching and sorting images about their desire to hold on to their incomes, and protect their territory from the new firms. They like the existing status quo way of doing things and the status quo distribution of income, and will do anything to maintain their incomes.

The universal human behavior that explains the actions of the knowledge-bearing units who create knowledge is survival and personal success. They want more income and incumbent firms who do not want to lose income oppose them. The quest for knowledge by both groups is like the quest for food because knowledge has the potential to create income.

The biological metaphor concerns competition for knowledge in a defined geographical territory because knowledge within the regional social structure has both an intrinsic value and an extrinsic value to humans in terms of obtaining income.

The value of knowledge and the competition for knowledge is not priced-based, it is income-based. Miyazawa's interrelational income multiplier matrix is a useful addition to Feser's matrix for analyzing this type of competition. Miyazawa's method shows how a direct change in the income of one social class results in a direct, indirect, and induced change in income in other social classes in a specific geographical region.[360]

According to this method, a change in the regional production mix alters the distribution of income, which in subsequent time periods, alters the pattern of consumption. As applied to the case of income competition and knowledge competition, the new method would allow an investigation into the dynamics of feed back effects from the final demand market which describe consumer preferences for new, technologically-advanced products, offered by new ventures, in comparison to the old existing products, offered by incumbent firms.

The income matrix developed by Miyazawa is a surrogate model of the social institutional structure of regional income, just like Feser's modified regional input output matrix serves as a surrogate model of the social institutional structure of the regional markets.

Both types of new regional input output matrices would be required to investigate the feed back and feed forward flows of knowledge to determine how new products created by new ventures lead the regional economy along a technological trajectory.

Or, alternatively, the two methods could be used to describe how incumbent firms act to resist technological innovation and the process of knowledge creation.

As Lazonic noted in 1994, "...because social structure is so important to the development and utilization of productive resources, former technological leaders may have problems responding to competitive challenges...and may pursue the alternative strategy of adapting on the basis of their traditional organizations and technologies...this adaptive strategy may augment rates of productivity growth in the short run, while making it impossible to sustain those rates of growth in the long run."[361]

Lazonic could have added an additional sentence that it would be impossible to sustain long run rates of economic growth because the incumbent firms had destroyed the regional environment's capacity for knowledge creation and diffusion.

Short run productivity improvements act to drop prices, which then drop profits, which then kills the company. In the absence of new knowledge, new technology, new firms, new products, and new complementary intermediate demand markets, there is no sustainable basis for regional economic growth.

The growth of new markets is both a function of knowledge, as a regional asset, and regional cultural and social values. John Zysman points out that "Markets...are the creation of government and politics...markets do not exist or operate apart from the rules and institutions that establish them and that structure how buying, selling and the very organization of production takes place."[362]

The most important social rules for explaining economic growth are the rules for individual initiative to create new ventures and appropriate profits. Those type of cultural rules are determined by the application of political power over knowledge creation and diffusion.

Incumbent firms that gain control over political power in order to protect their status quo distribution of income kill the regional knowledge base and the diversity of technology needed to create new ventures and new products.

In their resurrection of Schumpeterian endogenous growth theory, Aghion and Howitt list the top seven variables associated with economic growth. Three of their top seven variables involve the entry of new products, the creation of new intermediate markets and the creation of new ventures to service and supply the new intermediate markets.

These three variables are tied together by the knowledge variable, K, which reflects the marginal contribution of a vintage sector, s, to the rate of innovations, which is the "...rate which an old idea becomes obsolete and the rate of diffusion of older ideas into current general knowledge."[363]

They identify the market acceptance of an innovation as a "...Bayesian probability based upon hedonic characteristics of the new product compared to the old product..." Applying the biological metaphor to their work allow for a better explanation of their hypothesis that "...each time an innovation arrives implementing the GPT (new firm's technology) in a sector, it destroys a fraction of the capital that had previously been employed in that sector."[364]

New products created by new ventures do not compete directly for either knowledge or markets with the politically powerful incumbent firms. They feed for knowledge around the edges of the regional environment, in niches and eddies that are too unattractive to the incumbents.

Knowledge, as a regional asset, or regional resource, is a valuable asset to control because it is linked to control over incomes. The ability to control knowledge is a LaMarkian acquired characteristic, but in a negative way. Controlling knowledge is more like a de-acquired characteristic because when it is destroyed, it contributes to economic extinction in subsequent generations.

Placing knowledge in an evolutionary biological metaphor of regional economic growth begins to answer Blaug's complaint about the causal factors that explain economic growth and the emergence of new markets.

The central explanatory variable is an easy to understand concept called income. As William Baumol has noted, social rules and laws regarding appropriation of income set the economic reward structure of income for a regional economy.

Generally, in the absence of a constitutional mandate that points to the goal of open competition for income, the reward structure associated with the rules about income distribution are manipulated to the benefit of the most powerful set of elites who obtain power over setting the rules and the laws.

In other words, to return the conundrum known as "Arrow's Paradox," if the constitutional bedrock of laws does not contain the telos of upward occupational mobility and fair rules for the competition of income, then the subordinate laws that are passed will not provide logically consistent outcomes.

The economic consequence of the static income distribution is loss of economic diversity and, contingently, the elimination of the forces that contribute to economic growth.

Under one set of constitutional rules, increasing incomes can be obtained if new markets emerge which have new products that consumers favor over the old products. New products and new markets will emerge given a specific configuration of cultural values and laws that favor individual initiative and the appropriation of rewards based upon individual merit.

Under another set of constitutional rules, income distribution is static, and new markets, based upon the commercialization of new knowledge, do not emerge.

In a global economy, characterized by non-territorial networks of multinational corporate elites who have an entirely different set of financial objectives than ordinary citizens who live in geographically bounded regions, the issue raised by Arrow's Paradox on constitutional rules as they relate to the sovereignty of the nation and the wealth of citizens is no longer a trivial academic question.

Chapter VIII

Disruptive Technological Crossover and The Emergence of New Markets

R. C. Lewontin reminds us that Darwin called attention to actual genetic variation among "real" organisms, not synthetic versions of organisms. Darwin went to the Galapagos Islands to study real animals in order to better understand the obvious fundamental problem in the science of genetics, which was the origin of the species.[365] Darwin studied natural species in order to explain how their behavior adapted to environmental conditions.

As a result of inheritance, he theorized that the species with the best adaptation behavior survived, to pass genetics to the next generation. Darwin's theory involves a philosophy of science based upon a method of detailed cumulative causal explanations. For Darwin, as long as there is a phenotype population of species with imperfect inheritance of their parent's genetic characteristics, then some of the species will probably die or become extinct.[366]

Applying the biological metaphor to economics, the fundamental issue in economics is the origin, or the emergence, of new markets based upon the mechanism of inheritance of technology in products. Synthetic amalgamations of markets, comprised of three synthetic variables, Labor, Capital, and Land, do not lead to scientific explanations of how product technology is passed to the next generation in successful products nor how new markets emerge when entirely new products appear. And, while natural systems may not have a teleology, or end to which they are directed, neoclassical theory does have a telos of equilibrium.

Earlier efforts to employ the evolutionary metaphor to economics assumed that the firm was unit of analysis that evolved. Edith Penrose warned that firms, as biological organisms, do not evolve.[367] In her criticism of the application of the biological metaphor to economics, she suggested that Darwin's theory could not accommodate the deliberative and calculated economic behavior of the synthetic neoclassical amalgam of the firm.

In SERET, it is products that show evolutionary technological descendence, while executives of firms can be shown as adapting their firms to their environment. Product technology evolves, and product technology looks just like genetics in species. This assertion is in direct contrast to Ulrich Witt, who maintains that in economics, there is not a unit of analysis that has a clear or close analogy to genetics in biology.[368]

Markets, just like environments, have niches, which are comprised of a diversity of products and consumers, and each regional market is unique in the sense that the niches and units of analysis in each economic region exhibit differentiation and variety both within the geographical scope and history of the market and between one market and a distant market.

Markets, consumers and products, for very short periods of time, are related to each other, but not precisely in the way that Walras and Marshall speculated about prices and quantities. Markets are related to each other because for brief periods of time, consumers in a market "see" the same future, and share common expectations about each other's behaviors.

Part of the common set of expectations about the future is formed by the observance of current prices of products in distinct geographical markets. The current prices, for brief periods of time, are relevant in the way that Marshall and Walras, and the entire tradition of neoclassical equilibrium economics, postulates about prices bringing the economy to a point of equilibrium.

But, the introduction of technological novelty makes current prices irrelevant for postulating about the direction of the economy because novelty affects the mental imaging of humans. Novelty creates new expectations and new images about the future, as humans speculate on the right course of action to take, in conjunction with what they imagine other humans are likely to do.

In the final demand markets, it takes consumers time to learn about the new products, and it takes time for consumer preferences to shift. In contrast to Witt's assertion, Saviotti states, "A change in the design features of a product through innovation can thus be considered analogous to mutations in an organism which then gets selected by future markets based upon consumer preferences."[369]

The market niche, itself, as an environment, determines how fast or slow the information is transmitted, and the selection of new products versus old products, determines how the structure of relationships in the market will change. Each market niche is different and one price signal does not fit all.

Saviotti and his associates continue, "Niche theory predicts that the number of niches that may be created in a given habitat is proportional to the size of the habitat. The greater the span (in technological diversity) of the habitat, the greater the number of niches that can be created within it. An increase in the range (variety of product technologies) allows a technology to become more specialized and differentiated, thus leading to an increase in both production technology and product variety."[370]

As variety and diversity increase in a market, the birth rate of new ventures producing new products, which constitutes one of the indicators of economic environmental heath, would be expected to increase. Markets are comprised of relationships between humans. Economics is about the way these market relationships change over time. The changing relationships are often called the "structure" of the market, and economists sometimes use the term "market structure" to mean market relationships.

The behavior and adaptations of humans in markets change as a result of the introduction of novelty, which causes the "structure" of market relationships to change. Most of the novelty in markets, but not all of it, is related to the introduction of new technology in both products, and the way products are made.

The human response to novelty is contingent, and depends on the mental ability of humans to anticipate the future. What humans do in markets when new products are introduced depends on what humans anticipate other humans are going to do when they see the new product for the first time.

Most human economic activity is based on the biological ability of humans to anticipate what other humans are going to do, and imagine a course of action to take under different scenarios. And, to answer many economists who are critics of applying the biological metaphor, the human response to novelty in economics is "intentional."

Markets change when humans anticipate the behavior of other humans by imagining the future, and trying out, mentally, what may happen under different hypothetical scenarios. The behavior choices confronting humans are restricted and limited by laws and social customs, which vary by market and by geographical region.

Often, the future markets anticipated by humans have no prices, and consequently, the price-based utility optimization strategies hypothesized by neoclassical economics are irrelevant for explaining how new markets emerge. Alchian makes this same point when he states, "...where foresight is uncertain, profit maximization is *meaningless* as a guide to specifiable action."[371]

The rational choice set of behavior in future markets being imagined in the brains of humans depends on the freedom to choose, and the freedom to pursue an individual course of destiny, once the choices and decisions about the future have been determined.

Individuals who happened to born and live in regional markets characterized by greater individual freedoms would create a different future market environment, for themselves, than individuals who happened to be born and live in regions with less individual freedoms and liberty.

Markets characterized by property rights, and cultural values of trust and reciprocity would probably create a different set of imagined future choices in the brains of humans than markets that did not possess this resource set. Freedom in individualistic capitalist markets would probably generate different mental images than the absence of freedom in socialistic, or collectivistic markets where the future choice sets are determined by self-appointed elites.

Given a set of initial market conditions, the metaphor of biology asks the question: what happens next when new technology appears in the market? Technology is the biological equivalent of genetics and knowledge is the equivalent of food that gets eaten in a market to provide mental energy to apply technology.

Applying the biological metaphor of evolution, predicting what happens next in a market depends on what type of novelty is introduced into the environment. If the novelty is in the form of an existing asexual product technology, the genetics being passed on by the parent product may result in a form of competitive adaptation between the offspring competitor product and the parent product, with little effect on the aggregate final demand for both products.

If the novelty is in the form of an entirely new technological product, the entire final demand marketplace may change, which would cause changes in the other parts of the products and complementary products as the humans changed their relationships in order to adapt to each other's behavior.

The changes in behavior are reflected in choices and decisions made by consumers, and the behavior acts as a communication or signaling mechanism to other humans, in much the same role that neoclassical economists suppose that prices act as a signaling mechanism that equilibrates supply and demand. But, the object of inquiry in evolutionary economics is human behavior in the presence of novelty, not the behavior of prices, holding the behavior of humans constant.

Strategies that improve individual welfare over the long term require that humans anticipate the future and learn from mistakes in a life-long behavior modification process. A choice that looks rational and optimal at today's prices may turn out to be not optimal in the long run, and consequently, the behavior would be modified to overcome the mistake.

Short term price-based decisions made by consumers depend on temporary, fleeting, relationships that occur as the Walraisiain auctioneer instantaneously clears all markets at all times, both now and in the future.

Longer-term strategies are time-based, not price-based, and depend on how permanent relationships are modified. Most of the permanent relationships require the anticipation of who to trust in future exchanges based upon reciprocity and mutuality.

Predicting Technology

Given a certain set of civil rules and the rule of law, markets would evolve differently than under another set of civil rules or the absence of the rule of law. Laws and customs determine prices in the market, and consequently, also determine income distribution, not the other way around.

Markets are like natural ecological environments. Human behavior in the market environment can be observed, and certain types of generalizations about human behavior can be derived from the observations. Sometimes, the behavior takes on the form of regularities, which occur with high degrees of certainty, given certain environmental conditions.

When these behaviors occur with some high frequency, the behaviors can be described as having law-like properties that have the logical pattern: "If such-and-such environmental conditions occur, then we would expect humans to exhibit such-and-such behaviors."

A prior task to explaining and predicting human behavior in market environments involves describing what constitutes a "market." Lord Keynes made a distinction between the final demand markets, and the intermediate demand markets. Alfred Marshall described labor markets and capital markets.

Recent writers have described "knowledge" markets and "information" markets. These different descriptions of markets raise the scientific issue of whether there is any authoritative definition in economic literature that describes the concept of "market" that provides a common interpretation for all markets. If a common definition can be found of markets, then different markets can be compared, using a scientific method that analyzes the prior, existing, and future time periods.

A survey of economic literature reveals a surprising lack of attention to defining the concept of "market." Most articles and books begin by assuming that a Cobbs-Douglas production function adequately describes how products are made in a "market." Products are made with capital and labor, and consumers, based upon the lowest price, buy products. Labor performs both a production function in making products and a consumption function as households in buying products.

Capital also performs a dual function. Capital serves as equipment that produces goods, and serves as the intelligence function to guide investment capital to its highest and best use. Just as labor has a dual personality, capital has a dual personality, both as equipment on the manufacturing floor of the industrial plant, and as intelligence, embodied in the synthetic brains of "capitalists," who are conceived as a synthetic collectivist class of humans.

A better scientific approach is to carefully delineate the difference between an economy and a market. Professor Paul A. David observed that "…the full impact of technological change on the economy is revealed only after the technology has been embodied in a facilitating structure of cooperating and complementary technologies and organizational structures."[372]

Presumably, when David uses the term "structure" to describe both cooperating technologies and organizations, he means the structure of market relationships, but this interpretation is not clear from his writings.

Markets, the way that David uses the term, could mean something other than facilitating structures and organizational structures that cooperate. Humans cooperate sometimes, in certain kinds of relationships, but suggesting that technologies and organizations cooperate is a good example of anthropomorphic ascription, where synthetic variables are imagined to possess human characteristics.

Feser improves the precision of David's definition of markets by placing the behavior of cooperation in the context of human relationships that occur as "interrelationships between economic actors" within a geographic cluster of firms. Feser cites the work of Ben Chinitz who placed the term "structure" in the context of how humans learn from each other in industrial districts.

As Feser explained, "...it is not just the size of the district alone, but social, cultural, and political factors, including trust, business customs, social ties, and other institutional considerations."[373] Feser's improvement is to distinguish between economic production, which he defines in terms of input-output models and industrial clusters of economic producers, and the surrounding region, which constitutes the market environment.

Griliches notes, "technical change is the result of conscious economic investments and explicit decisions by many different economic *units*. (emphasis added.).[374]

"In the static model," states Winch, "we assume that technology is given and unchanging. Commodities can be produced only by use of scarce factors, and there are maximum amounts of products that can be produced from any given bundle of factor inputs."[375] The existing technology is held constant, while the resulting change in technology, if any, is assumed to be an externality.

In Holland's interpretation of hidden order, adaptations are rule based changes in behavior. Most of the adaptive behavior is based upon adapting to other humans, through a process of learning and mental anticipations. Humans anticipate the future just like they anticipate the possible sequences of moves in a game of chess.

In the presence of novelty, the old rules and routines may not be adequate for the situation, and humans combine time-tested old rules and routines with new hypothesis to anticipate what may happen next. Applying Holland's interpretation of hidden order to the workings of the market provides a contrast to the neoclassical equilibrium interpretation of technology as an external given that does not change.

"From the classical point of view, markets should always clear rapidly," states Holland, "moving in narrow ranges dictated by changing supply and demand...economic theory is built around agents of perfect rationality – agents that can perfectly foresee the consequences of their actions, including the reactions of other agents."[376]

In contrast to neoclassical theory, Holland's interpretation of markets is that they are complex adaptive systems where humans anticipate the future and attempt to make decisions based upon their mental hypothesis about what may happen next. New markets emerge when the old rules and old behavior adaptations do not fit the changing structure of relationships that humans have with each other as a result of the novel circumstances brought about by the introduction of new technology.

Individuals in markets are busy creating their own futures, and the markets that emerge in the future are a result of individual decisions that affect both their own life destiny and change the economic environment as their decisions are implemented. Markets emerge as a result of a growing common perception in the brains of humans in a defined geographical territory about the implications of the novelty.

Evolutionary processes within a complex adaptive system happen very slowly. Sometimes, for long periods of time, as Kimura reminds us, very little happens at all. It takes humans a long time to interpret and apply the implications of novelty.

The biological metaphor of markets begins with the assumption that users of goods in a market, and producers of goods in the market cannot be aware of the technological properties of new goods before they are created, and become aware of them very slowly once they are introduced into the market. "Consumer wants and preferences are created gradually by means of a learning process involving both producers and consumers," states Frenken.[377]

Berten Martens conceives of markets as trading systems that reduce uncertainty between the traders about what may happen next. For Martens, the market itself, provides a valuable function to traders for exchanging information and knowledge about the future. The sharing of information and knowledge reduces risk as a result of allowing traders to form common expectations about the future. Part of the common expectations involves gaining information about who to trust.

For Martens, markets are not about technology that gets passed on from generation to generation, it is behavior algorithms that get passed on.

"Societies that allow specialization and trading systems to emerge thus have an evolutionary advantage over societies that do not...Communication and trading systems require only the reproduction of a small subset of a "parents" behavioral algorithm to any other recipient."[378]

While the outcomes of the trading system in Martens' conception of the market are easily understood, in the sense that as transaction costs go down, the rate of information and innovation go up, if the real world operated like the ideal efficient, equilibrium world, "...the difference between private and social costs can never exceed the level of transaction costs."[379]

The logical philosophical linkage between declining transaction costs and what happens next is that product technological innovation depends on the exchange of loyalty, trust, and truth. In the presence of uncertainty about the future, and a lack of prices to guide decisions about who to trust, the values that are exchanged between traders are trust, not prices on products. Declining transaction costs, by themselves, do not create the conditions for information exchange.

Trust allows human imagination in the realm of economic behaviors to be fulfilled over a long period of time, which may eventually lead to the emergence of new markets, if the cultural value of trust is inherited over successive generations. Trust is a moral and cultural value that is inherited when the social and legal structure is characterized by a certain configuration of civil rules of exchange and laws regarding property and appropriation of profit.

For the Coase theorem to explain the future direction of the economy, prices in the current market would need to be related to the creation and transmittal of trust, not to the idealized return to harmony.

Current market selection leads to future market emergence very slowly because wants and preferences develop gradually, as consumers learn about product technology and as they shift preferences from older product technology to newer product technology. The learning process takes time, and in addition to learning about product technology, it takes humans much time to overcome earlier mistakes in selection because humans are slow to change personal behavior patterns.

The current learning process is informed and shaped by the future expectations and mental images each human is creating as the future options come slowly into mental focus.

As future options come slowly into mental focus, the economic environment may be changing to present even greater choice sets as complementary markets are created. A decision in the current time period may lead to an unexpected, unanticipated opportunity in the next time period as a result of the complex adaptive behavior that occurred in the mental images of other humans when they first saw the innovation.

When the current relationships encounter the new opportunities in the complementary market niches, the evolutionary environment becomes ripe for market bifurcation, where the new market environment looks completely different than what currently exists.

In addition to retaining Lord Keynes' description of final demand and intermediate demand markets, a new language of markets would include current markets, future markets, and complementary markets, and the bifurcation points of time between these time periods. Predicting what happens next, when the new products are created, depends on how humans respond to novelty.

The response is not based upon the price of the new product but on how the new product fits into the mental images of the humans as they gauge their future options. Often, the behavior would include not selecting the new product, but watching to see what happens to other humans who do buy the new product.

The most important economic fact is that the new product appears in the future market, not that the new product is assigned a price. The appearance of the new product may cause common expectations to form in the brains of individuals. The new common expectations about the future may cause humans to create complementary products related to the new product.

The complementary products provide an entirely new selection environment, where earlier decisions that may have been the best at that time, are no longer optimal, requiring behavior modification and behavior adaptation. There is a type of auto regressive evolutionary process involved in the emergence of new markets because the units of analysis themselves affect the rate of change of evolution in the market.

The direction of the philosophical inquiry for evolutionary economics shifts attention from prices and equilibrium to how and why new products, new technology and new firms are created. Product innovation, and the regional economy's ability to stimulate or thwart economic change become more important for understanding and predicting what may happen next.

The institutions of the regional economy, as observed in market relationships, provide the framework for observing "...the communications and interactions between people as well as between organizations and thus feeds the process of technical, organizational and institutional change."[380] The market, and its description as an environment, becomes the theoretical focal point for explaining economic behavior.

The structure of the relationships in the market provides the analytical framework for conducting the scientific inquiry of economic behavior in production of goods and services. The relationships of interest between markets and economics are those involving how firms and consumers communicate with each other and how their relationships change over time.

Within any distinct region, the mental images and perceptions about the future tend to be shared by firms and consumers. Part of the common perception about the future has the effect of reducing the risk associated with creating new firms and new products. Part of the common perception of the future within a region is based upon intermediate and complementary markets whose stability over any 20-year time period acts as an insurance policy to reduce risk associated with the creation of new products and new ventures.

Part of the dynamic market behavior within the region is that existing firms have a vested financial interest in creating common perceptions that continue the status quo into the future because their capital investments in current technology are so difficult to alter if they must compete with new technology.

Part of the analytical framework of neoclassical economics regarding the return to equilibrium is correct, but not because of the dynamics of prices that tend to equate supply and demand.

What happens in an environment when innovation occurs is that many different humans see the phenomena and use many different mental images to interpret the meaning of the innovation. The slow emergence of a common perception among different humans means that the market is providing the validity of the interpretation.

When many mental images reach the same conclusion and behavior is based upon the interpretation, the meaning of the innovation is validated across the market environment.

The market interpretation could easily be validated by common perceptions without being scientifically accurate or truthful. If everyone in a market "believes" the same thing, and sees the same future, then it is likely that much of the behavior will conform to the common perceptions.

This is somewhat similar to Jean Baptiste Say stating that supply creates its own demand, except in an evolutionary way, the future resembles the past because no one can imagine that the future could be different. If the future must look like the past, then there is no rational basis for trying to obtain high paying jobs or creating new ventures based upon technological innovations.

A diverse and changing income distribution in a market environment is an essential pre-condition for allowing the market structure to change and evolve. It is also, following the work of DeSoto, a pre-condition for eradicating poverty in third world countries.

As a part of the description of the analysis of economic change, the political forces which resist change must be modeled and understood, from within the theoretical framework of heredity and genetics. From a regional economic evolutionary perspective, the theory must answer the same question Edward Constant asks about technology: "What is it that evolves? What is the unit of heredity?"[381]

Technology evolves in products, and technical characteristics of products are inherited. Political power is also inherited as a result of laws enduring over generations and the units of analysis are humans whose behavior is defined by cultural values.

Given a certain type of prior social and political conditions in political power and cultural values, the economy could be predicted to take a certain type of trajectory. Given another constellation of political power, the economy would maintain the status quo. In terms of evolutionary logic, the social and political conditions represent the "environment" within which the units of analysis adapt or modify their behavior.

The units of analysis are born into their environment, and do not control where they are born. However, once they are born in the environment, each unit of analysis imagines the future differently, because mental images are unique to each individual. There is a Bayesian probability attached to each configuration of political power and cultural values, based upon the degree of belief about the future held in the mental images of humans in a distinct geography.

The general analytical terms used to describe the evolution of the market are: social structure, interindustry structure, information networks, industrial clusters, and metro regions. These analytical variables do not possess purposeful or intentional human behavior, and they do not describe units of analysis with mental reflexive capacity.

The terms are like scientific and analytical instruments in a laboratory used as tools by scientists use to measure and record the results of experiments. Only individual humans have mental reflective capabilities, and as a result of these natural capabilities, humans shape the evolutionary path of the market in a LaMarkian process. The analytical tools are the accounting and measurement categories that allow regional economic change to be recorded and described.

The analytical framework for economic evolution is based upon an analysis of how the social structure affects the economic structure as captured by coefficients in input-output accounting models as they change over time.

To provide a partial answer to Edward Constant's question, the structure of the institutional social structure is described by the following types of concepts. These institutional concepts represent assets or a stock of assets in a social structure, measured at different points in time, and the values associated with them are expected to change, based upon evolutionary principles. In order to gauge and measure how the changes in affects the genetic technology of products at future intervals of time, another set of market variables are measured and analyzed for rates of change.

In other words, the underlying premise or first assumption of SERET, is that as the conditions in the social environment change, new opportunities for genetic technological combinations and mutations appear, which can be tried out, or "selected" by the environment.

These types of variables represent flows of assets during periods of time, and the rates of change are expected to increase or decrease according to evolutionary principles. In order to evaluate the evolutionary changes in both the stocks and the flows of variables related to the market infrastructure, the concept of time, and the passage of time must be incorporated into the analysis.

In other words, in evolutionary theory, the basic premise is that some event or condition in a prior time period affects, or "maps on to" events in later time periods. The basic causal mechanism of mapping from the past to the future is the genetic transfer between generations. The prior conditions set the environmental constraints within which the "units of analysis" adapt or modify their behavior.

The preferred method of incorporating time is to create an imaginary boundary between prior conditions, current conditions and future conditions. These imaginary distinctions are shown in the diagram below along the vertical axis, moving from prior to future conditions within each structure. The lines separating the time boundaries represent the application of evolutionary principles.

Table 8.1. Concepts Used to Describe and Measure Changes in Market Structure.

1. Institutional Economic Interindustry Structural Concepts
   1. Degree of technological closeness within the regional intermediate matrix.
   2. Degree of technological diversity with the regional intermediate matrix.
   3. Number of industrial cluster niches in regional market.
   4. Location quotient of Multi National Corporations within the regional market.

2. Institutional Social/Political Structure Concepts
   1. Degree of individual civil liberties and civil rights.
   2. Degree of property ownership rights and rights to transfer title of property.
   3. Number of voluntary membership civic clubs and civic/ professional organizations.
   4. Degree of population ethnic diversity.
   5. Degree of occupational diversity.
   6. Degree of interlocking networks in civic, social and professional organizations.
   7. Number and diversity of non-government media and communication channels.

3. Institutional Information Network Structural Concepts
   1. Infrastructure of telecommunications and mass media.
   2. Number of mobile communication devices in use.
   3. Number of journals, newspapers, websites.

Table 8.2. Variables Used to Measure and Describe Changes to the Regional Market Structure.

1. Economic Units of Analysis
   1. Rate of venture capital profits from "exit" events.
   2. Rate of venture capital and angel investments in new products.
   3. Rate of institutional capital investment in new production technology.
   4. Birth rate of new ventures producing technologically new products.
   5. Birth rate of new ventures producing newer versions of older products.
   6. Rate of old product obsolescence and life-cycle.
   7. Death rate of companies producing older products.
   8. Death rate of new ventures creating new technological products.
   9. Rate of mass layoffs in multi national branch plants located in region.
   10. Rate of new jobs created in multi national branch plants located in region.
   11. Rate of commercial or other institutional bank loans to existing companies.

2. Social and Political Units of Analysis
   1. Rate of personal wealth creation.
   2. Rate of property or title transfers on personal or business property.
   3. Rate of per capita income growth or decline.
   4. Rate of political turnover in elected and appointed government positions.
   5. Rate of net population in-migration.
   6. Rate of personal property crime and business fraud.

3. Information Network Units of Analysis
   1. Rate of speed of information diffusion/contagion of new ideas.
   2. Rate of marketing or advertising expenditures on new products.
   3. Rate of political campaign contributions to incumbents.

In other words, the antecedent conditions changed into the current conditions as a result of some factors or forces, and the purpose of evolutionary economic theory is to provide the explanation of why historical conditions changed to evolve into the current conditions.

Then, based upon the application of rules and regularities that have scientific "law-like" properties, the future market structure is predicted, based upon the application of Bayesian statistical analysis of the prior beliefs about how humans "see" the future in a the defined geographical area.

At the same time that evolutionary principles are affecting the structural characteristics of the environment between the past and the present, evolutionary principles can be applied within a time period. Along the horizontal axis in the diagram below, the antecedent social institutional factors are described affecting the antecedent economic structure, for that same period of time.

In the logical theoretical framework of evolutionary economics described in the diagram, the social structure affects the economic structure, which is then shown affecting the market structure.

In an expanded diagram, the market structure would be shown in a feedback loop affecting the social and political structure, as a result of either bifurcations or adaptive behavior. The logical linkage from the market to the social political structure is a result of competition and rent seeking behavior related to income distribution, not prices.

Diagram 8.3. "Incorporating Passage of Time Into the Analytical Framework of Market Evolution," below is further broken into 12 components along the vertical and horizontal axis, and each component is labeled from one to twelve.

Each sub-component describes a set of hypothesis related to the effect one set of evolutionary principles has on the structural characteristics of the environment. For ease of explanation, each component in the diagram is shown with an abbreviation, such as C1, to describe the testable hypothetical relationships between the antecedent institutional structure and the antecedent economic structure.

Applying Bayesian statistical analysis for each component provides data values that can explain what is happening in the time period under analysis, and also answer the major theoretical question of what may happen next in terms of market emergence.

For example, the Bayesian analysis can be applied to both the average technological production coefficients under the current regional production feasibility frontier, in other words, the average production techniques currently in use, and to the "best practice" coefficients, when they first appear in the regional economy.

The relationship between the average a_{ij} and the best practice a_{ij} provides some estimates of probability distribution at future points in time of how the regional economy would evolve under adaptive behavior responses. Regional production technology improves over time as a result of local searches, in other words, adaptive behavior, by owners of firms, who imitate the most recent best practice of their competitors.

The imitation of best practice in production is akin to passing along genetics in the production side of the economy. Passing along best practice genetics is like a production efficiency improvement, which has the effect of dropping production costs, which drops profits, while the market is saturated with lower priced goods produced by the best practices.

The Bayesian statistical analysis would also be applied to beliefs and expectations in the current period that related to the appearance of entirely new technological coefficients in the regional economic interindustry matrix. The appearance of something new, in this case a new technological product, causes humans to imagine the future possibilities the new thing creates. The future that they are imagining creates the conditions of contingency that the Bayesian analysis can investigate.

Predicting Technology

Diagram 8.3.

Part I. Asexual Product Technology in an Adaptive Market Environment

Status Quo→Economic Decline

Antecedent Evolutionary Principles →maps Structure	Antecedent Evolutionary Economic Principles →maps Structure	Antecedent Institutional Market Structure

(transformation matrix)

Component I   *Component II*

Passage of time

↓ maps onto   ↓ maps onto   ↓ maps onto
Component III   *Component IV*   *Component V*

Current →maps onto Institutional Structure	Current →maps onto Economic Structure	Current Market Structure

Component VI   *Component VII*
Passage of time

↓ maps onto   ↓ maps onto   ↓ maps onto
Component VIII   *Component IX*   *Component X*

Future Institutional Structure	Future Economic Structure	Future Market Structure

Part II. Sexual Product Genetic Technology Cross Breeding with Contingent Market Selection Behavior

Bifurcation   →Emergence of New Markets

Current →maps onto Institutional Structure	Current →maps onto Economic Structure	Future Market Structure

Component XI   *Component XII*

Given a set of prior expectations about the future, the novelty may cause a new set of expectations, which can provide probability distributions or estimates of the most likely future that may emerge. The new thing may cause new coefficients to appear in the matrix of production coefficients as contingent and complementary markets are created to accommodate the new expectations of the future.

The market, which emerges in the future time period, as a result of sexual crossover in product technology, evolved from the market in current time period, but it is a different future market, as reflected by the different coefficients in the transactions table.

On the other hand, if habits do not change and resistance to the new thing are strong enough within the regional social and political institutional structure, expectations about the future may not change, in which case future markets will not emerge, and evolutionary processes will most likely cease, causing the regional market to decline.

The coefficients in the transaction table would disappear, reflecting a "hollowing out" of the regional economy, as it approached a future point of decline and possible economic extinction. Markets, viewed as a biological entity, can become hostile environments to the humans, which inhabit them, and can experience long periods of stagnation and decline.

Observing the emergence of a future market is like trying to focus on a small oscillating moving window of time, a type of threshold Bayesian event that becomes progressively clearer as the future market becomes the current market.

The Bayesian window is either evolving upwards, in terms of economic growth, through a threshold event, called a bifurcation, or it is devolving through another type of threshold event. The oscillations towards the future market become progressively smaller as the transition from the current to the future market is approached because fewer and fewer variables can change, and the rate and scope of change becomes progressively restricted.

Once the market slips through the Bayesian window, it can never go back in time, and for upward bifurcations, the future market will look nothing like the current market, except in historical terms to note that it evolved out of the current market.

The middle component in the diagram, the economic structure, can also be called the "transformation matrix" because this is where resources are transformed into products. The transformation matrix describes the regional production technology, or the recipe for using resources that are transformed into products, and is captured as production coefficients in the transaction tables of a regional input-output model.

In the initial stages of regional production, the regional recipe for making a product is different in a specific region, but as the product move down the life cycle towards a mass global market, production technology for producing the product becomes homogenized across all regions. Regional production technology evolves based upon adaptive behavior, but the causal mechanism for adaptive evolution of markets is products, not production.

Products evolve based upon the selection of consumers in market environment, and the products selected by consumers are determined by their incomes, not the costs of production. The costs of production, and therefore also their prices, are always in a timeless movement downward until they reach the point where it does not make any economic sense to produce them.

The basic concept described in the diagram is that in a market characterized by asexual adaptive behavior, the most recent technological version of the product displaces the parent product. The new and better version is bought first by the highest income classes because the new product's price is higher than the earlier version and it contains new technology that the highest income classes are most likely to have seen and used before.

The higher income classes have an income level that allows them to take the greatest risk in making a risky new version purchase.

As newer versions of the product enter the market, the earlier technological versions drift down in price and are bought by lower income classes. Even as the market widens, the contribution to net marginal profits from the earlier product version is declining.

At some point in the product's life cycle, the contribution of the earlier versions of the product to the firm's revenue are not sufficient to cover replacement of production equipment on the plant floor to produce it. This is the basic economic process captured by neoclassical marginal economic theory for an existing asexual market. In biology, Mueller's Ratchet of Inbreeding describes this process.

Taking just one of the components from Diagram 8.3. of the current market structure and expanding it to describe how incomes determine the evolution of the market can help explain this concept. Diagram 8.4., below, breaks the earlier diagram into 2 theoretical component parts and for each component part, issues testable hypothesis to explain how the economy at a point in time is evolving, and describes, for that moment in time, the trajectory that the economy is following to the future markets.

The hypothesis described in Diagram 8.4. explains how historical and current asexual behavior causes certain types of market configurations. The purpose of the application of biological evolutionary theory is to issue predictions for all the components in the following 12 diagrams about how the current time period evolves into the future time period based upon evolutionary principles.

Diagram 8.4. Current Market Demand in an Asexual Economic Environment Where Parent Products Compete With Technologically Superior Offspring.

Product X-1 Newest A_{ij} Best Practice Manufacturing	Selected by Highest Income Class	Highest Price Contributes Greatest Marginal Profit
Product X-2 Next Most Recent Product A_{ij}	Selected by Lower Income Classes as Price Drops	Declining Marginal Revenues, Even as Market Widens
Product X-3 Second Generation Product A_{ij} Mass Production for Mass Global Market	Lower Income Classes Buy Earlier Technological Versions of Product as Price Continues to Decline	Zero Marginal Revenues Contributed to Firm
Product X-4 First Generation, Earliest Version A_{ij} Parent Product Becomes Technologically Obsolete, Displaced by Offspring	Product is Thrown Away by Existing Users	No Legacy Marginal Revenues Exist from Prior Product Sales

Table 8.5. Component One. Asexual, Adaptive Environment.
Historical Institutional Structure to Economic Structure.

Antecedent Institutional Structure	Evolutionary Principles maps onto (aka *transformation matrix*)	Antecedent Economic Structure
Institutional Historical Hypothesis	*maps onto*	Economic Historical Hypothesis

C. 1. The region's historical institutional structure can be described in terms of rules and laws that govern property rights and appropriation of profits by private for-profit companies.	C. 1. The regional historical economic structure can be described in terms of the "closeness" of technological coefficients in the regional interindustry transaction table.
C. 1. A. The greater the historical endowment of constitutionally protected property rights and rights associated with the appropriation of profits, the greater the historical rate of knowledge creation and knowledge diffusion.	C. 1. A. New technological knowledge diffuses faster in regional economies characterized by closeness in the historical endowment of technological coefficients. The diffusion is associated with the rate of knowledge contagion within firms in the industrial cluster.
C. 1. B. The greater the extent and range of individual freedoms and constitutionally-protected rights associated with the administration of justice and the rule of law, the greater the upward occupational mobility of the population from generation to generation.	C. 1. B. The greater the "closeness" in economic structure, the greater the historical rates of knowledge creation and diffusion among private firms, the greater the rates of "adaptation" and imitation of production techniques among firms which share a similar production technology.
C. 1. C. The greater the rate of profit appropriation and the greater the rate of private property title transfers in the prior period, the greater the amount of legacy capital from historical exit events that serves as a potential source or supply of investments capital.	C. 1. C. The greater the historical rate of profits from exit events, the greater the potential rate of new venture creation in the regional industrial clusters.

C. 1. D. The greater the historical rate of upward occupational and social mobility the greater the rate of new venture creation.	C. 1. D. The greater the historical rate of new venture creation, the greater the technological diversity in both production and asexual product innovation and the faster the technological possibility frontier is depleted.
C. 1. E. The longer the duration and stability of income distribution in the region, the greater the potential for permanent income classes based upon political rent seeking in legislative affairs aimed at protecting the existing distribution of income.	C. 1. E. The more permanent the income class structure, the greater the rate of debt financed new ventures and debt financed production innovation in manufacturing technology compared to equity financed innovation.
C. 1. F. The more rent seeking behavior, the greater the political power of commercial bankers and financial institutional elites to direct the future trajectory of the technology of the regional industrial cluster. The more control bankers have over the direction of the regional economy, the more the economy shifts from innovation to a "rentier" economy.	C. 1. F. The greater the debt financed innovation the less diversity in the regional industrial clusters and the lower the rate of new technological knowledge creation the more economically dependent the region becomes on global sources of demand. The shift from an innovation economy to a rentier economy is accompanied by increased use of political mechanisms to recruit branch operations of global corporations.

Predicting Technology

Table 8.6. Component Two. Asexual, Adaptive Environment.
Historical Economic Structure to Historical Market Structure.

Antecedent Economic Structure	Evolutionary Principles maps onto (aka *selectin matrix*)	Antecedent Market Structure
C. 2. The regional historical economic structure can be described in terms of the "closeness" of technological coefficients in the regional interindustry transaction table		C. 2. The region's historical market structure can be described along two dimensions, one for intermediate and final demand products, and one for the income classes of consumers who select products.
C. 2. A. New technological knowledge diffuses faster in regional economies characterized by closeness in the historical endowment of technological coefficients. The diffusion is associated with the rate of knowledge contagion.		C. 2. A. The greater the rate of knowledge diffusion, the more likely consumers will have seen prior product variations, and the more likely they are to adapt new variations which they select over the prior variations.
C. 2. B. The greater the "closeness" in economic structure, the greater the historical rates of knowledge creation and diffusion among private firms, the greater the rates of "adaptation" and imitation of production techniques among firms which share a similar production technology.		C. 2. B. The closer the technological coefficients in the industrial cluster, the greater the historical rate of product imitation, and asexual product innovation in both intermediate and final demand markets.
C. 2. C. The greater the historical rate of profits from exit events, the greater the potential rate of new venture creation in the regional industrial clusters.		C. 2. C. The greater rate of entrepreneurial new venture creation, the larger the upper income classes and the more likely that new higher priced products will be selected when they first appear.

256

C. 2. D. The greater the historical rate of new venture creation, the greater the technological diversity in both production and asexual product innovation and the faster the technological possibility frontier is depleted.	C. 2. D. The faster the rate of asexual product selection of new products, the faster the product life cycle as product variations work their way through the lower income classes as prices on older versions drop.
C. 2. E. The more permanent the income class structure, the greater the rate of debt financed new ventures and debt financed production innovation in manufacturing technology compared to equity financed innovation.	C. 2. E. The greater the debt financing in production the greater the homogenization of products aimed at the global final demand market, and the more dependent consumers in the region become of products produced for the mass global market.
C. 2. F. The greater the debt financed innovation the less diversity in the regional industrial clusters and the lower the rate of new technological knowledge creation.	C. 2. F. The greater the historical rate of product selection of global mass produced products, the faster the decline in regional knowledge creation and diffusion within the regional intermediate demand market.

Predicting Technology

**Table 8.7. Component Three. Asexual, Adaptive Environment.
Antecedent Institutional Structure to Current Institutional Structure.**

Antecedent Institutional Structure	Passage of Time Evolutionary Principles maps onto	Current Institutional Structure
C. 3. The region's historical institutional structure can be described in terms of rulesand laws that govern property rights and appropriation of profits by private for-profit companies.		C. 3. The region's current institutional structure is described by the historical endowment of constitutional rights, and the divisions of social classes based upon wealth and unequal ability to manipulate laws and rules not subject to democratic procedures.
C. 3. A. The greater the historical endowment of constitutionally protected property rights and rights associated with the appropriation of profits, the greater the historical rate of knowledge creation and knowledge diffusion.		C. 3. A. Regional social structures characterized by the greatest individual freedoms and adherence to democratic rules of procedure have the greatest diversity and variety in knowledge creation and diffusion.
C. 3. B. The greater the extent and range of individual freedoms and constitutionally-protected rights associated with the administration of justice and the rule of law, the greater the upward occupational mobility of the population from generation to generation.		C. 3. B. Regional social structures with the greatest historical rates of upward occupational mobility have the greatest current rates of wealth creation and the fastest rates of economic growth, described by output per person.
C. 3. C. The greater the rate of profit appropriation and the greater the rate of private property title transfers in the prior period, the greater the amount of legacy capital from historical exit events that serves as a potential source or supply of investments capital.		C. 3. C. The greater the historical rates of profit appropriation from exit events the more concentrated the wealth and income is in the upper income classes. The more concentrated wealth becomes, the more political rent seeking is aimed at maintaining the existing distribution of wealth and patterns of income.

C. 3. D. The greater the historical rate of upward occupational and social mobility the greater the historical rate of new venture creation.	C. 3. D. The greater the historical rates of new venture creation the greater the current social conflict between the social classes that favor the status quo and those who favor social mobility and diversity.
C. 3. E. The longer the duration and stability of income distribution in the region, without new sources of genetic diversity, the greater the potential for permanent income classes based upon political rent seeking in legislative affairs aimed at protecting the existing distribution of income.	C. 3. E. The more laws that are passed protecting the current distribution of income the less sympathetic the regional economic environment is to technological innovation via new venture creation. The greater the political influence on income distribution, the more the level of prices is determined by political manipulation.
C. 3. F. The more rent seeking behavior, the greater the political power of commercial bankers and financial institutional elites to direct the future trajectory of the technology of the regional industrial cluster.	C. 3. F. The greater the current political power of commercial bankers and financial elites to control the debt versus equity investment of legacy pools of capital, the greater the allegiance to the existing status quo distribution of wealth and income.
C. 3. G. The greater the use of political rent seeking to direct the trajectory of the economy, the more risky and uncertain the environment becomes for new venture creation of technologically new products financed by equity.	C. 3. G. The greater the allegiance to the status quo distribution of income, the greater the rate of "harvesting" the existing firms for exit profits in the current period, and the greater the rate of genetic inbreeding.

Predicting Technology

Table 8.8. Component Four. Asexual, Adaptive Environment.
Antecedent Economic Structure to Current Economic Structure.

Antecedent Economic Structure	Passage of Time Application of Evolutionary Principles maps onto	Current Economic Structure
C4. The regional historical economic structure can be described in terms of the "closeness" of technological coefficients in the regional interindustry transaction table.		C4. The historical structure of interindustry relations as described by a regional input-output transaction matrix can be updated and modified by the Feser technique to describe technological linkages in current industrial technological clusters.
C. 4. A. New technological knowledge diffuses faster in regional economies characterized by closeness in the historical endowment of technological coefficients. The diffusion is associated with the rate of knowledge contagion within firms in the industrial cluster.		C. 4. A. The initial historical endowment of technological knowledge defines the boundaries of the regional production possibilities frontier, which is the region's current endowment of genetic technological variation which can be "expressed" as technology diffuses.
C. 4. B. The greater the "closeness" in economic structure, the greater the historical rates of knowledge creation and diffusion among private firms, the greater the rates of "adaptation" and imitation of production techniques among firms which share a similar production technology.		C. 4. B. The greater the historical rate of knowledge contagion the greater the current rate of imitation and adaptation of production technology among firms within regional technological clusters as a result of firms sharing knowledge when "boundary-crosser" returns to his firm.
C. 4. C. The greater the historical rate of profits from exit events, the greater the potential rate of new venture creation in the regional industrial clusters.		C. 4. C. New firm creation and existing firm death rates in the region are defined by a theoretical maximum based upon the speed at which the technological endowment in the PPF is used up as technological gene pool is expressed.

C. 4. D. The greater the historical rate of new venture creation, the greater the technological diversity in both production and asexual product innovation and the faster the technological possibility frontier is depleted.	C. 4. D. The historical rates of new venture creation and firm death rates determines the existing current level of possible investment opportunities for legacy capital to fund, based upon the historical "exit" events.
C. 4. E. The more permanent the income class structure, the greater the rate of debt financed new ventures and debt financed production innovation in manufacturing technology compared to equity financed innovation.	C. 4. E. The greater the rate of debt financing on both new ventures and existing companies, the more dependent the regional economy becomes on global final demand and the weaker the interindustry interindustrial linkages in the regional technological industrial cluster.
C. 4. F. The greater the historical rate of debt financed innovation the less diversity in the regional industrial clusters and the lower the rate of new technological knowledge creation. At a certain threshold value, there is a Bayesian probability that the loss of genetic diversity causes the regional environment to lose its ability to generate new technological knowledge.	C. 4. F. The lower current rates of knowledge creation the greater the current rate of economic decline as the regional production possibilities frontier is exhausted without replacing the genetic diversity as it moves through a bifurcation point into the future. The genetics of technological inbreeding causes the rate of loss of genetic diversity in the regional PPF to increase.

Predicting Technology

**Table 8.9. Component Five. Asexual, Adaptive Environment.
Antecedent Market Structure to Current Market Structure.**

Antecedent Market Structure	Passage of Time Application of Evolutionary Principles maps onto	Current Market Structure
C. 5. 1. The region's historical market structure can be described along two dimensions, one for intermediate and final demand products, and one for the income classes of consumers who select products.		C. 5. 1 The history and experience of consumers within the region making selections between new versions of products and between regional goods versus global goods can be described by a final demand matrix in the region's input-output transactions table
C. 5. A. The greater the historical rate of knowledge diffusion, the more experience upper income classes have in trying out new product variations, and therefore the more likely they are to adapt new variations which they select over the prior variations.		C. 5. A. The greater the historical rate of knowledge diffusion within the market, the greater the rate of new version product selection by higher income classes in the region. In Mokyr's words, the market environment is "sympathetic" to new products.
C. 5. B. The closer the technological coefficients in the industrial cluster, the greater the historical rate of product imitation, and asexual product innovation in both intermediate and final demand markets.		C. 5. B. The more the new product version looks like and functions technologically like the older version, the faster the market rate of selection in the current period both in intermediate and final demand markets.
C. 5. C. The greater rate of entrepreneurial new venture creation, the larger the upper income classes and the more likely that new higher priced products will be selected when they first appear.		C. 5. C. The greater the rate of selection of new products versus old products, the faster the rater of product obsolescence for a specific version and the greater the faster the product life cycle is completed.

C. 5. D. The faster the rate of asexual product selection of new products, the faster the product life cycle as product variations work their way through the lower income classes as prices on older versions drop.	C. 5. D. The faster the product life cycle in both intermediate and final demand markets, the more dependent the regional market becomes on rent-seeking behavior to maintain existing markets.
C. 5. E. The greater the debt financing in production the greater the homogenization of products aimed at the global final demand market, and the more dependent consumers in the region become of products produced for the mass global market.	C. 5. E. The more dependent the regional market becomes on global sources of economic growth, the less ability the market has for creating and diffusing technological growth.
C. 5. F. The greater the historical rate of product selection of global mass produced products, the faster the decline in regional knowledge creation and diffusion within the regional intermediate demand market.	C. 5. F. The loss of the regional market's ability to transmit knowledge among firms in the regional industrial cluster, the greater the rate of speed towards economic decline.

Table 8.10. Component Six. Asexual, Adaptive Environment.
Current Institutional Structure to Current Economic Structure.

Current Institutional Structure	Evolutionary Principles maps onto	Current Economic Structure
C. 6. The region's current institutional structure is described by the historical endowment of constitutional rights, and the divisions of social classes based upon wealth and unequal ability to manipulate laws and rules not subject to democratic procedures.		C. 6. The historical structure of interindustry relations as described by a regional input-output matrix can be updated and modified by the Feser technique to describe current industrial technological clusters.
C. 6. A. A current regional social structure characterized by individual freedoms and adherence to democratic rules of procedure has the greatest diversity and variety in knowledge creation and diffusion.		C. 6. A. The initial historical endowment of technological knowledge defines the boundaries of the regional production possibilities frontier, which is the region's current endowment of genetic technological variation which can be "expressed" as technology diffuses through the regional industrial clusters.
C. 6. B. Regional social structures with the greatest historical rates of upward occupational mobility have the greatest current rates of wealth creation and the fastest rates of economic growth, described by output per person.		C. 6. B. The greater the historical rate of knowledge contagion the greater the current rate of imitation and adaptation of production technology among firms within regional technological clusters as a result of firms sharing knowledge when a "boundary-crosser" returns to his firm with new knowledge.
C. 6. C. The greater the historical rates of profit appropriation from exit events the more concentrated the wealth and income is in the upper income classes.		C. 6. C. New firm creation and existing firm death rates in the region are defined by a theoretical maximum based upon the speed at which the technological endowment in the PPF is used up as technological gene pool is expressed.

C. 6. D. The greater the historical rates of new venture creation the greater the current social conflict between the social classes that favor the status quo and those who favor social mobility and diversity.	C. 6. D. The historical rates of new venture creation and firm death rates determines the existing current level of possible investment opportunities for legacy capital to fund, based upon the historical "exit" events. The current rate of investment must be sufficient to create new future demand within the regional industrial cluster.
C. 6. E. The more laws that are passed protecting the current distribution of income the less likely social and political forces that favor individual social mobility will have for creating an economic environment that is sympathetic to technological innovation via new venture creation.	C. 6. E. The greater the rate of debt financing on both new ventures and existing companies, the more dependent the regional economy becomes on global final demand and the weaker the interindustry interindustrial linkages in the regional technological industrial cluster that cause knowledge creation and diffusion.
C. 6. F. The greater the current political power of commercial bankers and financial elites to control the debt versus equity investment of legacy pools of capital, the greater the allegiance to the existing status quo distribution of wealth and income.	C. 6. F. The lower current rates of knowledge creation the greater the current rate of economic decline as the regional production possibilities frontier is exhausted without replacing the genetic diversity as it moves through a micro bifurcation point into the future. The greater rate of homogenous clustering in the economy, the greater the rate of technological inbreeding.

Predicting Technology

Table 8.11. Component Seven. Asexual Adaptive, Environment.
Current Economic Structure to Current Market Structure.

Current Economic Structure	Evolutionary Principles maps onto	Current Market Structure
C. 7. The historical structure of interindustry relations as described by a regional input-output matrix can be updated and modified by the Feser technique to describe technological linkages in current industrial technological clusters.		C. 7. 1 The history and experience of consumers within the region making selections between new versions of products and between regional goods versus global goods can be described by a final demand matrix in the region's input-output transactions table
C. 7. A. The initial historical endowment of technological knowledge defines the boundaries of the regional production possibilities frontier, which is the region's current endowment of genetic technological variation which can be "expressed" as technology diffuses through the regional industrial clusters.		C. 7. A. The greater the historical rate of knowledge diffusion within the market, the greater the rate of new version product selection by higher income classes in the region. In Mokyr's words, the environment is "sympathetic" to new products.
C. 7. B. The greater the historical rate of knowledge contagion the greater the current rate of imitation and adaptation of production technology among firms within regional technological clusters as a result of firms sharing knowledge when a "boundary-crosser" returns to his firm with new knowledge.		C. 7. B. The more the new product version looks like and functions technologically like the older version in product mutation, the faster the market rate of selection in the current period both in intermediate and final demand markets. The selection behavior of the nearly equivalent new product by consumers is purposeful, goal oriented, and non random.
C. 7. C. New firm creation and existing firm death rates in the region are defined by a theoretical maximum based upon the speed at which the technological endowment in the PPF is used up as non-expressed genes are "called-forth" from the technological PPF.		C. 7. C. The greater the rate of selection of new products versus old products, the faster the rate of product obsolescence for a specific version and the faster the product life cycle is completed. The entire product life cycle is usually completed within 28 years.

C. 7. D. The historical rates of new venture creation and firm death rates determines the existing current level of possible investment opportunities for legacy capital to fund, based upon the historical "exit" events. The current rate of investment must be sufficient to create new future demand within the regional industrial cluster.	C. 7. D. The faster the product life cycle in both intermediate and final demand markets, the more dependent the regional market becomes on rent-seeking behavior to maintain existing markets because past equity investments are insufficient at creating adequate levels of demand within the intermediate demand industrial clusters.
C. 7. E. The greater the rate of debt financing on both new ventures and existing companies, the more dependent the regional economy becomes on global final demand and the weaker the interindustry intermediate demand linkages in the regional technological industrial cluster that cause knowledge creation and diffusion.	C. 7. E. The more dependent the regional final and intermediate demand market becomes on global sources of economic growth, the less ability the regional intermediate demand market has for creating and diffusing technological growth within the regional industrial clusters.
C. 7. F. The lower the current rates of knowledge creation the greater the current rate of economic decline as the regional production possibilities frontier is exhausted without replacing the genetic diversity as it moves through a micro bifurcation point into the future.	C. 7. F. The greater the loss of the regional intermediate demand market's ability to transmit knowledge among firms, the greater the rate of speed towards a micro bifurcation point regional economic decline characterized by Mueller's Ratchet.

Predicting Technology

Table 8.12. Component Eight. Asexual, Adaptive, Environment.
Current Institutional Structure to Future Institutional Structure.

Current Institutional Structure	Passage of Time Application of Evolutionary Principles maps onto	Future Institutional Structure
C. 8. The region's current institutional structure is described by the historical endowment of constitutional rights, and the divisions of social classes based upon wealth and unequal ability to manipulate laws and rules not subject to democratic procedures.		C. 8. The region's future institutional structure can be predicted from the trends currently in place regarding constitutional rights of citizens versus the increasing authority of government agents whose power is not constrained by the democratic consent of the governed.
C. 8. A. Regional social structures characterized by the greatest individual freedoms and adherence to democratic rules of procedure have the greatest diversity and variety in knowledge creation and diffusion.		C. 8. A. A regional institutional structure characterized by increasing human and civil rights will have the greatest potential for creating future knowledge and greater technological diversity than regions where the agents of government are increasing their authority.
C. 8. B. Regional social structures with the greatest historical rates of upward occupational mobility have the greatest current rates of wealth creation and the fastest rates of economic growth, described by output per person.		C. 8. B. Regions with the greatest rates of upward occupational mobility and the greatest increases in knowledge have the greatest opportunity for future economic growth.
C. 8. C. The greater the historical rates of profit appropriation in asexual environments from exit events the more concentrated the wealth and income is in the upper income classes.		C. 8. C. Regions characterized by the greatest rates of increased wealth concentration in the upper social classes will experience the greatest future rates of civil conflict over wealth and income distribution.

268

C. 8. D. Changes in current regional income distribution occur more slowly than price declines on standardized mass produced homogeneous products. Regions with the greatest reliance on global markets experience the greatest declines in prices and the slowest rates of change in income class distribution.	C. 8. D. Regions with the slowest current rates of income change and economic growth have the greatest future application of political power in making laws and enforcing rules of justice to maintain the status quo equilibrium of income distribution.
C. 8. D. The greater the historical rates of new venture creation the greater the current social conflict between the social classes that favor the status quo and those who favor social mobility and diversity.	C. 8. D. The greater the rates of civil conflict over individual freedoms and civil rights the more the use of the police power of the state will be used in the future to maintain the existing distribution of wealth and income.
C. 8. E. The more laws that are passed protecting the current distribution of income the less likely social and political forces that favor individual social mobility will have for creating an economic environment that is sympathetic to technological innovation via new venture creation.	C. 8. E. The greater the current power of government to maintain the existing distribution of income and power not constrained by the consent of the governed the less the future rates of technological innovation and knowledge creation from the region's social institutional structure.
C. 8. F. The greater the current political power of commercial bankers and financial elites to control the debt versus equity investment of legacy pools of capital, the greater the allegiance to the existing status quo distribution of wealth and income.	C. 8. F. The greater the political power of bankers and their use of the police power of the state to enforce their debt liens, the faster the legacy pools of regional capital will be depleted leading to future economic decline in more distant future periods of time, what Myrdal called "cumulative causation" of economic backwardness.

Predicting Technology

Table 8.13. Component Nine. Asexual, Adaptive, Environment.
Current Economic Structure to Future Economic Structure.

Current Economic Structure	Passage of Time Application of Evolutionary Principles maps onto	Future Economic Structure
C. 9. The historical structure of interindustry relations as described by a regional input-output matrix can be updated and modified by the Feser technique to describe technological linkages in current industrial technological clusters.		C. 9. The future economic structure of regional interindustry relations can be predicted by applying the changing final demand trends in the market to the current Feser transaction table using traditional Leontief matrix inversion methods.
C. 9. A. The initial historical endowment of technological knowledge defines the boundaries of the regional production possibilities frontier, which is the region's current endowment of genetic technological variation which can be "expressed" as technology diffuses through the regional industrial clusters.		C. 9. A. The current rate of genetic expression describes the rate of speed of product life cycles within the region. Applying the rate of speed of product life cycles to the regional industrial clusters defines the time limit of future economic viability as applied to the inverted regional intermediate demand matrix.
C. 9. B. The greater the historical rate of knowledge contagion the greater the current rate of imitation and adaptation of production technology among firms within regional technological clusters as a result of firms sharing knowledge when a "boundary-crosser" returns to his firm with new knowledge.		C. 9. B. The loss of interindustry linkages within the regional industrial clusters destroys the neural pathways of knowledge transfer in the future, limiting the diversity of destinations within the cluster where the "boundary-crosser" can access technological knowledge. As the technological genetic diversity declines, the knowledge frontier declines.

Thomas E. Vass

C. 9. C. New firm creation and existing firm death rates in the region are defined by a theoretical maximum based upon the speed at which the technological endowment in the PPF is used up as technological gene pool is expressed. The crossover point in the current period is defined when death rates exceed birth rates of new ventures within the industrial cluster.	C. 9. C. As the death rate of existing firms goes up in the current period, combined with the faster evolutionary rate of gene expression in PPF, the future industrial matrix contains fewer and fewer coefficients among the matrix cells, a phenomenon called "hollowing-out" by regional economists.
C. 9. D. The historical rates of new venture creation and firm death rates determines the existing current level of possible investment opportunities for legacy capital to fund, based upon the rate of successful historical "exit" events. The current rate of investment must be sufficient to create new future demand within the regional industrial cluster.	C. 9. D. The increased death rate in the current period erodes the pools of legacy capital available for creating future new ventures. Insufficient investments in new ventures in the period of time 7 years earlier leads to insufficient regional intermediate demand in the future period of time, cumulatively leading to a faster future economic decline within the region.
C. 9. E. The greater the rate of debt financing on both new ventures and existing companies, the more dependent the regional economy becomes on global final demand and the weaker the interindustry intermediate demand linkages in the regional technological industrial cluster that cause knowledge creation and diffusion.	C. 9. E. The global sources of final demand for economic growth create fewer future interindustry linkages in the complementary service and support firms within the regional clusters because global firms buy services and products from sources internal to the global corporate supply chain, not from regional sources of services.

C. 9. F. The lower the current rates of knowledge creation the greater the current rate of economic decline as the regional production possibilities frontier is exhausted without replacing the genetic diversity as it moves through a micro bifurcation point into the future.	C. 9. F. The loss of complementary regional service and support industries in the region causes the regional income and employment multipliers to decline, leading to faster future rates of economic decline, which will be more difficult to overcome because the regional genetic diversity in knowledge creation and diffusion has been destroyed.
C. 9 G. The greater the current rate of genetic asexual inbreeding in the resulting gene pool, the faster the deleterious genetic mutations are expressed in technologically obsolete products.	C. 9. G. The greater the past rates of technological specialization within the production technologies of the industrial clusters, the faster the future rates of product extinction as the market becomes saturated with technologically-homogeneous mass produced cheap products. (Haldane's single parent hypothesis).

Table 8.14. Component Ten. Asexual, Adaptive, Environment. Current Market Structure to Future Market Structure.
Adaptation Leads to Micro Bifurcation At Lower Level of Equilibrium Economic Growth Oriented to Maintaining the Status Quo Distribution of Income.

Current Market Structure	maps onto Passage of Time Application of Evolutionary Principles bifurcation	Future Market Structure
C. 10. 1. The history and experience of consumers within the region making selections between old and new versions of products and between regional goods versus global goods can be described by a final demand matrix in the region's input-output transactions table		C. 10. 1. The projections from trends from the current rates of selection that consumers are making can be applied to the final demand matrix of the current regional transaction matrix to investigate how future market relationships may change when consumers are confronted with slightly new and better products.
C. 10. A. The greater the historical rate of knowledge diffusion within the market, the greater the rate of new version product selection by higher income classes in the region. In Mokyr's words, the market environment is "sympathetic" to new products.		C. 10. A. Regions with the greatest current rates of knowledge diffusion will have the greatest future rates of economic and wealth creation in the future, with markets characterized by growing income concentration in the top social classes.
C. 10. B. The more the new asexual product version looks like and functions technologically like the older version, the faster the market rate of selection in the current period both in intermediate and final demand markets.		C. 10. B. Regional markets with the fastest rates of adaptive product innovation will have markets with the fastest rates of product adaptation by lower income classes as older versions rapidly diffuse through lower income classes as market prices drop.

C. 10. C. The greater the rate of selection of new products versus old products, the faster the rate of product obsolescence for a specific version and the faster the product life cycle is completed. The entire product life cycle is usually completed within 28 years.	C. 10. C. The faster the rate of current product life cycle obsolescence, the less the birth rate of future new ventures within the regional industrial cluster, and the greater the barriers to upward occupational mobility based upon opportunities created by the entrepreneurial new venture creation process.
C. 10. D. The faster the product life cycle in both intermediate and final demand markets, the more dependent the regional market becomes on rent-seeking behavior to maintain existing markets because past equity investments are insufficient at creating adequate levels of demand within the intermediate demand industrial clusters..	C. 10. D. The greater the political rent-seeking process in the future for attracting global sources of final demand with tax incentives, the more politicized investment decisions become for directing the future trajectory of economic growth, which leads to global corporate control over the creation and diffusion of regional technological knowledge.
C. 10. E. The more dependent the regional final and intermediate demand market becomes on global sources of economic growth, the less ability the regional intermediate demand market has for creating and diffusing technological growth within the regional industrial clusters.	C. 10. E. The current market collapse of intermediate demand markets exacerbates the future collapse of complementary markets in the regional industrial cluster, and greater future applications of the police power of the state to maintain the status quo distribution of income as the economy declines.
C. 10. F. The loss of current period regional intermediate demand in the region's industrial cluster leads to increased rates of unemployment and increased death rates and business failure and a decreased birth rate of new ventures which serve as the home of "boundary-crossers" who transmit knowledge among firms.	C. 10. F. Future markets that lose intermediate demand linkages, (nerve ganglions), lose the ability to create and diffuse technological knowledge and are characterized by a skewed wealth distribution where mobility across class lines is severely restricted by laws and rules aimed at maintaining the new lower level equilibrium status quo.

Table 8.15. Component Eleven. New Market Emergence.
Contingent Market Selection Behavior In An Environment Characterized by
Sexual Genetic Cross-Breeding of Technology in Products.

Current Economic Structure	maps onto	Current Institutional Structure
C. 11. The region's current institutional structure is described by the historical endowment of constitutional rights, and the divisions of social classes based upon wealth and unequal ability to manipulate laws and rules not subject to democratic procedures.		C. 11. The current economic structure of interindustry relations as described by a regional input-output matrix can be updated and modified by the Feser technique to describe technological linkages in current industrial technological clusters.
C. 11. A. Regional social structures characterized by the greatest individual freedoms and adherence to democratic rules of procedure have the greatest diversity and variety in knowledge creation and diffusion.		C. 11. A. The initial historical endowment of technological knowledge defines the boundaries of the regional production possibilities frontier, which is the region's current endowment of genetic technological variation which can be "expressed" as technology diffuses through the regional industrial clusters.
C. 11. B. Regional social structures with the greatest historical rates of upward occupational mobility have the greatest current rates of wealth creation and the fastest rates of economic growth, described by output per person compared to regions which do not possess these social institutional endowments.		C. 11. B. The greater the historical rate of knowledge contagion the greater the probability that new technological knowledge, obtained from the "edge" of the cluster, will be crossbred into a product with similar technological production when a "boundary-crosser" returns to his firm with new knowledge.

C. 11. C. Regions with the greatest rates of knowledge creation and diffusion have the greatest rates of mental imagination of how to commercialize new technology when a novel event occurs within the industrial cluster.	C. 11. C. Regions with a greater experience in commercializing technological innovations have the greatest rates of new venture creation and the greatest rates of success in new venture profitability because the greater experience acts as a social insurance policy for spreading risk among many new ventures.
C. 11. D. The greater the current rates of profit appropriation from exit events in an environment characterized by rapid upward occupational mobility, the greater the pool of capital available for equity investments and the more likely it becomes for former entrepreneurs with exit capital to search for and fund new ventures in the population of potential entrepreneurs that is moving upward in social and income class.	C. 11. D. The sexual crossover of genetic production technology causes the production possibilities frontier to expand outward, creating new opportunities for new firm creation from the pool of new genetic technology that can be "expressed" by investments in new ventures that are producing new technological products in the expanding regional interindustrial technology clusters.
C. 11. E. The search for possible funding opportunities occurs within the geographical boundaries of the industrial cluster and within the technological clusters the former entrepreneurs have the greatest professional experience.	C. 11. E. Two distinct product species that share similar technological production features and are located close to each other in the regional cluster have the greatest probability of sexual interbreeding

C. 11. F. The greater the rate of upward occupational mobility combined with the greater the rate of income distribution spread among social classes the greater the political allegiance to the constitutional rule of law by social classes committed to social and economic diversity versus the social classes that favor the status quo distribution of income. (What rules are fair if I were to find myself on the bottom of the heap?)	C. 11. F. The greater the stability of the rule of law the greater the risk taking of potential entrepreneurs in creating new ventures in technologically risky new products, that may not be selected by consumers. The rate of new venture creation within the industrial cluster increases over time as more and more potential entrepreneurs become aware of the opportunity to create their own companies.
C. 11. G. The greater the current rate of equity investment in new venture creation the greater the political allegiance by the entrepreneurial class to the constitutional rule of law so that future profits can be obtained by future exit events made in the current period on risky new ventures. (Adherence to the rule of law acts as the social insurance policy that underwrites risky investments).	C. 11. G. The greater the current rate of investment in new ventures that "express" the new genetic technology, the greater the rate of variety in the complementary firms in the industrial cluster that service and support the new ventures. The development of the complementary ventures possess LaMarkian evolutionary characteristics, in which a current period development is immediately causing new evolutionary environmental changes.
C. 11. H. The more political power that resides in the social classes that favor technological diversity and upward occupational mobility the less likely will be the enactment of laws that protect the current distribution of income, and the more likely that those who favor allegiance to the status quo will resort to extra-legal methods of protecting their favored distribution of income.	C. 11. H. The greater the use of extra-legal measures to maintain the status quo, the more dependent the regional economy becomes on outside sources of capital and final demand, which are attracted to the region with tax inducements. The greater the political manipulation of the economic system, the more the current economic technological structure becomes fixed around a local stable equilibrium point.

C. 11. I. The greater the current political power of social forces committed to diversity, the more open the social and institutional pathways for creating and diffusing new technological knowledge among the socially upward mobile participants of the society as opposed to the use of extra-legal power to control the diffusion of knowledge as a method of protecting the status quo distribution of wealth and income.	C. 11. I. The greater the current rates of knowledge creation and diffusion are within the current industrial clusters the greater the current rate of economic growth as the regional production possibilities frontier is pushed outward through an upward micro bifurcation point into the future. The economic structure is changing and the future structure is looking less and less like the current structure.
C. 11. J. The longer the duration of time that the society adheres to the rule of law and constitutional procedures the more difficult it becomes for those who favor the status quo to protect their distribution of income via constitutional methods and consequently, the more intense and catastrophic the civil conflict achieved through the extra-legal methods.	C. 11. J. The longer the duration of stability within the industrial cluster, the more likely that debt financing will replace equity financings of existing firms because the potential rate of return in existing firms with older technology products is not favorable compared to the multiple equity investment opportunities in new firms. Reliance on debt financing in the existing, established firms will cause the death rate of those firms to increase.
C. 11. K. Regional social structures characterized by the greatest coefficients of income class inequality and the lowest rate of growth in coefficients of occupational mobility have the greatest social and political allegiance to the status quo distribution of income.	C. 11. K. Regional social structures with the greatest allegiance to the status quo distribution of income have the greatest range of rules and laws in place restricting upward occupational mobility and creating barriers to entry of new firms into the existing industrial clusters.

Thomas E. Vass

Table 8.16. Component Twelve. New Market Emergence.
Contingent Market Selection Behavior In An Environment Characterized by Sexual Genetic Cross-Breeding of Technology In Products.

Current Economic Structure	maps onto	Future Economic Structure

C. 12. The current economic structure of interindustry relations as described by a regional input-output matrix can be updated and modified by the Feser technique to describe technological linkages in current industrial technological clusters which share similar technological features in both production and use by consumers in the current environment.	C. 12. The future market structure can be predicted from the trajectory of coefficients at Bayesian micro bifurcation points given the prior set of beliefs and behavior of consumers in their selection of new products that are a "better fit" in the environmental selection space. The "better fit" selections are between older asexual technological products and new products which are created from sexual crossover from products which share similar technological genetic features both in production and in use by consumers.
C. 12. A. The initial historical endowment of technological knowledge defines the boundaries of the current regional production possibilities frontier, which is the region's current endowment of genetic technological variation which can be "expressed" as technology diffuses through the regional industrial clusters.	C. 12. A. Regional markets currently characterized by the greatest rates of genetic technology expression in the expanding PPF present consumers with the greatest variety of new technological products to select in the future. Regions with the greatest product genetic variety have the greatest potential for new market emergence.
C. 12. B. The greater the historical rate of knowledge contagion the greater the probability that new technological knowledge, obtained from firms located at the "edge" of the cluster, will be crossbred into a product with similar technological production when a "boundary-crosser" returns to his firm with new knowledge.	C. 12. B. The greater the initial number of industrial cluster which share similar technological features in production and use, the greater the Bayesian probability that new product genetic variations that have been created will be presented to consumers for them to contingently select in the future. Regions with the greatest diversity in product innovation have the greatest probability of new market emergence.

279

C. 12. C. The closer the technological linkages in production between firms that produce genetically different products, the greater the Bayesian probability that the new crossbred product's technological features will be similar to the technological features of the two parent products.	C. 12. C. The closer the technological features of the new product to the two parent products that consumers have seen and used before, the greater the rate of product selection and market acceptance of the risky new product by the upper income classes when the product first enters the market. However, the closer the product technological features are the slower the rate of income change and the slower the rate of change of the market towards the micro bifurcation window.
C. 12. D. The greater the current rate of market selection of technologically innovative in products created through genetic crossbreeding, the greater the rate of income growth and upward occupational mobility within the lower income classes in the region.	C. 12. D. The greater the rate of growth of upper income classes caused by entry from lower income classes, the greater the Bayesian probability that risky new products will be selected as the market demand grows from the purchasing patterns of newly arrived upper income class consumers.
C. 12. E. The greater the gap in technological features of products within the current industrial clusters, the less likely that genetic technology will be crossbred into a new product when the "boundary-crosser" returns with new technological knowledge.	C. 12. E. The greater the gap in technological features of new genetic products, the less likely they are to be selected by consumers in the future. Products with the greatest gap which happen to be selected cause the greatest changes in income distribution in the future leading to a faster approach of the Bayesian macro bifurcation window.

C. 12. F. The sexual crossover of genetic production technology in the current period causes the production possibilities frontier to expand outward, creating new opportunities for new firm creation from the pool of new genetic technology that can be "expressed" by investments in new ventures that are producing new technological products in the expanding regional interindustrial technology clusters.	C. 12. F. The greater the rate of new product selection by consumers the greater the probability that the industrial cluster will create new technological linkages in the service and support industries in intermediate final demand. Regional economies that create the greatest number of new nerve ganglions that connect the service and support firms have the greatest probability of creating a complementary market.
C. 12. G. The longer the duration and stability of the rule of law and fair democratic procedures of collective decision making, the greater the current period rate of new venture creation in technologically risky new products, that may, or may not, be selected by consumers.	C. 12. G. The longer the duration of stability of the rule of law, the more experience the upper income classes have in selecting new genetic variations of products. Regional economies characterized by consumers with the greatest experience in selecting new product variations have the greatest probability of new market emergence.
C. 12. H. The greater the current rate of investment in new ventures that "express" the new genetic technology, the greater the rate of variety in the complementary firms in the industrial cluster that service and support the new ventures.	C. 12. H. Regions with the greatest rates of intermediate demand growth in emerging complementary markets have the fastest rates of income growth from upwardly mobile entrepreneurial classes who enter the highest income classes.
C. 12. I. The greater the rate of equity financing on new ventures that are "expressing" new technology in the current period, the less dependent the regional economy becomes on global final demand for creating adequate economic rates of growth because the regional intermediate demand is sufficient for causing regional economic growth.	C. 12. I. Regions with the fastest rates of complementary market creation create wealth and incomes in new ventures within the industrial cluster that did not previously exist, creating entirely new patterns of both final and intermediate demand based upon the new income distribution. The less dependent the regional economy is on global sources of demand, the more probability of new market emergence.

C. 12. J. The greater the current rates of knowledge creation and diffusion are within the current industrial clusters the greater the current rate of economic growth as the regional production possibilities frontier is pushed outward through an upward micro bifurcation point into the future. The current economic structure is changing and the future economic structure is looking less and less like the current structure.	C. 12. J. The less the future market demand patterns look like the current demand patterns as the regional economy slips through the micro Bayesian bifurcation point window into the future the more likely that the regional economy will slip through some distant future attractor point of a macro bifurcation where the future market environment looks nothing like the current market in terms of product technology and income distribution.
C. 12. K. The longer the duration of stability within the industrial cluster, the more likely that debt financing will replace equity financings of existing firms because the potential rate of return in existing firms with older technology products is not favorable compared to the multiple equity investment opportunities in new firms. Reliance on debt financing in the existing, established firms will cause the death rate of those firms to increase.	C. 12. K. The greater the death rate of firms in the older technological clusters combined with an increased birth rate of new ventures in both the complementary markets and the intermediate demand markets, the faster the approach to the future distant attractor macro bifurcation point to the emergence of a new future market.

Without the introduction of technological novelty, a regional economy can experience periods of economic growth associated with increasing production efficiency, without adding economic genetic variety. Prices, used as indicators of economic activity, reflect the level of economic exchanges occurring in a time period without describing the trajectory of the economy.

Novelty starts in the brains of individuals as they imagine the future, and novelty is actualized when technology is commercialized in the form of new ventures. When the period of productivity improvements of declining price-based exchanges ends, the lack of novelty spells the end of economic growth for the regional economy.

The greater the technological homogeneity and standardization in production technology, the greater the rate of adaptation and imitation, and the faster the rate to product and market obsolescence.

The process of economic growth and the emergence of new markets can be described by a series of "then if" contingent logical statements:

- If exit events in the past create a pool of entrepreneurial profits, then if,
- The entrepreneurial profit is used to fund new ventures that create new products, then if,
- Technological genetic crossover occurs between two products, then if,
- Markets select new products, then if,
- Complementary markets are created, then if,
- New patterns of income distribution are created, then if,
- New technological knowledge is created, then if,
- New technological knowledge is diffused, then if,
- New genetic variety is "called forth" from the expanding production possibilities frontier, the new genetic variety has a greater probability of being "inherited" by subsequent generations of products, and the evolution of the market can continue through a macro bifurcation and the emergence of an entirely new market.[382]

In the case of genetic crossover, the initial rates of product mutation are very slow, as a result of the forces favoring the status quo arrangement. New genetic combinations of technology in new products that would be useful in future markets must be selected by consumers in current markets in order to have a chance of survival and passing on their genetics to future new product generations.

This contrast between future markets and current markets highlights one of the scientific philosophical differences between SERET and neoclassical economic theory. Neoclassical theory attempts to explain current market behavior by describing how prices on current market exchanges equilibrates supply and demand. SERET attempts to explain how asexual or sexual mating between technology creates an environment conducive to market emergence.

If the contingent market selection forces are strong enough after product genetic crossover occurs, the new genetic possibilities open up pathways that did not previously exist for other building blocks in technological complementary markets to form. Genetic crossover occurs on the outermost boundaries of industrial clusters that share certain technological features within a confined domain of interaction.

The genetic crossover occurs after the boundary- crossing agent brings back new knowledge. If, however, the new knowledge is deployed in the existing product technology, homeostasis arises, which leads to technological sclerosis. After some time of increasing production efficiency and fixed homogeneous production capacity, new investments in existing product technology do not make economic sense.

In any given region, the greater the initial technological genetic variation in the regional production possibilities frontier, the greater the potential product diversity that can be commercialized. Each region is different, and on a different trajectory.

As Alfred Marshall pointed out in 1890, "Every locality has incidents of its own which affect in various ways the methods of arrangement of every class of business that is carried on in it: and even in the same place and the same trade no two persons pursuing the same aims will adopt exactly the same routes. The tendency to variation is a chief cause of progress; and the abler are the undertakers in any trade the greater will this tendency be."[383]

Used in the context of Structural Evolutionary Regional Economic Evolution, Marshall's emphasis on variation as the chief cause of economic progress is exactly right. The chief cause of market emergence is technological genetic variation, and regional economic leaders who desire the type of economic growth that creates new markets need to shift their policy attention from productivity to the question of what causes technological genetic variety.

The two economic outcomes associated with the asexual genetic inbreeding versus a sexual genetic crossbreeding are described in the diagrams below.

Thomas E. Vass

Diagram 8.17. Interactive Model of Information Flows of Regional Economic Evolution: Asexual Single Parent Environment

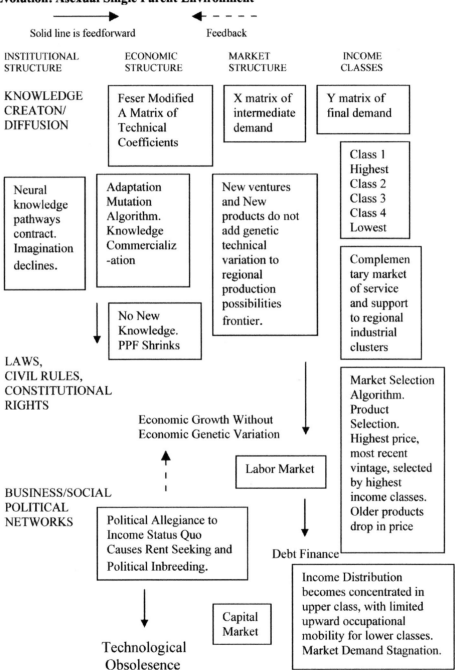

285

Predicting Technology

Diagram 8.18. Interactive Model of Information Flows of Regional Economic Evolution: Genetic Technological Cross Breeding In Two Parent Product Environment.

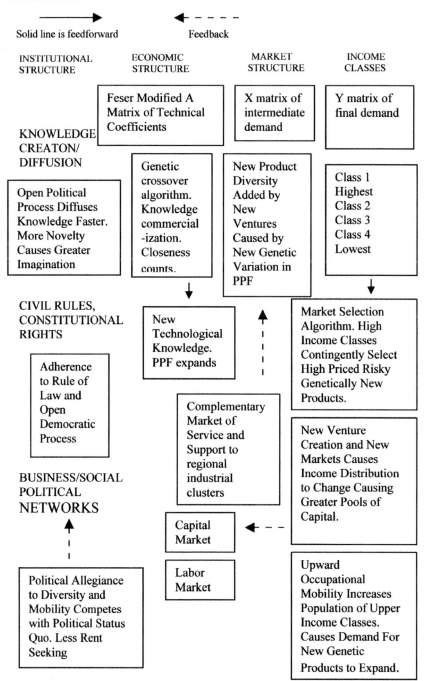

Diagram 8.19. Contrasting the Two Possible Evolutionary Economic Trajectories To Future Markets.

ASEXUAL SINGLE PARENT ENVIRONMENT

Mueller's Ratchet of product technology genetic inbreeding causes economy to pass through micro bifurcation points on downward trajectory of economic decline. Marginal rate of change in regional GNP at bifurcation point equals zero. Market contracts along trajectory path to new lower economic level of equilibrium .

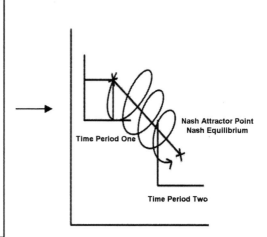

GENETIC TECHNOLOGICAL CROSS BREEDING IN TWO PARENT PRODUCT ENVIRONMENT

Genetic cross breeding of product technology causes increased genetic possibilities frontier. New PPF creates conditions for contingent market selection. Possible new markets emerge as market passes through upward micro bifurcation points to distant future attractor and macro bifurcation. Oscillations decrease in amplitude along trajectory of micro bifurcation points towards distant

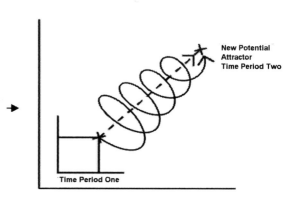

Chapter IX

Using The New Theory to Identify Future Market Opportunities and Disruptive Technologies

In an asexual market environment, the political forces that favor the status quo distribution of income would generally be engaged in rent-seeking political activity that inhibits open public knowledge creation and diffusion in favor of secret proprietary knowledge flows. That type of political control behavior ultimately leads to economic decline, which is a simple prediction to make from the perspective of SERET.

By gaining control over the price of capital, the elites who favor the status quo distribution of income impose a political constraint on the highest level of welfare achievable for lower income classes.

As soon as the financial and political elites are able to impose the income constraints, which are obtained through price-based market exchange manipulation, the economic outcome for the region can be predicted with accuracy.

Neoclassical equilibrium theory can also predict this outcome, given *the initial endowment of factors and goods.*[384] The outcome from the equilibrium perspective is that the initial endowment of income will become the future endowment of income, which is the telos of the theory.

It would not matter, from a scientific investigation of regional economic decline, if the units of analysis were primarily local economic and financial elites, or elites drawn from the population of senior executives of multinational corporations who had branch operations in the region under investigation. Their elite behavior in both cases would be the same.

In response to the global declining marginal efficiency of capital in the mass, global markets, a rational response by those who own current capital assets is to make their assets generate income for as long as possible, sometimes through political rent-seeking, but more importantly, by gaining control over the flow and direction of investment of capital so that the future market continues to function like the existing market.

It generally takes about 7 years from the time an investment in an asexual market environment to affect both the production of other firms and the market for the slightly better asexual product. Given an initial set of private property rights and rights to accumulate profits and rights of estate inheritance, an initial distribution of income can be shown, using standard neoclassical marginal analysis, to lead to a status quo distribution of income, holding the initial distribution of prices constant.

Using the implications of SERET in the case of a regional market characterized by asexual markets to predict the next likely market environment is relatively straightforward. The expected outcome of technological inbreeding is regional economic decline, and the first variable of decline is the rate of the marginal efficiency of capital in existing firms in the regional industrial clusters.

The key economic variables to be analyzed are rates of profits, income distributions, and the birth and death rates of firms in the regional economy. The economic variables must be gathered and analyzed in conjunction with social and political variables.

The key political variables to investigate are how long existing political representatives have been in office, the extent of corporate political contributions, the amount and type of corporate welfare, and an increase in the ambient level of special interest corruption.

All of the political variables of local elite behavior must be matched to variables aimed at measuring the increase in political alliances between local political elites and executives and lobbyists for the multinational corporations.

The goal of conducting this part of the political analysis is to identify how political allegiance to the status quo distribution of income may affect the future trajectory of the market. In an asexual environment not much is likely to change for periods of about 7 years in the regional economy, while in politics, the rate of official corruption is likely to increase.

Official corruption, in this case, is the use of government resources to promote private financial enterprises and the personal financial interests of business and political elites in the region.

The most significant benefit for business people in identifying the future market of an asexual environment is to gain an awareness that business projects that are inconsistent with the dominant political ethos, in other words, new ventures or new products that do not contribute to maintaining the status quo, are likely to be commercial failures. On the other hand, aligning business and financial interests with the dominant interests in an asexual environment could prove to be lucrative.

In the asexual environment, hourly manufacturing workers should expect that their jobs in either traditional domestic industry, such as tobacco and textiles in North Carolina, will be shipped to lower wage regions of the world. Hourly and mid-level salaried staff in the multinational corporations should anticipate that their jobs will be outsourced, or "right-sized," meaning eliminated, in response to the increased globalization of production processes.

Regions with the greatest reliance on global markets can be predicted to experience the greatest declines in prices and the slowest rates of change in income class distribution. The financial and political interests of global corporations will dominate decisions about the regional economic growth path. In the asexual environment, it would be expected that senior executives from the multinational corporations would move easily between private corporate positions and elected or appointed political positions in the region.

Local business groups and professional associations in the region would be expected to have leadership positions held by representatives of the largest corporations and that political and policy positions adopted by those groups would advocate the dominant ethos of the status quo.

Towards the end of the period of economic decline, official corruption gives way to increased criminal behavior at all levels and a general social breakdown in civil authority. Examples of this expected outcome can be seen in Detroit with the global decline in the fortunes of the big auto makers.

For similar reasons but with a different precipitating cause, the social and civil breakdown in New Orleans after Katrina fits this pattern predicted by SERET. The period of corruption would generally be followed by greater applications of the police power of the state to restore civil authority, consistent with the maintenance of the status quo distribution of income.

The hollowing out phenomena that occurs in the regional economic structure in the asexual environment is matched by a hollowing out in the political structure, with no one left in a position of authority that can execute responsibility on behalf of the public good, or the common wealth. In the aftermath of a catastrophe like Katrina, what can be expected of the corrupt phase of government is that no one is in charge.

The asexual environmental predictions of SERET are compatible with what William Greider calls "the race to the bottom." Used in his context, the asexual environment encompasses global trading relationships, with national economies viewed as the units of analysis.

"Globalization is entering a fateful new stage," writes Greider, "in which the competitive perils intensify for the low-wage developing countries much like the continuing pressures on high-wage manufacturing workers in the United States...As one economy after another sinks into contraction, output subsides nearly everywhere..."[385]

Applied to the context of regional economic decline, Greider's analysis predicts that national economies are headed on a downward trajectory. The benefit of adding SERET to Greider's analysis is that as the race to the bottom passes through a ratchet, the regional economy will not return to the previous "equilibrium."

The regional economy adjusts to the lower level of economic activity, and can stay in that new position for decades at a time. As long as the regional economy can generate income consistent with the status quo arrangement of political authority, the new lower level of equilibrium would not have any reasons, from an evolutionary point of view, to change.

Stephen Kobrin describes this phase of asexual technological innovation in terms of increasing dependency of the regional economy on the technology of the multinational corporations. "Globalization is a transition from a world ordered geographically...to an a-territorial, networked mode of organization."[386] Kobrin suggests that the future outcome of this shift in technological dependency is not clear.

He can see that the "...transfer of technology increases the dependency on the center and inhibits indigenous technological development." And, he can see that the "...dependent developing countries have little, if any, control over critical decisions affecting their economies and their societies."[387]

With the benefit of the analysis provided by SERET, Kobrin should be able to predict with more accuracy where the technological trajectory is taking the economy. In an asexual technological economy, the growing economic dependency of the regional economy on global multinational corporations as the engines of growth is leading to regional income distribution lock-in, and not simply to regional technological path dependency.

The loss of regional economic territorial sovereignty that Kobrin can see comes with the additional cost of lost opportunity for upward income and occupational mobility for the regional residents who are not plugged into the global mode of multinational corporate operations.

Geoffrey Jones also touches on the relationship between technological dependency and the loss of territorial sovereignty. "The borders of multinational corporations and nation states are not, by definition, identical. As a result, governments are confronted by economic entities whose ultimate control and ownership lies beyond their borders, while firms face multiple jurisdictions rooted in different political systems."[388]

Jones calls this condition "jurisdictional asymmetry," as seen from the eyes of the senior executives in multinational corporations.

With the benefit of SERET, the predictions about the future of the national economies can become more accurate. In an asexual technological global environment, technological production standards and interoperable modular production components become standardized, just like the global mass-produced products, that can be made anywhere in the world.

Predicting Technology

The global uniformity in technology is matched by the global uniformity in political systems that is required by corporations to overcome the political jurisdictional asymmetry. Hence, the desire by multinational corporate executives to implement global trade agreements and shift jurisdictional disputes from national courts to international trade courts.

What the multinational corporations need in an asexual technological environment is control over the direction of technology so that they do not get blown away by some type of disruptive technological product crossover that disrupts their markets and their incomes.

As Kogut and Zander point out, what the multinational corporations have come to specialize in is not simply global production standardization, it is specialization in knowledge creation and diffusion and uniformity in economic policies at the local level achieved through global political control over matters of trade and finance.

They gain control over the knowledge creation and diffusion process by locating certain types of facilities in geographical territories. "Multinationals specialize in the transfer of knowledge that is difficult to understand and codify…(Global) firms define a community in which their exists a body of knowledge regarding how to cooperate and communicate."[389]

From SERET's point of view, the desire to obtain a region's tacit knowledge in order to direct it to the benefit of the corporation's core technological competency is a rational response to the declining marginal profits from existing technology. The regional knowledge is useful to protect incomes, while at the same time allowing for greater control over the future direction of the market, both for the region and for the world's economy.

Control over technology allows the lower equilibrium level of economic activity to endure for decades at a time, entirely consistent with Kimura's theory nearly neutral genetic drift.

To answer the critics of Geoffrey Hodgson, who promotes a Darwinian interpretation of regional economic evolution, "…the idea that humans are (uniquely) intentional does not rule out the need or possibility of an evolutionary account of human intentionality."[390]

The interpretation of human intentionality, though, must be removed from the neoclassical economic theoretical framework and placed into a biological evolutionary framework in order to explain the intentional human behavior of the multinational corporate executives.

Controlling knowledge creation and diffusion is an intentional behavior that is both an adaptation to the declining marginal revenues, and a LaMarkian response that alters the next generation of knowledge in the asexual regional economic environment.

As early as 1960, economists such as Stephen Hymer, were trying to place the intentional behavior of multinational corporate executives into this more biological theoretical framework.

Hymer argued that multinational corporations entered host states because the host states possessed certain assets that complimented the corporation's technological knowledge. By entering a region to gain strategic knowledge, the corporation was able to gain property rights over future useful knowledge, gain rental payments on existing knowledge and politically influence the future direction of regional knowledge creation and diffusion to benefit the interests of the multinational corporation.[391]

As a result of the political influence of multinational executives, the host regional economies generally lose political control and democratic accountability over the future direction of the regional economy. Usha Haley has called the loss of economic and political sovereignty the "sovereignty at bay" effect.

In an interdependent global production process, the multinational corporations require uniform standards of trade and commerce in the political host regimes. The regional governments must be sympathetic to the needs of the global corporations, who are always in danger of sliding down the slope of declining marginal profits that are associated with mass global markets.

"Therefore," writes Haley, "dependent development encourages authoritarian regimes in host states and creates alliances between multinational (executives) and domestic reactionary elites."[392] The point of using SERET as the analytical tool to investigate the relationships between local political financial elites and multinational executives is to provide measurements of the strength of the affinities, which biologists would call symbiosis.

In the asexual environment, the symbiosis is strong, and getting stronger through time. As the regional economy passes through the ratchet, very little external genetic force exists in the regional production possibilities frontier to disrupt the strength of symbiosis between local autocratic political elites and the senior executives who manage the global corporations. As the asexual conditions persist over time, SERET's predictions about the future of the global economy are as accurate as the predictions for any single regional economy. In the absence of genetic variety, the environmental conditions of global genetic inbreeding will lead to global economic collapse.

Diagram 9.1. describes a set of testable hypothesis issued by SERET that can be used in an analytical framework to help investigators predict the future pathway of a regional economy. The hypothesis contains many of the elements described by contemporary regional scientists in terms of "path dependency" and "technological lock-in."

As noted by Greider, the trajectory described by the path dependency is like a "race to the bottom." Along the path to the bottom, there is a contingent point of equilibrium where economic forces can maintain the status quo for a considerable period of time.

Retracing an upward trajectory from this future lower level of economic equilibrium is not likely because of the effect of Mueller's Ratchet of genetic inbreeding. As bad as that future point of status quo economic equilibrium may be, it offers a superior welfare outcome to what comes next in the asexual economic environment.

The outcome predicted by SERET in the case of genetic crossbreeding within a regional economic environment is different than the asexual case. In the rare event of sexual, two parent product genetic crossover, conditions exist for the emergence of a new market at some vague new attractor point in the future. The purpose of the inquiry is to predict when and where that potential future market may emerge.

The first tool of analysis for looking for what may come next is a regional input-output model of the regional economy, describing the types of linkages within industrial clusters in the region. This detailed examination of the regional economy has been advocated as the first step in regional economic analysis for many years.

In 1958, for example, Albert Hirschman, in *The Strategy of Economic Development*, called for an analysis of "filling in of the missing linkages in the supply chain from extractive activities to the provision of final demand goods."[393]

Hirschman was calling for an analysis of the backward and forward linkages in the regional inter-industry relationships between firms. SERET uses the same concept and extends the idea to backwards and forward linkages from the values and incomes matrix associated with markets to the regional transaction matrix in order to describe both economic and knowledge flows.

The geographical location of economic activity has always been a constant in both classical economic theory, as expressed by Adam Smith, to neoclassical theory, as written by Alfred Marshall. The importance and significance of the geographical location, as viewed from the neoclassical tradition is modified somewhat by SERET, with its emphasis on predicting when and where a new market may emerge.

Diagram 9.1. Asexual Technology Innovation and Predicting the Economic Decline of A Regional Economy.©

SERET Hypothesis	Variables of Analysis of Decline	Predicted Outcome
The current rate of investment in new ventures must be sufficient to create new future demand within the regional industrial cluster or the region's economy will decline.	Profits from capital gain exit events. Balance between debt and equity investments in funding new ventures. Age of firms in region. Death rate of firms in region.	Low rates of reinvestment of capital gains into regional new ventures. Low supply of capital for starting new ventures or funding growth of existing firms.
The lower the current rates of knowledge creation the greater the current rate of economic decline as the regional production possibilities frontier is exhausted.	Number of open intellectual forums held n the region per quarter. Number of competitive political campaigns. Length of term incumbency for elected representatives. Number and diversity of professional organizations. Uniformity coefficients in public policy and opinions about regional economy.	An official doctrine of acceptable economic growth strategies becomes conventional wisdom. Bankers, lawyers and real estate elites occupy prestigious positions on economic development boards and chamber of commerce committees. University research becomes oriented to serving multinational corporations located in the region.

The greater the power of government to maintain the existing distribution of income the less the future rates of technological innovation.	Rate of criminal prosecution of election law campaign contributions. Rate of fraud prosecution in socially oriented non-profits organizations. Percentage of population eligible for government welfare assistance. Degree of stability in income distribution.	Income growth rates stagnate. Income disparity increases. Dependency on government for income increases. Jobs become a political end, not an economic function. Upward occupational mobility is based on political connections and not individual merit. Criminal behavior increases, including crimes against "property."
Mueller's Ratchet hollows out regional structure. The greater the rate of selection of asexual new products (sustaining innovation) versus old products, the faster the rate of product obsolescence for a specific version and the faster the product life cycle is completed. The entire product life cycle is usually completed within 28 years.	Variety of intermediate products in regional supply chain markets. Coefficients of cluster linkages. Regional income and multiplier effects. Rates of regional new product innovation. Rate of new venture creation. Age of existing firms. Death rate of existing firms. Factory closings.	Increased use of targeted real estate incentives for offices and industrial space for firms in the regional industrial cluster. Increased secret negotiations between local political and economic elites and multinational corporate elites on tax evasions and tax incentive schemes to attract the corporation to the region.

Gaps in distribution of income between upper income classes and lower income classes grows, which means economic activity shifts from production of goods to a politicized rentier-debt economy.	Rules and regulations on protections for private property and rights of individuals to appropriate profits from their work. Anti-union official rules and laws against collective bargaining.	New constitutional definitions and protection of private property against the taking of private property for the "public purpose" as opposed to "public use."
Regions with the greatest reliance on global markets experience the greatest declines in prices and the slowest rates of change in income class distribution. Global corporations dominate regional economic growth path.	Occupational and job classifications by local/ non-local groupings. Public relations expenditures advocating status quo economic policies. Public spending on private real estate facilities such as convention centers, football stadiums.	Industrial recruitment of multinational corporations to compliment and support the regional local business elites, primarily in law, finance and real estate.
Declining marginal efficiency of capital chokes off innovation.	Regional income and employment multipliers in the regional industrial clusters. Degree of factor analysis affinity between technical coefficients in regional industrial clusters.	Increased policy linkages between commercial bankers, occupational skill training customized to the specific needs of multinational branch operations, and increased debt financial transactions.

The greater the rates of civil conflict over individual freedoms and civil rights the more the police power of the state will be used in the future to maintain the existing distribution of wealth and income.	Open occupational licensing. Enactment of anti-trust regulations aimed at market manipulation of supply.	Increased restrictions on the rights of citizen civil action against monopolies and market concentration. Decreased reliance on statistical data on market concentration and relaxed anti-trust enforcement actions.
The greater the death rate of firms in the older technological clusters combined with a decreased birth rate of new ventures in the regional intermediate demand markets, the faster the rate of economic decline.	Birth rates of new ventures in all parts of the regional industrial clusters. Death rate of all ventures, with primary emphasis on the death rates between industrial cluster trading partners.	Increased constitutional support for the use of public tax revenues to support dying industries and to recruit multinational corporations to the region. Less publicly disclosed information about tax transactions between local and global elites.

As explained by Edgar Hoover, in *The Location of Economic Activity*, in 1948, the spatial industrial concentrations of industries was related to the vertical integration of the supply chain in complementary markets. As is always the case with neoclassical economic theory, Hoover's purpose in describing the agglomeration effect is to show how reduced costs and increased productivity of the faceless and timeless units of analysis are always working to bring the economy back to a natural point of equilibrium.

Hoover notes that "... the benefits of localization and agglomeration derived from concentration would induce enterprises to agglomerate, and to rationalize their operations by sharing and consolidating their input linkages."[394] When the input output analysis is freed from the neoclassical imperative to describe the telos of equilibrium, the same type of sharing and consolidation of input linkages can describe the potential emergence of new knowledge and possible new markets.

Rather than equilibrium as the end point of the analysis, SERET posits a possible new attractor point in the regional market that would have an entirely new set of regional inter-industrial relationships that evolved out of the current conditions, but then functioned to modify the economic environment.

Adna Ferrin Weber accurately described the importance of studying knowledge flows in relation to regional economic linkages in 1899. Her insights into the importance of that relationship are extended in SERET. In Weber's analysis, spatial economic activity and knowledge can be used to describe the future direction of the regional economy if they are viewed from a "biological analogy."

In her biological analogy, much like the metaphor described by SERET, the two key variables to look for are:

Increasing spatial heterogeneity in production units.
Increasing interdependence of heterogeneous elements, which share knowledge.[395]

In contrast to neoclassical theory's emphasis on specialization in production and increased productivity as the explanation of regional economic development, SERET agrees with Weber that the main variables to look for are increasing heterogeneity in products, production, and knowledge. The regional input output model is useful to describe all of these relationships.

The next step in the analysis of where the new market may emerge is to look for commercial activity in small, insignificant markets. This is how

Predicting Technology

Clayton Christensen explains the difference between sustaining innovations and disruptive technological innovations.

As Christensen describes the analysis, "Markets that do not exist cannot be analyzed. Suppliers and customers must discover them together."[396] Perhaps a better description would be that markets that do not exist couldn't be analyzed using traditional economic theory and marginal analysis based upon price movements.

The purpose or intent of Christensen's analysis is to figure out why big firms fail. Translating his concern into SERET's framework, the concern would be to explain and predict when and where a current small market activity leads to the extinction of species in the environment in the future period of time.

If the input-output transactions tables, which describe correlation coefficients of interdependence, are further analyzed with the benefit of factor analysis, the correlations can describe underlying technological affinities between industrial sectors.

Merely describing the underlying statistical affinities in regional technology is not significant, yet. As Christensen points out from Hewlett Packard's experience with their 1994 product launch of KittyHawk, the managers assumed that the product's functional characteristics would be so obvious that consumers would immediately switch their buying habits.

Upon retrospection, when consumers failed to conform to the marketing expectations, the managers agreed that if they had to do the project over again, "they would assume that neither they, nor anyone else knew for sure what kind of customers would want it or in what volumes."[397]

The reason future market emergence is contingent and difficult to predict is that the underlying causal factors are human behavior in the presence of novelty. The processes at work require small steps to judge what consumers are doing, and from each small step into the future, taking a further small step to see what may come next.

The first event in the technological innovation stage is a technological crossover between two parent products. After that crossover occurs, as would have been the case with the Hewlett Packard product, the question turns into a marketing analysis problem of answering the question "Where is the market of consumers that would use the technology that is embedded in this new product?"

What the analysts should be anticipating are small market niches of buyers who would value the functionality of the new technology and *be willing to risk paying the higher price to obtain the new good, knowing in advance the great uncertainty that the good will serve the anticipated need.*

The first iteration, or first step into the future, is to watch what the buyers do after their purchase of the first generation of product technology in order to assess how the technology fits the "mental image" of the buyer.

The feedback of information from the market informs the product design engineers on the modifications to the new product that must be made to meet the changing needs of the buyers, because as soon as the buyer starts using the new product, the buyer's brain starts spinning out new mental images associated with using the new product. In other words, the buyer starts imaging a different future.

As the feedback information flows from the market to production, the marketing challenge turns into a guessing game about how related, or what economists call, complementary markets are going to change, if buyers continue to buy the newer versions of the new product.

This is the stage of analysis that Christensen, and other business management professors like him, would describe as disruptive, if they adapted their analysis to the SERET framework. It is not the market effect of the initial product technology crossover that is disruptive, and ends up killing the big dinosaurs, it is the changed environment that the big dinosaurs find themselves in that has become hostile to their survival.

Diagram 9.2. describes the sequence of events that frame the analysis of predicting technology and market emergence. Along the left column are the types of regional economic and political analysis that would be used to conduct the inquiry. The right hand column describes what to look for in knowledge creation and diffusion, along with market selection.

The time elapse for the inquiry would encompass about 7 years for the first components of the analysis, always mindful that new technology could easily stall or be undermined by political forces.

The market crossover would occur about 5 to 7 years from the first appearance of the new technological product. Recall that this is not the case of asexual technology, where the offspring replaces the parent product in the market. The case described in the Diagram is more akin to the refrigerator replacing the ice box.

The four steps to the initial investigation are:

- Identify the small set of users or customers who would value the functionality of the new technology.

- Observe what the users do when they first see the product for the first time, and how they use the product to fulfill their needs.

- Observe what the users do when the second and third generation of product improvements occur.

- Watch for what other technologies are in the same geographical region that could potentially solve the same set of user needs.

Clayton Christensen makes an important distinction for marketing analysis that can be applied to the investigation based upon SERET. The functions and features of the new technology are what constitute the "market" for the new good, not the buying habits of the users. "It is the circumstances in which customers find themselves that is the critical unit of analysis," writes Christensen, "not the customer."[398]

Christensen uses the example of how workers on the morning commute to their jobs view the possible range of goods that fit into their mental image of what economists have called their utility function.

He notes "...In the customer's minds, the morning milkshake competes against boredom, bagels...etc."[399] The significance of Christensen's insight is that users who see the new product for the first time are engaged in a mental imagination process of trying out mentally how the new product may fit.

At this stage of the products life, if it is still alive, the process of marketing and advertising can be deployed to help potential users make the mental connection between the new technological functions, and the anticipated response by the users.

The underlying fundamental human behavior being investigated is how the human brain processes information in the presence of a novel event. The brain, in this case, is aiming at individual sovereignty, or as biologists may interpret the behavior, individual control over the environment. The small market niche to look for in the case of technological crossover is the population of potential users who can gain better control over their lives by adopting the new product.

If the small niche of users continues to buy the new product, the product may begin to undergo sustaining innovations, in the mode of asexual product innovations. At that time, as Christensen points out, "subsequent improvements typically create production efficiencies that enable price reductions that make the disruptive product or service available to wider customer groups."[400]

In other words, the product enters into the price competition phase that can be adequately described by neoclassical marginal theory. What neoclassical theory cannot help with is what happens in the market as a result of the changed environment created by the new consumer demand, which is causing new mental images in the brains of other potenial users.

Diagram 9.2 Schematic Diagram of Two Parent Product Technological and Market Crossover©

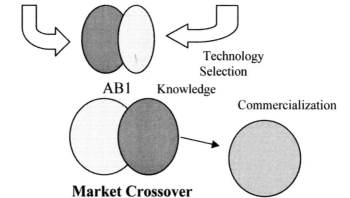

Regional Industrial Cluster Analysis	Industry A Firm 1 A1 Geographically close to B2	Industry B Firm 2 B2 Geographicall v close to A1

Knowledge Creation

Factor Analysis	A1 shares similar production technology as B2	B2 shares similar production technology as A1

Knowledge Diffusion

Knowledge Creation Social Business Network Analysis Technology Crossover In Products Creates New Product	Scientific and engineering staff of A1 meets in face to face social engagements with staff of B2. A1 staff boundary crossers bring knowledge back to A1	Scientific and engineering staff of B2 meet in face to face social engagements with staff of A1. B2 staff boundary crossers bring knowledge back to B2.

Technology Selection

AB1   Knowledge

Commercialization

Market Niche Market Selection Created For New Product

Market Crossover

303

Diagram 9.2., above would enter at this stage of the investigation, where the new product had displaced other products, called "market crossover."

In Diagram 9.3., the relationship between the new product's functionality is described in terms of the time elapse of the declining price. As the price declines, reliability from sustaining innovations increases, and convenience of use increases, while more potential users can buy the new product at the lower prices.

What investigators should be looking for at this stage, probably about 7 to 9 years out from the product's first appearance, is whether other technological innovations are occurring in the regional market that complement the technological functions of the first product.

Beyond the scientific application of SERET, the common sense evidence of the regional characteristics are simple enough to understand and can be applied by anyone who has not the slightest training in economic or biological theory. The investigator would look for the kind of regional environment that engineers and scientists like to live in.

Given those regional characteristics, the investigator would look for social and business events where engineers and scientists from different industries and disciplines attend. The investigator would determine if the political and economic rules are based upon individualistic cultural values that promote individual initiative and risk taking in creating new products and new ventures.

The investigator would then look at the types of consumers and the kinds of market relationships in the environment and decide if new products and new ventures have a fair opportunity for selection by consumers, and if consumers have exhibited a history of buying risky new products.

Regional metro market areas, which possessed all of these characteristics, are likely to have the greatest potential for new venture creation. They would be expected to have much higher rates of economic growth and wealth creation than regions that did not possess these characteristics.

In those metro regions which had these type of characteristics, the investigator would look for small traces of evidence that complementary markets and small niches in off-the-beaten paths in markets that were supporting or supplying the new products and new ventures.

The appearance of complementary markets is the first empirical evidence of the most rare of economic evolutionary events, called the emergence of a new market. It is the dynamics of market selection that is responsible for the disruption, not the technological crossover. And, the disruption of the market is caused by and facilitated by the disruption to the status quo distribution of political power and incomes in the regional economy.

And, the investigator does not need a Ph.D in economics, biology or political science to understand the forces in the environment that are hostile to that outcome.

Diagram 9.3. Market Relationship Between Function and Price in Technological Crossover New Product. ©

Consumer Selection Criteria From Product Introduction

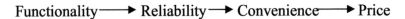

Functionality ⟶ Reliability ⟶ Convenience ⟶ Price

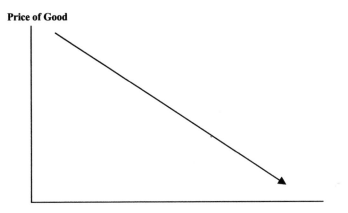

Price of Good

Regional Market ⟶ Mass Global Market
Product Introduction   Product Obsolescence

Chapter X

Strategies For Companies and Citizens: Seizing New Market Opportunities and Creating The Jobs and Wealth Creation Pipeline In Your Community

Regional economic development occurs as a result of technical change in production units, generally, manufacturing plants and high technology service units related to information and communication technology, (ICT). Technical change causes relationships between economic, social and political agents within the region to change.

One of the possible outcomes associated with technical change over time is that more wealth and greater per capita incomes are created in the region. There is nothing preordained or certain that this desirable outcome of more wealth or greater income will occur.

If you or your company are organized to take advantage of the opportunities and alert to the changes that are occurring in technology, you could benefit greatly from the creation of the new markets.

There are social, political and economic forces that favor technical change, and there are other forces that inhibit change. Economic development is a contingent outcome of technical change. It occurs in some regions, but not in others. It always occurs when companies and individuals identify new opportunities to make money and create a new business or new product to sell in a new market.

The theory explained in this book describes that technical change combined with regional economic growth occurs during favorable historical circumstances. As an example of the historical moment, Adam Smith noted that the American colonists seemed to occupy a unique place in history to apply their newly found individualistic ambitions.

"The colonists carryout a knowledge of agriculture and of other useful arts....Every colonist gets more land than he can possibly cultivate... He is eager, therefore, to collect labourers from all quarters, and to reward them with the most liberal wages. But those liberal wages, joined to the plenty and cheapness of the land, soon make those labourers leave him, in order to become landlords themselves, and to reward, with equal liberality, other labourers, who soon leave them for the same reason ...."[401]

One of the differences between the economic evolutionary theory described in this book, and Darwin's theory of evolution is that humans can positively influence economic outcomes. What exists today in the way of economic conditions could easily have been something else, if earlier decisions had been different. What will exist in the future in your community can be different than the status quo, if certain types of policies and programs are implemented today.

Your regional economy does not have to return to a point of historical equilibrium and you are not necessarily doomed to repeat past economic history.

Part of the challenge in creating the jobs and wealth creation pipeline in your community is seizing the historical opportunity presented at a unique moment in time. As the theory described in the book explained, the regional economy can pass through a small window of economic growth, but getting to the other side of the window is hard. Seizing the opportunity is difficult because there is no road map or theory that tells you how to go about the task.

Most economic theory assumes that the free market will automatically create regional wealth and prosperity. If you and other community leaders rely on existing economic theory to guide you in your policy decisions, your regional economy will probably not experience technical change. As the theory outlined in this book explained, the most likely outcome of allowing things to remain the same is regional economic decline.

At the beginning of this book, a series of questions were raised that the new economic theory could answer better than existing economic theory. The questions were written in the form of policy guidelines for citizens to implement to create and jobs and wealth creation pipeline. The policy guidelines are reviewed below, this time in the form of policy goal statements.

I. You Region Requires Competent Regional Innovation Management.

What organizational entity in your region promotes and performs knowledge creation? Part of the problem of finding strategies to promote regional economic growth concerns the fact that regions do not have the same organizational capacity and functionality as private corporations.

No organizational entity in the regional economy or community at large has a mission to create knowledge about technological innovation based upon the region's strategic strengths. Yet, knowledge creation is one of the most important variables for influencing the creation of future market opportunities.

In the case of private corporations, the inability to generate knowledge often leads to corporate economic decline. Alfred Chandler attributes RCA's downfall in the electronics industry to its lack of an "internal learning base". The company controlled the critical patents for radio technology, but did not have the in-house expertise to develop new products and push that technology into new markets.

A regional economy can have all the right attributes of land, capital and skilled labor, but without the framework for creating and diffusing technological knowledge, a region can easily go out of business, just like RCA.

If your region operated like a modern corporation, your region would implement an innovation management system to systematically take advantage of new markets. Clayton Christensen asked how industry leaders could reinvent themselves by developing and successfully commercializing disruptive innovations that challenge their existing business models.

The same question applies to regions, especially regions that are on the downward spiral because the traditional sources of economic growth have all died or left the community. How can regional economies continually reinvent themselves? The issue for regions is that disruptive economic innovation at the regional level disrupts the existing status quo distribution of wealth and power. In order to take advantage of a unique historical economic opportunity, some agency or entity in the region would need enough courage to disrupt the existing status quo.

Christensen called this problem the *innovator's dilemma*. As applied to private corporations, he argued that market leaders have difficulty diverting resources from the development of sustaining innovations, which address known customer needs in established markets, to the development of disruptive innovations, which often under perform established products in mainstream markets but offer benefits some emerging customers value.

The dilemma for private corporations is that the status quo arrangement with existing customers makes it difficult to give up on them in order to focus on new customers that do not exist yet.

The innovator's dilemma applies to regions for similar reasons as private corporations. In order to pass through the historical window of opportunity presented by technological innovation and the emergence of new markets, regional elected leaders must divert resources from the status quo. This is a risky proposition because there is no assurance that the future market opportunities will open up. The risk is one reason why politicians cannot be relied upon to lead the regional economy to a new structure.

Politicians are committed to the status quo. On the other hand, doing nothing has a great and certain risk that ends in regional economic decline. The regions that favor the status quo arrangement, as the theory in this book explained, are headed towards economic death.

Christensen's research focused primarily on *technological innovations*, broadly defined as those that introduce a different set of features, performance, and price attributes relative to existing products and technologies. He thought that technological innovations could occur in the ordinary course of corporate events, which he termed sustaining innovations, primarily directed making existing products better.

Regional economies in a steady-state condition also have something that looks like sustaining innovations, but most economists refer to this phenomenon as *"productivity improvements."* Existing products and processes are made better over time. Productivity improvements do not create regional economic growth. Productivity improvements simply allow the regional economy to run in place for an extended period of time.

When other parts of the world, or other regional economies catch up to a region that has been running in place with productivity improvements, the region becomes vulnerable to economic decline.

When private corporations create new technological knowledge, they tend to be more successful financially. For example, Griffin, et. al., reports that best-practice firms realize 49 percent of their sales from products developed and launched in the last five years and that new product performance accounts for one-fourth of the variability in organizational performance.[402]

That is, firms that are systematic innovators and earn profits above the average have a high probability to keep innovating and earning profits above the average, just as firms that are occasional innovators and earn profit below the average have a high probability to remain in the initial situation. The persistence in innovation seems to foster the persistence in profits, especially in the long run.

From an evolutionary economic perspective, the same types of results are probably true for regions. Successful regions in the future will continuously create new knowledge, which will, hopefully, create new markets.

According to research findings of Michael Camp, the most entrepreneurial regions in the United States had better economic performance in their local economies from 1990 to 2001 than the less entrepreneurial regions.

The more entrepreneurial regions had 125 percent higher employment growth, 58 percent higher wage growth and 109 percent higher productivity than the less entrepreneurial regions. The most entrepreneurial regions were associated with higher levels of technology. They expended nearly 54 percent more of R&D, recorded 67 percent more patents per labor force participant, had a 63 percent higher percentage of hi-tech establishments and had a 42 percent higher portion of college educated population than the least entrepreneurial regions.[403]

Importantly, from an evolutionary point of view, Camp documented a lag in time between the first appearance of an entrepreneurial activity in the region, and ensuing economic growth. Camp found a four year lag between measures of entrepreneurship activity and economic growth.

He stated, "The positive and significant coefficients for entrepreneurship activity and the relatively high levels of explained variation for each test suggest that entrepreneurship activity is a driver of regional economic growth."[404]

The economic growth that occurred in regions studied by Camp was caused by the formation of new markets. The goal of your jobs and wealth creation pipeline is the creation of entirely new markets. The new markets will create new flows of income. It does not particularly matter, in the beginning period, how small or disorganized the new markets appear to be.

The new markets will unleash an incredibly powerful force in the regional economy, but the outcomes of that event will not be felt for many years. Your region will require a regional innovation management system to manage the knowledge creation process in your region.

The existing status quo distribution of income and political power will be disrupted by the new flows of incomes, so you should anticipate political opposition from the wealthiest, most well-connected individuals and organizations in your community. You should never assume that the existing political parties or political organizations are going to help you. They would not constitute, as Mokyr's suggestion implies, the "sympathetic environment" for changing the status quo.

The main organizational ingredients that you need to create your own regional innovation management system for the jobs and wealth creation pipeline are:

- A social and business network of engineers and scientists who communicate regularly with each other about new products.

- A regional econometric model of the region's primary technological clusters that can show linkages and gaps in the local economic supply chain.

- A regional venture capital fund that directs capital to both new ventures and established ventures which need capital to grow.

- A supportive business and political environment for entrepreneurs.

- A regional e-commerce trading platform so that new ventures in the region can trade with each other in the regional supply chains.

- A business and political leadership that places primary allegiance on the wealth and prosperity of local residents.

The entire innovation management framework outlined above is designed to identify future market opportunities. The identification process does not occur quickly, and it does not occur in a single place or moment in time. It occurs because the individuals in the networks are communicating with each other about how things work in the regional economy. As a result of the discussions, new knowledge is being created.

The regional innovation management system is designed to organize the new knowledge into commercially viable ventures. The new ventures create new markets when the ventures trade goods and services with each other.

II. Your Region Must Function More Like A Private Corporation In Focusing on Job Creation.

Sarah J. Marsh and Gregory N. Stock in their article, *Creating Dynamic Capability: The Role of Intertemporal Integration, Knowledge Retention, and Interpretation,* describe how difficult it is for any single corporation to acquire external knowledge to benefit the corporation or even codify prior internal corporate knowledge.

"Uncertainty about the ability for technological knowledge to be transformed to meet market demands, lack of complementary technologies, the lack of developed markets for a given technical feature, and other types of uncertainty add significant challenges to organizations as they develop products for future markets,"[405] they state.

One technique that private corporations use to manage uncertainty is to adopt a strategic business plan that tells them what to do when things inside the company get out of whack. In the case of regions, there is even greater uncertainty because there is no unity of values or objectives about what the region is trying to accomplish. In the absence of any clearly defined goals or business plan, every policy can be seen in some politically expedient light to justify doing nothing.

Regions need to operate according to a strategic economic business plan. The people who implement the plan are small business owners and entrepreneurs, not government or non-profit agencies. The plan must not become the political vehicle for ambitious politicians or government bureaucrats that have their own agendas.

Predicting Technology

Once the components of the regional business plan are in place, they must be managed and administered, just like the regional economy was a business organization. The business plan of operation would be guided by the following set of principles:

- Product innovation and automated production are constants in a changing global economy. Local residents need a continuous stream of better information about the entire product development and commercialization process. In the future, most wealth will be created as a result of residents either working for, or creating, many different high technology companies, all of who sell new types of products, both to each other in the region and to consumers in the rest of the world.

- Residents need the regional new venture creation resources to be independent of global forces and local leaders need to adopt a policy that puts community financial interests above vaguely stated benefits of global trade agreements. Each region will need a "new venture creation pipeline," that has a huge number of new companies born each year as job growth shifts from the larger corporations to smaller companies. Part of the strategic plan recognizes that only a special type of multinational corporation makes sense to recruit to the region.

- Strong local economies will feature high income multiplier effects, as a dollar spent in each region stays in that region creating more jobs and incomes. Regional strength will be based upon regional industrial cluster relationships that are open to all residents, not just a selected few insiders. The regional plan of operation will foster the maximum degree of supply chain buying and selling between firms in the regional economy. The regional economy's primary linkage to the rest of the world will be through the larger corporations who have located branch operations in the region. Only a special type of large corporation that buys goods and supplies from local businesses should be a target of industrial recruitment.

- Knowledge about potential new market opportunities and information about "gaps" in technology can be defined with the assistance of sophisticated econometric models. The data from the models needs to be placed into the widest possible network of scientists, engineers and entrepreneurs to help them identify new venture opportunities.

Successful private companies produce profits. Successful regions produce jobs and wealth for the residents of the region. The unity of purpose for the region is the production of jobs and wealth, just like profits provide the unity of purpose for a private corporation.

Your new jobs and wealth creation business plan must give special support and consideration to individuals and families who have been disrupted, or are likely candidates to be disrupted, by the existing global economic and financial forces. They will be left with very little self-support or financial resources to take advantage of new market opportunities. Part of the help your can provide to them is in the time period before the regional economy enters the downward economic decline.

Individuals and families are usually too busy with daily events to focus on long-term economic trends and technological patterns. Your new regional business plan must continually inform families, and especially students in high school and college, about what is happening in the local economy and how the local economy is connected to the rest of the world.

Traditional media and news outlets do not usually generate this type of information in their daily newscasts; so one job of your innovation management system is to continually update citizens about the changing economic conditions in the region.

Your regional economy's greatest economic strength in the new world economy is its culture of individual initiative and reward based upon merit. Those attributes of individualism will serve your economy well in the global economy, but it will require a lot more work to help individuals identify new market opportunities. And, it will require the managers of the innovation system to continually identify potential new entrepreneurs and plug them into the regional innovation process.

Another part of the social network that will need special consideration is directed at helping poor individuals and minorities who do not have adequate education or resources to seize rapidly changing opportunities in a new entrepreneurial environment.

Your new regional innovation management system will contain a special type of econometric model that describes how parts of the economy are connected to each other. For example, manufacturing plants are connected to transportation companies that deliver the goods to wholesalers, who deliver the goods to retail stores. Part of the function of the new regional econometric model is to describe where and how service and support industries, like transportation, will be needed in the new regional economy.

The new firms that are created to service and support the emerging technological clusters will be the most likely opportunities to make certain that poor people do not get left behind in the global markets. The regional econometric model will identify gaps in the regional service and supply chain, a part of the economy that economist call indirect effects of investments.

Special policy steps will need to be taken in the area of indirect effects to plug poor people into the new markets so that they can benefit from the jobs and wealth.

The basic lesson is that all Americans will become entrepreneurs and captains of their own enterprises in order to survive and prosper. Job churn and loss of income is a likely economic outcome in a global economy for metro regions that do not focus on new venture creation and new product development. The alternative of doing nothing to change the status quo in America will be to experience greater levels of job churn and income loss, eventually leading large regions of this country to being reduced to the lowest living standards in the lowest wage areas of the world.

III. Your new regional economic business plan should help individuals and companies in specific ways:

Provide them ways to become a part of a local business/social network that discusses trends in local technology and commerce. These new organizations and networks would be different than the existing chambers of commerce, which are more oriented to satisfying the needs of the larger players in the regional economy.

Provide them with documents and research about the economic strengths and weaknesses of your local economy, and help them identify gaps in the market that may lead them to identify to new venture ideas.

Create public and political forums where citizens can demand that local elected leaders do a better job at helping residents identify future new markets that may arise in your city's industrial base.

Create a dialogue or forum for your business and banking leaders so that they understand the importance of doing a better job at creating the financial infrastructure that would help residents make a successful transition to owning their own company.

Provide avenues for residents to engage in continuous professional education and on-the-job skill training in the industrial sectors that have the highest regional rates of technological change.

Provide incentives to the local chamber of commerce and economic development organizations to focus more attention and resources on local new venture creation programs and small business development as a higher priority than recruiting outside industry.

Your strategic business plan must contain a section on competition, just like a private corporation's business plan. As the theory in this book described, competition is usually over incomes, not prices. In the future the most intense competition will be between global corporations seeking an advantage in gaining new knowledge to protect their profits. The competitive part of your business plan should address the competing interests over knowledge.

Part of the strategic nature of your regional business plan is understanding the dynamics of competition for knowledge and realizing that only a special type of multinational corporation will benefit the regional quest for knowledge creation. You regional economy has a strategic interest in having a certain type of multinational corporation located there.

IV. Your Metro Region Must Target A Special Type of Multinational Corporation For Industrial Recruitment Whose Presence Will Benefit Residents in the Region.

Technological knowledge diffusion is a social process of learning. There is a great act of faith involved in following this advice about knowledge creation, because there is no specific outcome involved that leaders can point to with certainty as the most likely outcome. Gaining the benefits of knowledge creation takes an act of faith, very similar in concept to the act of faith that most economists express about the theoretical benefits of the free market system.

In their case, most economists start out believing in the telos of perfect competition, and have faith that the real world will function just like the perfect world. In the case of knowledge creation, you would start out at the other end of the philosophical tunnel. You start out creating knowledge in the real world and have faith that the knowledge will end up creating jobs and wealth for regional residents. There is no certainty or guarantees involved in this process.

Your region could try to create knowledge and fail, or it could create knowledge but not have it diffused. Worse, it could create knowledge and have the benefits flow to other regions or to large private corporations that are desperate for new technological knowledge.

This is currently the biggest dilemma facing regional leaders. Most knowledge creation today, especially scientific knowledge created at major research universities, is absorbed by global corporations, with little economic benefit to most residents in the region.

If they happen to be the right type of corporation, there may not be a bad outcome for residents. For example, Intel establishes research partnerships with universities and consortia and then manages those partnerships very closely to make certain that the private corporation obtains a return on its investments. Contrary to the more common practice of giving money to a university and allowing it to pursue its own path, Intel assigns engineers to work directly with the students so the students have the advantage of the most current level of knowledge.

This practice is a case of knowledge creation, and diffusion, from the Intel engineers and scientists to students. In the theory explained in this book, the Intel engineers look like "boundary-crossers," who leave their own beehive and pollinate the university beehive. The role of boundary-crossers for the right type of multinational corporation is the creation of "open source knowledge," similar to the open source software coding associated with Linux.

In their research on how corporations generate knowledge, Marin and Bo describe how an idea turns into knowledge. "An idea to be realized," they write, "needs that the agent informed about the idea recruits another agent from a pool of uninformed people. This constraint generates a recursive effect of knowledge transmission via players' mobility across firms which affects simultaneously the players' payoffs and the number of active players engaged in market competition."[406]

In terms of your regional business plan, there is a certain type of multinational corporation that makes the most sense to invite into your region to create knowledge and produce new venture spin offs. These special types of multinational corporations should be the target of your regional industrial recruitment efforts.

While the corporations would like to gain your region's knowledge for their own private financial gain, they are willing participants in creating the open source knowledge networks that your region needs for knowledge creation and diffusion.

Not all corporations fit this description and you should never be lulled into the false assumption that your regional economic interests and the corporate financial interests are the same. They are not. However, the conflict of interest between regions and corporations over the benefits of technological knowledge, given this special type of corporation, do not prohibit your region from directing benefits to regional residents.

In their research on identifying certain types of knowledge creating multinational corporations, Marin Anabel and Giuliani Elisa categorized corporations according to their knowledge diffusion capacity. "We have advanced the idea," they write, "that only under certain organisational and managers' mental models, can subsidiaries be in a condition to diffuse technological knowledge locally. In our analysis, this occurs in the case of Globally Diversified and Independent subsidiaries."[407]

As is the case with all of evolutionary theory, under different environmental conditions, a different set of evolutionary events take place. "In contrast," (to the special kind of multi national corporation), they write, "when subsidiaries are dependent on the MNE group, they seem less likely to develop dense networks at the local level, leading these types of subsidiary to be considered as dead-ends in the global knowledge pipeline. Finally, Globally Isolated subsidiaries tend to behave in isolation also at the local level, not representing a valuable source of knowledge for other firms in the host country."[408]

Gunnar Hedlund described how large international businesses are ..."actively seeking advantages originating in the global spread of the firm" (rather than just exploiting centrally created technological assets). The early models of the MNE, as a centrally directed and closely integrated organisation, therefore, have lost relevance."[409] He outlined how the branch operations now function as "...a knowledge seeking affiliate, which taps into domestic sources of knowledge to develop products (or contributes to developing them) when the domestic environment provides the conditions."

The type of globally diversified corporations that are most valuable to regional economic development are those that are characterized by persistent innovation. The two valuable outcomes of persistent, or serial product innovation, are greater regional interindustry knowledge creation and a high rate of corporate spin-offs.

The knowledge creation effect of the multinational corporation occurs in an environment where technological information flows freely both inside the branch operations and between the branch and outside organizations composed of technical and professional employees. The regional knowledge creation infrastructure must be organized to promote and capture the benefit from this information flow.

The value of the spin-off effect for the region is that research demonstrates that spin-offs are generally superior to *de novo* new ventures in terms of lasting longer than 3 years. The evidence on the most successful spin-offs is that they originate from the most profitable large firms.

The evidence on spin-offs shows that the spin-off effect contributes to the development of regional industrial clusters. The evidence also shows that a certain type of multinational corporation does not generate spin-offs. The absence of spin-offs from large corporations in a region prevents regional industrial clusters from forming.

Marco A. Marin and Carlo Bo found both of the positive impacts of knowledge and spin-offs from a certain type of multinational corporation being located in a region.

They stated, "The findings suggest that communication behavior and fairness are positive contributors to trust. In contrast, conflicts during product development and perceived egoism of the partner appear to have a detrimental effect. High levels of trust were found to create the conditions for successful outcomes…Empirical results here suggest that collective, or organizationally controlled, knowledge is indeed statistically associated with service improvement and new service introduction. Collective knowledge can take the form of shared, or team, routines or service solutions and technologies."[410]

V. Your New Regional Business Plan Should Deliberately Target Financial Incentives and Benefits To Existing Small Business Owners in the Regional Industrial Cluster Supply Chains.

Business owners know about the effects of price competition that comes with the open global borders in trade and open illegal immigration. American small business owners realize that the one great advantage they have in the new global environment is out-thinking and out-innovating the competition. They know that competing on price in the new world market will not be a winning strategy.

Business owners are the primary economic agents in each metro region who will implement, or be the causal agents, to create the product innovation pipeline. They will be the first to perceive new market opportunities and the first to try out new mental ideas. But, more importantly, existing business owners already have a small pool of trust among each other and it is the presence of trust that allows new ideas to be commercialized.

Continuous technological innovation and commercializing new products will create new markets. New markets will generate new sources of income. Business owners must benefit from the new flows of income or else those flows of income will easily leave the regional economy. The business owners perform the essential economic function of keeping dollars flowing in the regional economy by continually buying and selling goods and services to each other and to local consumers.

However, new markets and new products do not happen by chance. They happen because the local economic environment is conducive to innovation and supports new venture creation. In order to benefit from technological change, business owners will need to create a new type of regional economic environment that is built on trust and truthful business dealings.

Your regional business plan must include explicit guidelines for plugging local small business owners into the new regional networks and alliances.

- Provide membership mechanisms for business owners to become a part of a new product development and technological innovation networks in your community so that they can gain insights into what new products may work for their company.

- Promote open registration at local private capital market meetings with angel investors and venture capitalists to allow business owners to find out what new ventures are being funded in your community. By attending these meetings, existing small business owners will gain valuable information on the structure of the deals that venture capitalists like to fund so that they can pitch the right type of deal to them when they are ready for private capital. The forums must be open, and not replicate the ordinary closed "by-invitation-only" events that are controlled by a handful of powerful local insiders.

- Provide open information access for small business owners to the data from the regional econometric model that forecasts trends in the local economy. In the same way that shareholders of public corporations have legal rights to see financial information about a company, local stakeholders in the region need to be able to monitor the strengths and weaknesses in the local supply chain networks.

- Provide easy membership for local business owners in a local e-commerce supply chain network so that they can obtain more dollars from every dollar spent in your local economy.

VI. Your Regional Innovation Management System Must Pursue Regional Technological Change.

Technology is often defined as a body of knowledge about how things work. In "*Technical Change as Cultural Evolution,*" Richard Nelson states that "...technology needs to be understood as consisting of both a set of specific designs and practices, and a generic knowledge that surrounds these and provides an understanding of how things work, the key variables affecting performance, the nature of currently binding constraints and promising approaches to pushing these constraints back."[411]

When Nelson describes "constraints," he is talking about scientific or technical constraints. But, as the theory explained in this book notes, the most severe constraint is from organized financial interests who benefit from the status quo arrangement of power and income. The pursuit of technological change means realizing there is competition for knowledge where financial interests of corporations are different than the financial interests of ordinary citizens.

319

Predicting Technology

The financial interests who could potentially benefit from technological change probably have never realized that they share a common interest in technological change. As Marsh and Stock point out, "Suppliers, customers, consultants, and the results of benchmarking and reverse engineering all provide sources of external knowledge that may be utilized in the new product development process, as do patent applications, scientific and trade publications, and conferences."

One goal of the regional innovation management system is to organize this set of economic agents in the region so that they realize their common interests. The new markets created by technical change represent an entirely different economic structure, with its own internal dynamic of growth, than the existing economic structure. The most important ingredient for creating technical change in your regional economy is an economic agent called an "entrepreneur."

VII. Individuals and Entrepreneurs.

While the existing small business community in your region will function to distribute regional income that results from technological change, the agents who create the new ventures are commonly called "entrepreneurs." Most entrepreneurs come from the ranks of the unemployed, the outsourced, the down-sized and the laid-offs.

In a well known passage of the Wealth of Nations, written in 1776, Adam Smith described the causes of prosperity of new American colonies as a "continuous process of transformation of initially subordinate workers into a group of independent producers. "

Your new regional business plan must help unemployed scientists, engineers, university professors, and budding entrepreneurs from every walk of life identify new venture opportunities and create a social climate that is environmentally-friendly for them to create new companies.

The likely supply of entrepreneurs is drawn from those employees who performed a boundary-spanning function prior to being laid off or catching the new venture fever. Prior to the regional economic disruption caused by rapid technological change and global price competition, these individuals were commonly the most individualistic in their ability to identify emerging patterns in the environment, with little or no direction from the organization. Because of their individualistic tendencies, they were also the first to be fired or laid-off for not being able to follow the company line.

Boundary spanners have been described as persons who operate at the periphery or boundary of a permeable organization, performing organizationally relevant tasks and relating the organization with elements outside it. In the theory explained in this book, the boundary-spanners are the individuals who bring knowledge back to their organization from sources outside their organization. Boundary spanners are the next generation nascent entrepreneurs.

Pier Saviotti describes why the supply of entrepreneurs is so important to the process of technical change in a region. "The knowledge of engineers, scientists, managers, technicians, etc., involved in the implementation of the technology becomes specialized around the process, technical and service characteristics used. This specialization creates networks of communication and power which reinforce the stability of the artifact dimension of the technology."[412]

In other words, in the region's existing social-business network of skilled individuals, there is a shared specialized knowledge about regional production processes. Within this network, potential entrepreneurs meet with each other and discuss technical problems and how to solve them. Often, the problems cannot be solved within the existing older firms, so the feasibility of starting a new venture is usually a topic of conversation.

Even more precious than the supply of local venture capital, the supply of nascent entrepreneurs is the region's greatest asset for creating the new venture creation pipeline. Identifying the potential supply of entrepreneurs and helping them solidify their ideas for new ventures should be job number one for your region.

You will find them at business social networking functions. They are the ones who are always at the different professional association meetings, and usually the ones who ask all the questions about how things work.

VIII. The Importance of Nurturing Your Regional Industrial Clusters.

Technological knowledge is not distributed uniformly across regions. Saviotti notes that innovative firms "...tend to cluster in those (areas) that were already innovating countries...this specificity can not be explained by factor endowments, but is more likely to be caused by specific institutional configurations, and by the cumulative, local and specific character of the knowledge that the institutions possess."[413]

Some regions have clusters of technological innovating firms and supportive social networks and some do not. The accumulation of technological knowledge and the pace of technical change are contingent outcomes of the social and political institutional structure of a region. For technological progress to occur, according to Mokyr, "...it must be born into a socially sympathetic environment."[414]

As used in the theory presented in the book, the concept of the industrial cluster is a precursor concept to regional markets. Regional markets are the most essential ingredient for promoting regional knowledge creation and diffusion. As has been mentioned several times, it is not so important that the regional market function perfectly. No market functions perfectly in reality. They only function perfectly in theory.

What is essential is that regional markets function, and have some independence from the global market. The regional industrial market should be the focus of policy attention in the regional innovation strategy because the regional market is the economic structure that changes shape over time as a result of economic evolution. It is the primary source of information on where new markets in the region are going to emerge.

Seizing New Market Opportunities

After years of academic research on entrepreneurship, Zoltan Acs recently came to the conclusion that no one had ever fully defined what an entrepreneurial opportunity looked like.[415]

As a way of addressing this gap in knowledge, Acs, who is arguably one of the world's greatest living scholars on entrepreneurship, organized a conference of academics, similar in concept to blind men feeling the body of an elephant in order to define what an elephant must be.

One blind man felt the trunk, and said that entrepreneurial "…opportunities and economic growth are strongly and explicitly linked to the evolution of science."

Another blind man felt the legs of the elephant and said "…entrepreneurial opportunities are those situations in which new goods, services, raw materials, and organizing methods can be introduced and sold at greater than their costs of production."

A very wise female academic, named Pamela Mueller rubbed the entire elephant and stated that, "…although the stock of knowledge in a region is an important determinant of local economic growth, it is new firms in general – seen as the exploitation of the opportunities that arise from R&D activities – and not public institutions that are the means by which knowledge contributes to the local economy."[416]

Mueller's research suggests that the contribution of public institutions and universities to regional growth pales in comparison with the contribution made by high-tech start-ups in particular. Mueller interprets the findings to suggest that new firms champion the innovations that drive economic growth and, as such, are far more likely to challenge the market positions of incumbent firms.

She noted, "Starting a firm in order to realize an entrepreneurial opportunity is assumed as a mechanism for knowledge diffusion and for the exploitation of knowledge. Ultimately, however, the firm is started with the purpose of introducing a new good or service."

The secret to success for your region is to start hundreds and hundreds of new ventures, based upon the unique technological knowledge in your regional industrial cluster. The new ventures, as Mueller suggests, are collectively what creates the new markets.

Your family, community and the local economy are being subjected to unprecedented changes in technology and markets. These trends are not going to change, and nothing can stop the trend in open global trading relationships. In order for you and your community to avoid economic decline, you will need to be able to predict the trends in technology and identify future market opportunities.

Once the entrepreneurs in your metro region "see" the new opportunities, they must "imagine" how a new venture can create a product that "fits" into the mental imaginations of future consumers, who do not yet exist.

You cannot depend on others to tell your nascent entrepreneurs about the future market gaps or to help them understand the economic effects of technology. The job of education is up to you and community leaders who place the welfare of the region first.

Disruptive technologies and rapid changes in global markets are a constant challenge today, and the more you read and educate yourself, the better your region's chances of financial survival will be in the coming years, and the greater the likelihood that you will seize the historical opportunity when it first appears.

BIBLIOGRAPHY

Acs, Zoltan, *Innovation and The Growth of Cities,* Cheltenham, Edward Elgar, 2002.

Acs, Zoltan, *Regional Innovation, Knowledge and Global Change,* London, Pinter, 2000.

Acs, Zoltan J. , McMullen, Jeffery S., Plummer, Lawrence A., "WHAT IS AN ENTREPRENEURIAL OPPORTUNITY?" Paper # 1007, Max Planck Institute of Economics, February, 2007.

Aghion, Philippe and Howitt, Peter, *Endogenous Growth Theory,* Cambridge, MIT Press, 1998.

Alchian, Armen, "Uncertainty, Evolution, and Economic Theory," Journal of Political Economy, Vol. 58, No. 3 (June, 1950),

Alderson, Wroe, *Dynamic Marketing Behavior,* Homewood, Richard D. Irwin, Inc., 1965.

Amick, Daniel, and Walberg, Herbert, *Introductory Multivariate Analysis For Educational, Psychological and Social Research,* Berkely, McCutchan Publishers, 1975.

Anabel, Marin, and Elisha, Giuliani, "Relating Global and Local Knowledge Linkages: The Case of MNC Subsidiaries in Argentina," Universidad Nacional de General Sarmiento, Argentina, 2006.

Appelbaum, Eileen, "The Economics of Technical Progress: Labor Issues Arising From the Spread of Programmable Automation Technologies," Automation and the Workplace, Washington, D. C., Office of Technology Assessment, ND.

Archibugi, Daniele, and Michie, Jonathan, *Technology, Globalisation and Economic Performance,* Cambridge, Cambridge University Press, 1997.

Arthur, Brian W., Durlauf, Steven, and Lane, David, *The Economy As An Evolving Complex System, II.,* Reading, Addison-Wesley, 1997.

Bagozzi, Richard, P., and Van Loo, M. Frances, "Motivational and Reasoned Processes In the Theory of Consumer Choice," Handbook of Behavioral Economics, (Vol. 2B), 1991.

Banzhuf, Wolfgang, and Reeves, Colin, *Foundations of Genetic Algorithms, 5th Edition,* San Francisco, Morgan Kaufmann Publishers, Inc., 1999.

Barnett, William, et. al., *Commerce, Complexity and Evolution,* London, Cambridge University Press, 2000.

Becker, Karen, and Feser, Edward, *Applying Cluster Analysis To North Carolina's Regions: Triangle Economic Development Partnership Region,* Chapel Hill, Institute for Economic Development, March 1997.

Beckman, M. J., (Editor), et. al., *Knowledge and Networks In A Dynamic Economy,* New York, Springer-Verlag, 1998.

Bennett, William, (Editor), et. al., *Commerce, Complexity and Evolution,* Cambridge University Press, London, 2000.

Bertuglia, Cristoforo, Lombardo, Silvana, and Nijkamp, Peter, *Innovative Behavior In Space and Time,* Berlin, Springer, 1997.

Best, Michael, *The New Competition: Institutions of Industrial Restructuring,* Cambridge, Harvard University Press, 1990.

Blaug, Mark, *Economic History and the History of Economics,* New York, New York University Press, 1986.

Bramanti, Alberto, (Editor), et. al., *The Dynamics of Innovative Regions: The GREMI Approach,* Aldershot, Ashgate, 1997.

Brennan, Geoffrey, and Buchanan, James M., *The Reason of Rules: Constitutional Political Economy,* London, Cambridge University Press, 1985.

Broemelinger, Lyle, and Tsurimi, Hiroki, *Econometrics and Structural Change,* New York, Marcel Dekker, 1987.

Bruno, A.V. and Tybjee, T.T., "The Environment for Entrepreneurship" In Kent, C.A., Sexton, D.L., and Vesper, K.H., (Eds.), *Encyclopedia of Entrepreneurship,* Prentice-Hall, Englewood Cliffs, NJ., 1982.

Burger, R., *The Mathematical Theory of Selection, Recombination and Mutation,* New York, John Wiley & Sons, 2000.

Camp, S. Michael, *The Innovation-Entrepreneurship NEXUS: A National Assessment of Entrepreneurship and Regional Economic Growth and Development,* Advanced Research Technologies, LLC, Powell, Ohio, April 2005.

Cantner, Uwe, Hanusch, Horst, and Klepper, Steven, *Economic Evolution, Learning, and Complexity,* Heidelberg, Physica-Verlag, 2000.

Carter, Anne P., *Structural Change In The American Economy,* Cambridge, Harvard University Press, 1970.

Chandler, Alfred, D. Jr., and Mazlish, Bruce, eds., *Leviathans: Multinational Corporations and the New Global History,* Cambridge, Cambridge University Press, 2005.

Chenery, Hollis, B., and Watanabe, Tsunehiko, "International Comparisons of the Structure of Production," <u>Econometrica</u>, 1958.

Christensen, Clayton M., *The Innovator's Dilemma: When New Technologies Cause Great Firms To Fail,* Boston, Harvard Business School Press, 1997.

Christensen, Clayton, and Raynor, Michael, *The Innovator's Solution: Creating and Sustaining Successful Growth,* Boston, Harvard Business School Press, 2003.

Christensen, Clayton, M., "The Rules of Innovation," Technology Review, June 2002.

Christensen, Claytom, M., Anthoney, Scott, D., and Roth, Erik, *Seeing What's Next: Using The Theories of Innovation To Predict Industry Change,* Boston, Harvard Business School Press, 2004.

Cialdini, Robert, *Influence: How and Why People Agree To Things,* New York, William Morrow & Co., 1984.

Cooke, Philip and Morgan, Kevin, *The Associational Economy: Firms, Regions and Innovations,* Oxford, Oxford University Press, 1998.

Czamanski, Stan, *Regional Science Techniques In Practice: The Case of Nova Scotia,* Lexington, D. C. Heath and Company, 1972.

Day, Richard, and Chen, Ping, *Nonlinear Dynamics and Evolutionary Economics,* New York, Oxford, 1993.

DeBresson, Christian, *Economic Interdependence and Innovative Activity: An Input-Output Approach,* Cheltenham, Edward Elgar, 1996.

Dennett, Daniel Clement, *Consciousness Explained,* 1st ed., Boston, Little, Brown and Co., 1991

DeSoto, Hernando, *The Mystery of Capital: Why Capitalism Triumphs in the West and Fails Everywhere Else,* New York, Basic Books, 2000.

Dewhurst, John, Hewings, Geoffrey, and Jensen, Rodney, *Regional Input-Output Modeling: New Developments and Interpretations,* Aldershot, Avebury. 1991.

Dobb, Maurice, *Theories of Value and Distribution Since Adam Smith: Ideology and Economic Theory,* Cambridge, Cambridge University Press, 1973.

Domar, Evsay, "Capital Expansion, Rate of Growth, and Employment," Econometrica, 1946, Vol. 14, No. 2.

Dorfman, Jeffrey, *Bayesian Economics Through Numerical Methods: A Guide To Econometrics and Decision Making With Prior Information,* New York, Springer, 1997.

Dosi, Giovanni, (Editor), et. al., *Technology, Organization, and Competitiveness: Perspectives on Industrial and Corporate Change,* Oxford, Oxford University Press, 1998.

Doucet, Paul, and Sloep, Peter, *Mathematical Modeling In the Life Sciences,* New York, Ellis Horwood, 1992.

Duchin, Faye, and Szyld, D. B., "A Dynamic I-O Model With Assured Positive Output," in *Input-Output Analysis, Volume I,* Kurtz, Henry, (Editor), et. al., Cheltenham, Edward Elgar, 1998.

Duchin, Faye, *Structural Economics: Measuring Change In Technology, Lifestyles and The Environment,* Washington, Island Press, 1998.

Dyson, Freeman, "Megaphone: The Darwinian Interlude," Technology Review, March 2005

Edquist, Charles, and McKelvey, Maureen, (Editors), *Systems of Innovation: Growth, Competitiveness, and Employment, Vol. I.,* Cheltenham, Edward Elgar, 2000.

Edquist, Charles, and McKelvey, Maureen, *Systems of Innovation: Growth, Competitiveness, and Employment, Vol., II,* Cheltenham, Edward Elgar, 2000.

Edquist, Charles, Hommen, Leif and McKelvey, Maureen, *Innovation and Employment: Process Versus Product Innovation,* Cheltenham, Edward Elgar, 2001.

Edquist, Charles, *Systems of Innovation: Technology, Institutions and Organizations,* London, Pinter, 1997.

Epstein, Joshua, *Nonlinear Dynamics, Mathematical Biology, and Social Science,* Reading, Addison-Wesley, 1997.

Evangelista, Rinaldo, *Knowledge and Investment: The Sources of Innovation In Industry,* Cheltenham, Edward Elgar, 1999.

Ferrell, O. C., and Brown, Charles Lamb, Jr., *Conceptual and Theoretical Developments in Marketing,* Chicago, American Marketing Association, 1979.

Feser, Edward, J., "Enterprises, External Economies and Economic Development," Journal of Planning Literature, (Vol. 12 #3), February 1998.

Feser, Edward, J., and Bergman, Ed., "National Industry Cluster Templates: A Framework For Applied Regional Analysis," Regional Studies, (Vol. 34 #1), 2000.

Feser, Edward, J., and Sweeney, Stuart, "A Test For the Coincident Economic and Spatial Clustering of Business Enterprises," Journal of Geographical Systems, (2, 4), 2002.

Feser, Edward, J., Bergman, Ed, and Sweeney, Stuart, *Targeting North Carolina Manufacturing: Understanding the State's Economy Through Industrial Cluster Analysis, Vol. 1.* Chapel Hill, Institute for Economic Development, March 1996.

Feser, Edward, J., *Technical Appendix To Kentucky Clusters: Derivation of Benchmark U.S. Clusters,* Edward Feser web site, www.unc.edu/depts/dcrpweb. April 2001.

Fischer, Manfred, "Innovation, Knowledge Creation and Systems of Innovation," The Annals of Regional Science, (Vol. 35 #2), 2001.

Fischer, Manfred, and Frohlich, Josef, *Knowledge, Complexity and Innovation Systems,* Berlin, Springer-Verlag, 2001.

Fischer, Manfred, Villa, Louis Suarez, and Steiner, Michael, *Innovation, Networks and Localities,* Heidelberg, Springer, 1999.

Friedman, Robert, and Schweke, William, *Expanding the Opportunity to Produce: Revitalizing The American Economy Through New Enterprise Development,* Washington, D. C., Corporation For Enterprise Development, 1981.

Fuhrer, Jeffrey, and Little, Jane Sneddon, *Technology and Growth: Conference Proceedings,* Conference Series #40, Boston, Federal Reserve Bank of Boston, 1996.

Glass, Leon, and Mackey, Michael, *From Clocks to Chaos: The Rhythms of Life,* Princeton, Princeton University Press, 1988.

Goel, Rajeev, K., *Economic Models of Technological Change: Theory and Application,* Westport, Quorum Books, 1999.

Greider, William, "A New Giant Sucking Sound," The Nation, December 31, 2001.

Griffin, A., "PDAM Research on New Product Development Practices: Updating Trends and Benchmarking Best Practices". Journal of Product Innovation Management, 1997.

Griliches, Zvi, (Editor), et.al., *Research And Development, Patents and Productivity,*" Chicago, University of Chicago Press, 1984.

Griliches, Zvi, *R & D, Patents and Productivity,* Chicago, University of Chicago Press, 1984.

Haley, Usha, C., *Multinational Corporations In Political Environments: Ethics, Values and Strategies,* Singapore, World Scientific Publishing, 2001.

Hall, Peter, *Innovation, Economics and Evolution: Theoretical Perspectives on Changing Technology in Economic Systems,* New York, Harvester Wheatsheaf, 1994.

Hansen, Bent, *A Survey of General Equilibrium Systems,* New York, McGraw Hill, 1970.

Hanusch, Horst, *Evolutionary Economics: Applications of Schumpeter's Ideas,* Cambridge, Cambridge University Press, 1988.

Harrington, Michael, *"Alliance Business Park Seen In Lead for Dell,"* Triad Business Journal, Greensboro, N. C., November 5, 2004.

Harrod, R., "An Essay in Dynamic Theory", The Economic Journal, 1939, Vol. 49, No. 193.

Hartl, Daniel, *A Primer on Population Genetics,* Sunderland, Sinauer Association, 1981.

Hartl, Daniel, *Principles of Population Genetics,* Sunderland, Sinauer Associates, 1980.

Harvey, Cambell, and Gray, Stephen, "Forward and Future Contracts," Global Financial Management, *www.finance.com* , Feb. 15, 1997.

Hedlund, Gunnar 'The Hypermodern MNC: A Heterarchy?' Human Resource Management, 1986.

Heertje, Arnold and Perlman, Mark, *Evolving Technology and Market Structure: Studies in Schumpeterian Economics,* Ann Arbor, University of Michigan Press, 1990.

Heertje, Arnold, *Economics and Technical Change,* New York, John Wiley & Sons, 1973.

Hekman, John, "The Future of High Technology Industry In New England," The New England Economic Review, Jan. – Feb., 1980.

Herbert, Robert, and Link, Albert, *The Entrepreneur,* New York, Praeger, 1982.

Hewings, Geoffrey, (Editor), et. al., *Understanding and Interpreting Economic Structure,* New York, Springer, 1999.

Higgins, Benjamin, and Savoie, Donald, *Regional Development Theories and Their Application,* New Brunswick, Transaction Publishers, 1997.

Hirschman, Albert, *The Strategy of Economic Development,* New Haven, Yale University Press, 1958.

Hodgson, Geoffrey, M., "Darwinism In Economics: From Analogy to Ontology," Journal of Evolutionary Economics, Springer Verlag, 2002, Vol. 12.,

Hodgson, Geoffrey and Screpanti, Ernesto, *Rethinking Economics: Markets, Technology and Economic Evolution,* Aldershot, Edward Elgar, 1991.

Hofbauer, Josef, and Sigmund, Karl, *The Theory of Evolution and Dynamical Systems: Mathematical Aspects of Selection,* Cambridge, Cambridge University Press, 1988.

Holland, John H., *Emergence: From Chaos To Order,* Reading, Helix Books, 1998.

Holland, John, H., *Genetic Algorithms,* www.arch.columbia.edu., 2001.

Holland, John, *Hidden Order: How Adaptation Builds Complexity,* New York, Helix Books, 1995.

Hollis, Martin, and Nell, Edward J., *Rational Economic Man,* London, Cambridge University Press, 1975.

Homans, George, C., *Social Behavior: Its Elementary Forms,* New York, Harcourt Brace Javanovich, Inc., 1974.

Hoover, Edgar, *The Location of Economic Activity,* New York, McGraw-Hill, 1948.

Hossfeld, Leslie, Legerton, Mac, Keuster, Gerald, "The Economic and Social Impact of Job Loss in Robeson County, North Carolina, 1993-2003," Sociation Today Volume 2, Number 2, Fall 2004.

Howson, Colin, and Urback, Peter, *Scientific Reasoning: The Bayesian Approach,* Second Edition, Chicago, 1993.

Hoyle, Fred, *Mathematics of Evolution,* Memphis, Acorn Enterprises, 1987.

Hughes, Austin, *Adaptive Evolution of Genes and Genomes,* New York, Oxford, 1999.

Hunt, E. K., and Schwartz, Jesse G., *A Critique of Economic Theory,* Baltimore, Penguin Books, 1972.

Hunt, E. K., *History of Economic Thought: A Critical Perspective,* New York, Harper Collins, 1992.

Hunt, Shelby D., *Marketing Theory: The Philosophy of Marketing Science,* Homewood, Richard D. Irwin, 1983.

Hunt, Shelby D., *Modern Marketing Theory: Critical Issues In the Philosophy of Marketing Science,* Cincinnati, South-Western Publishing Co., 1991.

Hymer, Stephen. H., (dissertation of 1960, published 1976), *The International Operations of National Firms: a Study of Direct Foreign Investment,* Cambridge, MIT Press, 1976.

Israilevich, Philip, and Hewings, Geoffrey, et. al., "Forecasting Structural Change With a Regional Econometric Input-Output Model," Journal of Regional Science, (Vol. 37, #4), 1997.

Jacobs, Jane, *Cities and the Wealth of Nations: Principles of Economic Life,* New York, Random House, 1984.

Johansson, Borje, (Editor), et. al., *Theories of Endogenous Regional Growth: Lessons For Regional Policies,* Berlin, Springer, 2001.

Jones, Geoffrey, *Multinational and Global Capitalism: From The Nineteenth to the Twenty-First Century,* Oxford, Oxford University Press, 2005.

Kachigan, Sam, K., *Multivariate Statistical Analysis: A Conceptual Introduction,* New York Radius Press, 1991.

Kamien, Morton, and Schwartz, Nancy, *Market Structure and Innovation.* Cambridge, Cambridge University Press, 1982.

Kaplan, Daniel, and Glass, Leon, *Understanding Nonlinear Dynamics,* New York, Springer-Verlag, 1995.

Katz, Ralph, "The S-Curve Explained," in <u>Managing Creativity and Innovation,</u> Boston, Harvard Business School Press, 2003.

Kent, Calvin, Sexton, Donald, and Vesper, Karl, *Encyclopedia of Entrepreneurship,* Englewood Cliffs, Prentice-Hall, Inc., 1982.

Kimura, Motoo, *The Natural Law of Molecular Evolution,* Cambridge, Cambridge University Press, 1983.

Kindleberger, Charles, P., *World Economic Primacy: 1500 to 1990.* New York, Oxford University Press, 1996.

Kirby, Peter, (Editor), *Entrepreneurship and Economic Development,* New York, The Free Press, 1971.

Kleiner, Art, "The World's Most Exciting Accountant," <u>Strategy & Business Issues,</u> #35. 2004.

Krahl, Dave, *"Modeling With Extend,"* <u>Proceedings of the 1999 Winter Simulation Conference,</u> No Date.

Krahl, David, *"The Extend Simulation Environment,* <u>Proceedings of the 2002 Winter Simulation Conference,</u> No Date.

Krugman, Paul, *Pop Internationalism,* Cambridge, MIT Press, 1996.

Krzanowski, Roman, and Roper, Jonathan, *Spatial Evolutionary Modeling,* New York, Oxford University Press, 2001.

Kurtz, Heinz, D., (Editor), et. al., *Input-Output Analysis, Volume I,* Cheltenham, Edward Elgar, 1998.

Kurtz, Heinz, D., (Editor), et. al., *Input-Output Analysis, Volume II,* Cheltenham, Edward Elgar, 1998.

Lambooy, Jan G., and Boschma, Ron, *"Evolutionary Economics and Regional Policy,"* <u>The Annals of Regional Science,</u> (#35), 2001.

Lancaster, K., "A New Approach To Consumer Theory," <u>Journal of Political Economy,</u> (#74), 1966.

Landau, Ralph, Taylor, Timothy and Wright, Gavin, (Editors), *The Mosaic of Economic Growth,* Stanford, Stanford University Press, 1996.

Landreth, Harry, and Colander, David, *History of Economic Theory,* 2cd Edition, Boston, Houghton Mifflin Co., 1989.

Larsen, Tors, and McGuire, Eugene, (Editors), *Information Systems Innovation and Diffusion: Issues and Directions,* Hershey, Idea Group Publishing, 1998.

Leontief, Wassily, *"Input-Output Data Base For Analysis of Technological Change,"* <u>Economic Systems Research,</u> (Vol. 1 #3), 1989.

Leontief, Wassily, *Essays In Economics, Theories, Facts and Policies, Volume II,* White Plains, M. E. Sharpe, Inc., 1977.

Leontief, Wassily, *The Structure of the American Economy, 1919 – 1939: An Empirical Application of Equilibrium Analysis,* New York, Oxford University Press, 1960.

Lewontin, R. C., *The Genetic Basis of Evolutionary Change,* New York, Columbia University Press, 1974.

Leydesdorff, Loet, and Van Den Besselaar, Peter, (Editors), *Evolutionary Economics and Chaos Theory: New Directions In Technology Studies,* London, Pinter Publishers, 1994.

Lorr, Maurice, *Cluster Analysis For Social Scientists: Techniques For Analyzing and Simplifying Complex Blocks of Data,* San Francisco, Josey-Bass Publishers, 1983.

Los, B., and Verspagen, B., *The Empirical Performance of a New Interindustry Technology Spillover Measure,* Working Paper, NP, 1999.

Malecki, Edward, and Oinas, Paivi, (Editors), *Making Connections: Technological Learning and Regional Economic Change,* Aldershot, Ashgate ,1999.

Malecki, Edward, J., *Technology and Economic Development: The Dynamic of Local, Regional and National Change,* Essex, Longman Scientific and Technical, 1991.

Mansfield, Edwin, (Editor), et. al., *Technology Transfer, Productivity, and Economic Policy,* New York, W. W. Norton and Company, 1982.

Mansfield, Edwin, (Editor), et. al., *The Production and Application of New Industrial Technology,* New York, W. W. Norton and Company, 1977.

Mantegna, Rosario, and Stanley, Eugene H., *An Introduction to Econophysics: Correlations and Complexity In Finance,* Cambridge, Cambridge University Press, 2000.

Marin, Marco A. Bo, Carlo, "The Value of a New Idea: Knowledge Transmission, Workers' Mobility and Market Structure," Faculty of Economics, University of Urbino, MPRA Paper No. 168710. July 2005.

Marsden, J. E., and McCracken, M., *The Hopf Bifurcation and Its Applications,* New York, Springer-Verlag, 1976.

Marsh, Sarah J., and Stock, Gregory N., "Creating Dynamic Capability: The Role of Intertemporal Integration, Knowledge Retention, and Interpretation," Journal of Product Innovation Management, 23 (5), September 2006

Marshall, Alfred, *Principles of Economics, 8ᵗʰ Edition,* New York, The MacMillan Co., 1949.

Marsili, Matteo, "*Dissecting Financial Markets: Sectors and States,*" Trieste, INFM, April 12, 2002.

McAdams, Robert C., *Paths of Fire: An Anthropologists Inquiry Into Western Technology,* Princeton, Princeton University Press, 1996.

Miernyk, William H., *The Elements of Input-Output Analysis,* New York, Random House, 1965.

Miller, Ronald, and Blair, Peter, *Input-Output Analysis: Foundations and Extensions,* Englewood Cliffs, Prentice-Hall, 1985.

Miller, Ronald, and Polenske, Karen, *Frontiers of Input-Output Analysis,* New York, Oxford University Press, 1989.

Mitchell, Melanie, *An Introduction To Genetic Algorithms,* Cambridge, MIT Press, 1996.

Mokyr, Joel, *The Gifts of Athena: Historical Origins of the Knowledge Economy,* Princeton, Princeton University Press, 2002

Mokyr, Joel, *The Lever of Riches: Technological Creativity and Economic Progress,* New York, Oxford University Press, 1990.

Morroni, Mario, *Production Process and Technological Change,* Cambridge, Cambridge University Press, 1992.

Mowery, David C., and Rosenberg, Nathan, *Paths of Innovation: Technological Change In the 20th Century America,* Cambridge, Cambridge University Press, 1998.

Mueller, H. J., "The Relation of Recombination To Mutational Advance," in Mutation Research, (Vol. 1), 1964.

Mueller, Pamela, "Exploiting Entrepreneurial Opportunities: The Impact of Entrepreneurship on Growth," cited in Acs, Zoltan J. , McMullen, Jeffery S., Plummer, Lawrence A., "WHAT IS AN ENTREPRENEURIAL OPPORTUNITY?" Paper # 1007, Max Planck Institute of Economics, February, 2007.

Nagle, Thomas, *The Strategy and Tactics of Pricing: A Guide To Profitable Decision Making,* Englewood Cliffs, Prentice-Hall, 1987.

Nelson, Richard R., *National Innovation Systems: A Comparative Approach,* New York, Oxford University Press, 1993.

Nelson, Richard R., *The Sources of Economic Growth,* Cambridge, Harvard Universtiy Press, 1996.

Nelson, Richard, and Winter, Sidney, *An Evolutionary Theory of Economic Change,* Cambridge, Belknap Press, 1982.

Nelson, Richard B "Technical Change As Cultural Evolution," in Ross, Thomson, (Ed.), Learning and Technical Change, New York, St. Martin's Press, 1993.

Parisi, Jurgen, (Editor), et. al., *A Perspective Look at Nonlinear Media: From Physics To Biology and Social Sciences,* New York, Springer, 1998.

Pasinetti, Luigi, *Structural Change and Economic Growth: A Theoretical Essay on the Dynamics of The Wealth of Nations,* Cambridge, Cambridge University Press, 1981.

Payson, Steven, *Economics, Science, and Technology,* Cheltenham, Edward Elgar, 2000.

Peterson, William, (Editor), *Advances in Input-Output Analysis: Technology, Planning and Development,* New York, Oxford University Press, 1991.

Porat, Mark Uri, *The Information Economy: Definition and Measurement,* Washington, D. C., U. S. Department of Commerce, OT Special Publication 77-12(1), 1977.

Porter, Michael, *The Competitive Advantage of Nations,* New York, The Free Press, 1990

Pryor, Frederick, *Economic Evolution and Structure: The Impact of Complexity in the US Economic System,* Cambridge, Cambridge University Press, 1996.

Raa, Thyis Ten, *Linear Analysis of Competitive Economies,* New York, Harvester Wheatsheaf, 1995.

Rees, John, *"Technological Change and Regional Shifts in American Manufacturing,"* Professional Geographer (Vol. 31 #1), Feb. 1979.

Ricardo, David, *On the Principles of Political Economy and Taxation,* London, John Murray, First published: 1817.

Rogers, E. M., *Diffusion of Innovations,* 3rd Edition, New York, Free Press, 1983.

Ronen, Joshua, (Editor), *Entrepreneurship,* Lexington, Lexington Books, 1982.

Rosenberg, Alexander, *Darwinism In Philosophy, Social Science and Policy,* Cambridge, Cambridge University Press, 2000.

Rosenberg, Alexander, *Philosophy of Social Science,* 2cd Edition, Boulder, Westview Press, 1988.

Rosenberg, Nathan, *Inside the Black Box: Technology and Economics,* Cambridge, Cambridge University Press, 1982.

Rosenberg, Nathan, Landau, Ralph and Mowery, David, *Technology and the Wealth of Nations,* Stanford, Stanford University Press, 1992.

Rosenberg, Nathan, *The Emergence of Economic Ideas: Essays in the History of Economics,* Cambridge, Edward Elgar Publishing, 1994.

Routh, Guy, *The Origin of Economic Ideas,* White Plains, M. E. Sharpe, Inc., 1975.

Rummel, R. J., *Understanding Factor Analysis,* R. J. Rummel web site, www. hawaii.edu/powerkills. December 11, 2002.

Saviotti, Pier Paolo, Walsh, Vivien, and Coombs, Rod, *Economic and Technological Change,* Totowa, N.J., Rowman & Littlefield, 1987.

Saviotti, Pier Paolo, *Technological Evolution, Variety and The Economy,* Cheltenham, Edward Elgar, 1996.

Schumacher, Randall, and Lomax, Richard, *A Beginner's Guide To Structural Equation Modeling,* Mahway, N. J., Lawrence Erlbaum Assoc., 1996.

Schumpeter, Joseph A., *The Theory of Economic Development,* New York, Oxford University Press, 1961.

Shapero, Albert, *The Role of Entrepreneurship In Economic Development at the Less-Than-National-Level,* Austin, University of Texas Press, 1977.

Sheth, Jagdish, (Editor), et. al., *Marketing Theory: Evolution and Evaluation,* New York, John Wiley & Sons, 1988.

Sheth, Jagdish, and Garrett, Dennis, *Marketing Theory: Classic and Contemporary Readings,* Cincinnati, South-Western Publishing, 1986.

Shionoya, Yuichi, and Perlman, Mark, *Innovation In Technology, Industry and Institutions: Studies In Schumpeterian Perspectives,* Ann Arbor, University of Michigan Press, 1994.

Simmie, James, (Editor), *Innovative Cities,* London, Spon Press, 2001.

Simpson, David, and Tsukui, Jinkichi, "The Fundamental Structure of Input-Output Tables: An International Comparison," Review of Economics and Statistics, 1965.

Smith, Adam, *An Inquiry into the Nature and Causes of the Wealth of Nations,* Methuen and Co., Ltd., ed. Edwin Cannan, London, 1904. Fifth edition. First published: 1776.

Smith, John Maynard, *Evolutionary Genetics,* Oxford, Oxford University Press, 1989.

Smith, John Maynard, *Evolutionary Genetics,* Second Edition, New York, Oxford University Press, 1998.

Spiegel, Henry William, *The Growth of Economic Thought: Revised and Expanded Edition,* Durham, Duke University Press, 1983.

Sraffa, Piero, *Production of Commodities by Means of Commodities: Prelude to a Critique of Economic Theory,* Cambridge, Cambridge University Press, 1960.

Staber, Udo, (Editor), et. al., *Business Networks: Prospects For Development,* Berlin, Springer, 1996.

Steiner, Michael, (Editor), et. al., *Clusters and Regional Specialisation: On Geography, Technology and Networks,* London, Pion, 1998.

Stiroh, Kevin, "What Drives Productivity Growth," Economic Policy Review, New York, Federal Reserve Bank of New York, March 2001.

Storper, Michael, *The Regional World: Territorial Development In a Global Economy,* New York, Guilford Press. 1997.

Suarez-Villa, Luis, *The Evolution of Regional Economies: Entrepreneurship and Macroeconomic Change,* New York, Praeger, 1989.

Sweeney, Stuart, and Feser, Ed, "Plant Size and Clustering of Manufacturing Activity," Geographical Analysis, (Vol. 30 #1), January, 1998.

Temin, Peter, "Entrepreneurs and Managers," in Higonnet, P., Landes, D. Rosovsky, H., (Eds.), *Favorites of Fortune*, Cambridge, Harvard University Press, 1991.

Thomson, Ross, (Editor), *Learning and Technological Change*, New York, St. Martin's Press, 1993.

Thwaites, A. T., and Oakley, R. P., (Editors), *The Regional Economic Impact of Technological Change*, New York, St. Martin's Press, 1985.

Tiebout, Charles M., "Interregional Input-Output Models: An Appraisal," Southern Economic Journal, (Vol. 24), October 1957.

Timmons, Jeffrey, Smollen, Leonard, and Dingee, Alexander, *New Venture Creation: A Guide To Small Business Development*, Homewood, Richard D. Irwin, Inc., 1977.

Vass, Thomas E., *Do Cities Still Matter? The Regional Geographical Imperative of Technological Progress in a Global Inter-Networked Market*, Houston, eBookstand, Inc., 2001.

Vesper, Karl H., *New Venture Strategies*, Englewood Cliffs, Prentice-Hall, Inc., 1980.

Wheeler, James, (Editor), et. al., *Cities In The Telecommunications Age: The Fracturing of Geographics*, New York, Routledge, 2000.

Wilbur, Charles, K., *The Political Economy of Development and Underdevelopment*, New York, Random House, 1973.

Winch, D. M., *Analytical Welfare Economics*, London, Penguin Education, 1971.

Winfree, Arthur, *The Geometry of Biological Time*, New York, Springer, 2000.

Wolff, Edward, N., "Spillovers, Linkages, and Technical Change," Economic Systems Research, (Vol. 9 #1), 1979.

Woodruff, Ronny, and Thompson, James, Jr., (Editors), *Mutation and Evolution*, Boston, Kluwer Academic Publishers, 1998.

Yan, Chiou-Shueng, *Introduction to Input-Output Economics*, New York, Holt, Rinehart & Winston, 1969.

Zhang, Wei-Bin, *Capital and Knowledge: Dynamics of Economic Structures With Non-Constant Returns*, Berlin, Springer-Verlag, 1999.

Ziman, John, *Technological Innovation As An Evolutionary Process*, Cambridge, Cambridge University Press, 2000.

ENDNOTES

(Endnotes)

1 Hossfeld, Leslie, Legerton, Mac, Keuster, Gerald, "The Economic and Social Impact of Job Loss in Robeson County, North Carolina, 1993-2003," <u>Sociation Today</u> Volume 2, Number 2, Fall 2004.

2 Hossfeld, Leslie, Legerton, Mac, Keuster, Gerald, "The Economic and Social Impact of Job Loss in Robeson County, North Carolina, 1993-2003," <u>Sociation Today</u> Volume 2, Number 2, Fall 2004.

3 Marsh, Sarah J., and Stock, Gregory N., "Creating Dynamic Capability: The Role of Intertemporal Integration, Knowledge Retention, and Interpretation," <u>Journal of Product Innovation Management,</u> 23 (5), September 2006. pps. 422–436.

4 Saviotti, Pier Paolo, <u>Technological Evolution, Variety, and The Economy,</u> Cheltenham, UK., Edward-Elgar. 1996. p. 78.

5 McAdams, Robert, Paths of Fire: An Anthropologists Inquiry Into Western Technology, Princeton, Princeton University Press, 1996. p. 91.

6 ⁶Temin, Peter, "Entrepreneurs and Managers," in Higonnet, P., Landes, D. Rosovsky, H., (Eds.), Favorites of Fortune, Cambridge, Harvard University Press, 1991. p. 339.

7 Nelson, Richard B "Technical Change As Cultural Evolution," in Ross, Thomson, (Ed.), <u>Learning and Technical Change,</u> New York, St. Martin's Press, 1993. p. 11.

8 Technological Evolution, Variety, and The Economy, p. 188.

9 The Lever of Riches, p. 191.

10 Paths of Fire, p. 87.

11 Bruno, A.V. and Tybjee, T.T., "The Environment for Entrepreneurship" In Kent, C.A., Sexton, D.L., and Vesper, K.H., (Eds.), Encyclopedia of Entrepreneurship, Prentice-Hall, Englewood Cliffs, NJ., 1982. pp. 288-316.

12 Technological Evolution, Variety, and The Economy, p. 188.

13 Kindleberger, Charles P., World Economic Primacy: 1500 - 1900, New York, Oxford University Press, 1996. p. 18.

14 Suarez-Villa, Luis, <u>The Evolution of Regional Economies: Entrepreneurship and Macroeconomic Change,</u> New York, Praeger, 1989. p. 22.

15 Christensen, Clayton M., <u>The Innovator's Dilemma: When New Technologies Cause Great Firms To Fail,</u> Boston, Harvard Business School Press, 1997. p. xiii.

16 Christensen, Clayton M., <u>The Innovator's Dilemma: When New Technologies</u>

Cause Great Firms To Fail, Boston, Harvard Business School Press, 1997. p. 133.

17 Alderson, Wroe, Dynamic Marketing Behavior, Homewood, Richard D. Irwin, Inc., 1965.

18 Christensen, Clayton M., The Innovator's Dilemma: When New Technologies Cause Great Firms To Fail, Boston, Harvard Business School Press, 1997. p. 150.

19 Christensen, Clayton, M., and Raynor, Michael, E., The Innovator's Solution: Creating and Sustaining Successful Growth, Boston, Harvard Business School Press, 2003. p. 74.

20 Kimura, Motoo, The Natural Law of Molecular Evolution, Cambridge, Cambridge University Press, 1983.

21 Katz, Ralph, "The S-Curve Explained," in Managing Creativity and Innovation, Boston, Harvard Business School Press, 2003. p. 15. Scholars at many business schools are fond of providing graphs, like the S Curve, that seem to bear no relationship to existing economic theory. The S Curve, as a concept, appears in print, as if it is an accepted part of the larger theoretical edifice of economic equilibrium, theory without the benefit of showing its philosophical lineage.

22 Kalecki, Michal, quoted in Dobb, Maurice, Theories of Value and Distribution Since Adam Smith: Ideology and Economic Theory, Cambridge, Cambridge University Press, 1973. p. 222.

23 Keynes, John Maynard, quoted in Dobb, Maurice, Theories of Value and Distribution Since Adam Smith: Ideology and Economic Theory, Cambridge, Cambridge University Press, 1973. p. 226.

24 Mill, J. S., quoted in Dobb, Maurice, Theories of Value and Distribution Since Adam Smith: Ideology and Economic Theory, Cambridge, Cambridge University Press, 1973. p. 130.

25 Domar, Evsay, quoted in Dobb, Maurice, Theories of Value and Distribution Since Adam Smith: Ideology and Economic Theory, Cambridge, Cambridge University Press, 1973. p. 229.

26 Christensen, Clayton, M., and Raynor, Michael, E., The Innovator's Solution: Creating and Sustaining Successful Growth, Boston, Harvard Business School Press, 2003. p. 5.

27 Kalecki, Michal, quoted in in Dobb, Maurice, Theories of Value and Distribution Since Adam Smith: Ideology and Economic Theory, Cambridge, Cambridge University Press, 1973. p. 233.

28 Porter, Michael, The Competitive Advantage of Nations, New York, The Free Press, 1990. p. 6.

29 Kaldor, cited in Dobb, Maurice, Theories of Value and Distribution Since Adam

Smith: Ideology and Economic Theory, Cambridge University Press, Cambridge, 1973. p. 239.

30 List, Friedrich, cited in Archibugi, Daniele and Michie, Jonathan, Technology, Globalisation and Economic Performance, Cambridge, Cambridge University Press, 1997. p. 6.

31 Archibugi and Michie, p. 11.

32 David, Paul, quoted in Rosenberg, Nathan, Inside The Black Box: Technology and Economics, Cambridge, Cambridge University Press, 1982, p. 16.

33 Rosenberg, Nathan, Inside the Black Box: Technology and Economics, Cambridge, Cambridge University Press, 1982. p. 27.

34 Christensen, Clayton, and Raynor, Michael, The Innovator's Solution: Creating and Sustaining Successful Growth, Boston, Harvard Business School Press, 2003. p. 78.

35 Rosenberg, p. 258.

36 Ricardo, David, On the Principles of Political Economy and Taxation, London, John Murray, First published: 1817.

37 Alderson, Wroe, Dynamic Marketing Behavior, Homewood, Richard D. Irwin, Inc., 1965.

38 Kaldor, cited in Dobb, Maurice, Theories of Value and Distribution Since Adam Smith: Ideology and Economic Theory, Cambridge, Cambridge University Press, 1973. p. 239.

39 Kaldor, cited in Dobb, Maurice, Theories of Value and Distribution Since Adam Smith: Ideology and Economic Theory, Cambridge, Cambridge University Press, 1973. p. 238.

40 Sraffa, Piero, Production of Commodities by Means of Commodities: Prelude to a Critique of Economic Theory, Cambridge, Cambridge University Press, 1960.

41 Dmitriev, cited in Dobb, Maurice, Theories of Value and Distribution Since Adam Smith: Ideology and Economic Theory, Cambridge, Cambridge University Press, 1973. p. 178.

42 Marshall, Alfred, Principles of Economics, 8th Edition, New York, The MacMillan Co., 1949. p. 421.

43 Fisher, Irving, quoted in Spiegel, Henry William, The Growth of Economic Thought: Revised and Expanded Edition, Durham, Duke University Press, 1983. p. 623.

44 Schumpeter, Joseph, A., The Theory of Economic Development, Oxford, Oxford University Press, 1961. p. 72.

45 Schumpeter, Joseph, A., The Theory of Economic Development, Oxford, Oxford University Press, 1961. p. 74.

46 Hollis, Martin, and Nell, Edward J., Rational Economic Man, Cambridge, Cambridge University Press, 1975. p. 255.

47 Schumpeter, Joseph, A., The Theory of Economic Development, Oxford, Oxford University Press, 1961. p. 216.

48 Say, Jean-Baptiste, cited in Pasinetti, Luigi, Structural Change and Economic Growth: A Theoretical Essay on the Dynamics of the Wealth of Nations, Cambridge, Cambridge University Press, 1981. p. 240.

49 Schumpeter, Joseph, A., The Theory of Economic Development, Oxford, Oxford University Press, 1961. pps. 66 and 78.

50 Schumpeter, Joseph, A., The Theory of Economic Development, Oxford, Oxford University Press, 1961. p. 8.

51 Schumpeter, Joseph, A., The Theory of Economic Development, Oxford, Oxford University Press, 1961. p. 9.

52 Schumpeter, Joseph, A., The Theory of Economic Development, Oxford, Oxford University Press, 1961. pps. 63 – 65.

53 Heertje, Arnold, "Schumpeter and Technical Change," in Evolutionary Economics: Applications of Schumpeter's Ideas, Hanusch, Horst, Editor, Cambridge, Cambridge University Press, 1988. pps.76 – 77.

54 Higgins, Benjamin, and Savoie, Donald, Regional Development Theories an Their Application, New Brunswick, N. J., Transaction Publishers, 1997. pps. 35 – 40.

55 Harrod, R., "An Essay in Dynamic Theory", The Economic Journal, 1939, Vol. 49, No. 193, pp. 14-33.

56 Domar, Evsay, "Capital Expansion, Rate of Growth, and Employment," Econometrica, 1946, Vol. 14, No. 2., pp. 137-147.

57 Schumpeter, Joseph, A., The Theory of Economic Development, Oxford, Oxford University Press, 1961. pps. 71- 72.

58 Marshall, Alfred, Principles of Economics, 8th Edition, New York, The MacMillan Co., 1949. p. 81 and p. 421.

59 Smith, John Maynard, Evolutionary Genetics, Second Edition, New York, Oxford University Press, 1998. p. 10.

60 Hughes, Austin, Adaptive Evolution, New York, Oxford University Press, 1999. p. 120.

61 Woese, Carl, "A New Biology For A New Century," cited by Dyson, Freeman, "Megaphone: The Darwinian Interlude," Technology Review, March 2005. p. 27.

62 Woese, Carl, "A New Biology For A New Century," cited by Dyson, Freeman, "Megaphone," Technology Review, March 2005. p. 27

63 Kimura, Motoo, The Neutral Theory of Molecular Evolution, Cambridge, Cambridge University Press, 1983. pps. 149 – 151.

64 Kimura, Motoo, The Neutral Theory of Molecular Evolution, Cambridge, Cambridge University Press, 1983. p. 164.

65 Doucet, Paul and Sloep, Peter, <u>Mathematical Modeling In The Life Sciences,</u> New York, Ellis Horwood, 1992. p. 149.

66 Doucet, Paul and Sloep, Peter, <u>Mathematical Modeling In The Life Sciences,</u> New York, Ellis Horwood, 1992. p. 151.

67 Nightingale, John, "Universal Darwinism and Social Research: The Case of Economics," in Barnett, William, et. al., eds., <u>Commerce, Complexity and Evolution,</u> London, Cambridge University Press, 2000. p. 29.

68 Nightingale, John, "Universal Darwinism and Social Research: The Case of Economics," in Barnett, William, et. al., eds., <u>Commerce, Complexity and Evolution,</u> London, Cambridge University Press, 2000. p. 34.

69 Beyer-Hans-Georg, "On The Dynamics of EAs Without Selection," in Banzhaf, Wolfgang, and Reeves, Colin, ed., <u>Foundations of Genetic Algorithms,</u> San Francisco, Morgan Kaufmann Publishers, Inc., 1999. pps. 7 – 9.

70 Beyer-Hans-Georg, "On The Dynamics of EAs Without Selection," in Banzhaf, Wolfgang, and Reeves, Colin, ed., <u>Foundations of Genetic Algorithms,</u> San Francisco, Morgan Kaufmann Publishers, Inc., 1999. p. 16.

71 Oster, G., and Guckenheimen, J., "Bifurcation Phenomena In Population Models," in Marsden, J. E., and McCracken, M., eds., <u>The Hopf Bifurcation and Its Application,</u> New York Springer-Verlag, , 1976. p. 328.

72 Oster, G., and Guckenheimen, J., "Bifurcation Phenomena In Population Models," in Marsden, J. E., and McCracken, M., eds., <u>The Hopf Bifurcation and Its Application,</u> New York, Springer-Verlag, 1976. p. 338.

73 Hoyle, Fred, <u>Mathematics of Evolution,</u> Memphis, Tenn., Acorn Enterprises, 1987. p. 12.

74 Hoyle, Fred, <u>Mathematics of Evolution,</u> Memphis, Tenn., Acorn Enterprises, 1987. p. 105.

75 Forst, Christian, "Molecular Evolutionary Dynamics," in Parisi, Jurgen, et. al., eds., <u>A Perspective Look At Nonlinear Media: From Physics to Biology and Social Sciences,</u> New York, Springer-Verlag, 1998. pps. 208 – 213.

76 Nagle, Thomas, <u>The Strategy and Tactics of Pricing: A Guide To Profitable Decision Making,</u> Englewood Cliffs, NJ, Prentice-Hall, 1987. p. 150.

77 Witt, Ulrich, "Reflections On The Present State of Evolutionary Economic Theory," in Hodgson, Geoffrey, and Screpanti, Ernesto, eds., <u>Rethinking Economics: Markets, Technology and Economic Evolution,</u> Aldershot, Edward Elgar, 1991. p. 91.

78 Farmer, Marty, and Mathews, Mark, "Cultural Differences and Subjective Rationality: Where Sociology Connects With The Economics of Technological Choice," in Hodgson, Geoffrey, and Screpanti, Ernesto, eds., <u>Rethinking Economics: Markets, Technology and Economic Evolution,</u> Aldershot, Edward Elgar, 1991. p. 114.

Predicting Technology

79 Arthur, Brian W., "Asset Pricing Under Endogenous Expectations in an Artificial Stock Market," in Arthur, Brian W., Durlauf, Steven, and Lane, David, The Economy As An Evolving Complex System II, Reading, Addison-Wesley, 1997. p. 21.

80 Johansson, Borje, and Andersson, Ake, "A Schloss Laxenburg Model of Product Cycle Dynamics," in Beckman, M. J., et. al., eds., Knowledge and Networks In a Dynamic Economy, Berlin, Springer-Verlag, 1998. pps. 189 – 192.

81 Johansson, Borje, and Andersson, Ake, "A Schloss Laxenburg Model of Product Cycle Dynamics," in Beckman, M. J., et. al., eds., Knowledge and Networks In a Dynamic Economy, Berlin,Springer-Verlag, 1998. p. 181.

82 Johansson, Borje, and Andersson, Ake, "A Schloss Laxenburg Model of Product Cycle Dynamics," in Beckman, M. J., et. al., eds., Knowledge and Networks In a Dynamic Economy, Berlin, Springer-Verlag, 1998. p. 185.

83 Johansson, Borje, and Andersson, Ake, "A Schloss Laxenburg Model of Product Cycle Dynamics," in Beckman, M. J., et. al., eds., Knowledge and Networks In a Dynamic Economy, Berlin, Springer-Verlag, 1998. p. 215.

84 Johansson, Borje, and Andersson, Ake, "A Schloss Laxenburg Model of Product Cycle Dynamics," in Beckman, M. J., et. al., eds., Knowledge and Networks In a Dynamic Economy, Berlin, Springer-Verlag, 1998. p. 190.

85 Homans, George C., Social Behavior: Its Elementary Forms, New York, Harcourt Brace Jovanovich, Inc., P. 361.

86 Schumpeter, Joseph A., The Theory of Economic Development, New York, Oxford University Press, 1961. pps. 72 and 132.

87 Schumpeter, Joseph A., The Theory of Economic Development, New York, Oxford University Press, 1961. p. 154.

88 Schumpeter, Joseph A., The Theory of Economic Development, New York, Oxford University Press, 1961. p. 66.

89 Schumpeter, Joseph A., The Theory of Economic Development, New York, Oxford University Press, 1961. p. 208.

90 Schumpeter, Joseph A., The Theory of Economic Development, New York, Oxford University Press, 1961. p. 108.

91 Schumpeter, Joseph A., The Theory of Economic Development, New York, Oxford University Press, 1961. p. 189.

92 Schumpeter, Joseph A., The Theory of Economic Development, New York, Oxford University Press, 1961. p. 196.

93 Burger, R., The Mathematical Theory of Selection, Recombination, and Mutation, New York, John Wiley & Sons, 2000. p. 27.

94 Olsen, Mancur, quoted in Mokyr, Joel, The Gifts of Athena: Historical Origins of the Knowledge Economy, Princeton, Princeton University Press, 2002. p. 227.

95 Mokyr, Joel, The Gifts of Athena: Historical Origins of the Knowledge Economy, Princeton, Princeton University Press, 2002. p. 296.

96 Mokyr, Joel, <u>The Gifts of Athena: Historical Origins of the Knowledge Economy,</u> Princeton, Princeton University Press, 2002. p. 220.

97 Hall, Peter, <u>Innovation, Economics and Evolution: Theoretical Perspectives On Changing Technology In Economic Systems,</u> New York, Harvester Wheatsheaf, 1994. p. 149.

98 Christensen, Clayton, M., Anthony, Scott, D., and Roth, Erik, <u>Seeing What's Next: Using The Theories of Innovation To Predict Industry Change,</u> Boston, Harvard Business School Press, 2004. p. xvi.

99 Storper, Michael, <u>The Regional World: Territorial Development In a Global Economy,</u> New York, Guilford Press, 1997.

100 Mokyr, Joel, <u>The Gifts of Athena: Historical Origins of the Knowledge Economy, Princeton,</u> Princeton University Press, 2002. p. 251.

101 Mokyr, Joel, <u>The Gifts of Athena: Historical Origins of the Knowledge Economy, Princeton,</u> Princeton University Press, 2002. p. 276.

102 Homans, George C., <u>Social Behavior: Its Elementary Forms,</u> New York, Harcourt Brace Jovanovich, Inc., 1974. p. 17.

103 Homans, George C., <u>Social Behavior: Its Elementary Forms,</u> New York, Harcourt Brace Jovanovich, Inc., 1974. p. 37.

104 Homans, George C., <u>Social Behavior: Its Elementary Forms,</u> New York, Harcourt Brace Jovanovich, Inc., 1974. p. 40.

105 Homans, George C., <u>Social Behavior: Its Elementary Forms,</u> New York, Harcourt Brace Jovanovich, Inc., 1974. p. 361.

106 Granovetter, Mark, quoted in Dosi, Giovanni, et. al., eds., <u>Technology, Organization, and Competitiveness: Perspectives on Industrial and Corporate Change,</u> Oxford, Oxford University Press, 1998. p. 3.

107 Cialdini, Robert, <u>Influence: How and Why People Agree To Things,</u> New York, William Morrow & Co., 1984. pps. 29 – 60.

108 Homans, George C., <u>Social Behavior: Its Elementary Forms,</u> New York, Harcourt Brace Jovanovich, Inc., 1974. p. 68.

109 Burger, R., <u>The Mathematical Theory of Selection, Recombination and Mutation,</u> New York, John Wiley & Sons, , 2000. p. 2.

110 Scherer, F. M., "Inter-Industry Technology Flows and Productivity Growth," in Griliches, Zvi, et. al., eds., <u>Research And Development, Patents and Productivity,</u> Chicago, University of Chicago Press, 1984. p. 627.

111 Scherer, F. M., "Using Linked Patent and R & D Data to Measure Interindustry Technology Flows," in Griliches, Zvi, et.al., eds., <u>Research And Development, Patents and Productivity,"</u> Chicago, University of Chicago Press, 1984. p. 418.

112 Hall, Peter, <u>Innovation, Economics and Evolution: Theoretical Perspectives on Changing Technology in Economic Systems,</u> New York Harvester Wheatsheaf, 1994. pps. 267 – 272.

113 Burger, R., The Mathematical Theory of Selection, Recombination and Mutation, New York, John Wiley & Sons, 2000. p. 303.

114 Burger, R., The Mathematical Theory of Selection, Recombination and Mutation, New York, John Wiley & Sons, 2000. pps. 285 – 303.

115 Vass, Thomas E., Do Cities Still Matter? The Regional Geographical Imperative of Technological Progress in a Global Inter-Networked Market, Houston, eBookstand, Inc., 2001.

116 Harrington, Michael, "Alliance Business Park Seen In Lead for Dell," Greensboro, N. C., Triad Business Journal, November 5, 2004.

117 Mitchell, Melanie, An Introduction to Genetic Algorithms, Cambridge, M. I. T. Press, 1996. p. 89.

118 Frenken, Koen, Saviotti, Pier Paolo, and Trommetter, Michel, "Variety and Economic Development: Conceptual Issues and Measurement Problems," in Cantner, Uwe, et. al. eds., Economic Evolution, Learning and Complexity, Heidelberg, Physica-Verlag, 2000. pps. 223 – 234.

119 Frenken, Koen, Saviotti, Pier Paolo, and Trommetter, Michel, "Variety and Economic Development: Conceptual Issues and Measurement Problems," in Cantner, Uwe, et. al. eds., Economic Evolution, Learning and Complexity, Heidelberg, Physica-Verlag, 2000. pps. 234 – 238. (text in parenthesis is added).

120 Blair, Peter, and Wyckoff, Andrew, "The Changing Structure of the U. S. Economy: An Input-Output Analysis," in Miller, Ronald, Polenske, Karen, and Rose, Adam, Frontiers of Input-Output Analysis, New York, Oxford University Press, 1989. pps 296 – 297.

121 Blair, Peter, and Wyckoff, Andrew, "The Changing Structure of the U. S. Economy: An Input-Output Analysis," in Miller, Ronald, Polenske, Karen, and Rose, Adam, Frontiers of Input-Output Analysis, New York, Oxford University Press, 1989. p. 296.

122 Minsky, Hyman, "Schumpeter: Finance and Evolution," in Heertje, Arnold, and Perlman, Mark, eds., Evolving Technology and Market Structure: Studies in Schumpeterian Economics, , Ann Arbor, University of Michigan Press, 1990. p. 72.

123 Tichy, G., "Clusters: Less Dispensable and More Risky Than Ever," in Steiner, Michael, Clusters and Regional Specialization: On Geography, Technology and Networks, London, Pion, Ltd., 1998. p. 229.

124 Burger, R., The Mathematical Theory of Selection, Recombination and Mutation, New York, John Wiley & Sons, 2000. pps. 267 – 284.

125 Burger, R., The Mathematical Theory of Selection, Recombination and Mutation, New York, John Wiley & Sons, 2000. pps. 285 – 303.

126 Mueller, H. J., "The Relation of Recombination To Mutational Advance," in Mutation Research, Vol. 1, 1964. pps 2 – 9.

127 Witt, Ulrich, "Emergence and Dissemination of Innovations: Some Principles of Evolutionary Economics," in Day, Richard, and Chen, Ping, Nonlinear Dynamics and Evolutionary Economics, New York, Oxford University Press, 1993. p. 93.

128 Baumol, William, cited in Hall, Peter, Innovation, Economics and Evolution: Theoretical Perspectives on Changing Technology In Economic Systems, New York, Harvestor-Wheatsheaf, 1994. pps. 364- - 365.

129 Dobb, Maurice, Theories of Value and Distribution Since Adam Smith: Ideology and Economic Theory, Cambridge, Cambridge University Press, 1973. p. 217.

130 Wilbur, Charles, K., The Political Economy of Development and Underdevelopment, New York, Random House, 1973. p. 225.

131 Wilbur, Charles, K., The Political Economy of Development and Underdevelopment, New York, Random House, 1973. p. 224.

132 Wilbur, Charles, K., The Political Economy of Development and Underdevelopment, New York, Random House, 1973. p. 227.

133 Wilbur, Charles, K., The Political Economy of Development and Underdevelopment, New York, Random House, 1973. p. 228.

134 Hollis, Martin, and Nell, Edward J., Rational Economic Man, , London, Cambridge University Press, 1975. pps. 225- 260.

135 DeSoto, Hernando, The Mystery of Capital: Why Capitalism Triumphs in the West and Fails Everywhere Else, New York, Basic Books, 2000.

136 Martens, Berten, "Toward A Generalized Coase Theorem: A Theory of the Emergence of Social and Institutional Structures Under Imperfect Information," in Barnett, William, et. al., eds., Commerce, Complexity, and Evolution, London, Cambridge University Press, 2000. p. 7.

137 Martens, Bertens "Toward A Generalized Coase Theorem: A Theory of the Emergence of Social and Institutional Structures Under Imperfect Information," in Barnett, William, et. al., eds., Commerce, Complexity, and Evolution, London, Cambridge University Press, 2000. p. 8.

138 Martens, Berten, "Toward A Generalized Coase Theorem: A Theory of the Emergence of Social and Institutional Structures Under Imperfect Information," in Barnett, William, et. al., eds., Commerce, Complexity, and Evolution, London, Cambridge University Press, 2000. p. 8.

139 Lancaster, K., "A New Approach To Consumer Theory," Journal of Political Economy, #74. (1966). pps. 132 – 157.

140 Rosen, Sherwin, "Economics and Entrepreneurs," in Ronen, Joshua, Entrepreneurship, Lexington, Lexington Books, 1982. p. 303.

141 Rosen, Sherwin, "Economics and Entrepreneurs," in Ronen, Joshua, Entrepreneurship, Lexington, Lexington Books, 1982. p. 303

142 Keaz, Modecai, "Entrepreneurial Activity in a Complex Economy," in Ronen, Joshua, Entrepreneurship, Lexington, Lexington Books, 1982. p. 300.

143 Martens, Berten, "Toward A Generalized Coase Theorem: A Theory of the Emergence of Social and Institutional Structures Under Imperfect Information," in Barnett, William, et. al., eds., Commerce, Complexity, and Evolution, London, Cambridge University Press, 2000. p. 13.

144 Schnell, Hermann, "Evolutionary Patterns of Multisectoral Growth Dynamics," in Barnett, William, et. al., eds., Commerce, Complexity, and Evolution, London, Cambridge University Press, 2000. p.226.

145 Schnell, Hermann, "Evolutionary Patterns of Multisectoral Growth Dynamics," in Barnett, William, et. al., eds., Commerce, Complexity, and Evolution, London, Cambridge University Press, 2000. p.231.

146 Lambooy, Jan G., and Boschma, Ron, "Evolutionary Economics and Regional Policy," The Annals of Regional Science, (2001) #35. p. 114.

147 Kaldor, Nicholas, quoted in Dobb, Maurice, Theories of Value and Distribution Since Adam Smith: Ideology and Economic Theory, Cambridge, Cambridge University Press, 1973. pps. 237 – 238.

148 Dobb, Maurice, Theories of Value and Distribution Since Adam Smith: Ideology and Economic Theory, Cambridge, Cambridge University Press, 1973. pps 258 – 259.

149 Leontief, Wassily, "The Economy as a Circular Flow," 1928. in Kurtz, Heinz, D., et. al., eds., Input-Output Analysis, Volume I, Cheltenham, Edward Elgar, 1998., p. 112.

150 Leontief, Wassily, "The Economy as a Circular Flow," 1928. in Kurtz, Heinz, D., et. al., eds., Input-Output Analysis, Volume I, Cheltenham, Edward Elgar, 1998., p. 112.

151 Dobb, Maurice, Theories of Value and Distribution Since Adam Smith: Ideology and Economic Theory, Cambridge, Cambridge University Press, 1973. p. 178.

152 Arthur, Brian, W., Durlauf, Steven, and Lane, David, "Introduction," The Economy As An Evolving Complex System, II, Reading, Addison-Wesley, 1997. p. 2.

153 Arthur, Brian, W., et. al.,"Asset Pricing Under Endogenous Expectations In An Artificial Stock Market," in Arthur, Brian, W., Durlauf, Steven, and Lane, David, The Economy As An Evolving Complex System, II, Reading, Addison-Wesley, 1997. p. 21.

154 Nagle, Thomas, The Strategy and Tactics of Pricing: A Guide to Profitable Decision Making, Englewood Cliffs, N. J., Prentice-Hall, 1987. p. 139.

155 Alderson, Wroe, Dynamic Marketing Behavior, Homewood, Il., Richard D. Irwin, 1965. p. 66.

156 Alderson, Wroe, Dynamic Marketing Behavior, Homewood, Il., Richard D. Irwin, 1965. p. 146.

157 Alderson, Wroe, <u>Dynamic Marketing Behavior,</u> Homewood, Il., Richard D. Irwin, 1965. pps. 207 – 291.

158 Kryzanowski, Roman, and Raper, Jonathan, <u>Spatial Evolutionary Modeling,</u> Oxford, Oxford University Press, 2001. p. 9.

159 Kryzanowski, Roman, and Raper, Jonathan, <u>Spatial Evolutionary Modeling,</u> Oxford, Oxford University Press, 2001. pps. 23 –26.

160 Kryzanowski, Roman, and Raper, Jonathan, <u>Spatial Evolutionary Modeling,</u> Oxford, Oxford University Press, 2001. p. 21.

161 Enis, Ben and Mokiva, Michael, "The Marketing Management Matrix: A Taxonomy For Strategy Comprehension," in Ferrell, O. C., et. al. eds. <u>Conceptual and Theoretical Developments in Marketing,</u> Chicago, American Marketing Association, 1979. pps. 492 – 497.

162 Feser, Edward, J., and Sweeney, Stuart, "A Test For the Coincident Economic and Spatial Clustering of Business Enterprises," <u>Journal of Geographical Systems,</u> (2, 4), 2002.

163 Burger, R., <u>The Mathematical Theory of Selection, Recombination, and Mutation,</u> New York, John Wiley and Sons, 2000. pps. 267 – 303.

164 Burger, R., <u>The Mathematical Theory of Selection, Recombination, and Mutation,</u> New York, John Wiley and Sons, 2000. p. 303.

165 Nash, cited in Hall, Peter, <u>Innovation, Economics and Evolution: Theoretical Perspectives on Changing Technology in Economic Systems,</u> New York, Harvester Wheatsheaf, 1994. p. 232.

166 Epstein, Joshua, <u>Nonlinear Dynamics, Mathematical Biology, and Social Science,</u> Reading, Mass., Addison-Wesley, 1997. p. 75.

167 Epstein, Joshua, <u>Nonlinear Dynamics, Mathematical Biology, and Social Science,</u> Reading, Mass., Addison-Wesley, 1997. pps. 75 – 76.

168 Aghion, Phillippe, and Howitt, Peter, <u>Endogenous Growth Theory,</u> Cambridge, MIT Press, 1998. p. 180.

169 Aghion, Phillippe, and Howitt, Peter, <u>Endogenous Growth Theory,</u> Cambridge, MIT Press, 1998. p. 186.

170 Aghion, Phillippe, and Howitt, Peter, <u>Endogenous Growth Theory,</u> Cambridge, MIT Press, 1998. p. 212.

171 Cappellin, R., "The Transformation of Local Production Systems: International Networking and Territorial Competitiveness," in Steiner, M., ed., <u>Clusters and Regional Specialization: On Geography, Technology and Networks,</u> London, Pion Ltd., 1998. p. 63.

172 Aghion, Phillippe, and Howitt, Peter, <u>Endogenous Growth Theory,</u> Cambridge, MIT Press, 1998. p. 154.

173 Fontela, E., and Pulido, A., "Input-Output, Technical Change, and Long Waves," in Peterson, William, ed., <u>Advances in Input-Output Analysis: Technology, Planning and Development,</u> New York, Oxford University Press, 1991. p. 140.

174 Allen, Peter, "Evolutionary Complex Systems: Models of Technology Change," in Leydesdorff, Loet, and Van den Besselaar, Peter, eds., Evolutionary Economics and Chaos Theory: New Directions in Technololgy Studies, London, Pinter Publishers, 1994. p. 14.

175 Allen, Peter, "Evolutionary Complex Systems: Models of Technology Change," in Leydesdorff, Loet, and Van den Besselaar, Peter, eds., Evolutionary Economics and Chaos Theory: New Directions in Technololgy Studies, London, Pinter Publishers, 1994. p. 16.

176 Piore and Sable quoted in Staber, Udo, "Networks and Regional Development: Perspectives and Unsolved Issues," in Staber, Udo, and Schaefer, Norbert, et. al., eds., Business Networks: Prospects for Regional Development, Berlin, Walter de Gruyter, 1996. p. 8.

177 Staber, Udo, "A Social Embeddedness of Industrial District Networks," in Staber, Udo, and Schaefer, Norbert, et. al., eds., Business Networks: Prospects for Regional Development, Berlin, Walter de Gruyter, 1996. p 152.

178 Staber, Udo, "A Social Embeddedness of Industrial District Networks," in Staber, Udo, and Schaefer, Norbert, et. al., eds., Business Networks: Prospects for Regional Development, Berlin, Walter de Gruyter, 1996. p 155.

179 Staber, Udo, "A Social Embeddedness of Industrial District Networks," in Staber, Udo, and Schaefer, Norbert, et. al., eds., Business Networks: Prospects for Regional Development, Berlin, Walter de Gruyter, 1996. p 155.

180 Nagle, Thomas, The Strategy and Tactics of Pricing: A Guide to Profitable Decision Making, Englewood Cliffs, Prentice-Hall, 1987. p. 195.

181 Rosenberg, Alexander, Philosophy of Social Science, Second Edition, Boulder, Col., Westview Press, 1988. p. 103 – 114.

182 Rosenberg, Alexander, Philosophy of Social Science, Second Edition, Boulder, Col., Westview Press, 1988. p. 164.

183 Rosenberg, Alexander, Philosophy of Social Science, Second Edition, Boulder, Col., Westview Press, 1988. p. 175

184 Christensen, Clayton, M., Anthony, Scott, D., and Roth, Erik, Seeing What's Next: Using The Theories of Innovation To Predict Industry Change, Boston, Harvard Business School Press, 2004. p. 207.

185 Holland, John, H., Emergence: From Chaos To Order, Reading, Mass., Helix Books, 1998. p. 208.

186 Lewontin, R. C., The Genetic Basis of Evolutionary Change, New York Columbia University Press, 1974. p. 5.

187 Kimura, Motoo, The Neutral Theory of Molecular Evolution, Cambridge, Cambridge University Press, 1983.

188 Hoyle, Fred, The Mathematics of Evolution, Memphis, Tenn., Acorn Enterprises, 1987. p. 8.

189 Stankiewicz, Richard, "The Concept of Design Space," in Ziman, John, ed., Technological Innovation As An Evolutionary Process, Cambridge, Cambridge University Press, 2000. p. 250.

190 Lewontin, R. C., The Genetic Basis of Evolutionary Change, New York, Columbia University Press, 1974. p. 160.

191 Hoyle, Fred, The Mathematics of Evolution, Memphis, Tenn., Acorn Enterprises, 1987. p. 105. Hoyle was explaining his interpretation of Darwin and how that interpretation could be reduced to mathematical formulas.

192 Hoyle, Fred, The Mathematics of Evolution, Acorn Enterprises, Memphis, Tenn., 1987. p. 108.

193 Reggiani, Aura, and Nijkamp, Peter, "Evolutionary Dynamics In Technological Systems: A Multi-Layer Niche Approach," in Leydesdorff, Loet, and Van den Besselaar, Peter, eds., Evolutionary Economics and Chaos Theory: New Directions In Technology Studies, London, Pinter Publishers, 1994. p. 94.

194 Hartl, Daniel, A Primer on Population Genetics, Sunderland, Mass., Sinauer Associates, 1981. pps. 10-14.

195 Christensen, Clayton, M., Anthony, Scott, D., and Roth, Erik, Seeing What's Next: Using The Theories of Innovation To Predict Industry Change, Boston, Harvard Business School Press, 2004. p. xvi.

196 Rosenberg, Alexander, Darwinism In Philosophy, Cambridge, Cambridge University Press, 2000. p. 126.

197 Allen, Peter, "Evolutionary Complex Systems: Models for Technological Change," in Leydesdorff, Loet, and Van den Besselaar, Peter, eds., Evolutionary Economics and Chaos Theory: New Directions In Technology Studies, London, Pinter Publishers, 1994. p. 14.

198 Stankiewicz, Richard, "The Concept of Design Space," in Ziman, John, ed., Technological Innovation As An Evolutionary Process, Cambridge, Cambridge University Press, 2000. pps. 234-235.

199 Stankiewicz, Richard, "The Concept of Design Space," in Ziman, John, ed., Technological Innovation As An Evolutionary Process, Cambridge, Cambridge University Press, 2000. p. 246.

200 Wolff, Edward N., "Spillovers, Linkages and Technical Change," Economic Systems Research, Vol.9, No. 1, (1997). pps. 7- 21.

201 Rosenberg, Alexander, Darwinism In Philosophy, Cambridge, Cambridge University Press, 2000. p. 169.

202 Holland, John, Hidden Order: How Adaptation Builds Complexity, New York, Helix Books, 1995. p. 8.

203 Holland, John, Hidden Order: How Adaptation Builds Complexity, New York, Helix Books, 1995. p. 8.

204 Holland, John, <u>Hidden Order: How Adaptation Builds Complexity,</u> New York, Helix Books, 1995. p. 163.

205 Holland, John, <u>Hidden Order: How Adaptation Builds Complexity,</u> New York, Helix Books, 1995. p. 10.

206 Holland, John, <u>Hidden Order: How Adaptation Builds Complexity,</u> Helix Books, New York, 1995. p. 29.

207 Holland, John, <u>Hidden Order: How Adaptation Builds Complexity,</u> Helix Books, New York, 1995. p. 33.

208 Brennan, Geoffrey, and Buchanan, James M., <u>The Reason of Rules: Constitutional Political Economy,</u> Cambridge University Press, London, 1985. p. 7.

209 Holland, John, <u>Hidden Order: How Adaptation Builds Complexity,</u> New York, Helix Books, 1995. pps. 51-54.

210 Dennett, Daniel Clement, <u>Consciousness Explained,</u> 1st ed., Boston, Little, Brown and Co., 1991. pps. 111 – 132.

211 Doucet, Paul, and Sloep, Peter, <u>Mathematical Modeling In the Life Sciences,</u> New York, Ellis Horwood, 1992. p. 86.

212 Doucet, Paul, and Sloep, Peter, <u>Mathematical Modeling In the Life Sciences,</u> New York, Ellis Horwood, 1992. p. 93.

213 Doucet, Paul, and Sloep, Peter, <u>Mathematical Modeling In the Life Sciences,</u> New York, Ellis Horwood, 1992. p. 149.

214 Doucet, Paul, and Sloep, Peter, <u>Mathematical Modeling In the Life Sciences,</u> New York, Ellis Horwood, 1992. p. 151.

215 Rosenzweig, M. L., "Paradox of Enrichment," Science, 171, 1971, cited in Doucet, Paul, and Sloep, Peter, <u>Mathematical Modeling In the Life Sciences,</u> New York, Ellis Horwood, 1992. p. 410.

216 Doucet, Paul, and Sloep, Peter, <u>Mathematical Modeling In the Life Sciences,</u> New York, Ellis Horwood, 1992. p. 398.

217 Lewontin, R. C., <u>The Genetic Basis of Evolutionary Change,</u> New York Columbia University Press, 1974. p. 19.

218 Lewontin, R. C., <u>The Genetic Basis of Evolutionary Change,</u> New York Columbia University Press, 1974. p. 160.

219 Ziman, John, "Selections and Complexity," in Ziman, John, ed., <u>Technological Innovation As An Evolutionary Process,</u> Cambridge Cambridge University Press, 2000. p. 42.

220 Lewontin, R. C., <u>The Genetic Basis of Evolutionary Change,</u> New York, Columbia University Press, 1974. p. 269.

221 Lewontin, R. C., <u>The Genetic Basis of Evolutionary Change,</u> New York, Columbia University Press, 1974. p. 269.

222 Hartl, Daniel, <u>Principles of Population Genetics,</u> Sunderland, Mass., Sinauer Associates, 1980. p. 269.

223 Hartl, Daniel, <u>Principles of Population Genetics,</u> Sunderland, Mass., Sinauer Associates, 1980. p. 150.

224 Banzhaf, Wolfgang, and Reeves, Colin, eds., <u>Foundations of Genetic Algorithms,</u> San Francisco, Morgan Kaufmann Publishers, Inc., 1999. p. 16.

225 Banzhaf, Wolfgang, and Reeves, Colin, eds., <u>Foundations of Genetic Algorithms,</u> San Francisco, Morgan Kaufmann Publishers, Inc., 1999. p. 15.

226 Banzhaf, Wolfgang, and Reeves, Colin, eds., <u>Foundations of Genetic Algorithms,</u> San Francisco, Morgan Kaufmann Publishers, Inc., 1999. p. 7.

227 Hughes, Austin, <u>Adaptive Evolution of Genes and Genomes,</u> New York, Oxford University Press. 1999. p. 226.

228 Kimura, Motoo, <u>The Neutral Theory of Molecular Evolution,</u> Cambridge, Cambridge University Press. 1983. pps. 151 – 164.

229 Hoyle, Fred, <u>Mathematics of Evolution,</u> Memphis, Tenn., Acorn Enterprises, 1987. p. 38.

230 Hoyle, Fred, <u>Mathematics of Evolution,</u> Memphis, Tenn., Acorn Enterprises, 1987. p. 108.

231 Hartl, Daniel, <u>Principles of Population Genetics,</u> Sunderland, Mass., Sinauer Associates, 1980. p. 344.

232 Hafbauer, Josef, and Sigmund, Karl, <u>The Theory of Evolution and Dynamical Systems: Mathematical Aspects of Selection,</u> Cambridge, Cambridge University Press, 1988. p. 31

233 Charlesworth, Brian, and Charlesworth, Deborah, "Some Evolutionary Consequences of Deleterious Mutations," in Woodruff, Ronny, and Thompson Jr., James, eds., <u>Mutation and Evolution,</u> Boston, Kluwer Academic Publishers, 1998. p. 12. "The ratchet will move faster if there is a large class of mutations with small effects on fitness, but the rate of decline in fitness will be greatly reduced if selection coefficients are reduced."

234 Garrish, Philip, and Lenski, Richard, "The Fate of Competing Beneficial Mutations in An Asexual Population," in Woodruff, Ronny, and Thompson, Jr., James, eds., <u>Mutation and Evolution,</u> Boston, Kluwer Academic Publishers, 1998. p. 128.

235 Garrish, Philip, and Lenski, Richard, "The Fate of Competing Beneficial Mutations in An Asexual Population," in Woodruff, Ronny, and Thompson, Jr., James, eds., <u>Mutation and Evolution,</u> Boston, Kluwer Academic Publishers, 1998. p. 128.

236 Smith, John Maynard, <u>Evolutionary Genetics,</u> Second Edition, New York, Oxford University Press, 1998, p. 36.

237 Mueller, H. J., quoted in Smith, John Maynard, <u>Evolutionary Genetics,</u> Second Edition, New York, Oxford University Press, 1998. p. 236.

238 Smith, John Maynard, <u>Evolutionary Genetics</u>, Second Edition, New York, Oxford University Press, 1998. p. 163.

239 Smith, John Maynard, <u>Evolutionary Genetics</u>, Second Edition, New York, Oxford University Press, 1998. p. 173.

240 Mitchell, Melanie, <u>An Introduction to Genetic Algorithms</u>, Cambridge, MIT Press, 1996. p. 6.

241 Mitchell, Melanie, <u>An Introduction to Genetic Algorithms</u>, Cambridge, MIT Press, 1996. p. 86.

242 Mitchell, Melanie, <u>An Introduction to Genetic Algorithms</u>, Cambridge, MIT Press, 1996. p. 147.

243 Burger, R., <u>The Mathematical Theory of Selection, Recombination, and Mutation</u>, New York John Wiley & Sons, 2000. p. 267.

244 Mueller, H. J., "The Relation of Recombination to Mutational Advance," cited in Burger, R., <u>The Mathematical Theory of Selection, Recombination, and Mutation</u>, New York, John Wiley & Sons, 2000. p. 303.

245 Leven, H., "Genetic Equilibrium When More Than One Ecological Niche Is Available," cited in Burger, R., <u>The Mathematical Theory of Selection, Recombination, and Mutation</u>, New York, John Wiley & Sons, 2000. p. 284.

246 Burger, R., <u>The Mathematical Theory of Selection, Recombination, and Mutation</u>, New York, John Wiley & Sons, 2000. p. 303.

247 Burger, R., <u>The Mathematical Theory of Selection, Recombination, and Mutation</u>, New York, John Wiley & Sons, 2000. p. 303..

248 Burger, R., <u>The Mathematical Theory of Selection, Recombination, and Mutation</u>, New York, John Wiley & Sons, 2000. p. 303.

249 Garrish, Philip and Lenski, Richard, "The Fate of Competing Beneficial Mutations In an Asexual Population," in Woodruff, Ronny and Thompson, Jr., James, eds., <u>Mutation and Evolution</u>, Boston, Kluwer Academic Publishers, 1998. p.128.

250 Garrish, Philip and Lenski, Richard, "The Fate of Competing Beneficial Mutations In an Asexual Population," Woodruff, Ronny and Thompson, Jr., James, <u>Mutation and Evolution</u>, Boston, Kluwer Academic Publishers, 1998. p. 128.

251 Garrish, Philip and Lenski, Richard, "The Fate of Competing Beneficial Mutations In an Asexual Population," in Woodruff, Ronny and Thompson, Jr., James, <u>Mutation and Evolution</u>, Boston, Kluwer Academic Publishers, 1998. p. 130.

252 Garrish, Philip and Lenski, Richard, "The Fate of Competing Beneficial Mutations In an Asexual Population," in Woodruff, Ronny and Thompson, Jr., James, <u>Mutation and Evolution</u>, eds., Boston, Kluwer Academic Publishers, 1998. p. 132.

253 Garrish, Philip and Lenski, Richard, "The Fate of Competing Beneficial Mutations In an Asexual Population," in Woodruff, Ronny and Thompson, Jr., James, eds., <u>Mutation and Evolution</u>, Boston, Kluwer Academic Publishers, 1998. p. 134.

254 Garrish, Philip and Lenski, Richard, "The Fate of Competing Beneficial Mutations In an Asexual Population," in Woodruff, Ronny and Thompson, Jr., James, eds., Mutation and Evolution, Boston, Kluwer Academic Publishers, 1998. pps. 138-139.

255 Hartl, Daniel and Taubes, Clifford, "Towards A Theory of Evolutionary Adaptation," in Woodruff, Ronny and Thompson, Jr., James, eds., Mutation and Evolution, Boston, Kluwer Academic Publishers, 1998. p. 526.

256 Woodruff, Ronny and Thompson, Jr., "Requisite Mutational Load, Pathway Epistasis and Deterministic Mutation Accumulation in Sexual vs. Asexual Populations," in James Woodruff, Ronny and Thompson, Jr., James, eds., Mutation and Evolution, Boston, Kluwer Academic Publishers, 1998. p. 74.

257 Hartl, Daniel, Principles of Population Genetics, Sunderland, Mass., Sinauer Associates, 1980. p. 269.

258 Hartl, Daniel, Principles of Population Genetics, Sunderland, Mass., Sinauer Associates, 1980. p. 300.

259 Hartl, Daniel, Principles of Population Genetics, Sunderland, Mass., Sinauer Associates, 1980. p. 335.

260 Holland, John, quoted in Mitchell, Melanie, An Introduction to Genetic Algorithms, Cambridge, MIT Press, 1996. p. 118.

261 Smith, John Maynard, Evolutionary Genetics, Oxford, Oxford University Press, 1989. p. 181.

262 Smith, John Maynard, Evolutionary Genetics, Oxford, Oxford University Press, 1989. p. 274.

263 Blaug, Mark, Economic History and the History of Economics, New York, New York University Press, 1986. p. 278.

264 Blaug, Mark, Economic History and the History of Economics, New York, New York University Press, 1986. p 266.

265 Blaug, Mark, Economic History and the History of Economics, New York, New York University Press, 1986. p 278.

266 Von Thunen, Johan, cited in Blaug, Mark, Economic History and the History of Economics, New York, New York University Press, 1986. p. 222.

267 Von Thunen, Johan, cited in Blaug, Mark, Economic History and the History of Economics, New York, New York University Press, 1986. p. 223.

268 Schumpeter, Jospeph A., The Theory of Economic Development, New York, Oxford University Press, 1961. p. 154.

269 Schumpeter, Jospeph A., The Theory of Economic Development, New York, Oxford University Press, 1961. p. 249.

270 Marshall, Alfred, Principles of Economics, 8th Edition, New York, The MacMillan Co., 1949. p. 210.

271 De Von Graaf, Jon, cited in Cantner, Uwe, Hanusch, Horst, and Klepper, Steven, eds., Economic Evolution, Learning, and Complexity, Heidelberg, Physica-Verlag, 2000. pps. 130 – 136.

272 List, Friedrich, quoted in Archibugi, Daniele, and Michie, Jonathan, eds., Technology, Globilisation, and Economic Performance, Cambridge,Cambridge University Press, 1997. p. 6.

273 Polanyi, Michael and Veblen, Thorstein, both cited in, Hodgson, Geoffrey, "Socio-Economic Disruption and Economic Development," in Hodgson, Geoffrey, and Screpanti, Ernesto, eds., Re-Thinking Economics: Markets, Technology and Economic Evolution, Aldershot, Edward Elgar, 1991. pps. 157 – 158.

274 Winch, D. M., Analytical Welfare Economics, London, Penguin Education, 1971. p. 165.

275 Winch, D. M., Analytical Welfare Economics, London, Penguin Education, 1971. p. 131.

276 Winch, D. M., Analytical Welfare Economics, London, Penguin Education, 1971. p. 198.

277 Prigogine, Ilya, "Bounded Rationality: From Dynamical Systems to Socio-Economic Models," in Day, Richard, and Chen, Ping, eds., Nonlinear Dynamics and Evolutionary Economics, New York, Oxford University Press, 1993. p. 9.

278 Allen, Jonathan, P., "Information Systems In Continuously Innovative Organizations," in Larsen, Tor, and McGuire, Eugene, Information Systems, Innovation and Diffusion: Issues and Directions, Hershey, Pa., Idea Group Publishing, 1998. p. 33.

279 Allen, Jonathan, P., "Information Systems In Continuously Innovative Organizations," in Larsen, Tor, and McGuire, Eugene, Information Systems, Innovation and Diffusion: Issues and Directions, Hershey, Pa., Idea Group Publishing, 1998. p. 40.

280 Swan, Jacky, et.al., "Inter-Organizational Networks and Diffusion of Information Technology: Developing a Framework," in Larsen, Tor, and McGuire, Eugene, Information Systems, Innovation and Diffusion: Issues and Directions, Hershey, Pa., Idea Group Publishing, 1998. p. 223.

281 Mansfield, Edwin, Technology Transfer, Productivity, and Economic Policy, New York, W. W. Norton and Company, 1982. p. 1.

282 Schmookler cited in Hall, Peter, Innovation, Economics and Evolution: Theoretical Perspectives on Changing Technology in Economic Systems, New York, Harvester Wheatsheaf, 1994. p. 1.

283 Kline, Stephen, and Rosenberg, Nathan, "An Overview of Innovation," in Edquist, Charles, and McKelvey, Maureen, eds., Systems of Innovation: Growth, Competitiveness and Employment, Vol. II, Cheltenham, Edward Elgar, 2000. p. 16.

284 Lundvall, Bengt-Ake, cited in Edquist, Charles, and McKelvey, Maureen, eds., Systems of Innovation: Growth, Competitiveness and Employment, Vol. II, Cheltenham, Edward Elgar, 2000. p. 61.

285 Evangelista, Rinaldo, Knowledge and Investment: The Sources of Innovation In Industry, Cheltenham, Edward Elgar, 1999. p. 5 and p. 91.

286 Hall, Peter, Innovation, Economics and Evolution: Theoretical Perspectives on Changing Technoogy in Economic Systems, New York, Harvester Wheatsheaf, 1994. p. 136.

287 Karlsson Charlie and Manduchi, Agostino, "Knowledge Spillovers In a Spatial Context: A Critical Review," in Fischer, Manfred, and Frohlich, Josef, eds., Knowledge, Complexity, and Innovation Systems, Berlin, Springer-Verlag, 2001. p. 103.

288 Karlsson Charlie and Manduchi, Agostino, "Knowledge Spillovers In a Spatial Context: A Critical Review," in Fischer, Manfred, and Frohlich, Josef, eds., Knowledge, Complexity, and Innovation Systems, Berlin, Springer-Verlag, 2001. p. 105.

289 Echeverrie-Carroll, Elsie, "Knowledge Spillovers in High Technology Agglomerations: Measurement and Modeling," in Fischer, Manfred, and Frohlich, Josef, eds., Knowledge, Complexity, and Innovation Systems, Berlin, Springer-Verlag, 2001. p. 159.

290 Thomson, Ross, "Epilogue: Institutions, Learning and Technological Change," in Thomson, Ross, ed., Learning and Technological Change, New York, St. Martin's Press, 1992. p. 268.

291 Nelson, Richard, R., The Sources of Economic Growth, Cambridge, Harvard University Press, 1996. p. 56.

292 Nelson, Richard, R., The Sources of Economic Growth, Cambridge, Harvard University Press, 1996. p. 21.

293 Nelson, Richard, R., The Sources of Economic Growth, Cambridge, Harvard University Press, 1996. p. 155.

294 Mowery, David, and Rosenberg, Nathan, "The U. S. National Innovation System," in Nelson, Richard, N., ed. National Innovation Systems: A Comparative Approach, New York, Oxford University Press, 1993. pps. 36 – 48.

295 Martens, Bertin, "Toward A Generalized Coase Theroem: A Theory of the Emergence of Social and Institutional Structures Under Imperfect Information," in Barnett, William, ed. Commerce, Complexity and Evolution, Cambridge, Cambridge University Press, 2000. p. 13.

296 Nelson, Richard, R., The Sources of Economic Growth, Cambridge, Harvard University Press, 1996. p. 268.

297 Saviotti, Pier Paolo, Technological Evolution, Variety and the Economy, Cheltenham, Edward Elgar, 1996. pps. 65 – 78.

298 Audretsch, David, and Feldman, Maryann, "The Telecommunications Revolution and the Geography of Innovation," in Wheeler, James, et. al., eds., Cities In the Telecommunications Age: The Fracturing of Geographics, New York, Routledge, 2000. p. 181.

299 Audretsch, David, and Feldman, Maryann, "The Telecommunications Revolution and the Geography of Innovation," in Wheeler, James, et. al., eds., Cities In the Telecommunications Age: The Fracturing of Geographics, New York, Routledge, 2000. p. 190.

300 Standish, Russell, cited in "Introduction," Bennett, William, et. al., eds., Commerce, Complexity, and Evolution, London, Cambridge University Press, 2000. p. xiv.

301 Saviotti, Pier Paolo, "Networks, National Innovation Systems and Self-Organisation," in Fischer, Manfred and Frohlich, Josef, eds. Knowledge, Complexity and Innovation Systems, Berlin, Springer-Verlag, 2001. p. 39.

302 Saviotti, Pier Paolo, "Networks, National Innovation Systems and Self-Organisation," in Fischer, Manfred and Frohlich, Josef, eds. Knowledge, Complexity and Innovation Systems, Berlin, Springer-Verlag, 2001. p. 41.

303 Witt, Ulrich, "Emergence and Dissemination of Innovations: Some Principles of Evolutionary Economics," in Day, Richard, and Chen, Ping, eds., Nonlinear Dynamics and Evolutionary Economics, New York, Oxford University Press, 1993. pps. 93 – 94.

304 North, Douglass, C., "Some Fundamental Puzzles In Economic History and Development," in Arthur, W. Brian, and Durlauf, Steven, The Economy As An Evolving Complex System, Vol. II., Reading, Addison-Wesley, 1997. p. 229.

305   Juniper, James, "Uncertainty, Risk, and Chaos," in Bennett, William, et. al., eds., Commerce, Complexity and Evolution, London Cambridge University Press, , 2000. p. 42.

306 Mitchell, Melanie, An Introduction to Genetic Algorithms, Cambridge, MIT Press, 1996. p. 6.

307 Lancaster, K., "A New Approach to Consumer Theory," Journal of Political Economy, 74. (1966), pps. 132- 157.

308 Freeman, Christopher, "Schumpeter's Business Cycle Revisited," in Heertje, Arnold, and Perlman, Mark, Evolving Technology and Market Structure, Ann Arbor, University of Michigan Press, 1990. p. 25.

309 Czamanski, Stan, Regional Science Techniques In Practice: The Case of Nova Scotia, Lexington, Mass., Lexington Books, 1972.

310 Feser, Edward, and Sweeney, Stuart, "A Test For Coincident Economic and Spatial Clustering of Business Enterprises," Journal of Geographical Systems, (2), pps. 349 – 373.

311 Bergman, Ed, Feser, Edward, and Sweeney, Stuart, "Targeting North Carolina Manufacturing: Understanding the State's Economy Through Industrial Cluster Analyses," Volume I, Summary, Chapel Hill, N. C., Institute for Economic Development, UNC-CH, March 1996. p. 4.

312 Feser, Edward, J., and Bergman, Edward, M., "National Industry Cluster Templates: A Framework For Applied Regional Cluster Analysis," <u>Regional Studies</u>, Vol. 34. #1, 2000. p. 12.

313 Saviotti, Pier Paolo, <u>Technological Evolution, Variety and the Economy</u>, Cheletenham, Edward Elgar, 1996. p. 188.

314 Saviotti, Pier Paolo, <u>Technological Evolution, Variety and the Economy</u>, Cheltenham, Edward Elgar, 1996. p. 188.

315 Carlsson, Bo, "Technological Systems and Economic Development Potential: Four Swedish Case Studies," in Shionoya, Yuichi, and Perlman, Mark, <u>Innovation in Technology, Industries and Institutions: Studies In Schumpeterian Perspectives</u>, University of Ann Arbor, Michigan Press, 1994. p. 64.

316 Krugman, Paul, cited in "Innovation and Agglomeration Theory," Simmie, James, ed., <u>Innovative Cities</u>, London, Spoon Press, 2001. p. 34.

317 Leontief, Wassily, "Input-Output Data Base For Analysis of Technological Change," <u>Economic Systems Research</u>, Vol. 1 #3, 1989.

318 Leontief, Wassily, "Input-Output Data Base For Analysis of Technological Change," <u>Economic Systems Research</u>, Vol. 1 #3, 1989. p. 293.

319 Duchin, Faye, <u>Structural Economics: Measuring Change in Technology, Lifestyles and the Environment</u>, New York, Island Press, 1998. p. 6.

320 Duchin, Faye, <u>Structural Economics: Measuring Change in Technology, Lifestyles and the Environment</u>, New York, Island Press, 1998. p. 82.

321 Carter, Anne, P., <u>Structural Change in the American Economy</u>, Cambridge, Harvard University Press, 1970. p. 33.

322 Carter, Anne, P., <u>Structural Change in the American Economy</u>, Cambridge, Harvard University Press, 1970. p. 20.

323 Yan, Chiou-Shuang, <u>Introduction to Input-Output Economics</u>, New York, Holt Rinehart & Winston, 1969. p. 29.

324 Saviotti, Pier Paolo, "Networks, National Innovation Systems and Self-Organization," in Fischer, Manfred and Frolich, Josef, eds., <u>Knowledge, Complexity and Innovation Systems</u>, Berlin, Springer-Verlag, 2001. p. 37.

325 Storper (1997) cited in Fischer, Manfred and Frolich, "Knowledge, Complexity, and Innovation Systems: Prologue," in Fischer, Manfred and Frolich, Josef, eds., <u>Knowledge, Complexity and Innovation Systems</u>, Berlin, Springer-Verlag, 2001. p. 8.

326 Rogers, E. M., <u>Diffusion of Innovations</u>, 3rd Edition, New York, Free Press, 1983.

327 Nelson, Richard, and Winter, Sidney, <u>An Evolutionary Theory of Economic Change</u>, Cambridge, Belknap Press, 1982. p. 172.

328 Nelson, Richard, and Winter, Sidney, <u>An Evolutionary Theory of Economic Change</u>, Cambridge, Belknap Press, 1982. p. 258.

329 Nelson, Richard, and Winter, Sidney, An Evolutionary Theory of Economic Change, Cambridge, Belknap Press, 1982. p. 267.

330 Mansfield, Edwin, The Production and Application of New Industrial Technology, New York, W. W. Norton and Company, 1977. p. 108.

331 Mansfield, Edwin, The Production and Application of New Industrial Technology, New York, W. W. Norton and Company, 1977. p. 109.

332 Mansfield, Edwin, The Production and Application of New Industrial Technology, New York, W. W. Norton and Company, 1977. p. 110.

333 Mansfield, Edwin, The Production and Application of New Industrial Technology, New York, W. W. Norton and Company, 1977. p. 142.

334 Lev, Baruch, cited in Kleiner, Art, "The World's Most Exciting Accountant," Strategy & Business Issues, #35. 2004. p. 29.

335 Mansfield, Edwin, The Production and Application of New Industrial Technology, New York, W. W. Norton and Company, 1977. p. 116.

336 Rosenberg, Nathan, cited in Hall, Peter, Innovation, Economics and Evolution: Theoretical Perspectives on Changing Technology in Economic Systems, New York, Harvester Wheatsheaf, 1994. p. 160.

337 Evangelista, Rinaldo, Knowledge and Investment: The Sources of Innovation In Industry, London, Edward Elgar, 1999. p. 5.

338 Evangelista, Rinaldo, Knowledge and Investment: The Sources of Innovation In Industry, London, Edward Elgar, 1999. pps. 32 –33.

339 Eliasson, Gunnar and Taymaz, Erol, "Institutions, Entrepreneurship, Economic Flexibility and Growth: Experiments On An Evolutionary Micro-to-Macro Model," in Canter, Uwe, et.al., eds. Economic Evolution, Learning, and Complexity, Heidelberg, Physica-Verlag, 2000. pps. 274 – 275.

340 Saviotti, Pier Paolo, "Networks, National Innovation Systems and Self-Organisation," in Knowledge, Complexity and Innovation Systems, Fischer, Manfred and Frohlich, Josef, eds., Berlin, Springer-Verlag, 2001. p. 40.

341 Chinitz, Benjamin, cited in "Feser, Edward, "Enterprises, External Economies, and Economic Development," Journal of Planning Literature, Vol. 12, #3. (Feb., 1998), p. 293.

342 Broemeling, Lyle and Tsurumi, Hiroki, Econometrics and Structural Change, New York, Marcel Dekker Publishing, 1987. p. 136.

343 Leontief, Wassily, "Input-Output Data Base For Analysis of Technological Change," Economic Systems Research, Volume 1, #3, 1989. p. 293.

344 Greiner, Alfred and Kugler, Friedrich, "A Note On Competition Among Techniques In The Presence of Increasing Returns to Scale," in Leydesdorff, Loet, and Besselaar, Peter Van Den, eds., Evolutionary Econmics and Chaos Theory: New Directions In Technology Studies, London, Pinter Publishers, 1994. pps. 83 – 87.

345 Enos, John, (1958) cited in Edquist, Charles, and McKelvey, Maureen, eds., Systems of Innovation: Growth, Competitiveness and Employment, Vol. II., Cheltenham, Edward Elgar, 2000. p. 11.

346 Mansfield, Edwin, et. al., Technology Transfer, Productivity, and Economic Policy, New York, W. W. Norton and Company, 1982. p. 141.

347 Evangelista, Rinaldo, Knowledge and Investment: The Sources of Innovation In Industry, London, Edward Elgar, 1999. p. 182.

348 Audretsch, David and Feldman, Maryann, "The Telecommunications Revolution and the Geography of Innovation," in Wheeler, James, et. al., Cities In The Telecommunications Age: The Fracturing of Geographics, New York. Routledge, 2000. p. 183.

349 Archibugi, Daniel, "On The Definition and Measurement of Product and Process Innovations," in Shionoya, Yuichi, and Perlman, Mark, eds., Innovation In Technology, Industries and Institutions: Studies In Schumpeterian Perspectives, Ann Arbor, University of Michigan Press, 1994. p. 20.

350 Rees, John, cited in Karlsson, Charlie, et. al., "Introduction: Endogenous Regional Growth and Policies," in Johansson, Borje, et. al., Theories of Endogenous Regional Growth: Lessons For Regional Policies, Berlin, Springer, 2001. p. 9.

351 Saxenian, Anna Lee, "Regional Networks and Innovation In Silicon Valley and Route 128," in Acs, Zoltan, Regional Innovation, Knowledge and Global Change, London, Pinter. 2000. pps. 125 – 131.

352 Saxenian, Anna Lee, "Regional Networks and Innovation In Silicon Valley and Route 128," in Acs, Zoltan, Regional Innovation, Knowledge and Global Change, London, Pinter. 2000. p. 137.

353 Danson, M., and Whittam, G., "Networks, Innovation and Industrial Districts: The Case of Scotland," in Steiner, M., ed. Clusters and Regional Specialization: On Geography, Technology and Networks, London, Pion Ltd., 1998. pps. 201 – 204.

354 Evangelista, Rinaldo, Knowledge and Investment: The Sources of Innovation In Industry, London, Edward Elgar, 1999. p. 91.

355 Evangelista, Rinaldo, Knowledge and Investment: The Sources of Innovation In Industry, London, Edward Elgar, 1999. p. 97.

356 Lundvall, Bengt-Ake, "Innovation As An Interactive Process: From User-Producer Interaction to The National System of Innovation," in Edquist, Charles, and McKelvey, Maureen, eds., Systems of Innovation: Growth, Competitiveness and Employment, Vol. II. Cheltenham, Edward Elgar, 2000. p. 52.

357 Hansen, Niles, "Knowledge Workers, Communication and Spatial Diffusion," in Johansson, Borje, et.al., eds., Theories of Endogenous Regional Growth: Lessons For Regional Policies, Berlin, Springer, 2001. p. 322.

358 Christensen, Clayton M., "The Rules of Innovation," Technology Review, June 2002. p. 34.

359 Christensen, Clayton M., "The Rules of Innovation," Technology Review, June 2002. p. 34.

360 Hewings, J. D. Geoffrey, et. al., "Interregional Multipliers For The U. S. Economy: An Application to Welfare Reform," in Hewings, J. D. Geoffrey, et. al. eds., Understanding and Interpreting Economic Structure, Berlin, Springer-Verlag, 1999. p. 347.

361 Lazonic, William, "Learning and the Dynamics of International Competitive Advantage," in Shionoya, Yuichi, and Perlman, Mark, eds., Innovation In Technology, Industries and Institutions: Studies In Schumpeterian Perspectives, Ann Arbor, University of Michigan Press, 1994. p. 208.

362 Zysman, John, "How Institutions Create Historically Rooted Trajectories of Growth," in Edquist, Charles, and McKelvey, Maureen, eds., Systems of Innovation: Growth, Competitiveness and Employment, Vol. II. Cheltenham, Edward Elgar, 2000. p. 188.

363 Aghion, Philippe, and Howitt, Peter, Endogenous Growth Theory, Cambridge, MIT Press, 1998. pps. 429 – 432.

364 Aghion, Philippe, and Howitt, Peter, Endogenous Growth Theory, Cambridge, MIT Press, 1998. p. 264.

365 Lewontin, R. C., The Genetic Basis of Evolutionary Change, New York, Columbia University Press, 1974. p. 159.

366 Hodgson, Geoffrey, M., "Darwinism in Economics: From Analogy To Ontology," Journal of Evolutionary Economics, Springer Verlag, 12, 2002. pps. 260 –270.

367 Penrose, Edith T., "Biological Analogies In the Theory of the Firm," American Economic Review, 42 (4) 1952. pps. 804 – 819.

368 Witt, Ulrich, quoted in Hodgson, Geoffrey, M., "Darwinism in Economics: From Analogy To Ontology," Journal of Evolutionary Economics, Springer Verlag, 12, 2002. p. 263.

369 Frenken, Koen, Saviotti, Pier Paolo, and Trommetter, Michel, "Variety and Economic Development: Conceptual Issues and Measurement Problems, in Cantner, Uwe, et. al., eds., Economic Evolution, and Complexity, Heidelberg, Physica-Verlag, 2000. p. 232.

370 Frenken, Koen, Saviotti, Pier Paolo, and Trommetter, Michel, "Variety and Economic Development: Conceptual Issues and Measurement Problems, in Cantner, Uwe, et. al., eds., Economic Evolution, and Complexity, Heidelberg, Physica-Verlag, 2000. p. 238.

371 Alchian, Armen, "Uncertainty, Evolution, and Economic Theory," Journal of Political Economy, Vol. 58, No. 3 (June, 1950), pps. 211 – 221.

372 David, Paul A., cited in Edquist, Charles, Hommen, Leif, and McKelvey, Maureen, Innovation and Employment: Process versus Product Innovation, Cheltenham, Edward Elgar, 2000. p. 92.

373 Feser, E. J., "Old and New Theories of Industry Clusters," in Steiner, Michael, et. al., eds., Clusters and Regional Specialization, London, Pion, 1998. pps. 31 – 32.

374 Griliches, cited in Feser, E. J., "Old and New Theories of Industry Clusters," in Steiner, Michael, et.al., eds., Clusters and Regional Specialization, London, Pion, 1998. p. 34.

375 Winch, David M., Analytical Welfare Economics, London, Penguin Education, 1971. p. 37.

376 Holland, John, Hidden Order: How Adaptation Builds Complexity, New York, Helix Books, 1995. p. 85.

377 Frenken, Koen, Saviotti, Pier Paolo, and Trommetter, Michel, "Variety and Economic Development: Conceptual Issues and Measurement Problems, in Cantner, Uwe, et. al., eds., Economic Evolution, and Complexity, Heidelberg, Physica-Verlag, 2000. p. 210.

378 Martens, Berten, "Toward A Generalized Coase Theorem: A Theory of the Emergence of Social and Institutional Structures Under Imperfect Information," In Bennett, William, et. al., eds., Commerce, Complexity and Evolution, London, Cambridge University Press, 2000. p. 13.

379 Martens, Berten, "Toward A Generalized Coase Theorem: A Theory of the Emergence of Social and Institutional Structures Under Imperfect Information," In Bennett, William, et. al., eds., Commerce, Complexity and Evolution, London, Cambridge University Press, 2000. p. 15.

380 Gregersen, Birgitte, and Johnson, Bjorn, "How Do Innovations Affect Economic Growth?" in Edquist, Charles, and McKelvey, Maureen, eds., Systems of Innovation: Growth, Competitiveness and Employment, Vol. 1, Cheltenham, Edward Elgar, 2000. p. 340.

381 Constant, Edward, "Recursive Practice and the Evolution of Technological Knowledge," in Ziman, John, ed., Technological Innovation As An Evolutionary Process, Cambridge, Cambridge University Press, 2000. p. 224.

382 Hughes, Austin, Adaptive Evolution of Genes and Genomes, New York, Oxford University Press, 1999. p. 144.

383 Marshall, Alfred, Principles of Economics, 8th Edition, New York, The MacMillan Co., 1949. p. 335.

384 Winch, D. M., Analytical Welfare Economics, Penguin Education, London, 1971. pps. 162 – 189.

385 Greider, William, "A New Giant Sucking Sound," The Nation, December 31, 2001.

386 Kobrin, Stephen, "Multinational Corporations, the Protest Movement and the Future of Global Governance," in Chandler, Alfred, D. Jr., and Mazlish, Bruce, eds., Leviathans: Multinational Corporations and the New Global History, Cambridge, Cambridge University Press, 2005. p. 219.

387 Kobrin, Stephen, "Multinational Corporations, the Protest Movement and the Future of Global Governance," in Chandler, Alfred, D. Jr., and Mazlish, Bruce, eds., Leviathans: Multinational Corporations and the New Global History, Cambridge, Cambridge University Press, 2005. p. 223.

388 Jones, Geoffrey, Multinational and Global Capitalism: From The Nineteenth to the Twenty-First Century, Oxford, Oxford University Press, 2005. p. 201.

389 Kogut and Zander (1993) quoted in Jones, Geoffrey, Multinational and Global Capitalism: From The Nineteenth to the Twenty-First Century, Oxford, Oxford University Press, 2005. p. 13.

390 Hodgson, Geoffrey, M., "Darwinism In Economics: From Analogy to Ontology," Journal of Evolutionary Economics, Springer Verlag, 2002, Vol. 12., p. 276.

391 Hymer, Stephen. H., (dissertation of 1960, published 1976), The International Operations of National Firms: a Study of Direct Foreign Investment, Cambridge, MIT Press, 1976.

392 Haley, Usha, C., Multinational Corporations In Political Environments: Ethics, Values and Strategies, Singapore, World Scientific Publishing, 2001. p. 36.

393 Hirschman, Albert, The Strategy of Economic Development, New Haven, Yale University Press, 1958.

394 Hoover, Edgar, The Location of Economic Activity, New York, McGraw-Hill, 1948.

395 Weber, Adna Ferrin, quoted in Suarez-Villa, Luis, The Evolution of Regional Economics: Entrepreneurship and Macroeconomic Change, New York, Praeger, 1989. p. 52.

396 Christensen, Clayton, M., The Innovator's Dilemma: When New Technologies Cause Great Firms To Fail, Boston, Harvard Business School Press, 1997. p. 147.

397 Christensen, Clayton, M., The Innovator's Dilemma: When New Technologies Cause Great Firms To Fail, Boston, Harvard Business School Press, 1997. p. 153.

398 Christensen, Clayton, and Raynor, Michael, The Innovator's Solution: Creating and Sustaining Successful Growth, Boston, Harvard Business School Press, 2003. p. 75.

399 Christensen, Clayton, and Raynor, Michael, The Innovator's Solution: Creating and Sustaining Successful Growth, Boston, Harvard Business School Press, 2003. p. 78.

400 Christensen, Clayton, Anthony, Scott, D., and Roth, Eric, Seeing What's Next: Using Theories of Innovation To Predict Industry Change, Boston, Harvard Business School Press, 2004.

401 Smith, Adam, An Inquiry into the Nature and Causes of the Wealth of Nations, Methuen and Co., Ltd., ed. Edwin Cannan, London, 1904. Fifth edition. First published: 1776. Book IV, Part II, Ch. VII.

402 Griffin, A., "PDAM Research on New Product Development Practices: Updating

Trends and Benchmarking Best Practices". Journal of Product Innovation Management, (1997) 14:429-458.

403 Camp, S. Michael, The Innovation-Entrepreneurship NEXUS: A National Assessment of Entrepreneurship and Regional Economic Growth and Development, Advanced Research Technologies, LLC, Powell, Ohio, April 2005.

404 Camp, S. Michael, The Innovation-Entrepreneurship NEXUS:A National Assessment of Entrepreneurship and Regional Economic Growth and Development, Advanced Research Technologies, LLC, Powell, Ohio, April 2005.

405 Marsh, Sarah J., and Stock, Gregory N., "Creating Dynamic Capability: The Role of Intertemporal Integration, Knowledge Retention, and Interpretation," Journal of Product Innovation Management ,23 (5) 2006. pps. 422–436.

406 Marin, Marco A. and Bo, Carlo, The Value of a New Idea: Knowledge Transmission, Workers' Mobility and Market Structure, Faculty of Economics, University of Urbino, MPRA Paper No. 168710. July 2005.

407 Anabel, Marin, and Elisha, Giuliani, "Relating Global and Local Knowledge Linkages: The Case of MNC Subsidiaries in Argentina," Universidad Nacional de General Sarmiento, Argentina, 2006.

408 Anabel, Marin, and Elisha, Giuliani, "Relating Global and Local Knowledge Linkages: The Case of MNC Subsidiaries in Argentina," Universidad Nacional de General Sarmiento, Argentina, 2006.

409 Hedlund, Gunnar 'The Hypermodern MNC: A Heterarchy?', Human Resource Management, 1986. 25. pps. 9-35.

410 Marin, Marco A. Bo, Carlo, "The Value of a New Idea: Knowledge Transmission, Workers' Mobility and Market Structure," Faculty of Economics, University of Urbino, MPRA Paper No. 168710. July 2005.

411 Nelson, Richard, B., "Technical Change As Cultural Evolution," in Thomson, Ross, (Ed.), Learning and Technical Change, NewYork, St. Martin's Press, 1993. p. 11.

412 Saviotti, Pier Paolo, Technological Evolution, Variety, and The Economy, Cheltenham, UK., Edward-Elgar, 1996. p. 78.

413 Technological Evolution, Variety, and The Economy, p. 188.

414 The Lever of Riches, p. 191.

415 Acs, Zoltan J. , McMullen, Jeffery S., Plummer, Lawrence A., "WHAT IS AN ENTREPRENEURIAL OPPORTUNITY?" Paper # 1007, Max Planck Institute of Economics, February, 2007.

416 Mueller, Pamela, "Exploiting Entrepreneurial Opportunities: The Impact of Entrepreneurship on Growth," cited in Acs, Zoltan J. , McMullen, Jeffery S., Plummer, Lawrence A., "WHAT IS AN ENTREPRENEURIAL OPPORTUNITY?" Paper # 1007, Max Planck Institute of Economics, February, 2007.